AutoCAD 2011
for the Interior Designer

Dean Muccio

ISBN: 978-1-58503-593-9

SDC

PUBLICATIONS

Schroff Development Corporation

www.SDCpublications.com

SDC Publications
P.O. Box 1334
Mission KS 66222
(913) 262-2664
www.SDCpublications.com

Publisher: Stephen Schroff

Examination Copies:

Books received as examination copies are for review purposes only and may not be made available for student use. Resale of examination copies is prohibited.

Electronic Files:

Any electronic files associated with this book are licensed to the original user only. These files may not be transferred to any other party.

Acknowledgements

This book is a compilation of the many handouts created for my AutoCAD® Interior Design class over the past several years. Those handouts were originally meant to supplement the multiple textbooks that I had tried for the course. Eventually, the amount of handouts overcame the need for a textbook. Thanks to the students that provided good feedback from those handouts, the work has resulted in this textbook.

I would also like to thank my family, and especially my beautiful wife Mary, for encouraging me to contact a publishing house and for having the patience with the many hours that were spent on this project.

About the Author

Dean Muccio is an adjunct Assistant Professor at Fairfield University in Fairfield, CT, and has been teaching since the late 1980's. He has taught a variety of Engineering Graphics and Computer Aided Design and Manufacturing courses, and for the past several years, has taught AutoCAD® for the Interior Design program.

In addition to teaching part-time, Dean is a full-time Engineering Manager at Sikorsky Aircraft Corporation in Stratford, CT. He holds a B.S. degree in Mechanical Engineering from Norwich University, and an M.S. degree in Mechanical Engineering from Yale University.

Dean is a DIY homeowner who has tackled many remodeling projects. He has applied his engineering knowledge to refine his woodworking skills and to develop creative design solutions for space planning. The remodeling projects have provided a practical insight into what an Interior Designer must deal with when creating a design.

Notes:

Table of Contents

Notes:

Chapter 1
Getting Comfortable with AutoCAD®

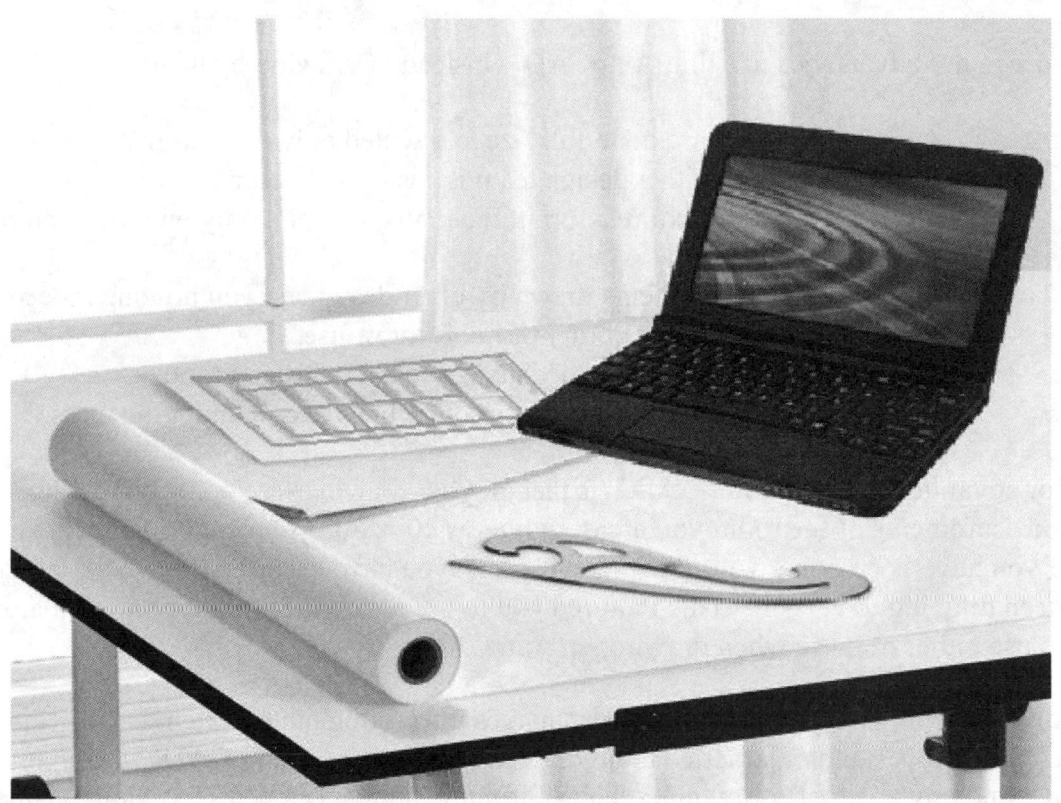

Learning Objectives:

- Going from drafting to CAD – Ground rules of using AutoCAD®
- Getting familiar with the AutoCAD® Workspace screens
- Understanding AutoCAD® Toolbars
- Getting AutoCAD® Help
- Customizing your screen color and right mouse button
- Using a Flash Drive
- Opening and Saving drawings
- Managing your files on your computer

Introduction to AutoCAD®

Congratulations on your decision to use the computer to draw your interior designs. AutoCAD® is an excellent product that is very popular. Having your designs in AutoCAD® format allows you to make changes easier, and also allows you to integrate your interior design with the architect's design. In fact, if an architectural drawing is already available on AutoCAD®, you can use that to build upon for your interior design.

There are many advantages to using AutoCAD® instead of drawing by hand:

- Drawings are done full size and scaled only for printing.
- Working with a design team is easier with AutoCAD®.
- You draw fixtures, furniture, appliances, etc. only one time and re-use them for other drawings.
- You can use items drawn by other designers; you no longer need to trace.
- You can have a library of items for re-use.
- You can use layers to visualize select items at a time.
- You can create/erase construction lines, etc. without the mess.

A major advantage to using AutoCAD® is that all your drawings are done in full scale. For example, if the measurements of the room you are designing is 20′ x 20′, you actually draw the room as 20′ x 20′. If you have been doing your drawings by hand, you have been drawing to scale. Perhaps you have been drawing to ¼″ = 1′. This required you to use an architect scale or a calculator. You do not have to use either of these when drawing on AutoCAD®.

Not only does this save you time, but it also makes integrating other drawings into your design very simple. Since it is standard practice to do drawings full scale on AutoCAD®, the architectural drawing, and any available drawings such as furniture, appliances, etc. are readily available for your use. Sharing your designs with other designers and vice versa is made easy by drawing to full scale. In fact, there are several Internet sites that have pre-drawn AutoCAD® items such as furniture, plants, appliances, etc. Some are available for free; others are available for a small charge.

The AutoCAD® LT version is for 2D drafting, which is all the Interior Designer needs to complete floor plan and elevation type drawings. It is more economical than buying the complete AutoCAD® version, which includes 3D. Either version works the same in the 2D mode (there is some advanced functionality that is not included in the LT version, but is not a necessity for the Interior Designer).

The AutoCAD® program has been upgraded over the years to include many enhancements. Since the AutoCAD® 2004 version, most improvements were in the appearance of some command dialog boxes, and right mouse-click functionality. As of this writing, the latest version is AutoCAD® 2011. For the most part, the instructions within this text can be used for versions 2004 through 2011. There may be some differences in the look of things, but the same basic procedures and functions have remained the same. The designer can easily adapt to these differences without the need for a completely new course or text.

Hand Drawing vs. AutoCAD®

Using the computer to create your drawings may seem intimidating. This may be true especially if have not done it before and only use a computer for e-mail, family photos, and shopping. Perhaps you have used it to touch up some photographs using one of the many programs available.

You may be surprised at first that AutoCAD® does not treat drawings the same as touching up photos. That is because AutoCAD® recognizes the items on your drawing screen as specific objects such as lines, circles, arcs, etc. This is similar to how a word processing program recognizes the characters on the screen as letters, numbers, etc. – especially when you are using a spellchecker.

When you create your designs using drafting techniques, you strive for accuracy. This is necessary because items must fit properly. It can be discouraging (and expensive) when the carpenter tells you that the cabinets don't fit properly (or any other item) and to make up for it you have to revise the design. Had your measurements and drafting been accurate in the first place, this mistake could have been avoided. Although AutoCAD® cannot help you in measuring your client's rooms correctly, once you have the measurements, they are accurately reflected on the computer.

Accuracy in AutoCAD® is achieved by the fact that it uses X and Y coordinates to determine exactly where lines, circles, arcs, etc. are on the drawing. Fortunately, we do not have to burden ourselves with this fact, and we can create our designs in confidence knowing that AutoCAD® is working to keep it precise.

Throughout this book, we will do our best to avoid using X and Y coordinates. Instead, the intention is to keep the method of drawing as similar as possible to how you are currently creating drawings using your drafting equipment.

For example:

- We will draw lines longer than needed and trim them as required
  - o Trimming will be like using your erasing shield to remove the excess line and have a clean intersection
- We will use circles and trim them to become arcs
  - o Just like when you use a circle template or compass, sometimes you draw an arc bigger than needed and have to clean it up with your erasing shield

The best part is that we will not have eraser debris all over the place!

Clarifications and Ground Rules

Before we begin, it is best to clarify how to interact with the computer so that AutoCAD® interprets your intentions correctly. Because it is a computer, it is looking at specific ways in which you communicate with it. You will be primarily using your mouse to pick locations on your drawing and selecting commands via icons or pull-down menus. You will also use your keyboard to key in specific values, and also for command shortcuts.

The following may help you throughout this book and with using AutoCAD®. Some of the rules will be needed as we progress, so you may wish to refer back to them, as we get further along.

Clarifications:

1. The words Pick, or Select, are meant to indicate that you must use your mouse/cursor and left click. For instances where a right mouse click is needed, it will be specifically stated to right-click.
2. Whenever it is required to type in a value or option letter, this must be followed by pressing the ↵ Enter key. AutoCAD® will not recognize what you have typed on the command line until the ↵ Enter key is pressed.

AutoCAD® Ground Rules:

1. AutoCAD® is based on an X-Y coordinate system. The horizontal direction, starting from left and going right, is the positive X direction. Starting from right and going left is the negative X direction. The vertical direction, starting from the bottom of the screen and moving up, is the positive Y direction. Starting from the top of the screen and moving down is the negative Y direction. This book will attempt to avoid referring to X and Y directions; instead, it will refer to horizontal and vertical directions.

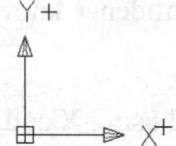

2. Positive angles are measured by starting from the positive X-axis and rotating in a counterclockwise direction. Note that you can use negative angles. For example, -90° is the same as 270°.

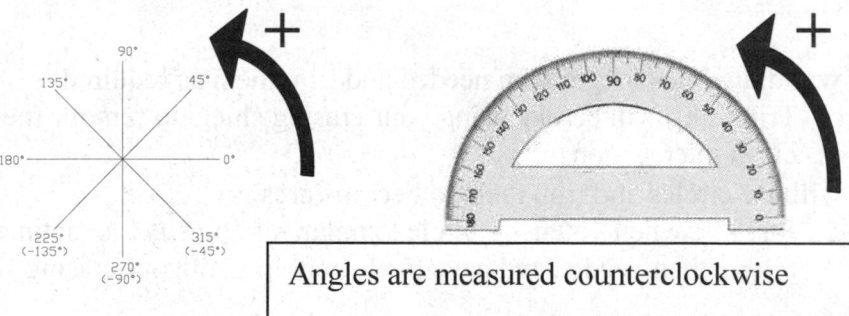

Angles are measured counterclockwise

3. To exit a command, press the ↵ Enter key or space bar. The Escape key (Esc) can also be used, but sometimes the Escape key will not work (depending on the command).
4. To repeat the previous command you used, press the ↵ Enter key. This comes in handy for fillets and offsets.
5. The default measurement is inches. When keying in distance values for feet, remember to use the foot symbol.
6. Standard practice is to draw everything full scale.
7. If you select objects with no command in the command line, AutoCAD® will show grips on that object (little blue boxes). Grips can be removed by pressing the Escape key.

The AutoCAD® Screen

To help guide you through learning AutoCAD®, it is a good idea to get familiar with the AutoCAD® screen. Various toolbars, menus, and screen areas are mentioned throughout this text. The following figure will help you get familiar with the names of these items.

Menu Browser – Pull-down Menu Items can be accessed using this

The Ribbon Tabs – Each tab is used to select a toolbar by group

Quick Access Toolbar – Contains frequently used Windows icons

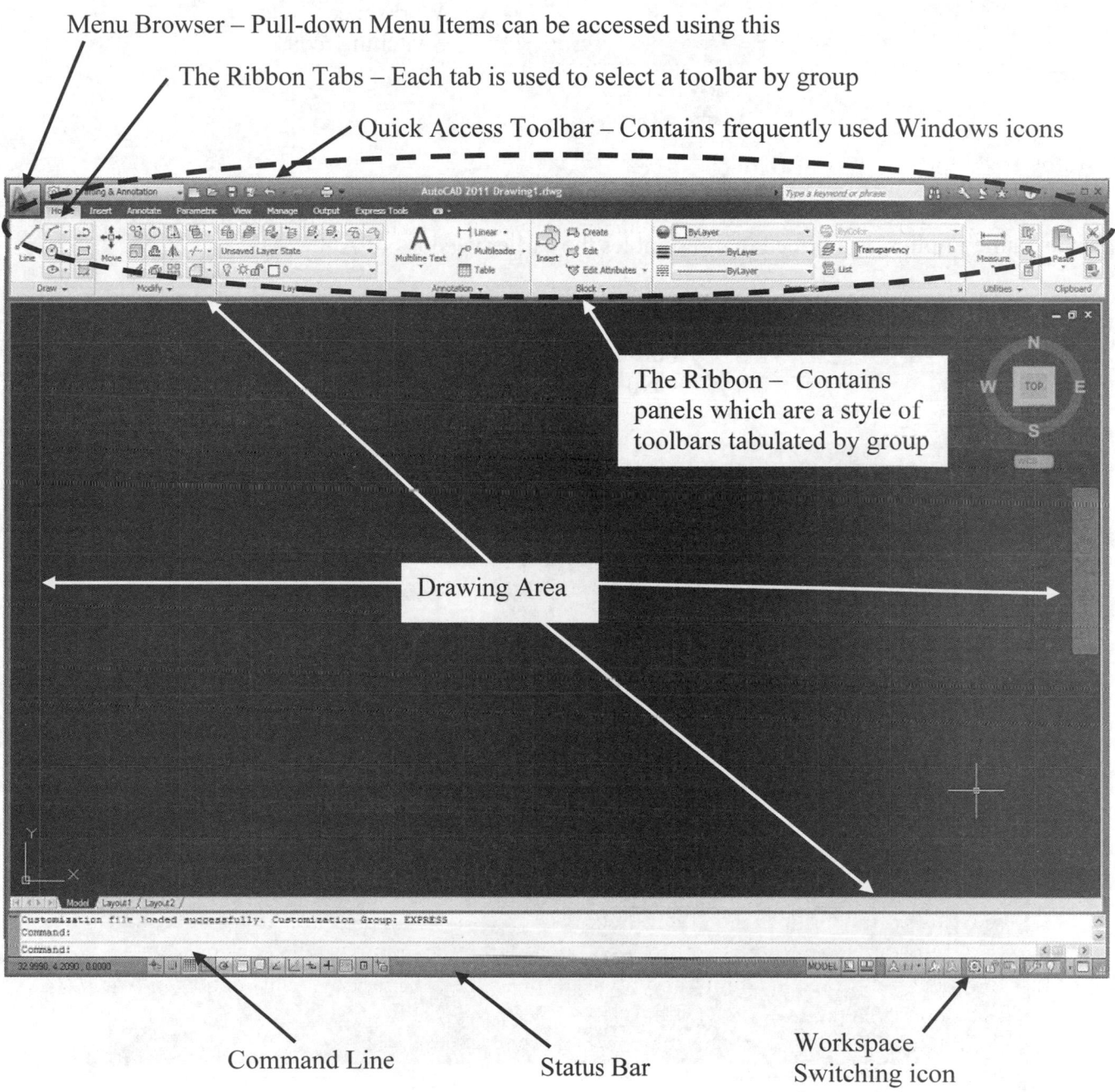

The Ribbon – Contains panels which are a style of toolbars tabulated by group

Drawing Area

Command Line

Status Bar

Workspace Switching icon

Default 2D drafting & Annotation AutoCAD screen

The default AutoCAD® screen is the 2D Drafting & Annotation screen. This can be changed to the AutoCAD® Classic screen by using the Workspace Switching icon found on the lower right side of the status bar.

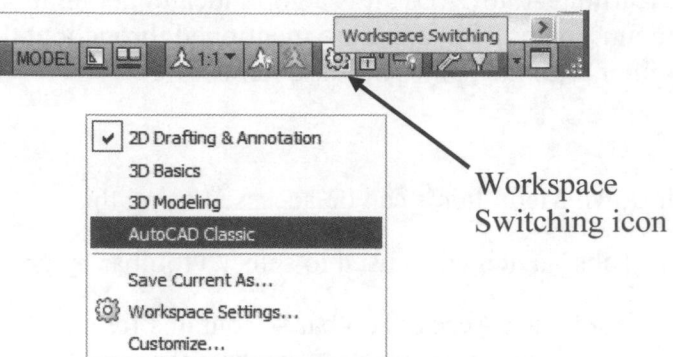

Workspace Switching icon

Throughout this text, we will be primarily using the AutoCAD® classic screen. The classic screen, as its name implies, is a screen that resembles the earlier versions of AutoCAD®.

Pull-down menus are available on the screen – No need to use the menu browser.

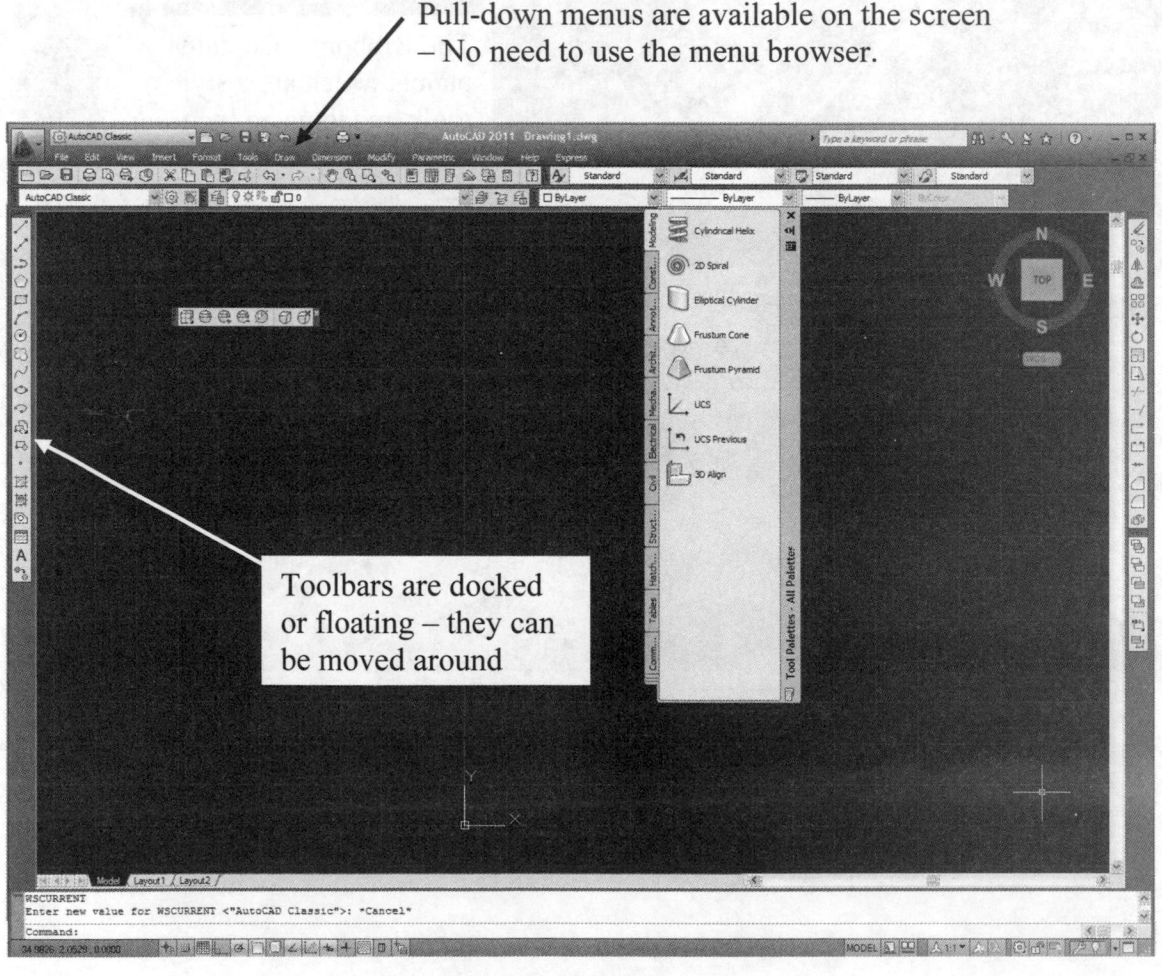

Toolbars are docked or floating – they can be moved around

AutoCAD Classic screen

Status Bar icons

Before we begin drawing, let's turn off the icons on the status bar. These are like switches – left click once to turn on, left click again to turn off. When they are turned on, they appear blue, when off, they are gray. The only icon to leave on is the Object Snap. We will discuss this more in later chapters.

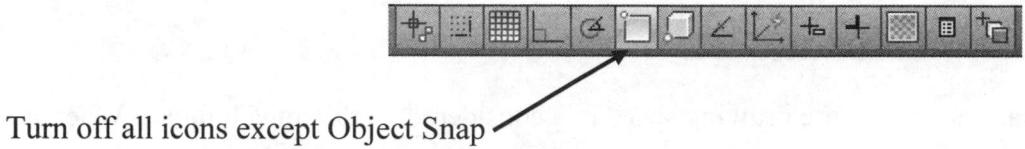

Turn off all icons except Object Snap

Toolbars

AutoCAD® has numerous toolbars, but not all toolbars are shown on your screen. Toolbars can be used via the Ribbon (for the 2D Drafting and Annotation workspace), or can be brought up individually. To bring up an individual toolbar, pick on the Pull-Down Menu and select Tools, then Toolbars, then AutoCAD®.

An easier way to bring up additional toolbars that are not currently shown on the screen is to right-click on any toolbar. This will bring up a list of available toolbars. Some items on the list will have a checkmark in front of them. Those are the ones that are currently on the screen.

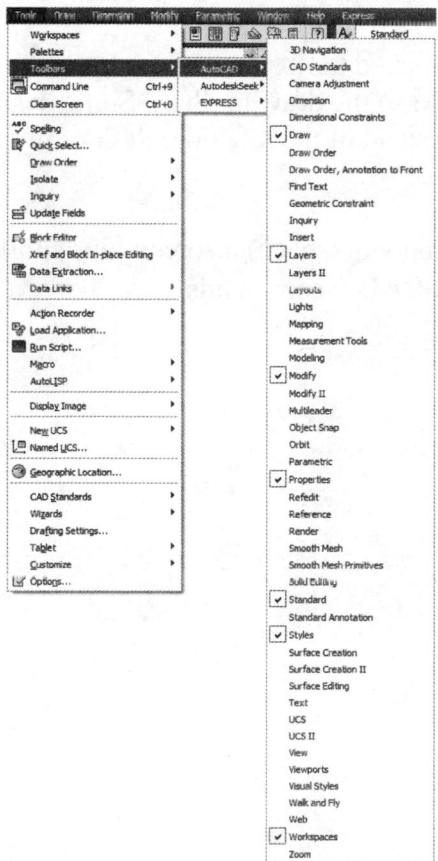

In order to display an additional toolbar, move the cursor over the name of the toolbar you want and pick it.

As an example, let's bring up the Inquiry toolbar. Move the cursor over the list of toolbars until Inquiry is highlighted. Pick (left-click) on the word Inquiry. An Inquiry toolbar will appear on the drawing screen and the list of toolbars will disappear.

When the toolbar appears on the drawing space it is considered a "floating" toolbar. When it is off to the side it is "docked".

The floating toolbar can be moved around the drawing screen by picking it on the end bar portion and dragging it to a new location. If you drag it close enough to any of the four edges of the drawing screen, the outline of the toolbar will change orientation to vertical or remain horizontal – depending on which edge you dock it to. This indicates that it will dock to that edge if you let go of the mouse button. You can move a docked toolbar by picking the end bar portion and dragging it to a new location.

To turn off a toolbar, you can right click on any toolbar and pick the toolbar that you want to turn off from the list of toolbars. The toolbar that you want to turn off must already be turned on. This is indicated by the check mark in front of it on the list. If you want to turn off a floating toolbar, you can simply pick the "X" on the upper right portion of the bar.

AutoCAD® allows the flexibility to relocate docked toolbars. This is a personal preference. Many designers prefer to have the modify toolbar next to the draw toolbar. Some designers prefer to have those toolbars on the right side of the screen instead of the left side. It does not matter where the toolbars are located, they will still work.

The Ribbon (for the 2D Drafting and Annotation workspace) also contains similar toolbars and is simply a different option of accessing the AutoCAD® commands.

Options – Screen Color & Right-Click

When you start up AutoCAD® 2011 for the first time, you will notice that the background is black with white gridlines. If you like this look, then you won't need to review this section. If you would like to change the background to a different color, such as white, then the following information will help you achieve that.

Customizing Screen Background Color

To change your drawing space background color, use the Tools pull-down menu and select Options.

The Options dialog box will pop up. Make sure the Display tab near the top of the dialog box is selected. Select the Colors button.

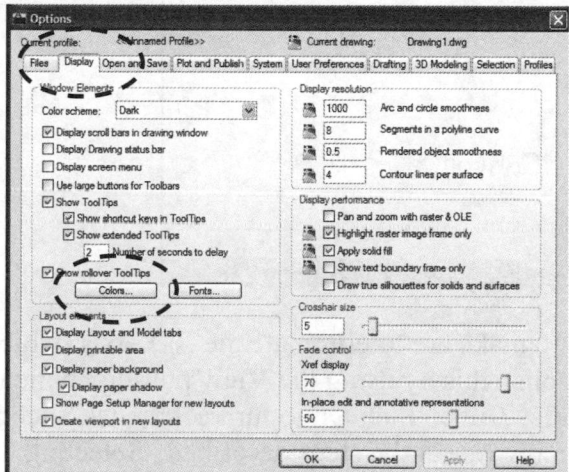

The Drawing Window Colors dialog box pops up. Use the pull down selection for 2D model space. Change the color of the Uniform background, Grid major lines, Grid minor lines, and Grid axis lines, to White by using the pull-down selection under Color. The color change needs to be done for each Interface element individually.

When done, select the Apply & Close button. Pick the OK button to close the Options dialog box.

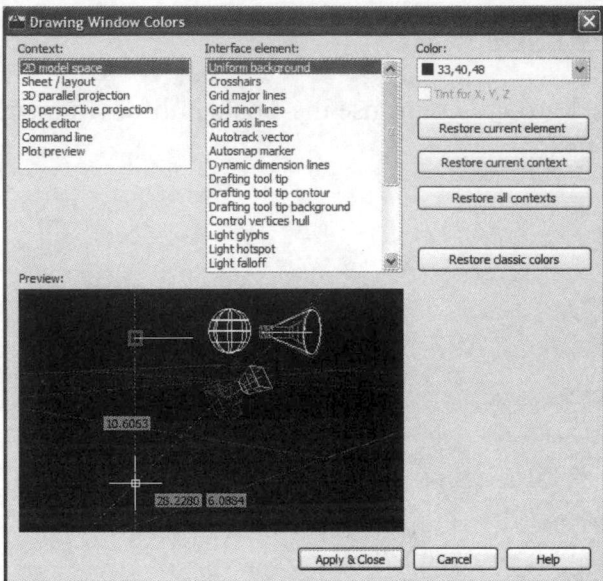

After you exit the dialog box, you will now have a white screen background. Of course, if you prefer a different color, the steps to make the changes are the same as described.

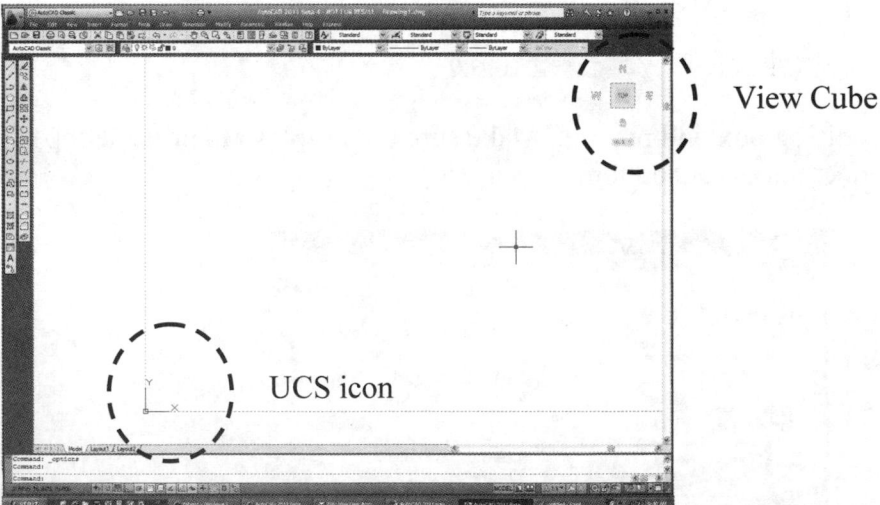

Additional display changes you may desire to make are to eliminate the X-Y axis (which is called the UCS icon) and the View Cube. You accomplish this by using the View pull-down menu and selecting Display then either UCS Icon or ViewCube. Pick On to turn off the UCS icon or View Cube. If you want to turn these back on, simply repeat the steps described. Selecting On will toggle from on to off and vice-versa.

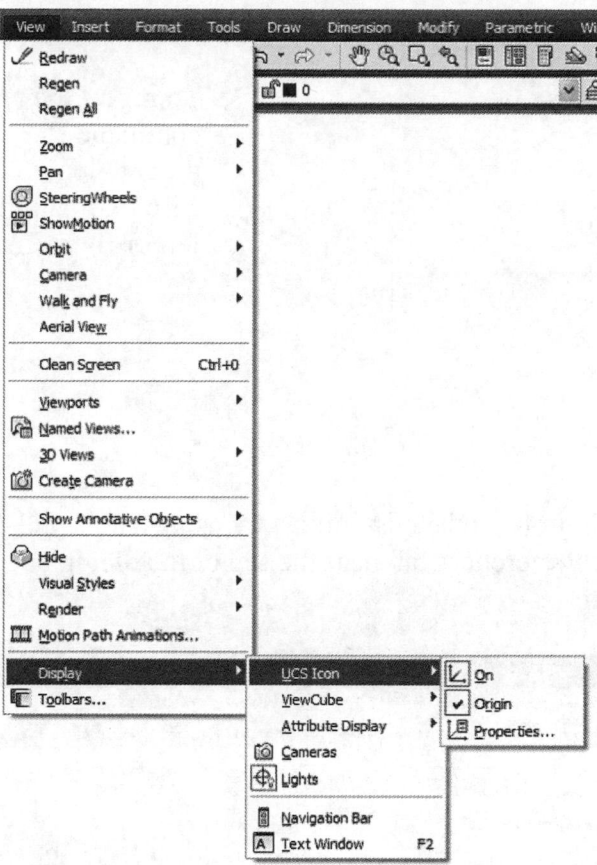

Customizing Right-Click

The default setting for AutoCAD® Right-Click (in the drawing space) is to bring up the shortcut menu. Since repeating the previous command by pressing the ↵ Enter key requires a keyboard operation, it can be more convenient to use the right mouse button to repeat the previous command instead.

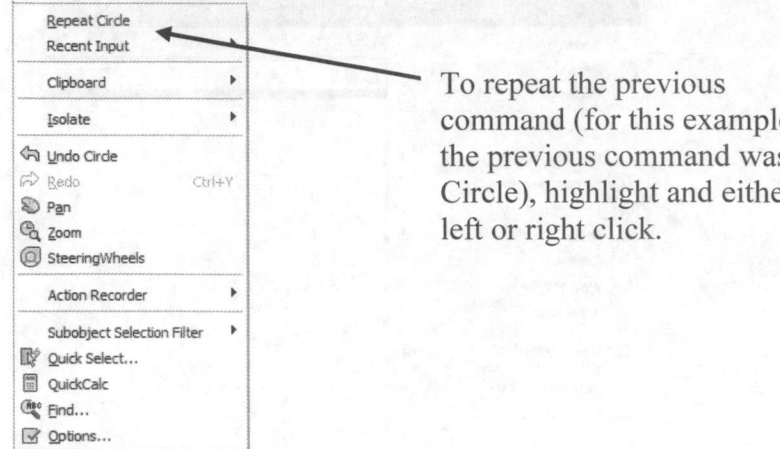

Shortcut menu is default setting

To repeat the previous command (for this example the previous command was Circle), highlight and either left or right click.

The function of the right mouse button can be customized by using Tools pull-down menu and selecting Options. Pick the User Preferences tab near the top of the dialog box is selected. Select the Right-click Customization button.

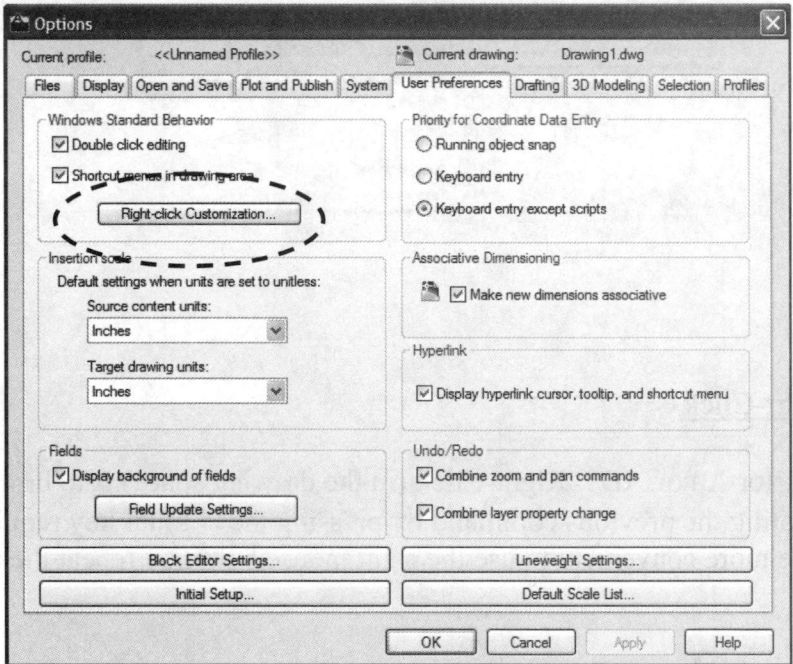

The Right-Click Customization dialog box pops up. Pick to place a checkmark to turn on time-sensitive right-click. When done, select the Apply & Close button. Pick the OK button to close the Options dialog box.

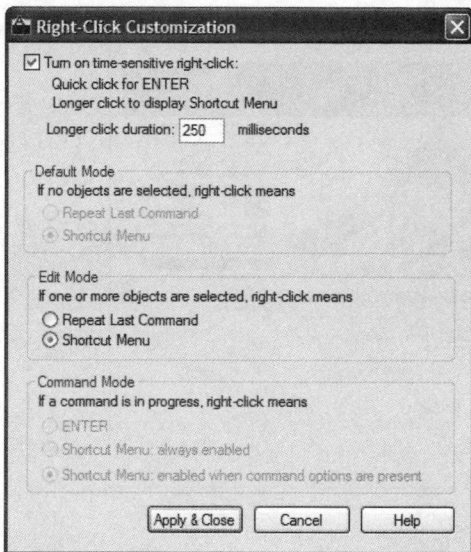

This option allows you use the right mouse button to repeat the last command without bringing up the shortcut menu, unless you press and hold the button for longer.

AutoCAD® Help

The intention of this book is not to cover every command in complete detail. Instead, it will provide enough information for the new user to be productive using AutoCAD® as quickly as possible. There are some textbooks available that attempt to provide a comprehensive instructional guide on how to use AutoCAD®, and there may still be some things that are not covered. Or, you may be seeking a different explanation of how a command works. Fortunately, AutoCAD® has provided a very good Help menu, which can be searched by topic. Like most other AutoCAD® functions, there are several ways to access the Help screen. You can use the Help icon or pull-down, or simply press the F1 key.

Using any of these methods will get you to the Help screen.

There are many methods available to find the information on a topic that you are seeking. I typically type in a key word under the Search tab on the left side of the Help screen.

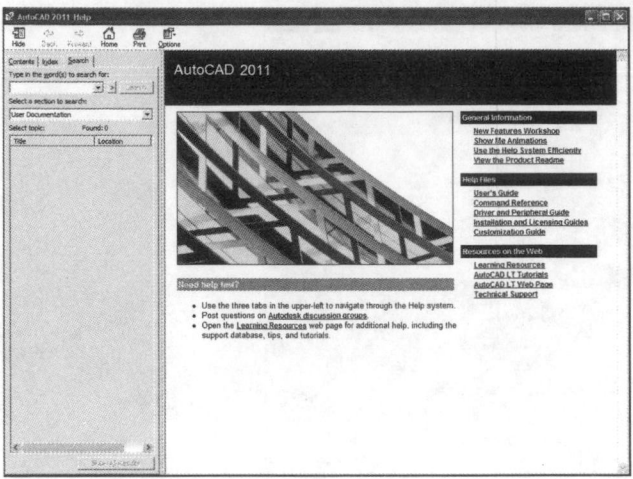

Example:

As an example, let's try searching on "circle". First, make sure the Search tab is selected. Then type in the word "circle" in the white space provided.

Pick on
Search tab

Type in a key word
for your search

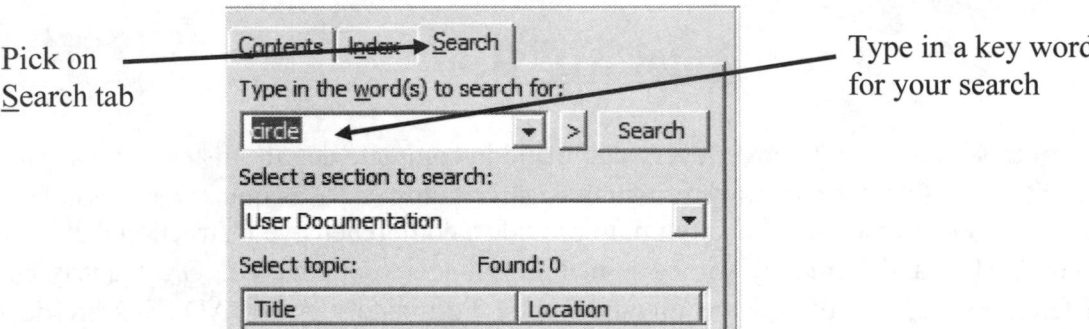

After you type in the key word (in this example that key word is "circle"), pick on the Search button. A listing of topics will appear that are related to the key word search. These are ranked in order of the highest to lowest validity to the chosen topic.

Let's choose Draw Circles from the list. You could either double-left-click on the item, or single-left-click and then choose the Display button.

Pick the item on
the list by either
double-clicking

<u>Search</u>
button

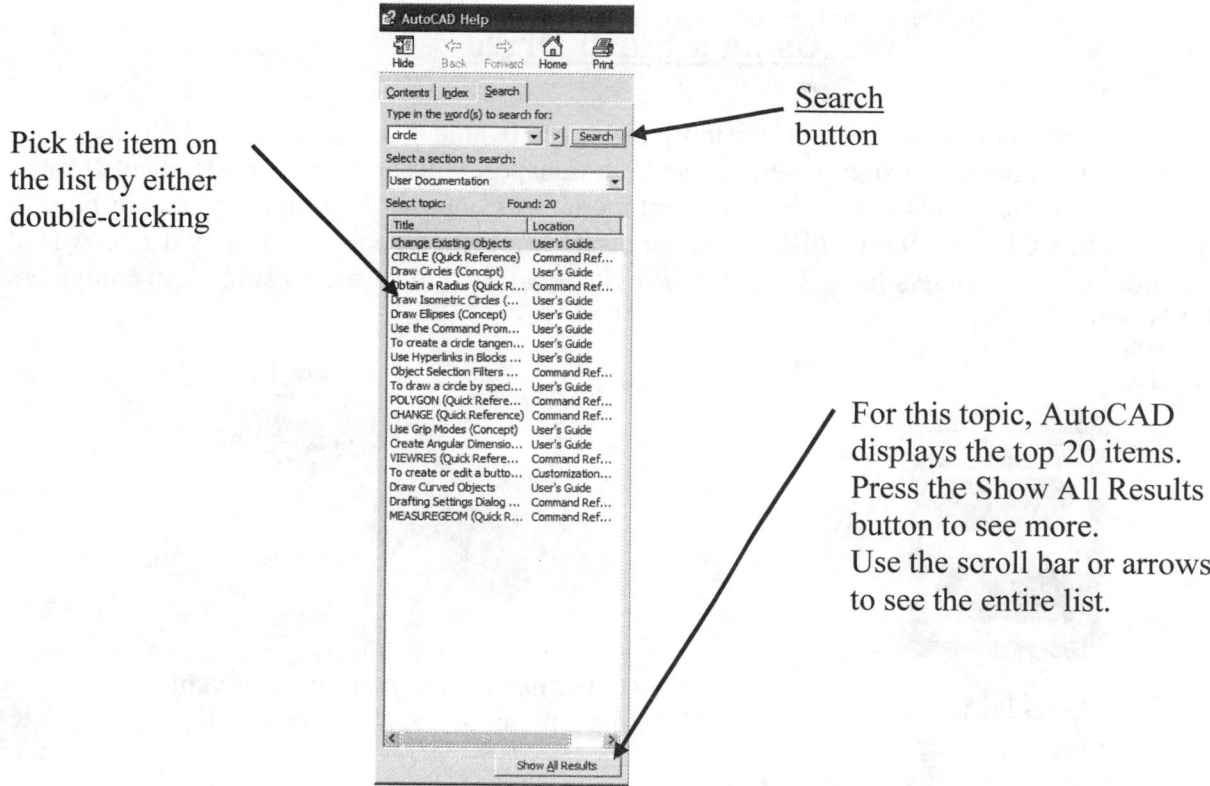

For this topic, AutoCAD
displays the top 20 items.
Press the Show All Results
button to see more.
Use the scroll bar or arrows
to see the entire list.

Information about the topic is displayed on the right side of the Help screen:

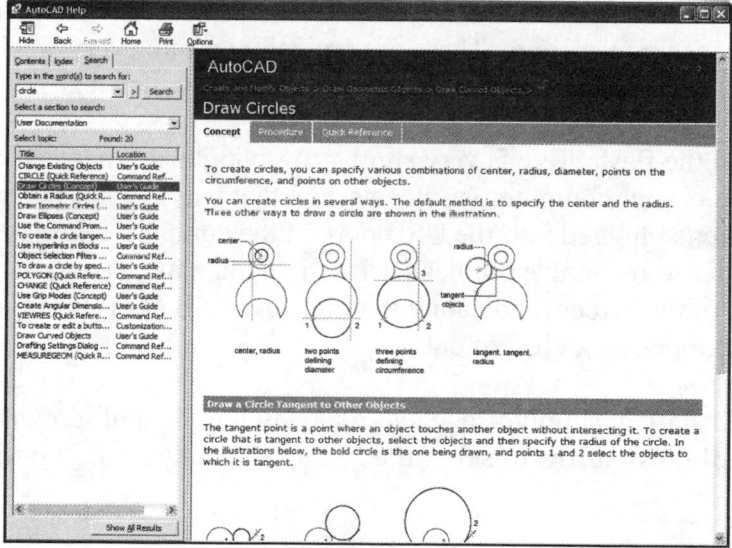

Since we chose Draw Circles from the list of topics found, that is what is displayed. In this example, this has three tabs to choose from: Concepts, Procedures, and Quick Reference. You can explore each tab on your own.

As you can see, the Help menu is self-explanatory. Try other tabs besides the Search tab. You may find your personal preference of finding things to be different than what was demonstrated here. AutoCAD® offers the flexibility of doing things in multiple ways. Choose which is best for you.

Using a Flash Drive

A Flash Drive (other names for this include: jump drive, removable disk, travel drive, USB mass storage device, etc.) comes in handy when you want to transport your drawings or documents from one computer to another. This is a very convenient method, as opposed to e-mailing them or burning the information to a CD, or a floppy disk. Most modern computers do not have floppy disk drives anymore, and not all computers have the ability to write to a CD. However, most modern computers have a USB port.

USB Ports on
the computer

Flash Drive
Other names: jump drive, removable disk, travel drive, USB mass storage device, etc.

Flash drives come in different shapes, sizes, and colors. They also come in different memory capacity ranging from 128 MB to 4 GB and larger. As with most electronic items, prices come down and memory capacity goes up over time. These are typically on sale every week at any office product store, computer store, or other electronic store, including large retailers that sell electronics.

Saving your drawings to the flash drive is very similar to saving them in the My Documents folder on the C: drive (or D: drive if your computer has been set up that way). Prior to saving your drawing, make sure the flash drive is plugged into the USB port on the computer. It may take a minute (more or less) for your computer to recognize the flash drive, and you may get a message in your Windows Tray (on the lower part of the screen) indicating that the new USB Mass Storage Device was detected. If a dialog box opens up, close it out.

Once the flash drive is installed, simply use "Save As…" in the File pull-down menu. A dialog box will appear. Use the pull-down arrow to select the "Save in" location for your drawing.

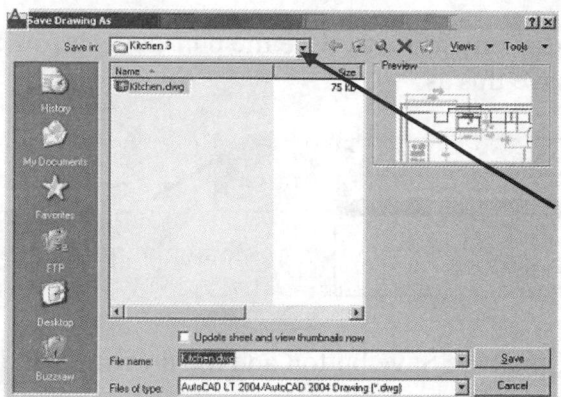

Use the pull-down arrow
to select "save in" location

Pick the Removable Disk. Note that the drive letter is automatically assigned by your computer. It will use the next available drive letter. In this example the drive letter assigned is (H:).

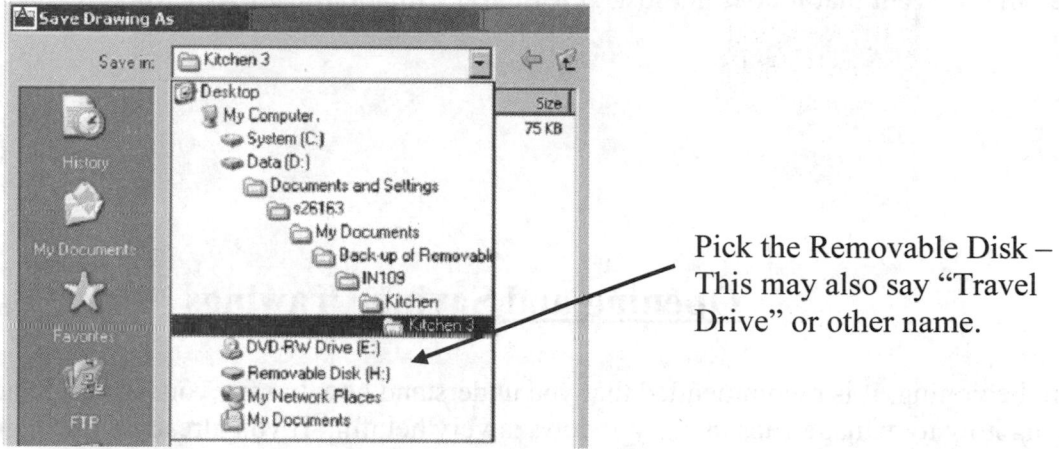

Pick the Removable Disk –
This may also say "Travel
Drive" or other name.

The "Save in" location is now the Removable Disk. You can rename your drawing if you wish as shown:

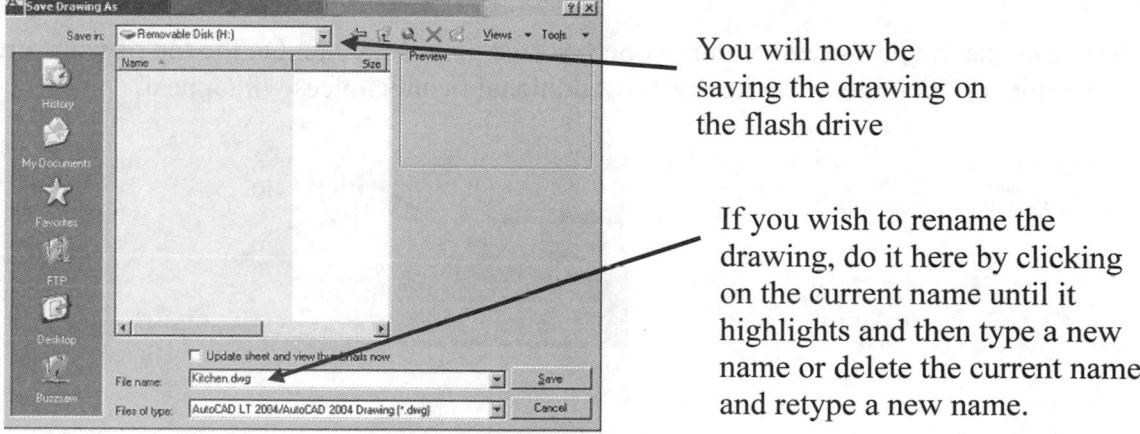

You will now be
saving the drawing on
the flash drive

If you wish to rename the
drawing, do it here by clicking
on the current name until it
highlights and then type a new
name or delete the current name
and retype a new name.

You can also change the file type to accommodate older versions of AutoCAD® (*.dwg) or other PC based CAD system using Drawing Exchange Format (*.dxf). Or you can save this as a template file

(*.dwt), which is typically used for drawing formats. Use the pull-down arrow for "Files of type:" to choose the type of file you wish to save this as:

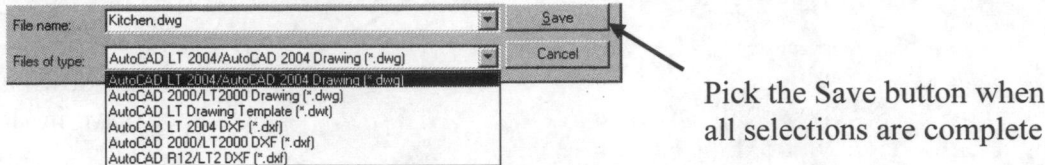

Pick the Save button when all selections are complete

Once all selections have been made, pick the Save button and the drawing will be saved to the flash drive.

Recommendation: Don't forget to take you Flash Drive out when done! Because this is so small it is easy to forget it or lose it. It is a good idea to make a back-up copy (periodically) of your Flash Drive. In the event that it does get lost, at least you will not lose all your work.

Opening and Saving Drawings

Before beginning, it is recommended that you understand how to save your work. In addition, knowing how to manage files using Windows is very helpful. If you already know how to do that, this section will be a review for you.

Using Pull-Down Menu

You can use the pull-down menu to open or save your drawing. On the top of your screen is the pull-down menu. Pick the menu item File. Additional menu choices will appear.

Pick File

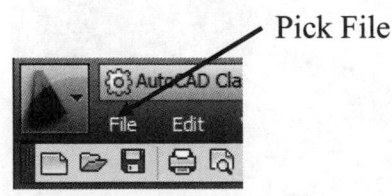

The following selections will be the ones we are initially interested in:

New... – Allows you to create a new drawing. You choose an existing template to begin your drawing, or use the default template. *Note: Template drawings will be covered later.*

Open – Allows you to open an existing drawing.

Close – Allows you to close the current drawing, but does not shut down the AutoCAD program.

Save – Allows you to save the drawing you are currently working on. If this is the first time you are saving the drawing, it will work the same as the **Save As...** command.

Save As... – Allows you to save the current drawing under a new name and/or to a new memory location (hard drive, different folder, flash drive, etc.)

Available shortcuts:
Example: pressing the **Ctrl key** and the letter **S key** simultaneously is another way to select **Save**

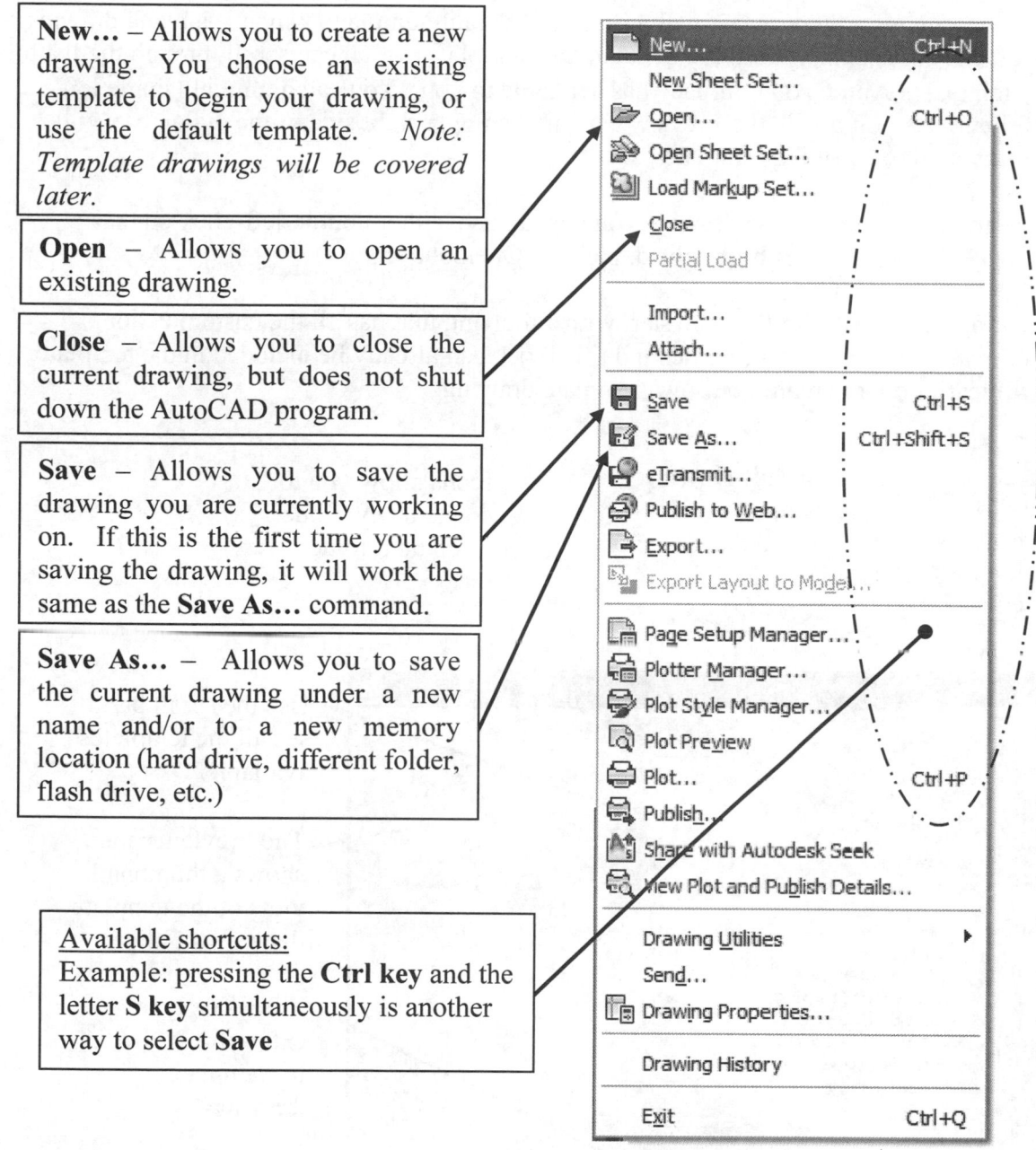

Selecting New...

When you select the New... option, AutoCAD® displays a Select template dialog box. The default location that it will look in is the template folder which is part of the AutoCAD® software package installed on the computer. AutoCAD® will pre-select a default template, which is a blank drawing. Otherwise, you can choose many of the other available templates. You can scroll through the list to see the many templates AutoCAD® already has available to you. You can highlight (single left-click) any of them. As you do so, the Preview pane in the upper right side of the dialog box will show you a thumbnail view of the template.

Once you determine which template drawing you wish to use, either double-left-click on that template, or, once that template is highlighted, pick the Open button.

Template drawings are helpful in that you start with a drawing that has all the customization included. For example, the drawing border and title block can already be included in the template. Later, you will learn how to create your own template drawing.

Look in: shows you which folder you are looking for the template

Using Pull-Down arrow allows you to choose the folder to look in

Icons allow you to create a new folder or go up a folder, etc.

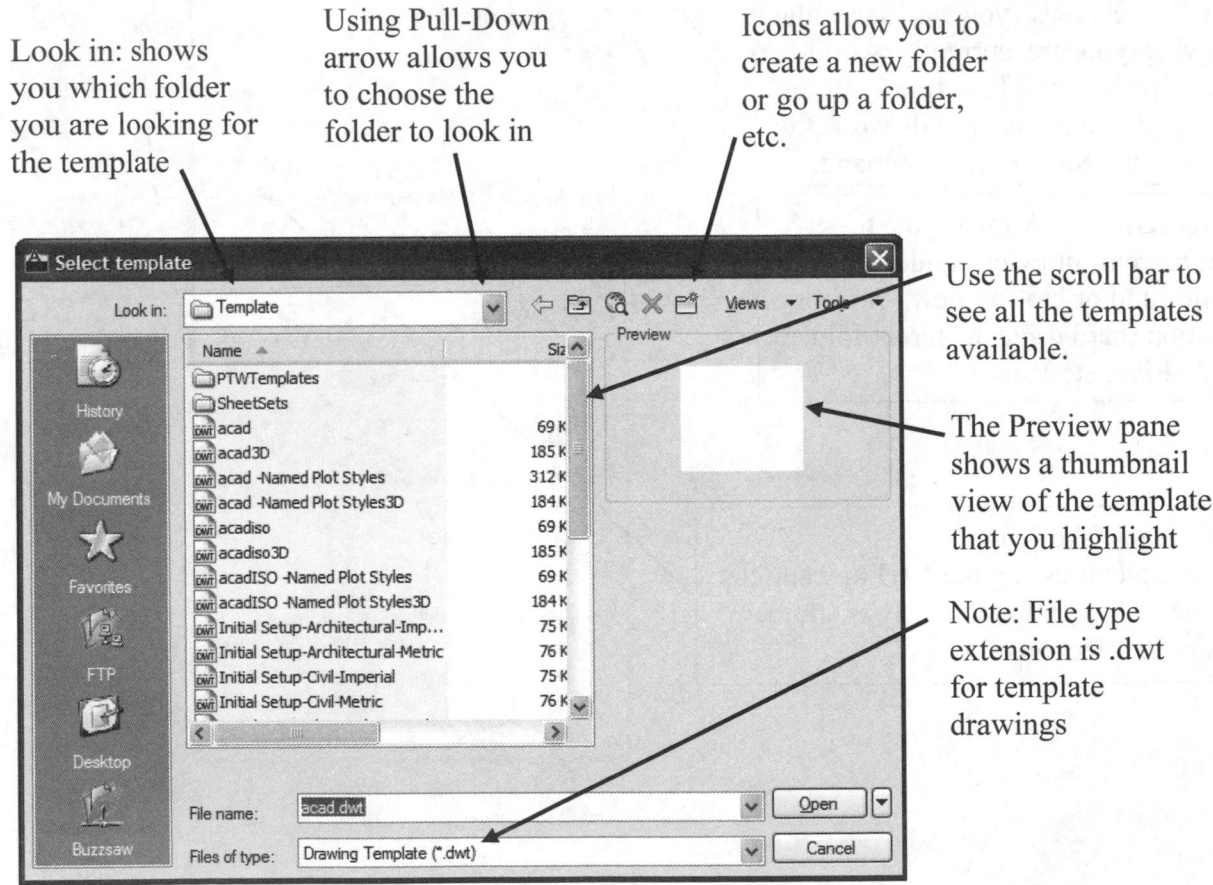

Use the scroll bar to see all the templates available.

The Preview pane shows a thumbnail view of the template that you highlight

Note: File type extension is .dwt for template drawings

Selecting Open

Selecting Open is very similar to selecting New… because AutoCAD® will be looking for an existing drawing. But instead of looking for a template drawing, which has a .dwt file extension, it will be looking for an AutoCAD® drawing with a .dwg file extension. You can change the file type extension that you wish to open by using the pull-down arrow in the "Files of type:" box.

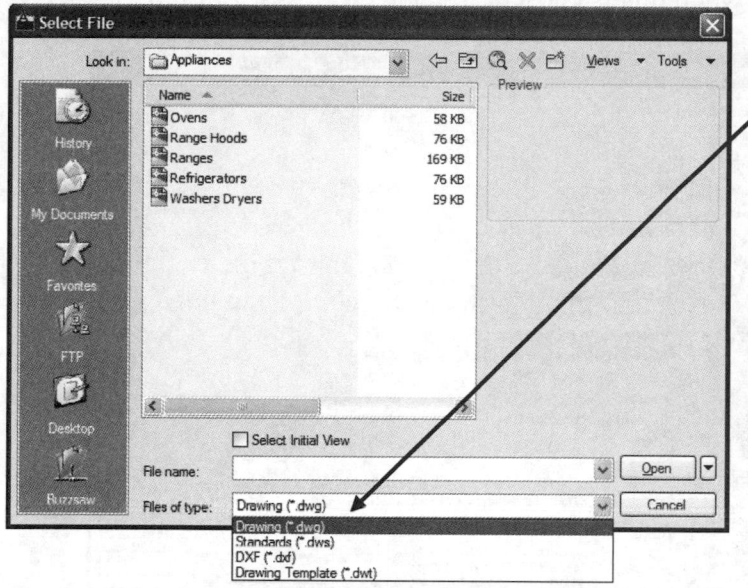

File types

.dwg is the standard extension used for an AutoCAD drawing

.dxf is a universal Drawing eXchange File type that allows drawings created by a non-AutoCAD program, that were saved as a .dxf file type, to be usable by AutoCAD

.dwt is the standard extension used for an AutoCAD template drawing

Selecting Close

When you select Close, the current drawing will close. If you have more than one drawing open at a time, the remaining drawings will still be open. If this was the only drawing you had open, AutoCAD® will close the drawing and all menus and will display the following on the upper left hand side of the screen:

Selecting Save

When you select **Save**, a dialog box will appear if this is the first time you are saving your drawing, and the command works the same as the **Save As…** command. This is because a new drawing is given a default name by AutoCAD®, such as Drawing1.dwg, and it is likely you would not want to save it under that name.

If this is not the first time saving the drawing, selecting **Save** will replace the existing version that was saved previously with the current version. In that case, no dialog box will appear, but the command line will show _qsave. This is what AutoCAD® refers to as a Quick Save.

Selecting Save As...

Use Save As... to save your drawing under a new name or to save it in a different location. This is useful if you wish to modify a drawing, but still want to preserve the original version. It is also useful if you want to save a duplicate copy to a separate folder or to a Flash Drive.

A Save As... dialog box will appear when this is chosen:

Save in: shows you which folder you are saving the drawing in.

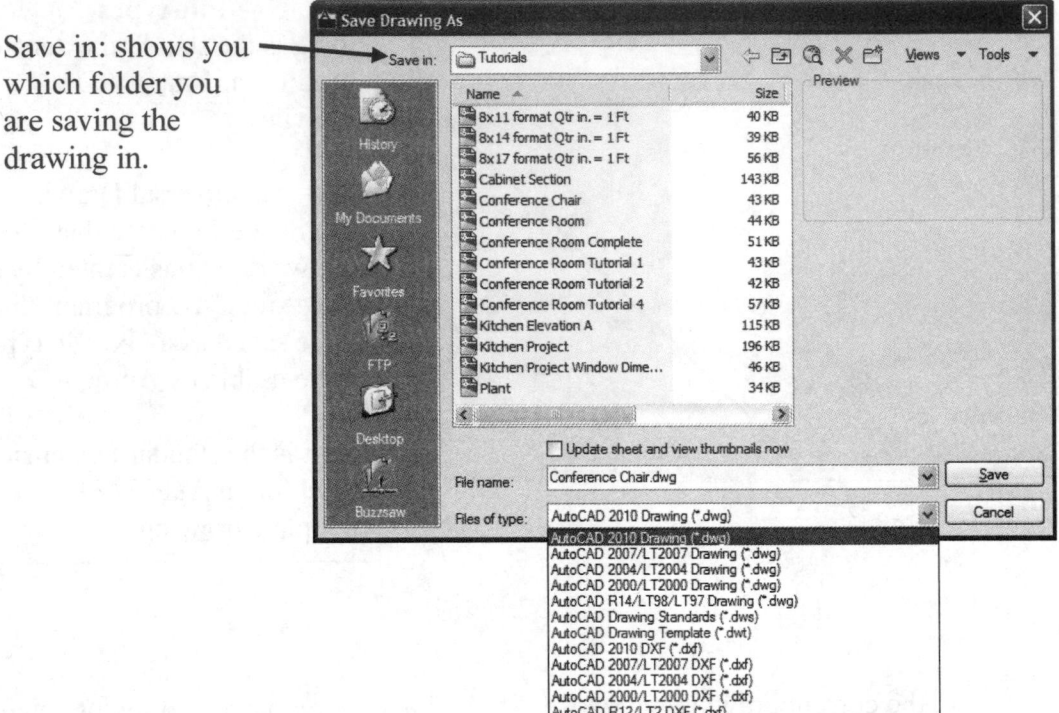

File types

You can choose to save your drawing as the current or earlier version of AutoCAD® as a .dwg, .dwt, or .dwt.

Saving your drawing as an earlier version allows sharing your files with other AutoCAD® users that are using an older version of AutoCAD®

Look in:/Save in: & Icons

The "Look in:" or "Save in:" work the same way. Understanding where your drawing is being saved, or where the drawing is located so that you can open it, is very important. You want to be able to locate your drawing later to make changes, etc. The pull-down arrow and the Icons help you manage that. A more detailed explanation can be found in File Management.

Getting Organized – File Management

Managing and organizing your drawings is very important. It allows you to easily find them when you need them. This is also true for non- AutoCAD® items such as text documents, spreadsheets, presentation slides, pictures, or any other computer data. Since AutoCAD® runs on a Windows operating system, file management will be easy if you have been using Windows based programs on your computer. If that is the case, this section can be skipped.

Your computer and drives

Your computer has one or more memory locations to store information and programs. Sometimes these are referred to as "drives". The following figure shows a typical layout of folders on the computer. Note: your computer may not be exactly the same as shown, but the organization concept is the same.

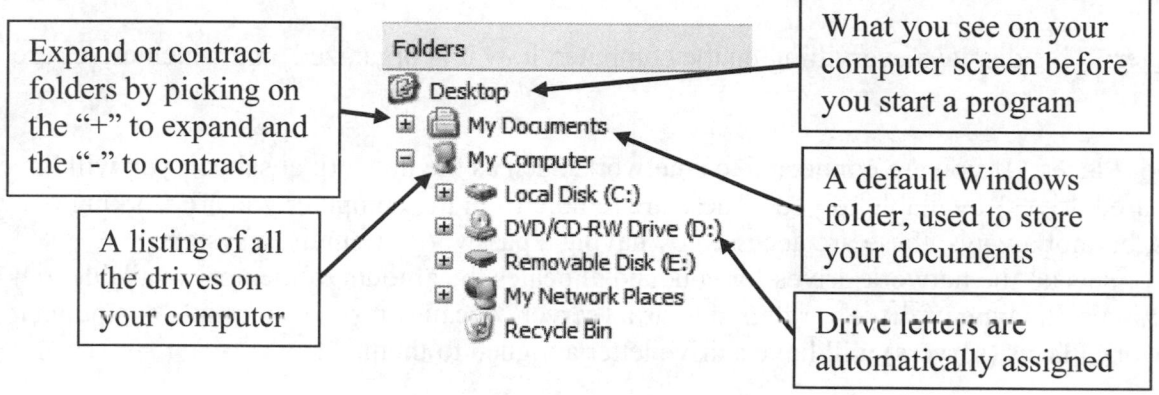

Expand or contract folders by picking on the "+" to expand and the "-" to contract

A listing of all the drives on your computer

What you see on your computer screen before you start a program

A default Windows folder, used to store your documents

Drive letters are automatically assigned

Desktop: The desktop is what is on your computer screen when you first turn the computer on. It has various icons, and the "wallpaper" background.

Various icons for whichever programs are installed on the computer

Wallpaper background of my the desktop – Yours most likely is different

<u>Drive Letters:</u> The letter in the parenthesis is the name of the drive on the computer. You may have heard the term "hard drive" before. This typically refers to the "C:" drive. This is a carry-over from the "old" days of the PC when two floppy drives were named "A:" and "B:" and the permanent internal drive was named "C:".   Any additional drive letters are automatically assigned in sequence (unless you have set a preference – usually for network drives).

In this example, drive "D:" is for the DVD/CD-RW. Since my computer is a laptop, this drive is removable. It is capable of reading DVD's and reading/writing compact discs (CD's). In addition, drive "E:" was automatically assigned to my flash drive when I installed it in the USB port. It is displayed as a Removable Disk.

<u>My Documents:</u> This is a default folder that is provided with Windows. It was provided as a convenient place to hold documents, drawings, pictures, etc. This avoids storing them in a location that holds your program files. You can add folders within the My Documents folder to help you organize your work.

<u>My Computer:</u> This displays everything on the computer, how it is organized, and which drives are available.

<u>My Network Places:</u> If you are connected to a network, such as the network at school, you will have various "shared drives" available to you. These are remote from the computer you are working on. Sometimes, but not always, these are accessed by having a password. Usually, a system administrator sets up the network drives for you, and allocates the amount of memory available to you. Sometimes this type of drive is referred to as a "server" because it serves multiple computers. These Network Places (servers) will have a drive letter assigned to them.

A convenient feature of a "shared drive" is that you can save your work on them, and other people will have access to that work. So, if you are working with a design team, you can share your portion of the design with other team members, without the need to e-mail them, or sending a CD copy to them.

Creating Folders

You can organize your work by creating folders, and sub-folders. This can be done within My Documents, on your Flash Drive, the Network Drive, or any other memory location. How you organize your work is up to you. One method I would recommend is to try to think of items as major topics with sub-topics. For example, if you have multiple clients, you could create a folder named "Clients" and name a folder for each client within the Clients folder. Let's use Smith and Jones for client names.

<u>Procedure:</u>

1. Double-left-click on the My Computer icon on your desktop.
2. My Computer will open up.

Folders icon   Views icon

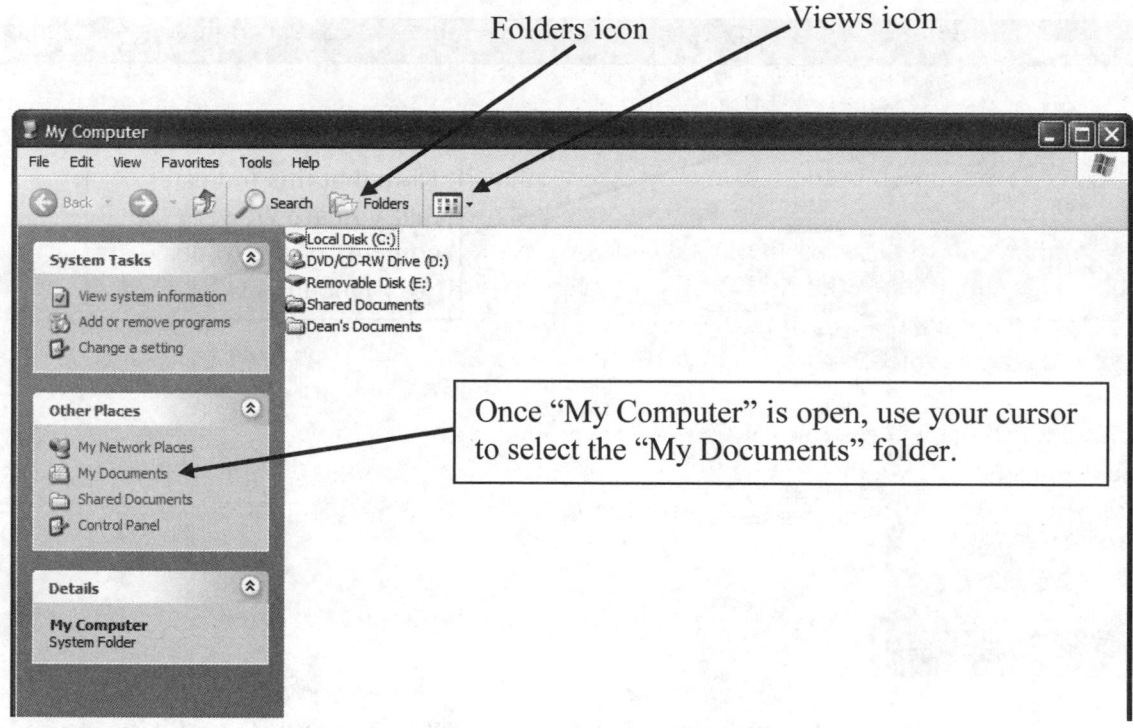

This is the list view of My Computer. How the view looks can be changed by selecting the Views icon.

Once that is selected, your choices will be displayed.

| Thumbnails |
| Tiles |
| Icons |
| • List |
| Details |

You can select a view type, depending on what you are after:

- Thumbnails come in handy for pictures
- Details can come in handy for checking dates and file sizes.

It is a personal preference which display you choose.

We will start out by creating the Client folder in My Documents (or you can create this folder on your flash drive instead). After the Client folder is set up, we can then create two folders within the Client folder; one named Smith and the other named Jones.

3. Select My Documents from the list shown. Your screen should now look similar to that shown below. Of course, your file folders will be different than mine.

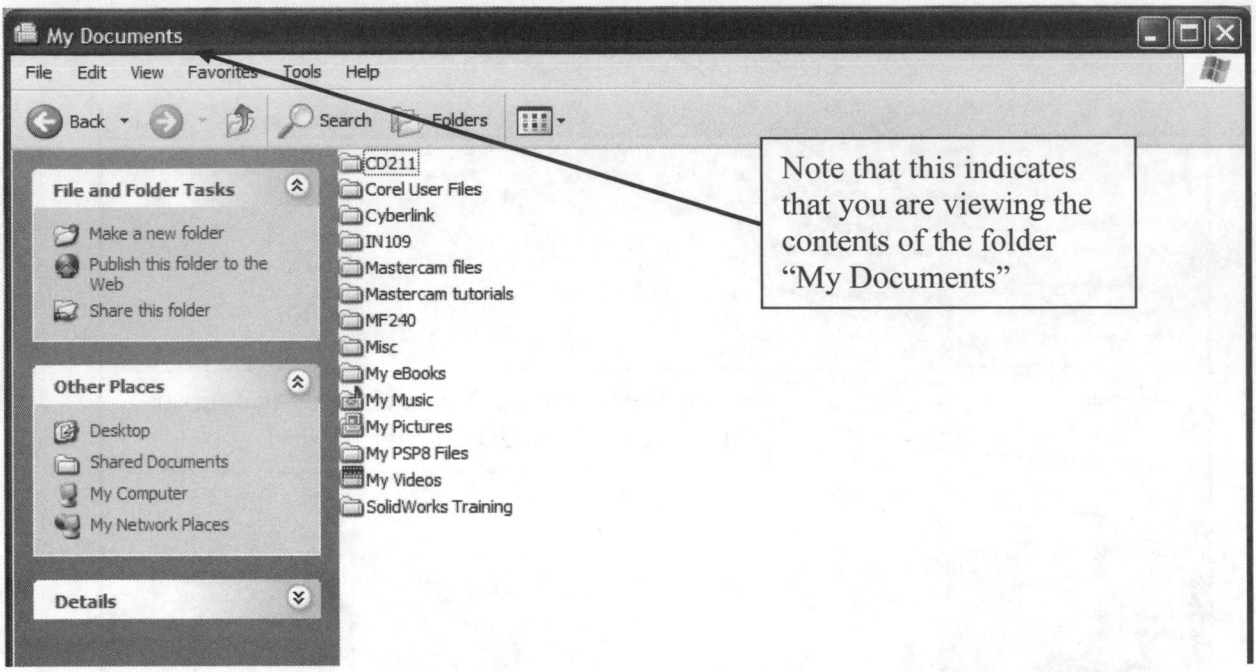

Note that this indicates that you are viewing the contents of the folder "My Documents"

4. Create a new folder within "My Documents" by selecting the pull-down File menu, select New, then select Folder:

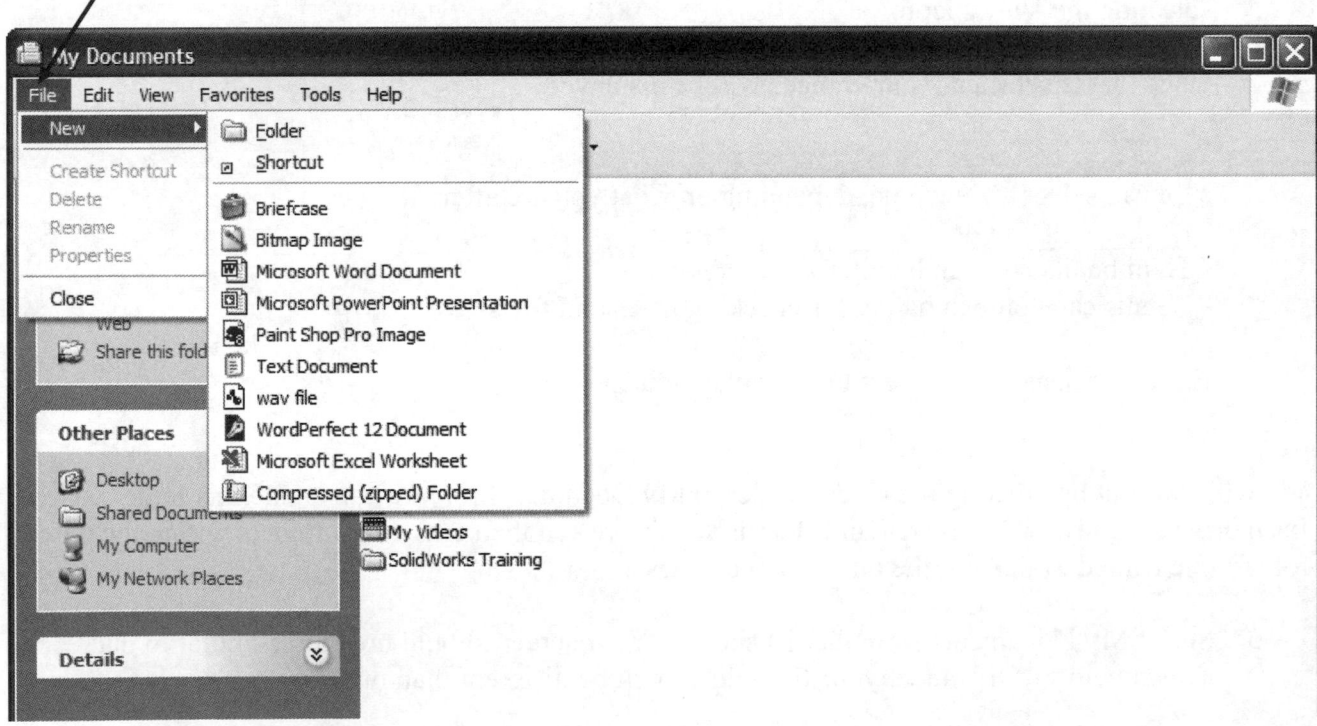

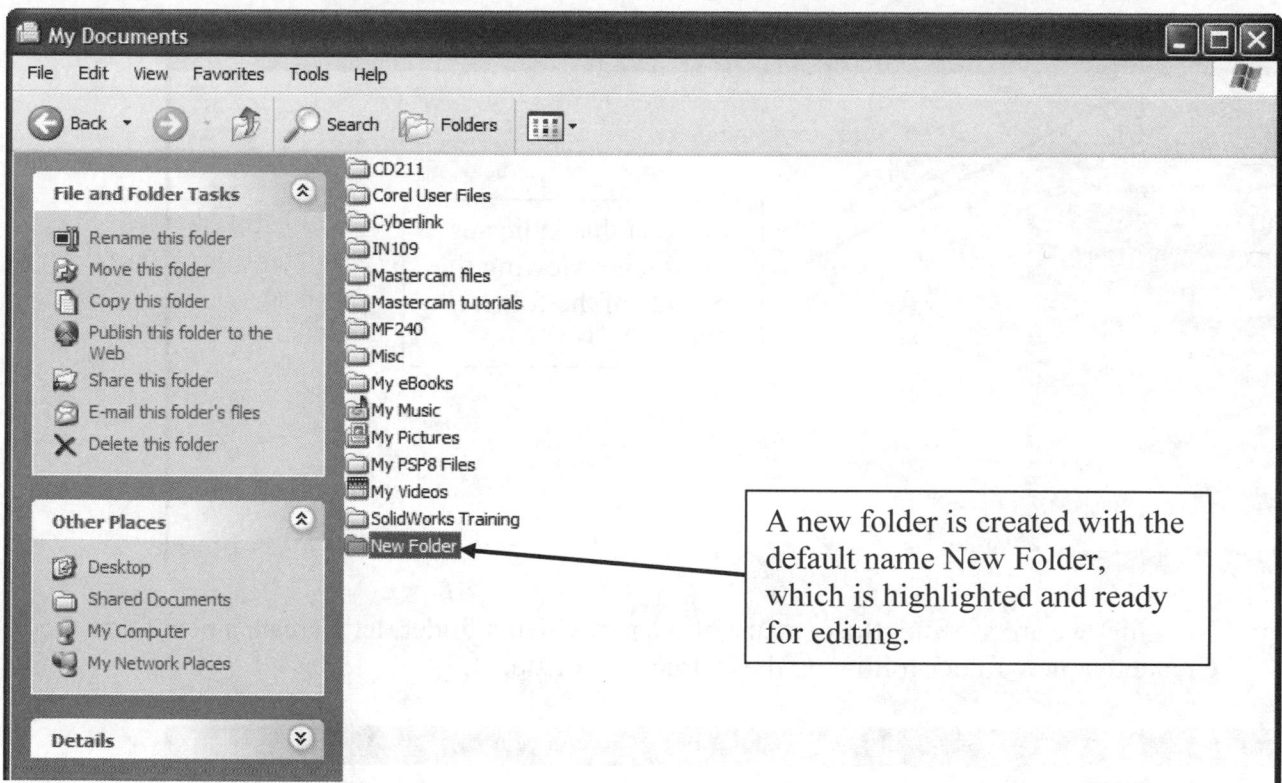

A new folder is created with the default name New Folder, which is highlighted and ready for editing.

5. Rename the New Folder to Clients. Note, since the New Folder is highlighted and the cursor is flashing within the highlight, it is ready for you to type the new name. Press the ⏎ Enter key when done.

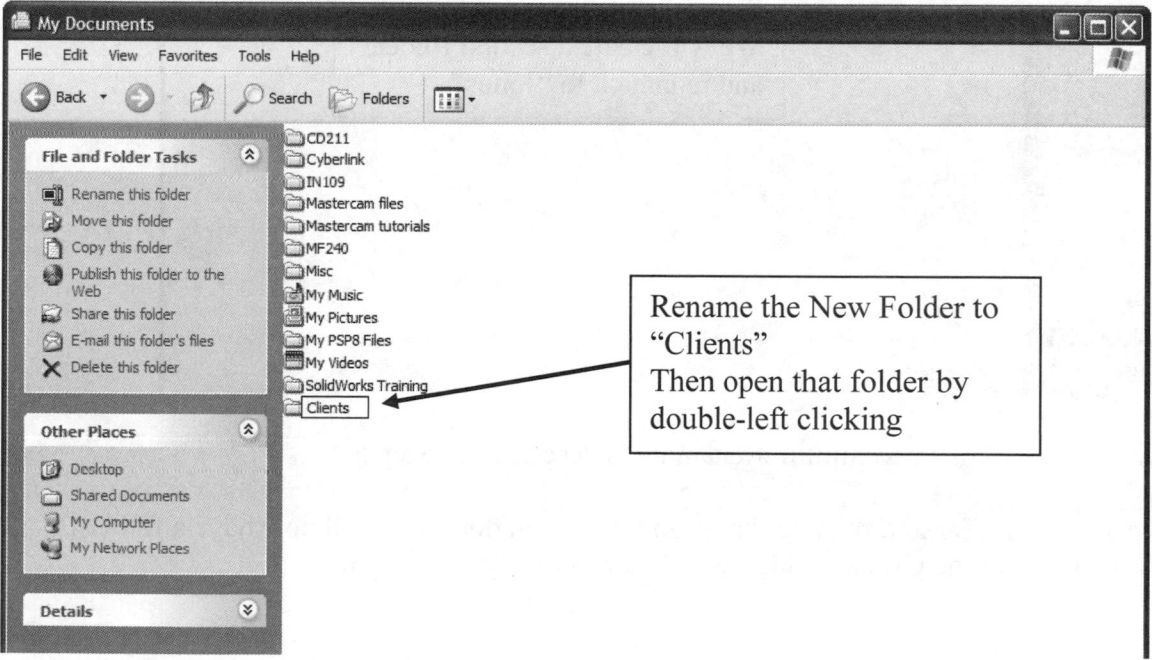

Rename the New Folder to "Clients"
Then open that folder by double-left clicking

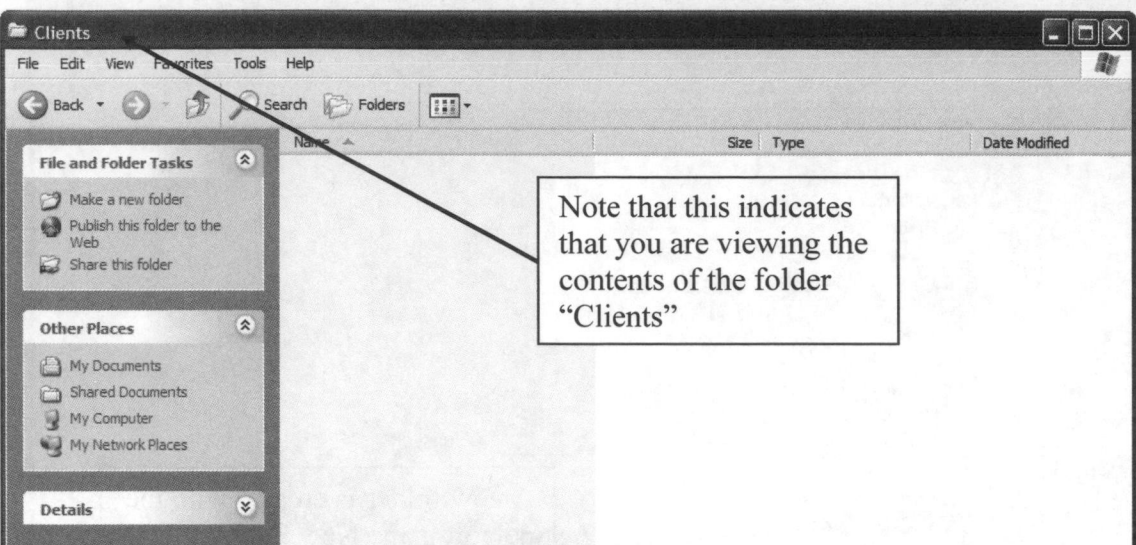

6. Now that we are viewing the contents of the new Clients folder, let's create a new folder here. Create that new folder following the instructions of step 4.

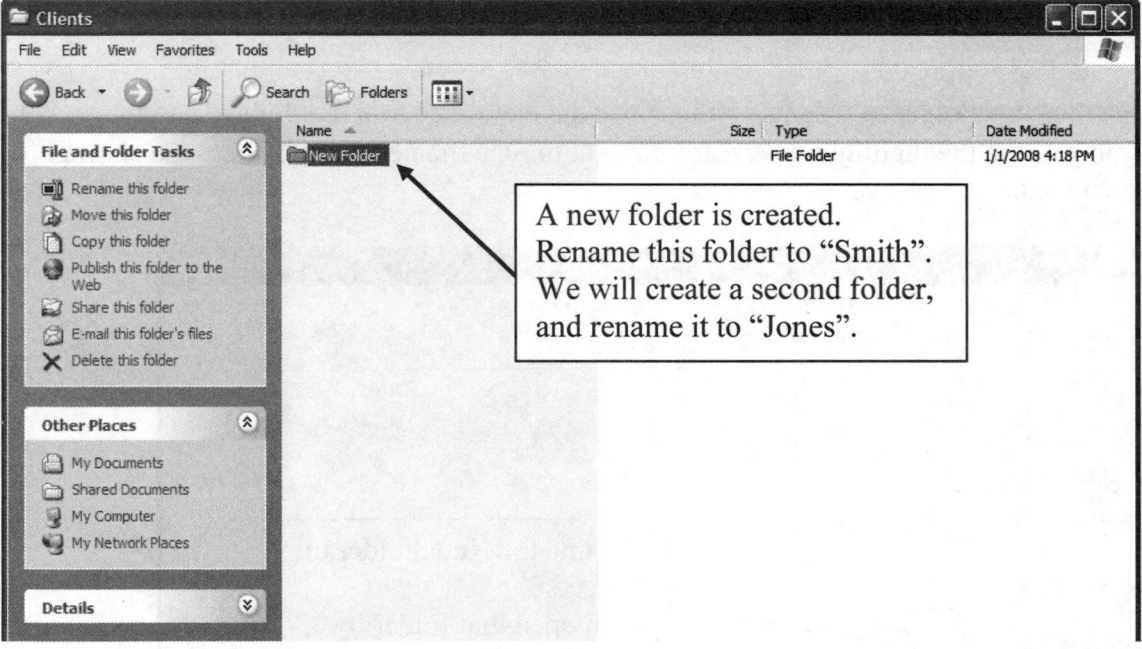

7. Rename the new folder to Smith. Renaming is described in Step 5.

8. Create another folder and rename that to Jones. When done you will now have a folder for each client within the Clients folder, which is within My Documents.

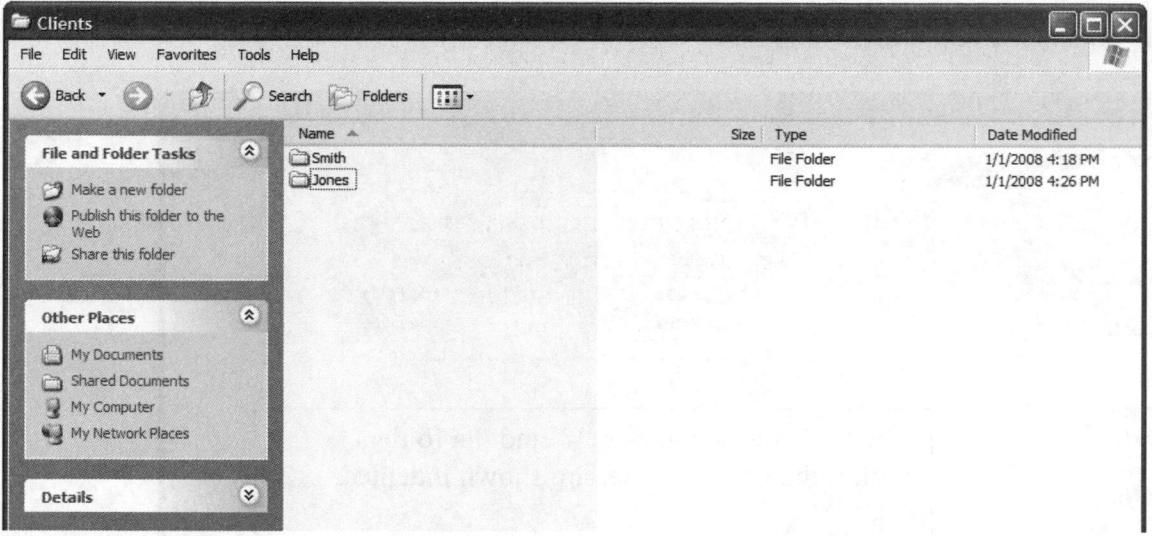

9. Turn on the Folders view and you will see the hierarchy tree (on the left side of your screen) of where these folders reside on your computer. Pick the "+" in front of the Clients folder to expand it.

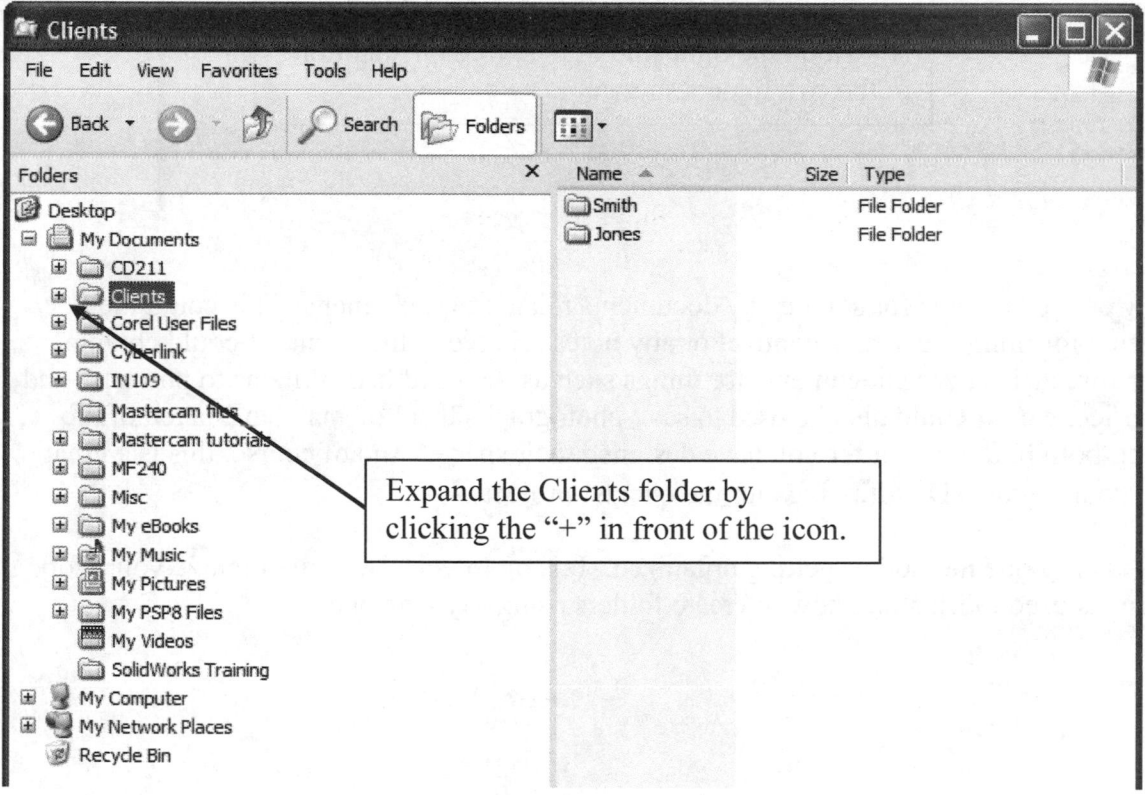

Expand the Clients folder by clicking the "+" in front of the icon.

The following shows the expanded view:

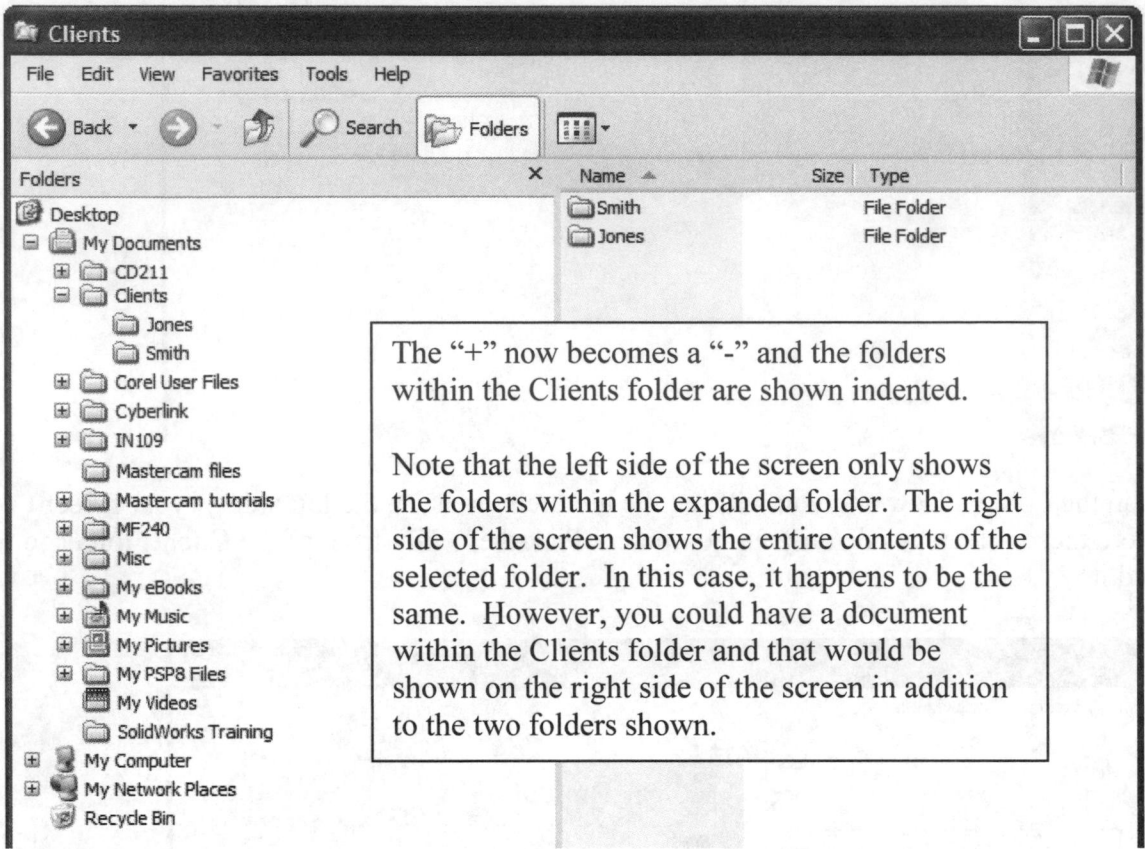

The "+" now becomes a "-" and the folders within the Clients folder are shown indented.

Note that the left side of the screen only shows the folders within the expanded folder. The right side of the screen shows the entire contents of the selected folder. In this case, it happens to be the same. However, you could have a document within the Clients folder and that would be shown on the right side of the screen in addition to the two folders shown.

You have now created a place for saving any documents related to each client. This could include Word documents for things such as a contract or any notes relative to the client. It could contain Excel or other spreadsheet type documents for things such as itemized lists of items to purchase and the purchase price, etc. It could also be used to save photographs that you may have taken of the clients' project, both before and after you have designed their space. And of course, this is a great place to store your AutoCAD® drawings for the clients' project.

Note that this is only one method of getting organized. It is up to you how you organize your work. This example was used to illustrate how to create folders using My Computer.

Summary

The topics covered in this chapter are meant to be an introduction to the AutoCAD® working environment. It is meant to help you feel more comfortable creating drawings on the computer. When you have completed this chapter, you should now have an understanding of the following:

- Differences between drawing by hand vs. using AutoCAD®
- Different ways of selecting AutoCAD® commands
- The different AutoCAD® Workspaces available
- Toolbars – how to bring them up and dock them
- Using the Help feature
- Customize your screen colors and your right mouse button
- Using a Flash Drive
- Opening, saving, and organizing your drawings

Review Questions

1. What are the advantages of using AutoCAD® instead of drawing by hand?

2. Why do you always draw full scale in AutoCAD®?

3. Which direction are angles measured in AutoCAD®?

4. What are the different Workspaces called that you can work in?

5. How can you bring up a different toolbar?

6. How do you access the Help feature?

7. Which pull-down menu and option do you use to change the screen color and customize the right mouse button?

8. What is a Flash Drive and how do you use it?

9. How do you open and save AutoCAD® drawings?

10. What Windows command is used to manage your files?

Notes:

Chapter 2
Setting-up and Intro to AutoCAD®

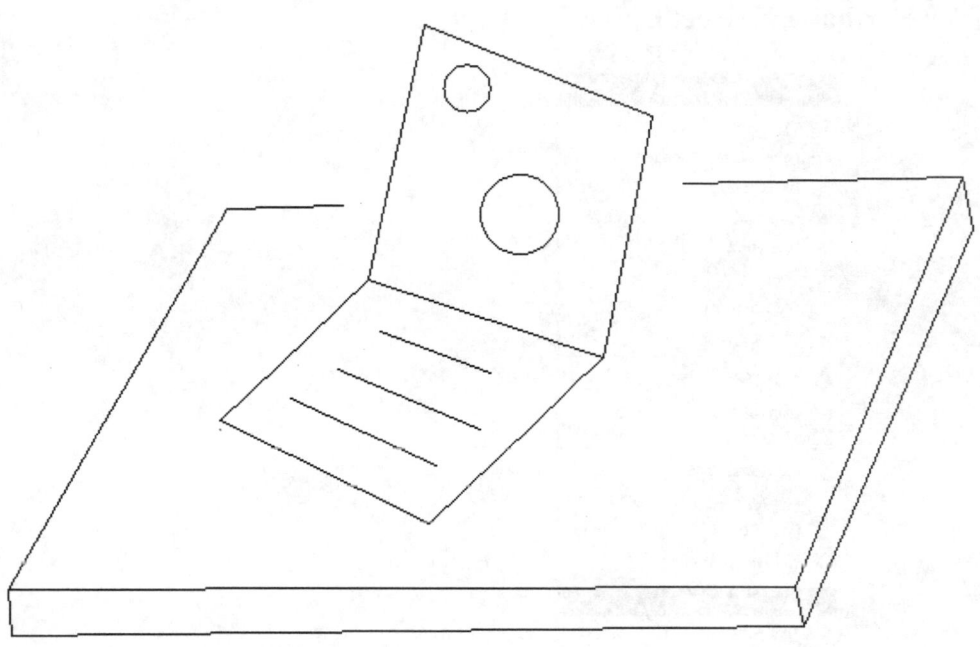

Learning Objectives:

- **Changing from Decimal to Architectural Units**
- **Increasing the size of your drawing space – Changing Drawing Limits**
- **Three basic commands to get started**
  - o **Line**
  - o **Circle**
  - o **Erase**
- **Methods of selecting objects**
- **Getting around your drawing by using Zoom and Pan**

Units

The Units command allows you to set the unit of measure for your drawing. For Interior Design, we want units of Feet and Inches. AutoCAD® names this style of units Architectural. The default style is Decimal, with a precision of 4 decimal places, so you will need to change it to Architectural.

Procedure:

Pick (left click): **Format** and select **Units…**

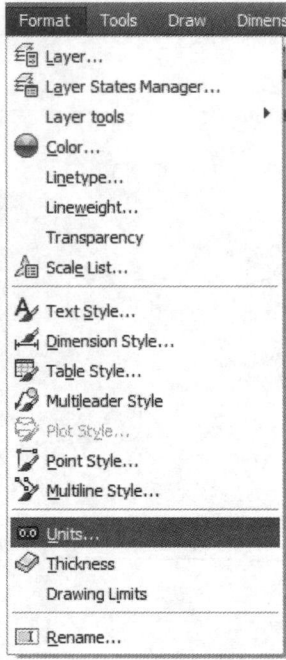

A dialog box will appear:

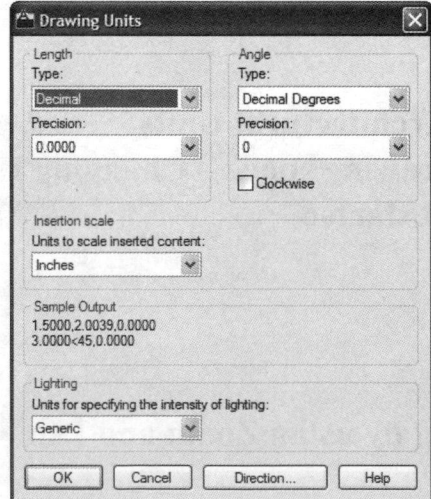

The dialog box contains pull-down selections for Length, Angle, and Insertion scale. We will not change the insertion scale. Within Length and Angle choices, there are also pull-down selections for Precision. Changing the precision only affects the displayed values of the coordinates and values shown when using Distance or List Commands (both to be discussed in later chapters). It does not change the true value of the object, which is stored in the AutoCAD® model at a very high precision.

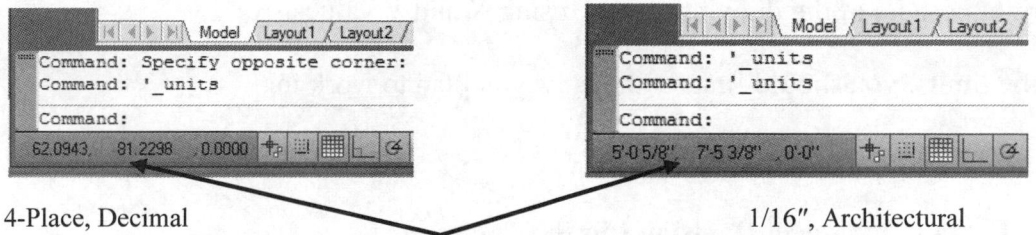

4-Place, Decimal   1/16″, Architectural

X,Y, & Z Coordinate Values of the cursor location
are displayed in the selected precision and unit type

Change the units for Length to Architectural:

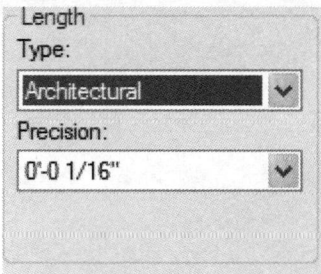

The Precision will automatically change to fraction style. Ensure that 1/16″ is the precision. If not, use the pull-down selection to change it.

Leave the default values for Angle at Decimal Degrees with 0 Precision, with the Clockwise check box unchecked. Note that the default direction for angles is counterclockwise, which we will leave alone.

Feel free to explore different styles and precisions. When you are done exploring, set the values to those shown in the above figure.

Drawing Limits

The Drawing Limits command allows you to set the size of the area for you to draw. Since you will be drawing everything full size, this should be done prior to doing your drawing. The default drawing size is 12″ wide by 9″ tall. AutoCAD® specifies the drawing limits by defining the lower left and upper right corners of the drawing area by using X and Y values.

Before setting the limits, you should first set the units you plan to work in.

Procedure:

Pick (left click): **Format** and select **Drawing Limits**.

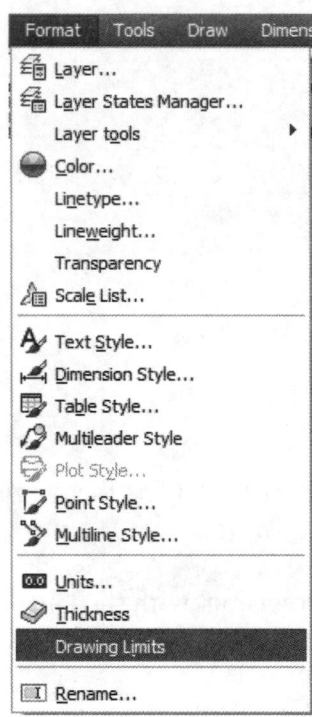

The command line prompts you with the following:
Specify lower left corner or [ON/OFF] <0'-0",0'-0">:

Specify lower left corner or [ON/OFF] <0'-0",0'-0">: ↵
(Note: ↵ represents pressing the ↵ Enter key)

> Press the ↵ Enter key to accept the default values (shown between brackets < >)

A new prompt appears on the command line with the following:

Specify upper right corner <1'-0", 0'-9">:

Key in new values for the upper right corner. As an example, if you have a 15′x15′ room, you may want your drawing space to be 20′x20′:

Specify upper right corner <1'-0", 0'-9">: **20′,20′**↵

> Type the values for the horizontal direction and vertical direction. Separate the values with a comma. Press the ↵ Enter key so AutoCAD can read the values you typed.

Remember to use the foot symbol (′) to represent feet. Without it, AutoCAD® defaults to inches. Also, remember to use a comma between the X and Y values. When complete, AutoCAD® ends the Drawing Limits command.

Three Easy Commands to Help Get You Started

Line

The Line command creates a point-to-point line. AutoCAD® allows you to create multiple end-to-end lines within the single command. The Line command is a very basic AutoCAD® command.

Procedure:

Pick (left click): **Line icon** from the Draw toolbar.

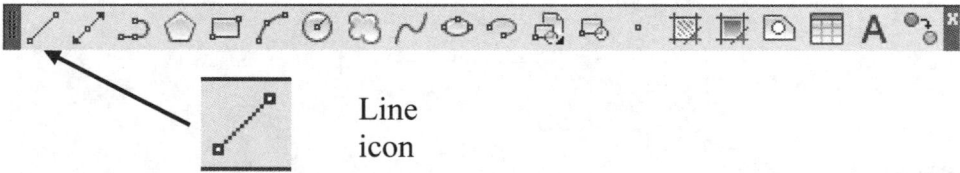

Line icon

The command line prompts you with the following:

Command: _line Specify first point:

Pick anywhere on your screen to begin to draw a line.

After you specify the first point, the line will appear on the screen, anchored at the point you just picked, and will "rubber-band" to follow your cursor. The command line prompts you with the following:

Specify next point or [Undo]:

Left click on the screen again and a line will be created. A second line will begin, anchored at the second point you just picked, and will "rubber-band" again to follow your cursor. Because AutoCAD® does not know how many lines you intend to draw, the command line will continue to prompt you with the following:

Specify next point or [Undo]:

When you are done drawing lines, press the ↵ Enter key to exit the Line command.

AutoCAD® will exit the line command and display a command prompt.
Command:

Although other methods of putting lines on your drawing exist, they will not be covered here. You can explore these on your own using the help menu.

Recommendation:

The Line command has limited use. It is recommended to use this command when you want to draw lines between two existing points (such as endpoints of existing lines). Otherwise, using the Construction Line command and trimming is a much more intuitive approach. The Construction Line and Trim commands will be covered in the next chapter.

Try it:

Draw 3 lines to form the letter "Z".

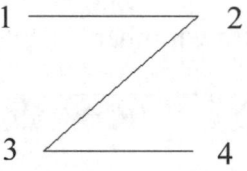

(Pick the Line icon)

Command: _line Specify first point: ***(Pick a point on the screen at location 1)***
Specify next point or [Undo]: ***(Pick a point on the screen at location 2)***
Specify next point or [Undo]: ***(Pick a point on the screen at location 3)***
Specify next point or [Close/Undo]: ***(Pick a point on the screen at location 4)***
Specify next point or [Close/Undo]: ↵
Command:

Remember, for the Line command, AutoCAD® does not know when your done drawing lines until you exit the command by pressing the ↵ Enter key.

Circle

The Circle command creates a circle. Creating a circle and trimming it can be an easy way to create an arc. A circle can be defined in multiple ways. The default method of creating a circle using the icon is to define the center and the radius.

Procedure:

Pick (left click): **Circle icon** from the Draw toolbar.

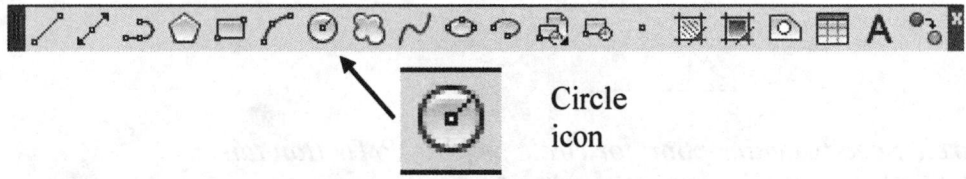

Circle
icon

The command line prompts you with the following:
Command: _circle Specify center point for circle or [3P/2P/Ttr (tan tan radius)]:

For a simple circle, pick a location for the center point:

(Pick anywhere on the screen to define the center of the circle)

After you specify the center point, the command line prompts you with the following:
Specify radius of circle or [Diameter]:

You can specify the radius of the circle by typing a value (followed by the ↵ Enter key) or by picking a second point on the screen.

If you prefer to specify the diameter instead of the radius, type the letter "**d**" (followed by the ↵ Enter key) which is for the diameter option. After doing so, the command line will prompt you with the following:
Specify diameter of circle:

After you define the radius (or diameter, if that option was used), a circle will be created and AutoCAD® will exit the Circle command and display a command prompt.
Command:

Recommendation:

The Circle command is a very useful, easy to use tool. Circles can be used as an alternative to arcs, especially when the center point and radius are known, because a circle will become an arc after it is trimmed.

Although using circles and trimming may actually take more steps than drawing arcs using exact starting and ending points, it allows the designer not to have to think in terms of starting and ending points. After some practice, it can actually be quicker to draw this way, since less thought is involved.

Try it:

Draw a 1″ radius circle to the right of the lines you just created.

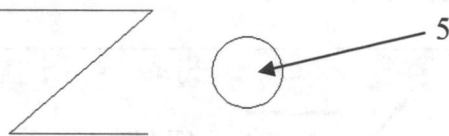

Command: _circle Specify center point for circle or [3P/2P/Ttr (tan tan radius)]: **(Pick a point on the screen at location 5)**

Specify radius of circle or [Diameter]: **1↵ (Key in the value 1 and press the ↵ Enter key)**
Command:

AutoCAD® will automatically end the Circle command.

Erase

The Erase command allows you to eliminate an object from your drawing.

Procedure:

Pick (left click): **Erase icon** from the Modify toolbar.

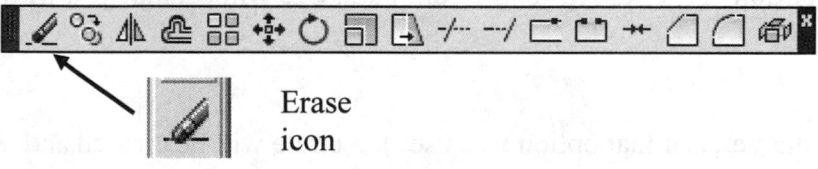

Erase
icon

The command line prompts you with the following:

Command: _erase
Select objects:

Select the object you want to erase by moving your cursor over the object and left-clicking the mouse to pick the object.

After you pick the first object, your command line will look like the following:

Select objects: 1 found
Select objects:

> As you pick objects to be erased, the
> line type changes from solid to dashed

AutoCAD® will continue to prompt you for more objects to erase. When you are done selecting objects to erase, press the ↵ Enter key to exit the command.

Try it:

Erase the lines and circle you just created.

(Pick the Erase icon)
Command: _erase
Select objects: (Pick one of the lines)1 found
Select objects: (Pick another line) 1 found, 2 total
Select objects: (Pick the last line)1 found, 3 total
Select objects: (Pick the circle) 1 found, 4 total
Select objects: ↵
Command:

Your screen will no longer have the lines and circle on it.

When using the Erase command, you can select objects individually or you can use either a Selection Window or a Crossing Window to select multiple objects. The following section describes the different methods of selecting objects.

Methods of Selecting Objects

Objects can be selected individually by picking them (using the left mouse button), or by using either a Selection Window or a Crossing Window. A Selection or Crossing Window allows you to select objects by picking opposite corners of a "window" around the objects you want to select. The direction in which the opposite corners are chosen determines whether you are using a Selection Window or a Crossing Window.

Selection Window (LEFT to RIGIIT)

A Selection Window is used during a command and the direction of picking the opposite corners is Left to Right. When a Selection Window is used, only those objects that are completely bounded by the window are selected. If only a portion of an object is in the window, it will not be part of the selection set.

The following example of selecting one of two lines to be erased illustrates this. The area inside the Selection Window will be shaded. Only the line that is completely bounded by the window will be selected. Picking on the screen in the order shown will result in the following:

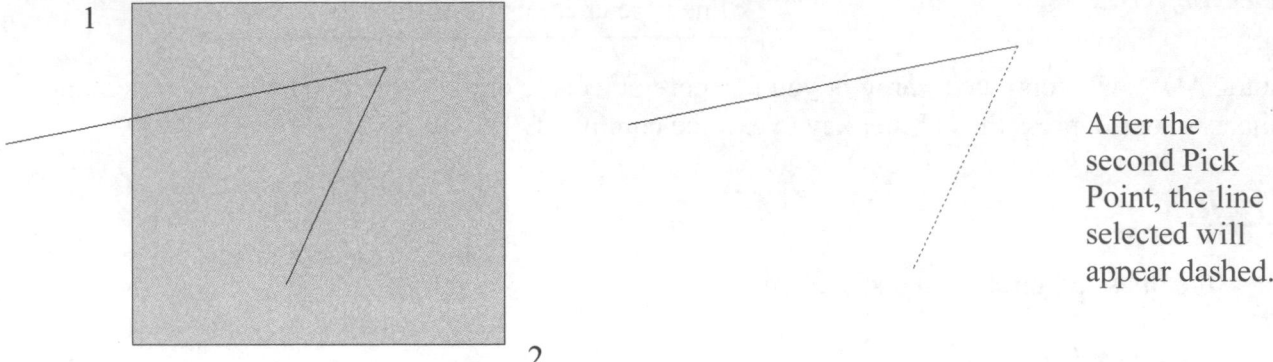

After the second Pick Point, the line selected will appear dashed.

Crossing Window (RIGHT to LEFT)

A Crossing Window is used during a command and the direction of picking the opposite corners is <u>Right to Left.</u> When a Crossing Window is used, objects that are bounded by the window are selected, including those that only a portion of which <u>crosses</u> the window.

The following example of selecting two lines to be erased illustrates this. The area inside the Crossing Window will be shaded. Although only a portion of one line is completely bounded by the window, a portion of it will be selected. Picking on the screen in the order shown will result in the following:

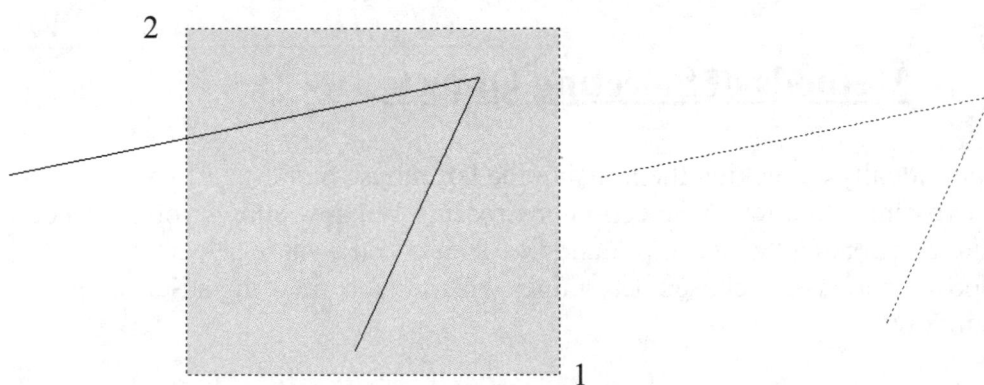

Notice that the Selection Window boundary is shown as a solid line and a Crossing Window boundary is shown as a dashed line. In addition, the color of the area inside the Crossing Window is different from the color of the Selection Window.

Removing objects from the selection set

When selecting multiple objects, you may have selected more objects than was intended. To remove objects from the selection set, simply hold the shift key and select the objects to remove. The selection method is the same: individual, selection window, or crossing window.

Using the same example as above (both lines were selected with Crossing Window during the Erase command), we can remove one of the two lines selected before completing the command. The following is the command line sequence:

Command: _erase
Select objects:

Use a Crossing Window to select both lines

Specify opposite corner: 2 found

Once the 2 lines are selected, hold the shift key and pick the line you want to remove from the selection set.

Select objects: 1 found, 1 removed, 1 total

Select objects: ↵
Command:

Pressing the ↵ Enter key completes the Erase command.

Grips

Sometime while trying out AutoCAD®, you may occasionally notice that your objects are highlighted and have little blue boxes attached to them. Or you may have moved your cursor on the screen and found that AutoCAD® appears to be drawing a rectangle (it isn't).

This can occur when you do not have a command in the command line and you left-click somewhere on your screen. After you do this, your command line will prompt you to specify the opposite corner. AutoCAD® is attempting to create a selection window or a crossing window. If there are objects selected without a command in the command line, the grips will appear.

Picking objects without having an active command will place grips on them.

Grips can be used to change object locations and sizes. For example, a line will have three grips attached to it: one at each end, and one at the mid-point. Picking the grip at the midpoint will allow you to relocate the line on your screen. Picking either end grip will allow you to change the length and angle of the line – this occurs because you are moving only one endpoint while the other endpoint stays fixed.

If you have no intention of using grips and you accidentally get them on your screen, simply press the Escape (Esc) key to make them go away.

> Pressing the Esc key will remove the grips from your objects.

Zoom and Pan

The Zoom and Pan features within AutoCAD® allow you to view the drawing you are creating at different sizes and locations. Imagine that the drawing you are creating is similar to the paper on a drawing board and you are viewing your drawing through a lens. The Zoom feature allows you to get a close-up look at an area or get a wider view, depending on whether you zoom in on a specific area or zoom out. The Pan feature moves the camera side-to-side or top-to-bottom.

There are several methods to Zoom and Pan around your drawing. One of the easiest methods of zooming in and out and panning is to use the wheel on the wheel mouse.

Zoom and Pan Using the Wheel Mouse

Wheel

Wheel Mouse

Rolling the wheel forward and aft allows you to zoom in and out of the drawing. Pressing the wheel down will change the cursor from a pointer to a hand. Moving the mouse around, while pressing the wheel down, allows you to "pan" around your drawing. This feature can come in handy because you do not need to select an icon or key in a command. In addition, you can zoom and pan using the wheel while you are in the middle of a command.

You can also fill your drawing screen with all the objects you have drawn by double-clicking the wheel on the mouse. This is referred to as Zoom Extents.

Typing the Zoom Command

One method of zooming is to type the command. Typing the letter "z" is the shortcut for the zoom command.

Command: z
ZOOM
Specify corner of window, enter a scale factor (nX or nXP), or
[All/Center/Dynamic/Extents/Previous/Scale/Window/Object] <real time>:

AutoCAD® will default to a Zoom Window command. A Zoom Window allows you to pick opposite corners of a selected area on your drawing to enlarge that area to fill your screen.

You can choose one of the multiple options shown in the square brackets. For instance, if you wanted to zoom the entire drawing, type the letter "a" for All. Each option is the same as previously explained.

Example of Zoom Window:

If you had the following items on your screen and you want to zoom in on just the circles, select the Zoom command by typing the letter "z" and then pressing the ↵ Enter key. This will begin the Zoom command. Now simply pick opposite corners around the circles (shown here at locations 1 and 2):

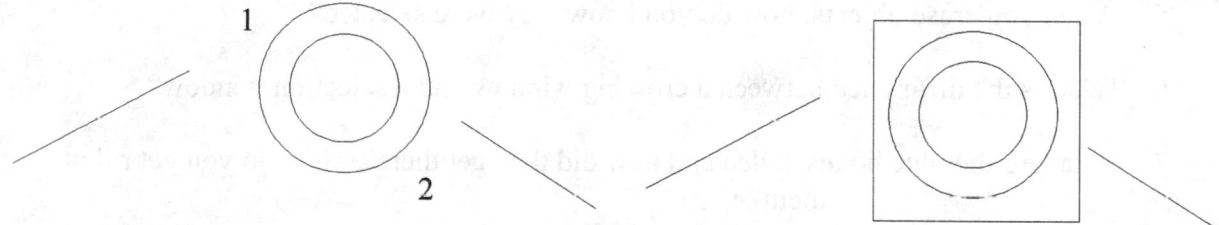

As you move your cursor from location 1 to location 2, you will notice what looks like a rectangle growing on the screen as it follows your cursor. That is the Zoom Window. Only those items in that window will now fill the screen. Depending on the shape of the Zoom Window, some additional pieces of other items may also appear on your screen.

Recommendation:

I have found that using the wheel mouse is the easiest way to zoom and pan around the drawing. In addition, double-clicking the wheel mouse is the easiest way to see the extent of everything you have drawn.

Summary

In this chapter you have learned to:

- Change the units from decimal to feet and inches.
- Change the size of your drawing space
- Create lines and circles
- Erase objects
- Select objects or remove objects from a selection set
- Get grips and make them disappear
- Navigate through your drawing using the Zoom command and mouse wheel

Review Questions

1. How do you change the units from decimal to feet and inches?

2. How do you change the size of the drawing space?

3. How does the line command end?

4. How does the circle command end?

5. When you erase objects, how do you know they were selected?

6. What is the difference between a crossing window and a selection window?

7. What are the blue boxes called and how did they get there? How do you get rid of them?

8. How do you use the wheel on your mouse to move around the drawing?

9. What is the shortcut key for the Zoom command?

10. What is a Zoom Window?

Exercises

1. Draw the star. Do not concern yourself with size or location.

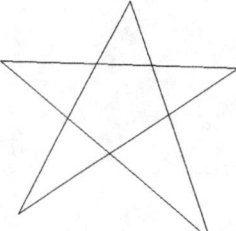

2. Draw the patch. Do not concern yourself with size or location.

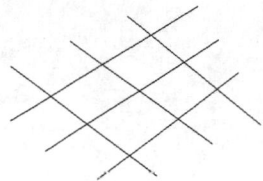

3. Draw the circles. Do not concern yourself with size or location.

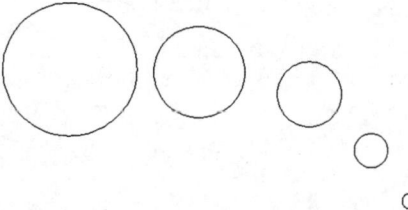

4. Draw the lines and circle. Do not concern yourself with size or location.

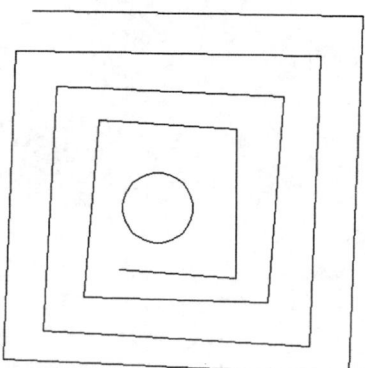

Notes:

Chapter 3
Commands – Set 1: Drawing Construction
- Getting Started

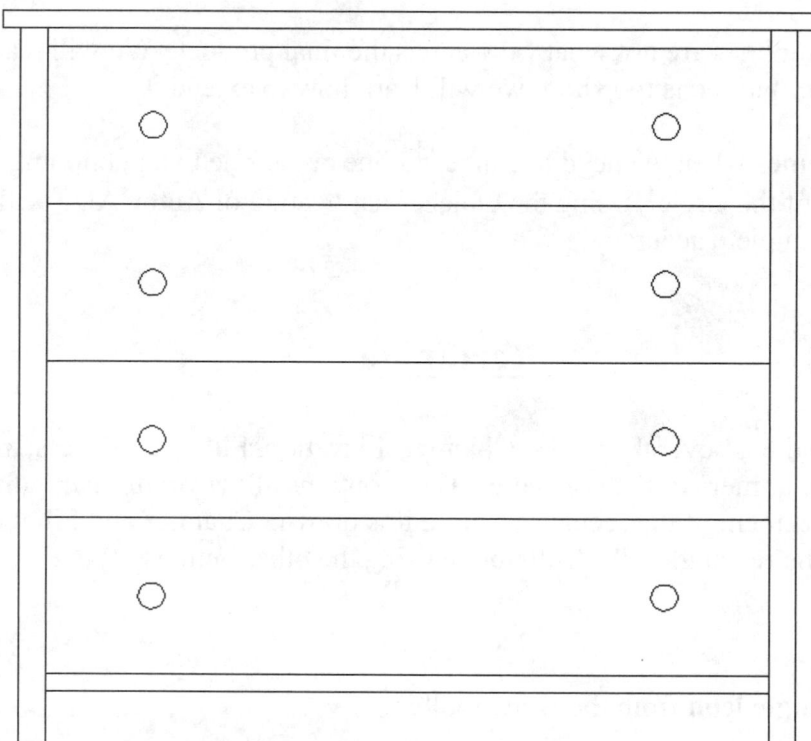

Learning Objectives:

- **A familiar shape: Rectangle**
- **Change rectangles to lines by using Explode**
- **Creating parallel or concentric objects using Offset**
- **Creating Horizontal, Vertical, Angled, and Offset Construction Lines**
- **Improving drawing accuracy using Object Snap**
- **Changing the objects limits using Trim and Extend**

In Chapter 2 we learned two basic drawing commands and one modify command to help us get started drawing: Line, Circle, and Erase. Not enough information was given in that chapter to allow you to create a drawing with accuracy. In this chapter we will learn more commands that will help us create an accurate drawing. We will also learn AutoCAD® construction techniques that will help you to make drawings quickly.

We will start with a shape that is most familiar to us: the rectangle. From there, we will move on to creating infinitely long lines, known as construction lines. The nice part about construction lines is that you can make them horizontal, vertical or at a specific angle. This can also be done with the line command, however, I have found that the construction lines are much easier to work with.

Of course, infinitely long lines are not what we want as the final product. We will learn how to trim those lines. In addition, if a line is too short, we will learn how to extend it.

And finally, there are times when we need to connect a line or a circle to an endpoint, or maybe draw a line through a center of the circle. Using the Object Snap feature of AutoCAD® will allow us to create drawings with complete accuracy.

Rectangle

The Rectangle command has several options: Chamfer, Elevation, Fillet, Thickness, and Width, as well as a prompt for the corners of the rectangle. These options allow you to manipulate the appearance and the placement of the rectangle before it is drawn. Chamfer and Fillet are options that change the corners of the rectangle. We will not be using the other options.

Procedure:

Pick (left click): **Rectangle icon** from the Draw toolbar.

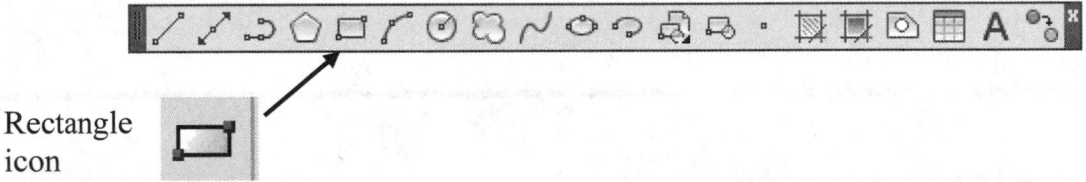

Rectangle icon

The command line prompts you with the following:
Specify first corner point or [Chamfer/Elevation/Fillet/Thickness/Width]:

For a simple rectangle, anchor the first corner by picking anywhere on the screen or by picking a point on existing objects (must have OSNAP turned on or select an object snap override before picking – more about this later).

After you specify the first corner point, the command line prompts you with the following:

Specify other corner point or [Area/Dimensions/Rotation]:

You can specify the second corner by simply picking a second point on the screen. Of course, this will not let you know the size of the rectangle that was created.

A recommended method to create a rectangle of a specific size is to type "d" for *Dimensions* and then press the ↵ Enter key. In the command line, AutoCAD® will prompt you for the size of the rectangle in two steps. The first prompt is for the horizontal direction. The second prompt is for the vertical direction. Unfortunately, the wording of the prompts is confusing.

AutoCAD® prompts for the horizontal direction as follows:

Specify length for rectangles <X'-X">:

At this prompt type in the distance for the rectangle in the horizontal direction and press the ↵ Enter key.

AutoCAD® prompts for the vertical direction as follows:

Specify width for rectangles <Y'-Y">:

At this prompt type in the distance for the rectangle in the vertical direction and press the ↵ Enter key.

AutoCAD® has one more prompt. Because we have specified the location of one corner and the size of the rectangle, there still remain 4 choices for the opposite corner. The prompt is as follows.

Specify other corner point or [Area/Dimensions/Rotation]:

Using your cursor, pick the location of the second corner of the rectangle. Note that there are four locations that can be picked (upper right, upper left, lower left, lower right). As you move your cursor around, the rectangle will follow for each location.

After you pick the second corner point, the rectangle command is complete and you are back to the command prompt.

The rectangle is considered to be a single object, and as such can be erased completely by picking anywhere on the rectangle.

Recommendation:

Use rectangles for the start of the room walls, format borders, furniture or other rectangular shaped objects. The advantage of using rectangles is that they can be offset by using a single Offset command (more info on Offset appears later in this chapter). All four sides will be offset and trimmed at once. This is a time saver for walls. For ease of drawing, use the dimension option for the second corner. Doing it this way allows the designer not to have to think in X-Y coordinates.

If you use rectangles, it is recommended that you then convert them to lines (after you are done offsetting them). This is done by using the Explode command. Lines are then treated as individual objects and are easier to modify.

Try it:

Draw an 8′x16′ rectangle.

(Pick the Rectangle icon)
Command: _rectang
Specify first corner point or [Chamfer/Elevation/Fillet/Thickness/Width]:
(Pick a point on the screen at location 1)

Specify other corner point or [Area/Dimensions/Rotation]: **d↵**
(Key in the letter "d" and press the ↵ Enter key)

Although it is prompting for length, AutoCAD® is looking for the value for the horizontal direction:
Specify length for rectangles <8′-0″>: **16′↵ (Key in 16′ and press the ↵ Enter key)**

Although it is prompting for width, AutoCAD® is looking for the value for the vertical direction
Specify width for rectangles <16′-0″>: **8′↵ (Key in 8′ and press the ↵ Enter key)**

Specify other corner point or [Area/Dimensions/Rotation]: (Pick a point on the screen at location 2)
Command:

AutoCAD® ends the command and your rectangle is on the screen.

Explode

The Explode command allows you to break down a compound object to its basic components. As an example, a rectangle is made up of 4 lines. However, AutoCAD® treats a rectangle as a single object. If you explode a rectangle, it will still appear as a rectangle on your screen, but AutoCAD® now treats it as 4 separate lines.

Procedure:

Pick (left click): **Explode icon** from the Modify toolbar.

Explode
icon

The command line prompts you with the following:

Command: _explode
Select objects:

Select the object to explode by moving your cursor over the object and left-clicking the mouse to pick the object.

After you pick the first object, your command lines will look like the following:

Select objects: 1 found
Select objects:

AutoCAD® will continue to prompt you for more objects to explode. When you are done selecting objects to Explode, press the ↵ Enter key to exit the command.

Recommendation:

Typically used for converting rectangles to lines. If you use rectangles, it is recommended that you then convert them to lines (after you are done offsetting them). This is done by using the Explode command. Lines are then treated as individual objects and are easier to modify.

Explode is also useful for converting Blocks to individual objects. Blocks will be covered in a later chapter.

Try it:

Hold your cursor over the rectangle that you just created. The rectangle will be highlighted and become bold lines and a tip will pop up identifying this object as a Polyline. A Polyline is what AutoCAD® names the rectangle.

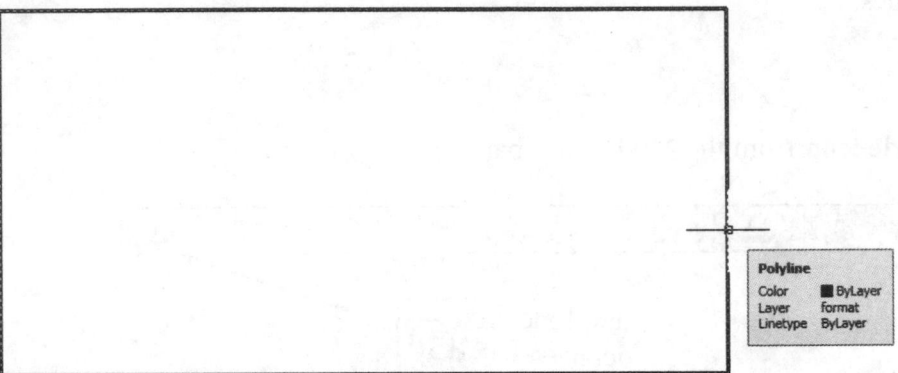

Now let's break down the rectangle into 4 separate lines by using the Explode command.

(Pick the Explode icon)

Command: _explode
*Select objects: **(Pick the rectangle)** 1 found*
Select objects: ↵
Pressing the ↵ Enter key exits the command and the command prompt returns.
Command:

Now hold your cursor over any of the lines of the rectangle and your pop up tip will tell you that it found a line. The line will be highlighted, not the whole rectangle.

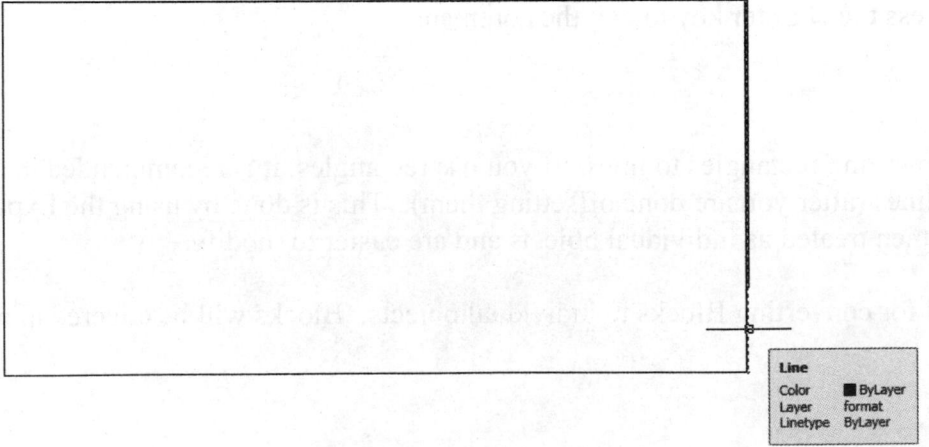

Offset

The Offset command creates parallel lines or curves, and concentric circles or rectangles/polygons, a specified distance away or through a specified point. This is used to create new objects from existing ones.

Procedure:

Pick (left click): **Offset icon** from the Modify toolbar.

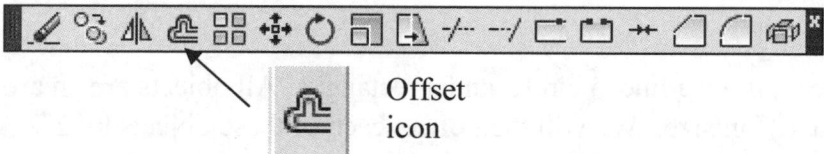

Offset
icon

The command line prompts you with the following:

Specify offset distance or [Through] <X'-XX>:

Key in a specified distance you wish to offset, followed by pressing the ↵ Enter key.
You can also accept the default of *<X'-XX>* by pressing the ↵ Enter key.

Note that the value inside the brackets is the value that was previously used in an Offset command. If this is the first time the Offset command is used for the drawing, the value would be *Through*.

After specifying the distance, the command line prompts you with the following:

Select object to offset or <exit>:
Select the object by left-clicking the mouse when the cursor is over the object you wish to select.

After selecting the object you wish to offset, the command line prompts you with the following:

Specify point of side to offset:

There are two choices that can be made here. As an example, a vertical line can be offset to the left or to the right. A circle, rectangle, or polygon, can be offset inside or outside. To specify which side to offset, left-click the mouse when the cursor is on the side of the object you wish to offset.

AutoCAD® will continue to prompt for more objects to offset:
Select object to offset or <exit>:

To exit the command, press the ↵ Enter key.

Recommendation:

The Offset command is a very useful tool, and likely the most used command. If you have lines on the drawing to offset, but they are not as long as you would like them to be after they are offset, then it is more convenient to use the Construction Line command (next topic) with the Offset option. An example would be if you had the interior walls drawn and want to construct the exterior walls. Using Offset would leave a gap at the corners. Trimming/Extending cannot be used. You can use Fillet with a Radius=0 (Fillet command will be covered in the next chapter) to close them, however, it is easier to avoid this situation by using a Construction Line Offset instead.

Try it:

Anywhere on your screen, draw a line, a circle, and a rectangle. All objects are an arbitrary size, but should at least be about 12″ in size. We will then offset each of these objects by 2″.

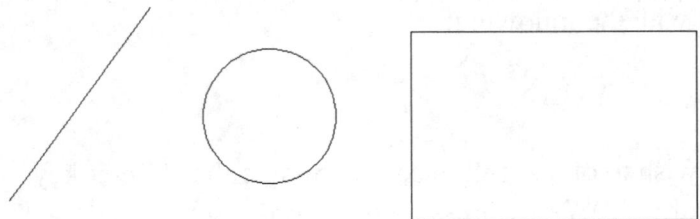

(Pick the Offset icon)

Command: _offset
Current settings: Erase source=No Layer=Source OFFSETGAPTYPE=0
Specify offset distance or [Through/Erase/Layer] <0'-1">: **2↵**
(Type "2" and press the ↵ Enter key)

Select object to offset or [Exit/Undo] <Exit>: ***(Pick the line)***

Specify point on side to offset or [Exit/Multiple/Undo] <Exit>: ***(Pick to the right of the line)***
Select object to offset or [Exit/Undo] <Exit>: ***(Pick the circle)***

Specify point on side to offset or [Exit/Multiple/Undo] <Exit>: ***(Pick outside the circle)***
Select object to offset or [Exit/Undo] <Exit>: ***(Pick the rectangle)***

Specify point on side to offset or [Exit/Multiple/Undo] <Exit>: ***(Pick outside the rectangle)***
Select object to offset or [Exit/Undo] <Exit>: ↵ **(Press the ↵ Enter key to exit the command)**
Command:

When you are done, your drawing will look like this:

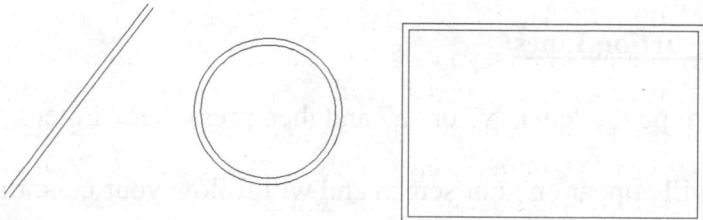

Construction Line

The Construction Line command creates a line (through a point that you select) that extends infinitely in both directions from the first point selected. You can select options at the command prompt to draw a horizontal, vertical, or angled construction line, or to offset the construction line by a distance from the object that you specify.

<u>Procedure:</u>

Pick (left click): **Construction Line icon** from the Draw toolbar.

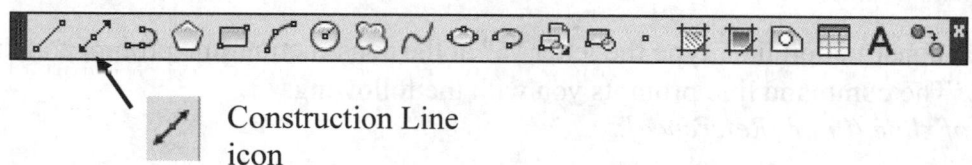

Construction Line
icon

The command line prompts you with the following:
Specify a point or [Hor/Ver/Ang/Bisect/Offset]:

For a simple construction line, anchor the first point by either picking anywhere on the screen (with or without grid/snap turned on), or picking a point on existing object (must have OSNAP turned on or select an object snap override before picking).

After you specify the first point, the command line prompts you with the following:
Specify through point:

You can specify the second point, or "through point" by picking anywhere on the screen or picking a specific point on an existing object.

After you select the "through point", the construction line will be created and another one will follow your cursor. AutoCAD® will continue prompting for more "through points":
Specify through point:

When you are finished with putting construction lines on your drawing, press the ↵ Enter key to exit the Construction Line command.

Construction Line Options

Horizontal and Vertical Construction Lines

For a horizontal or vertical line, type the letter "v" or "h" and then press the ↵ Enter key.

Note that the construction line will appear on your screen and will follow your cursor and prompt you as follows:
Specify through point:

The methods of specifying the "through point" are the same as previously described.

After you select the "through point", the construction line will be created and another one will follow your cursor. AutoCAD® will continue prompting for more "through points":
Specify through point:

When you are finished with putting construction lines on your drawing, press the ↵ Enter key to exit the Construction Line command.

Angled Construction Lines

For an angled construction line, type the letter "a" at the construction line prompt and then press the ↵ Enter key. The command line prompts you with the following:
Enter angle of xline (0) or [Reference]:

Type in the desired angle of the construction line and then press the ↵ Enter key. The command line prompts you with the following:
Specify through point:

From here on, the command acts the same as the horizontal or vertical line options.

Offset Option

This option works the same as the Offset command, only it puts construction lines in. You must key in the distance and select the direction to offset.

Recommendation:

The Construction Line command is a very useful tool. Horizontal, vertical, and angled lines are the most commonly used options. The Offset option can also be very useful. The Bisect option is rarely used and is not described here. It is left to the student to explore this option if so desired.

After construction lines are put on the drawing, it is necessary to trim them using the Trim command (discussed in the next section).

Although using construction lines and trimming may actually take more steps than drawing lines exactly where you want them by using X-Y coordinates, it allows the designer not to have to think in terms of X-Y coordinates. After some practice, it can actually be quicker to draw this way, since less thought is involved.

Try it:

1. **Draw 5 horizontal lines anywhere on your screen.**

(Pick the Construction Line icon)

Command: _xline Specify a point or [Hor/Ver/Ang/Bisect/Offset]: **h⏎**
(Type "h" and press the ⏎ Enter key)

Specify through point: (Pick a location anywhere on your screen)
Specify through point: (Pick a location anywhere on your screen)
Specify through point: (Pick a location anywhere on your screen)
Specify through point: (Pick a location anywhere on your screen)
Specify through point: (Pick a location anywhere on your screen)
Specify through point: ⏎ **(Press the ⏎ Enter key to exit the command)**
Command:

2. **Draw 5 vertical lines anywhere on your screen.**

(Pick the Construction Line icon)

Command: _xline Specify a point or [Hor/Ver/Ang/Bisect/Offset]: **v⏎**
(Type "v" and press the ⏎ Enter key)

Specify through point: (Pick a location anywhere on your screen)
Specify through point: (Pick a location anywhere on your screen)
Specify through point: (Pick a location anywhere on your screen)
Specify through point: (Pick a location anywhere on your screen)
Specify through point: (Pick a location anywhere on your screen)
Specify through point: ⏎ **(Press the ⏎ Enter key to exit the command)**
Command:

3. **Draw a 45° angled line anywhere on your screen.**

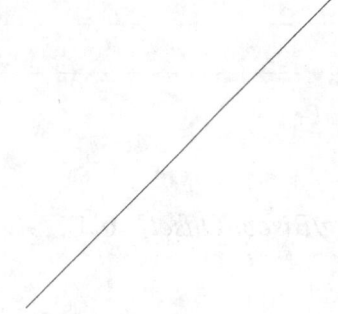

(Pick the Construction Line icon)

Command: _xline Specify a point or [Hor/Ver/Ang/Bisect/Offset]: **a⏎**
(Type "a" and press the ⏎ Enter key)
Enter angle of xline (0) or [Reference]: **45⏎**
(Type "45" and press the ⏎ Enter key)

Specify through point: (Pick a location on the screen for your line)
Specify through point: ⏎ **(Press the ⏎ Enter key to exit the command)**
Command:

4. **Draw a 4″ Construction Line offset.**

Draw a line anywhere on your screen. The length and angle is arbitrary.

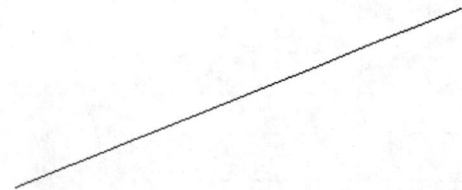

Now we will create an infinitely long line parallel to this one.

(Pick the Construction Line icon)

Command: _xline Specify a point or [Hor/Ver/Ang/Bisect/Offset]: **o⏎**
(Type "o" and press the ⏎ Enter key)
Specify offset distance or [Through] <0'-2">: **4⏎**
(Type "4" and press the ⏎ Enter key)

Select a line object: **(Pick the line)**
Specify side to offset: **(Pick to the right of the line)**
Select a line object: **⏎ (Press the ⏎ Enter key to exit the command)**
Command:

When you are done, your drawing will look like this:

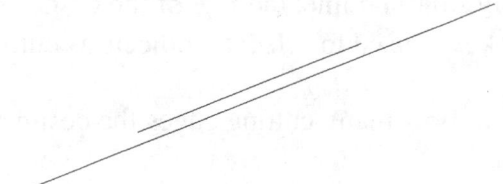

Changing Object Limits

The Trim command and the Extend command allow you to change the limits of existing objects. Trimming will shorten or cut out a section of an object. Extending will allow you to increase the length of an object (within the limits of the objects definition). One command can be used to perform the same as the other by holding the shift key during the object selection process.

Trim

Trim is a 2-part command; the first part is to select cutting edges, the second part is to select the objects to trim to those cutting edges. In order to trim an object, AutoCAD® requires the designer to first identify a "cutting edge". You can think of a cutting edge as a knife that will slice through the object you plan to trim. The cutting edge does not have to pass through the object you plan to trim; it can also project through the object (as long as *Edge=Extend* is set). The Trim command can also perform as an Extend command by holding the shift key down while picking the object to extend (it will treat the cutting edge as a boundary edge instead).

Procedure:

Pick (left click): **Trim icon** from the Modify toolbar.

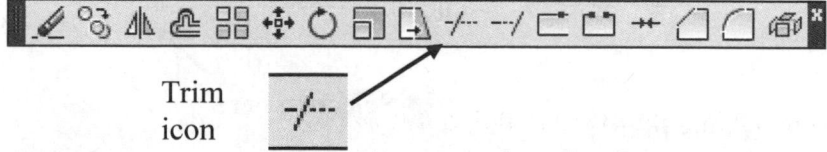

Trim
icon

The command line prompts you with the following:

Current settings: Projection=UCS, Edge=None
Select cutting edges ...
Select objects or <select all>:

There can be more than one cutting edge. These can be selected by the following methods:

1. Individually
2. Using a Selection Window or Crossing Window
3. Pressing the ↵ Enter key to select all objects as cutting edges

When an object is found as a cutting edge, AutoCAD® will highlight that object by changing its appearance to a dashed line. If it is already a dashed line, the size of the dashes becomes smaller. The exception to this is when the ↵ Enter key is used to select all objects as cutting edges.

Since AutoCAD® does not know in advance how many cutting edges the designer wishes to select, it will continue to prompt with the following:

Select objects: 1 found
Select objects:

After selecting all the cutting edges desired, press the ↵ Enter key. This will bring you to the second part of the command, which will prompt you with the following:

Select object to trim or shift-select to extend or [Project/Edge/Undo]:

You now have several options:

1. Pick the object to trim, or
2. Hold down the shift key and select an object to extend (the cutting edge will now act as a boundary edge), or
3. Choose one of the options in the [ ] brackets by typing the letter of the option that is capitalized.

Option 1

To select the object to trim, move the cursor to the object you wish to trim, on the portion of the object you want to eliminate, and use the left mouse button to pick that object.

Example:

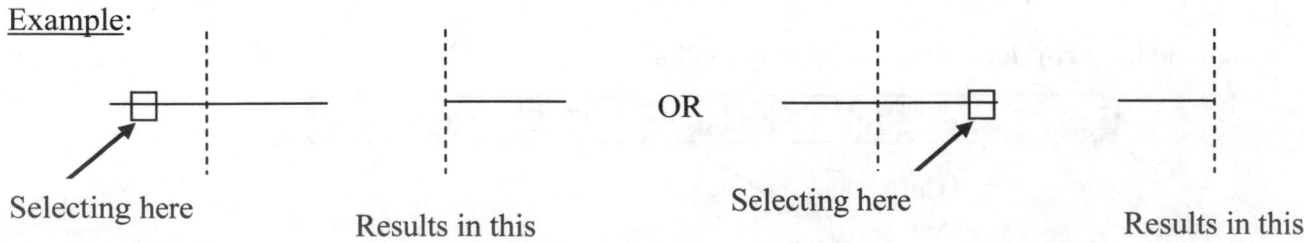

Selecting here

Results in this

OR

Selecting here

Results in this

You can also select a portion of an object to trim that is between two cutting edges:

Example:

Selecting here   Results in this

Option 2

This option works the same as the Extend command. Refer to the instructions for that command.

Option 3

We will describe only one of the choices in the square brackets: [*Undo*]
Use this choice if an object was trimmed in error. This must be done after an object was trimmed and while you are still in the command. Simply type the letter "u" followed by the ↵ Enter key.

Select object to trim or shift-select to extend or [Project/Edge/Undo]: **u** ↵

Try it:

Draw any size rectangle anywhere on your screen. Draw a horizontal construction line passing through the rectangle.

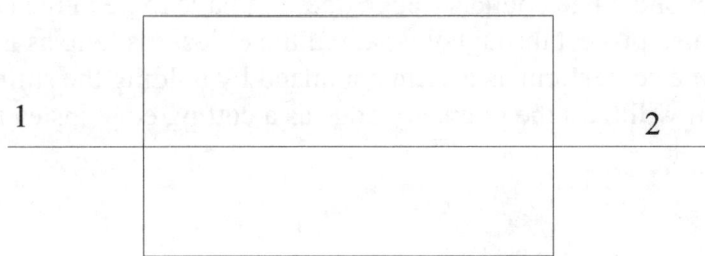

Now we will use the Trim command to trim the construction line to the rectangle.

(Pick the Trim icon)

Command: _trim
Current settings: Projection=UCS, Edge=None
Select cutting edges ...
Select objects or <select all>: (Pick the Rectangle) 1 found
Select objects: ↵ **(Press the ↵ Enter key to get to the second part of the command)**

Select object to trim or shift-select to extend or
[Fence/Crossing/Project/Edge/eRase/Undo]: **(Pick the Construction Line near point 1)**

Select object to trim or shift-select to extend or
[Fence/Crossing/Project/Edge/eRase/Undo]: **(Pick the Construction Line near point 2)**

Select object to trim or shift-select to extend or
[Fence/Crossing/Project/Edge/eRase/Undo]: ↵ **(Press the ↵ Enter key to exit the command)**
Command:

When you are done, your drawing will look like this:

Extend

Extend is a 2-part command: the first part is to select boundary edges; the second part is to select the objects to extend to those boundary edges. In order to extend an object, AutoCAD® requires the designer to first identify a "boundary edge". You can think of a boundary edge as a wall that will stop the object from extending beyond. The boundary edge does not have to be in the path of the object you plan to extend; it can also project through the path of the object (as long as *Edge=Extend* is set). The Extend command can also perform as a Trim command by holding the shift key down while picking the object to trim (it will treat the boundary edge as a cutting edge instead).

Procedure:

Pick (left click): **Extend icon** from the Modify toolbar.

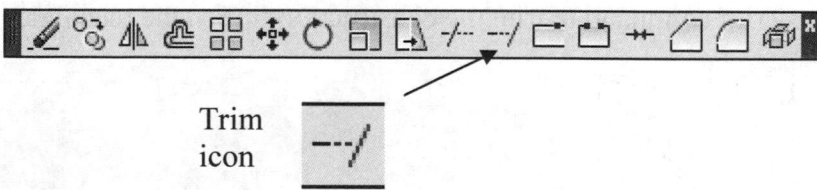

Trim
icon

The command line prompts you with the following:

Current settings: Projection=UCS, Edge=None
Select boundary edges ...

Select objects:
There can be more than one boundary edge. These can be selected by the following methods:

1. Individually
2. Using a Selection Window or Crossing Window
3. Pressing the ↵ Enter key to select all objects as boundary edges

When an object is found as a boundary edge, AutoCAD® will highlight that object by changing its appearance to a dashed line. If it is already a dashed line, the size of the dashes becomes smaller. The exception to this is when the ↵ Enter key is used to select all objects as boundary edges.

Since AutoCAD® does not know in advance how many boundary edges the designer wishes to select, it will continue to prompt with the following:

Select objects: 1 found
Select objects:

After selecting all the boundary edges desired, press the ↵ Enter key. This will bring you to the second part of the command, which will prompt you with the following:

Select object to extend or shift-select to trim or [Project/Edge/Undo]:

You now have several options:

1. Pick the object to extend, or
2. Hold down the shift key and select an object to trim (the boundary edge will now act as a cutting edge), or
3. Choose one of the options in the [ ] brackets by typing the letter of the option that is capitalized.

Option 1

To select the object to extend, move the cursor to the object you wish to extend, on the portion of the object you want to increase in length, and use the left mouse button to pick that object.

Example:

Selecting here   Results in this

Option 2

This option works the same as the Trim command. Refer to the instructions for that command.

Option 3

We will describe only one of the choices in the square brackets: [*Undo*]
Use this choice if an object was extended in error. This must be done after an object was extended and while you are still in the command. Simply type the letter "u" followed by the ↵ Enter key.

Select object to extend or shift-select to trim or [Project/Edge/Undo]: **u** ↵

Try it:

Draw two lines on your screen like these:

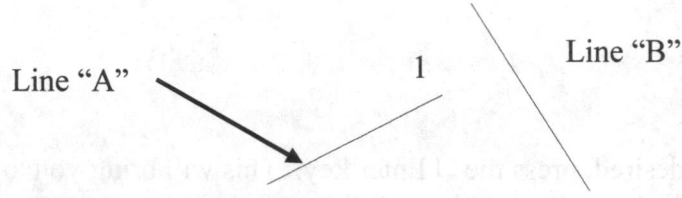

Line "A"   1   Line "B"

Now extend Line "A" to Line "B".

(Pick the Extend icon)

Command: _extend
Current settings: Projection=UCS, Edge=None
Select boundary edges ...
(Pick the line that you will extend to)
Select objects or <select all>: ***(Pick Line "B")****1 found*
Select objects: ↵ **(Pressing the ↵ Enter key will get you to the second part of the command)**

Select object to extend or shift-select to trim or
[Fence/Crossing/Project/Edge/Undo]: ***(Pick Line "A" near the endpoint marked 1)***
Select object to extend or shift-select to trim or
[Fence/Crossing/Project/Edge/Undo]: ↵ **(Pressing the ↵ Enter key will end the command)**
Command:

When you are done, your drawing will look like this:

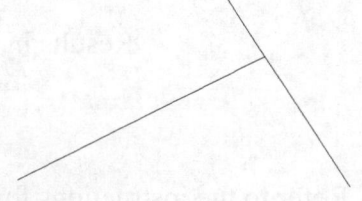

Object Snap – OSNAP

A major advantage of using AutoCAD®, or most Computer Aided Design programs, is the precision in which you can draw. To place objects in a precise location, such as the end of a line, the center of a circle, etc., AutoCAD® provides two methods: OSNAP and Object Snap. OSNAP is an abbreviation for Object Snap.

OSNAP icon

On the lower part of your screen, you will see the following:

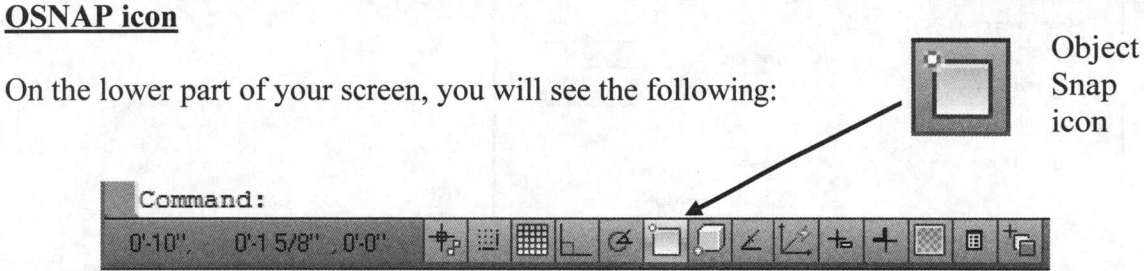

Object Snap icon

The Object Snap icon is a button that can be turned on and off. Move your cursor over the Object Snap icon and left-click to turn on the OSNAP feature. When OSNAP is turned on, the button will appear shaded blue.

There are many settings within OSNAP that can be turned on. To change those settings, hold your cursor over the OSNAP button and right-click. A pop-up box will appear by your cursor:

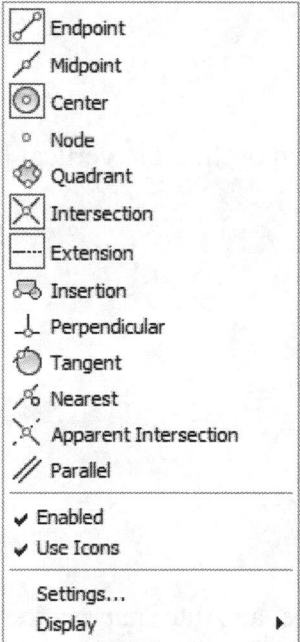

Each choice has an icon to the left of it. If the icon has a square box around it, that choice is selected. In this example, Endpoint, Center, Intersection, and Extension are selected. To select or de-select, pick on the icon. These are done one at a time. However, this method can be a little confusing and you may accidentally turn the OSNAP feature off.

A surer method of selecting which Object Snap choices you want is to pick Settings…

A Drafting Settings dialog box will appear. You can individually select your choice by picking the check box so that a check mark appears. Pick the OK button to exit the dialog box.

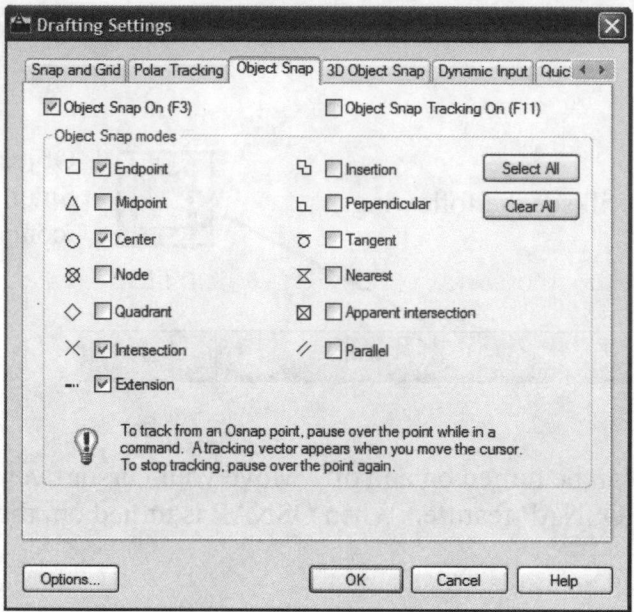

Using the OSNAP feature

Example 1. - Endpoint

In this example, let's place the center of a circle at the end of the right vertical line of the three lines shown:

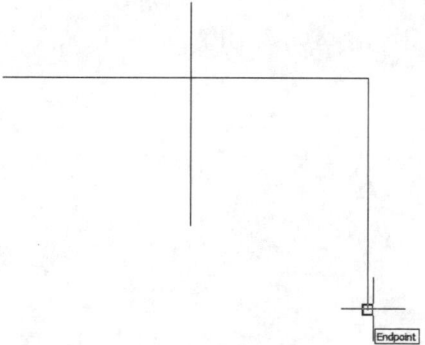

Notice that as the cursor gets near the endpoint of the line, an AutoSnap marker will appear at the end of the line, and a "tip" will indicate "Endpoint". Once the AutoSnap marker appears, left-click to pick the end of the line.

Pick anywhere away from that endpoint to complete the circle.

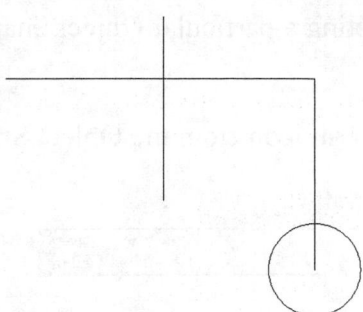

Example 2. – Intersection

Now let's place the center of a circle at the intersection of the left vertical line and the horizontal line:

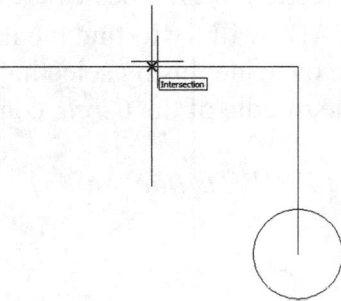

Notice that as the cursor gets near the intersection of the two lines, an AutoSnap marker will appear at the intersection, and a "tip" will indicate "Intersection". Once the AutoSnap marker appears, left-click to pick the intersection.

Pick anywhere away from that endpoint to complete the circle.

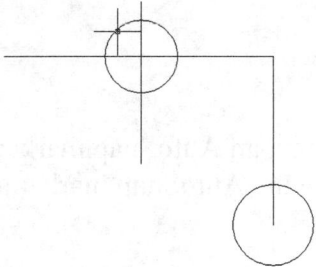

Object Snaps – Override

Object Snaps work very similar to OSNAP, except that these are one-time use overrides. Use Object Snaps when you are in the middle of a particular command to make your selection snap to a particular portion of an object. This can be done with OSNAP turned off or on. If OSNAP is turned on, you can override the OSNAP selection by selecting a particular Object Snap command from the Object Snap toolbar.

Object Snaps can be typed in during a command, or an icon from the Object Snap toolbar can be selected.

Object Snap Toolbar

Example 3.

Let's add another circle to the horizontal line, but we need to add it to the midpoint of the line. Note that the midpoint of the line is very close to the intersection of the lines where the circle was created in example 2. If we leave OSNAP turned on, AutoCAD® will try to find the intersection of the two lines as the cursor gets near the intersection. We can override this by selecting the Snap to Midpoint icon from the Object Snap toolbar while we are in the middle of the *Circle* command.

Command: _circle Specify center point for circle or [3P/2P/Ttr (tan tan radius)]: **(Pick Snap to Midpoint)**

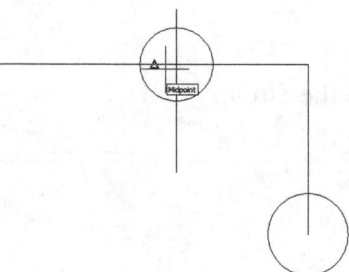

Command: _circle Specify center point for circle or [3P/2P/Ttr (tan tan radius)]: _mid of **(Pick the midpoint of the horizontal line)**

Notice that as the cursor gets near the midpoint of the line, an AutoSnap marker will appear at the intersection, and a "tip" will indicate "Midpoint". Once the AutoSnap marker appears, left-click to pick the midpoint.

Pick anywhere away from the midpoint to complete the circle.

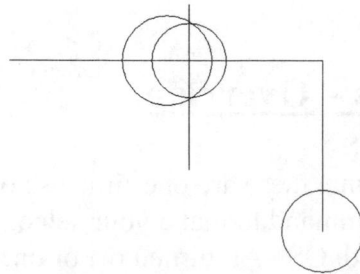

Try it:

Locate the circle inside the rectangle by using Construction Line Offset:

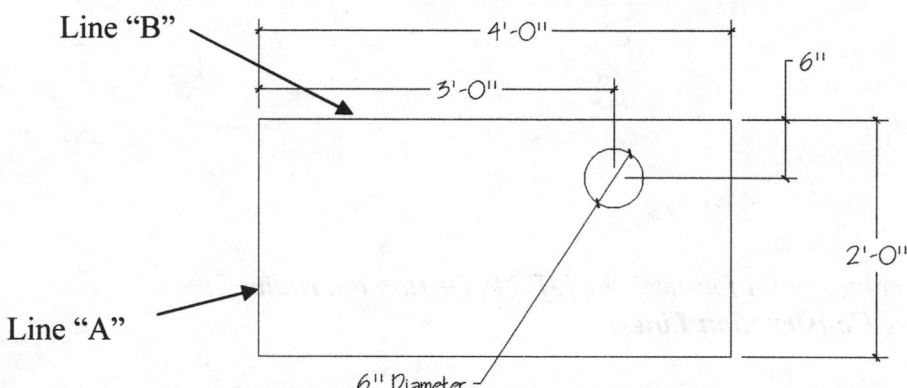

Before beginning, make sure that Object Snap icon on your Status Bar is turned on and that Intersection is selected. Ignore the default values shown:

(Pick the Rectangle icon)

Command: _rectang
Specify first corner point or [Chamfer/Elevation/Fillet/Thickness/Width]:
Specify other corner point or [Area/Dimensions/Rotation]: **d.⏎**
Specify length for rectangles <16'-0">: **4'⏎**
Specify width for rectangles <8'-0">: **2'⏎**
Specify other corner point or [Area/Dimensions/Rotation]: **⏎**
Command:

(Pick the Construction Line icon)

Command: _xline Specify a point or [Hor/Ver/Ang/Bisect/Offset]: **o⏎**
Specify offset distance or [Through] <0'-4">: **3'⏎**
Select a line object: **(Pick the rectangle line "A")**
Specify side to offset: **(Pick to the right of the selected line)**
Select a line object: **⏎**
Command:

Press the ⏎ Enter key to repeat the Construction Line command

XLINE Specify a point or [Hor/Ver/Ang/Bisect/Offset]: **o⏎**
Specify offset distance or [Through] <3'-0">: **6⏎**
Select a line object: **(Pick the rectangle line "B")**
Specify side to offset: **(Pick below the selected line)**
Select a line object: **⏎**
Command:

We now have intersecting construction lines that define the center of the circle. With OSNAP turned on and set to look for Intersections, we can proceed to put the circle in the exact location.

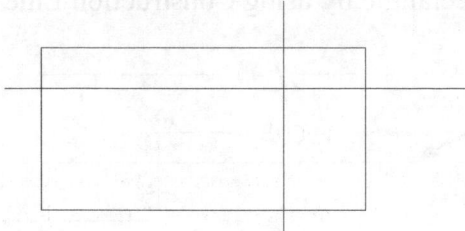

(Pick the Circle icon)

Command: _circle Specify center point for circle or [3P/2P/Ttr (tan tan radius)]:
(Pick the Intersection of the Construction Lines)

Specify radius of circle or [Diameter] <0'-3">: **d↵**
Specify diameter of circle <0'-6">: **6↵**
Command:

The circle is now drawn exactly 6″ diameter exactly located in the rectangle. All we need to do now is to eliminate the construction lines to complete the drawing. Use the Erase command to do this.

(Pick Erase icon)

Command: _erase
Select objects: **(Pick the vertical construction line)** *1 found*
Select objects: **(Pick the horizontal construction line)** *1 found, 2 total*
Select objects: ↵
Command:

When you are done, your drawing will look like this:

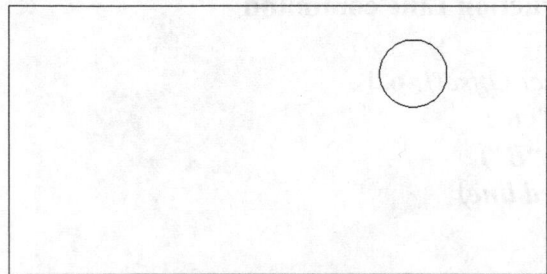

Summary

In this chapter you have learned to:

- Create rectangles of specific size
- Change the rectangle object to individual lines using Explode
- Create parallel lines and concentric rectangles or circles using Offset
- Create infinitely long lines that are horizontal, vertical, or at a specific angle
- Create an infinitely long line parallel to an existing line object using the Offset option of the Construction line command
- Change the length of lines using either Trim or Extend
- Place your objects at precise locations using the OSNAP or Object Snap tools

Review Questions

1. What is the option in the Rectangle command that allows you to create a rectangle of a specific size?

2. After you type in the size of the rectangle, what is the final step needed to complete the Rectangle command?

3. What command do you use to convert a rectangle into 4 separate lines?

4. What command is used to create a line parallel to another line?

5. How do you create an infinitely long parallel line?

6. How many steps are involved with creating an Offset?

7. How do you create horizontal, vertical, or angled lines that are infinitely long?

8. To change the length of a line, which two commands can be used?

9. Which icon on the Status Bar must be turned on to draw accurately?

10. Which toolbar is used to override the OSNAP selection?

Exercises

1. Draw the Mirror

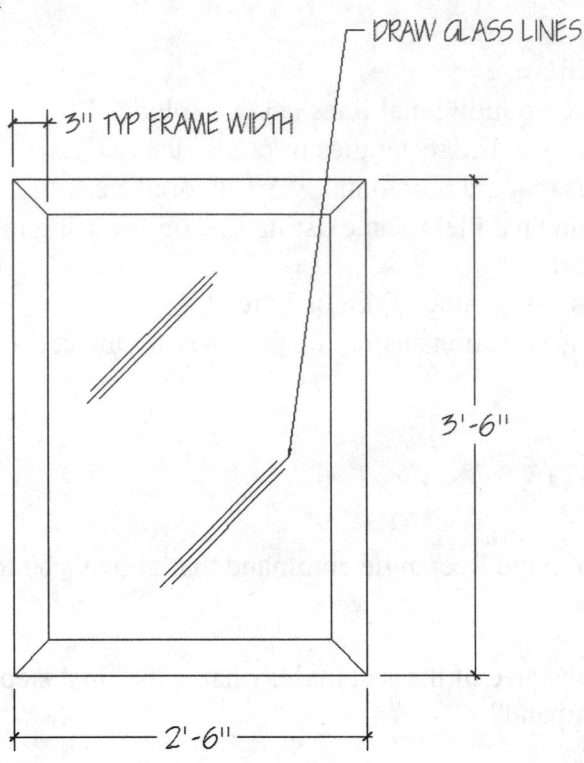

2. Draw the Luggage Rack (Use Offset or Construction Line Offset, with OSNAP turned on to locate each feature)

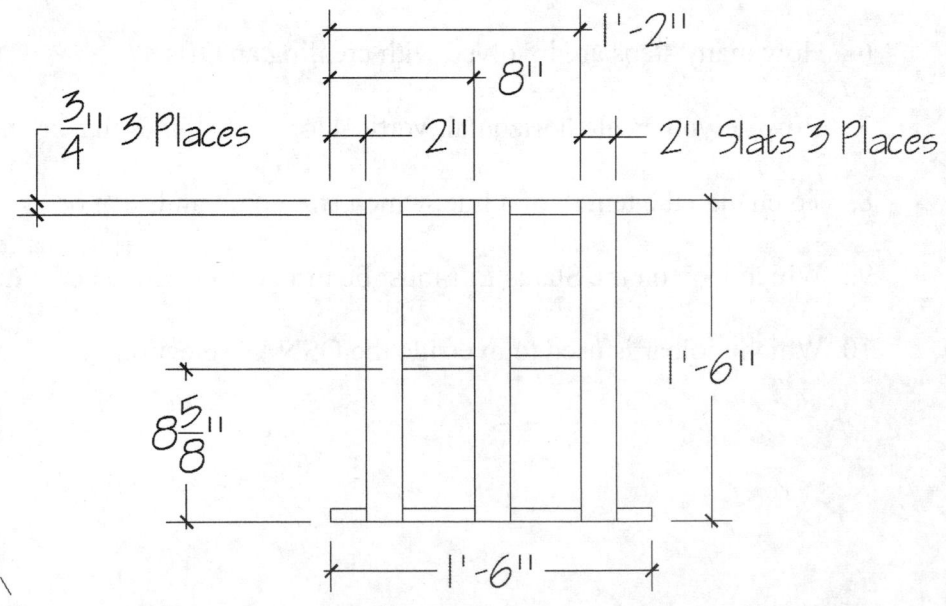

3. Draw the Floor Lamp – Spokes start at 45° and are 90° apart.

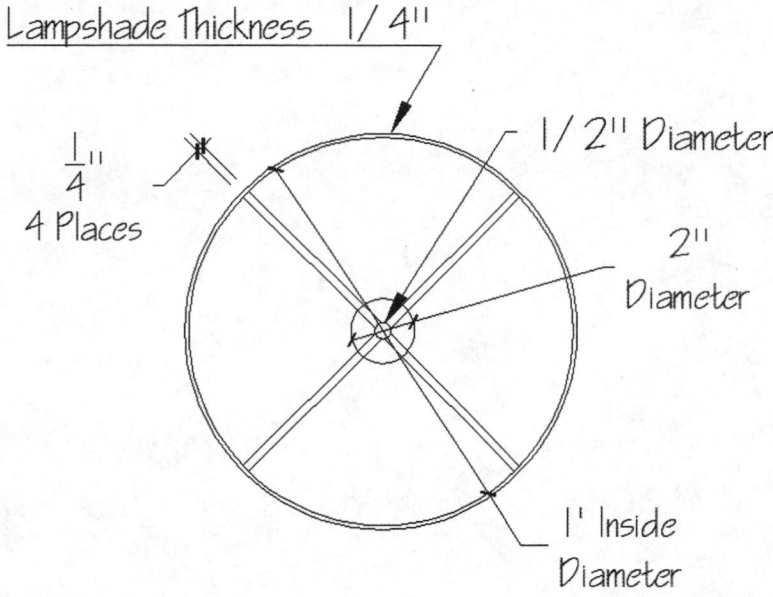

4. Draw the Dresser – Knobs are located the same for each drawer (Use Offset or Construction Line Offset, with OSNAP turned on to locate each feature)

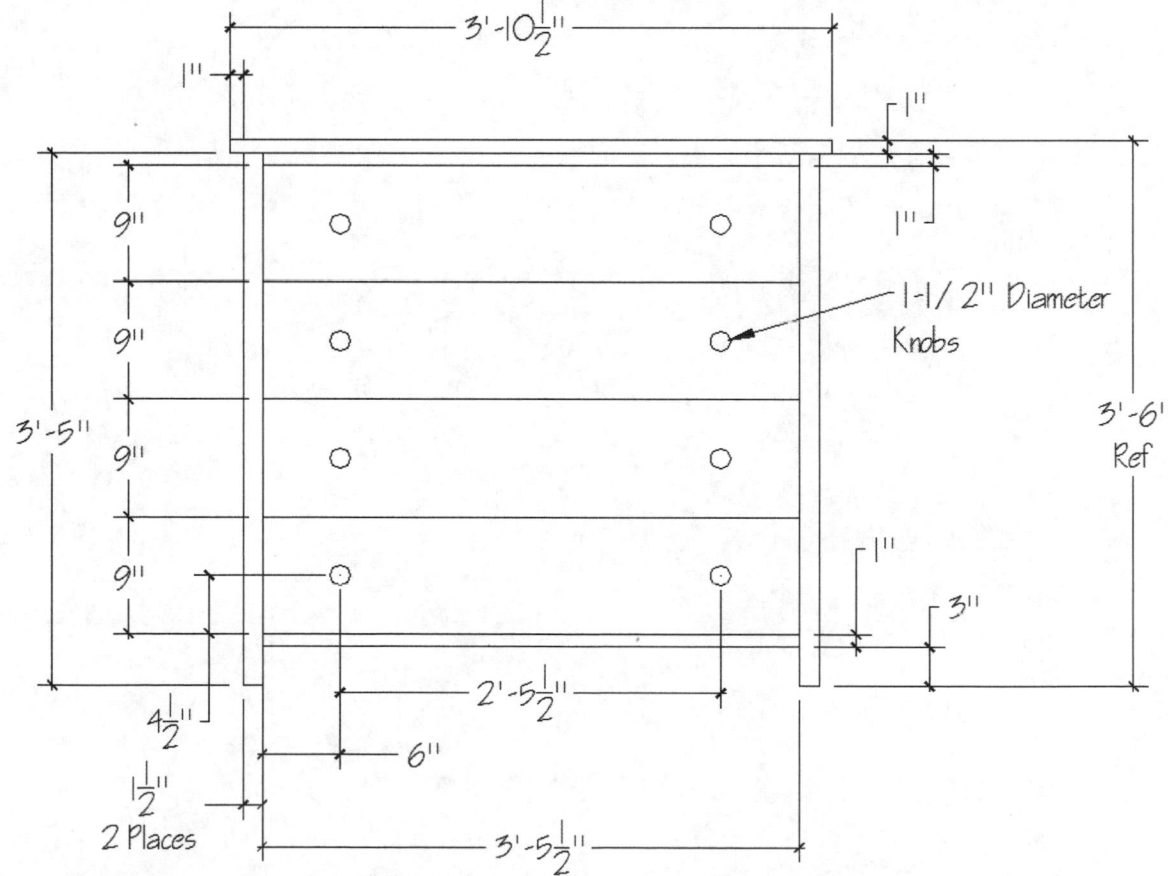

Notes:

Chapter 4
Hotel Suite Project – Tutorial 1

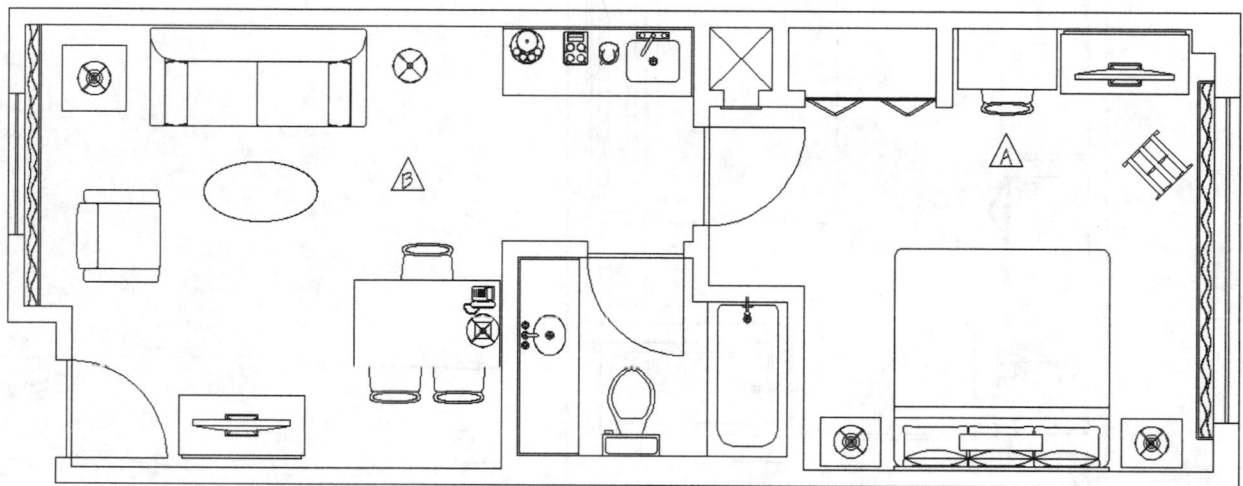

Learning Objectives:

- **To create a drawing of a real-world application of AutoCAD®**
  - o **Create the plan view of the outside walls of the hotel suite**
- **To utilize and reinforce the use of the AutoCAD® commands learned in the previous chapters**

Hotel Suite Project

For our project, we will draw a hotel suite that will include a bedroom, bathroom, and a living room area. This project will utilize the majority of commands that will be covered throughout this book. The project will be broken down into multiple tutorials and each tutorial emphasizes commands covered in the preceding chapter.

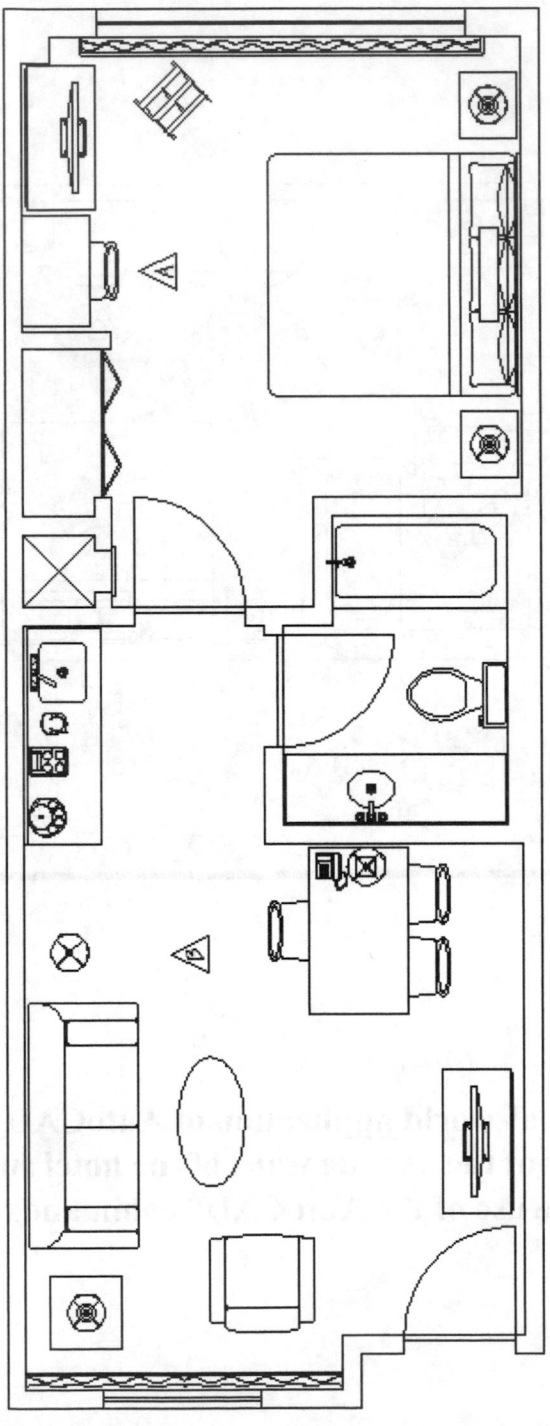

The Hotel Suite

This tutorial covers the creation of the plan view of the hotel suite outside walls.

<u>Commands & Techniques:</u>

- Starting a new drawing
- Units
- Drawing Limits
- Zoom - All
- Rectangle
- Offset
- Explode
- Construction Line – Offset
- Trim
- Extend
- Repeating commands by using the ↵ Enter key
- Erase
- Save

To help guide you through these tutorials, the following method is used to represent mouse and keyboard operations:

Bold font represents a keyboard operation.

Bold/Italic font in parenthesis represents a mouse operation.

Italic font represents AutoCAD® generated command line text.

Because the majority of the steps are repetitive, after the first several steps, the tutorial will not repeat every detail and prompt. When a new command is used, then the details will be given.

If you have already set up your mouse for customized right-click, everywhere the tutorial instructs you to press the ↵ Enter key, you can substitute that instruction with "right mouse-click".

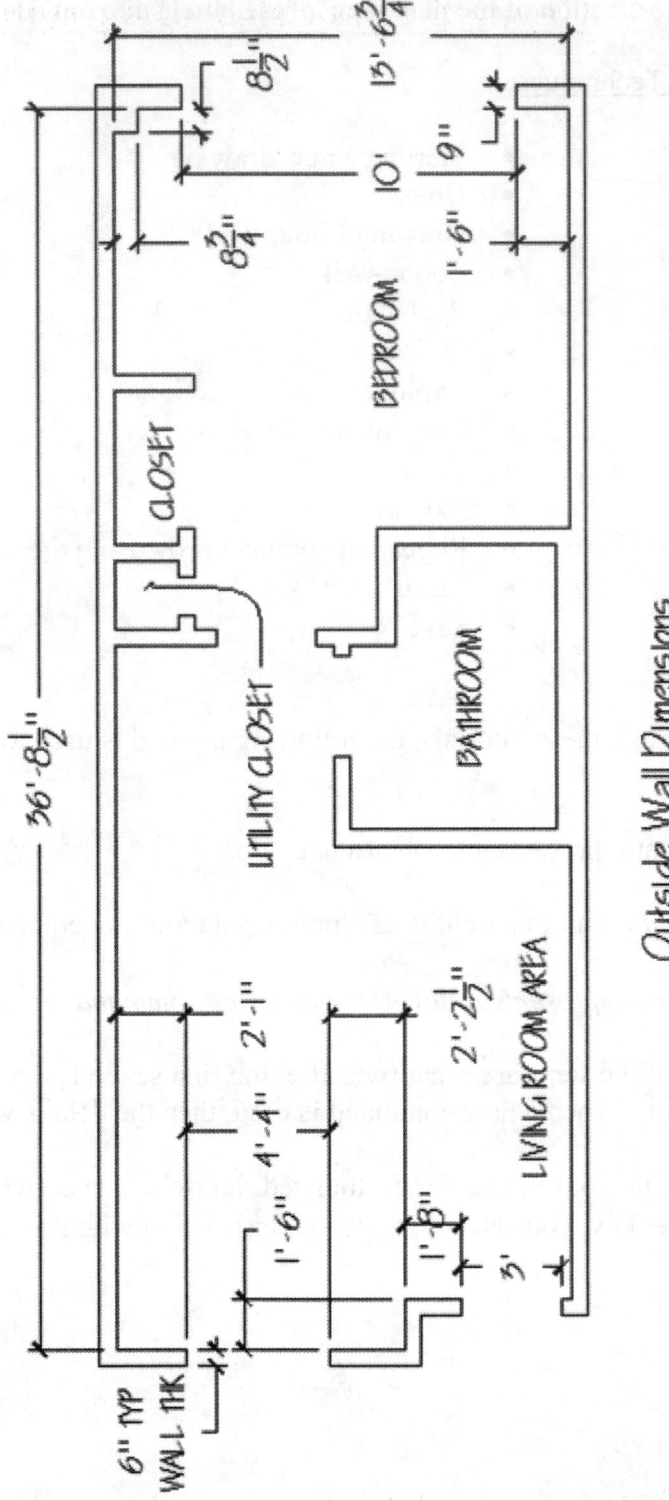

Outside Wall Dimensions

Create the basic shell of the suite

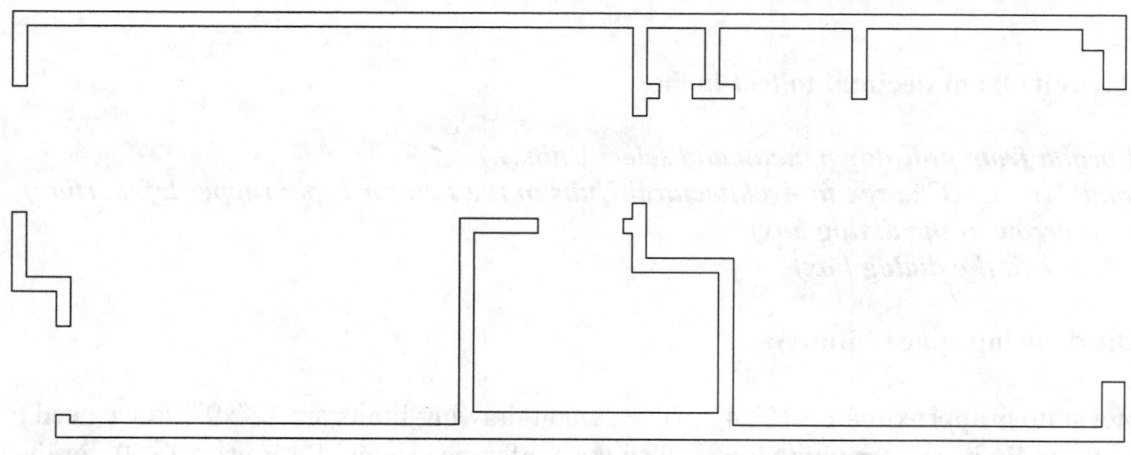

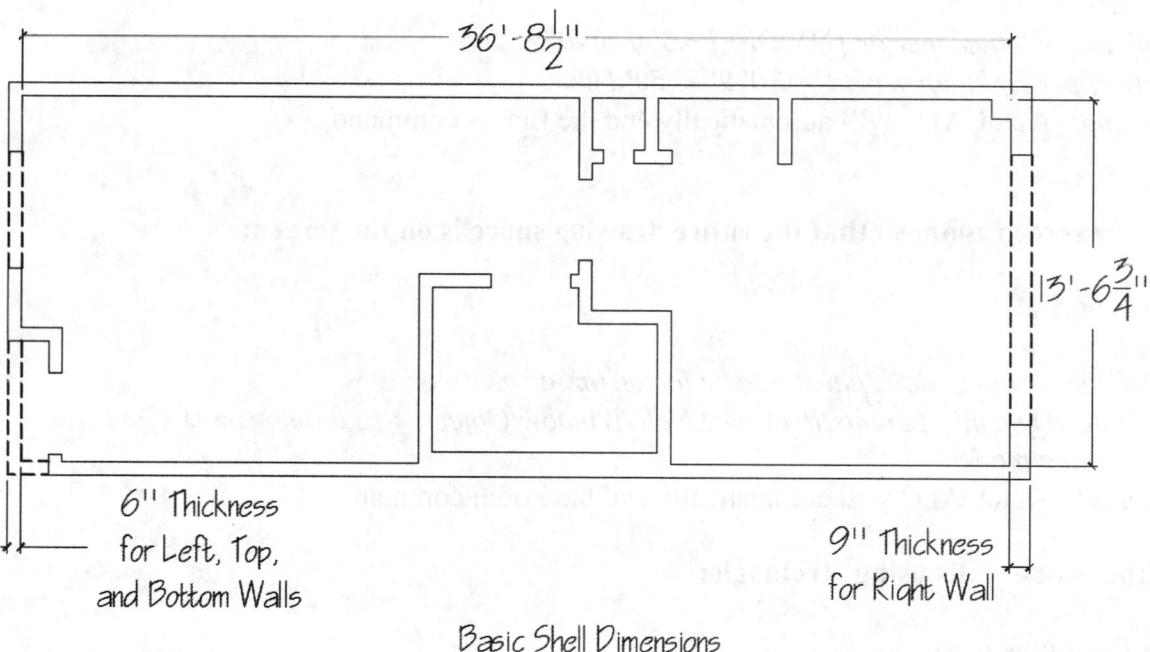

Basic Shell Dimensions

6" Thickness for Left, Top, and Bottom Walls

9" Thickness for Right Wall

The dashed lines are shown to illustrate that we can start this drawing by using rectangles.

- Before beginning, start up a new drawing, use the <u>Format</u> pull-down menu and change the <u>Units</u> to **Architectural** and set the <u>Drawing Limits</u> upper right corner to **50′,50′**.

1. **Change the units from decimal to feet-inches:**

    (Pick Format from pull-down menu and select Units…)
    Command: '_units (Change to Architectural Units in the Length Type: (upper left portion)
    pull-down arrow in the dialog box)
    (Pick OK to exit the dialog box)

2. **Expand the drawing space (limits):**

    The hotel suite is approximately15′x40′. The default drawing limits are 12″x9″, so we need to increase those limits to something bigger than the conference room. Let's use 50′x50′ for the drawing limits.

    (Pick Format from pull-down menu and select Drawing Limits)
    Command: '_limits
    Reset Model space limits:
    Specify lower left corner or [ON/OFF] <0'-0",0'-0">: ↵
    Specify upper right corner <1'-0",0'-9">: **50',50'**↵
    Command: (AutoCAD® will automatically end the Limits command)

3. **Change the screen zoom so that the entire drawing space is on the screen:**

    Command: **z** ↵
    ZOOM
    Specify corner of window, enter a scale factor (nX or nXP), or
    [All/Center/Dynamic/Extents/Previous/Scale/Window/Object] <real time>: **a** ↵
    Regenerating model.
    Command: (AutoCAD® will automatically end the Zoom command)

4. **Create the inside walls using Rectangle:**

    (Pick Rectangle icon)

    Command: _rectang
    Specify first corner point or [Chamfer/Elevation/Fillet/Thickness/Width]: **(Pick a point on the screen, below and to the left of the center)**

    Use the Dimensions option to define the 36′8-1/2″ width and the 13′6-3/4″ height. AutoCAD® uses confusing definition for length and width; "length" = Horizontal direction, "width" = Vertical direction.

> Note: when specifying Rectangle dimensions:
> - Length is the horizontal direction
> - Width is the vertical direction

Specify other corner point or [Area/Dimensions/Rotation]: **d**↵
Specify length for rectangles <0'-10">: **36'8-1/2** ↵
Specify width for rectangles <0'-10">: **13'6-3/4** ↵
Specify other corner point or [Area/Dimensions/Rotation]: **(Pick to the upper right of the 4 choices given)**

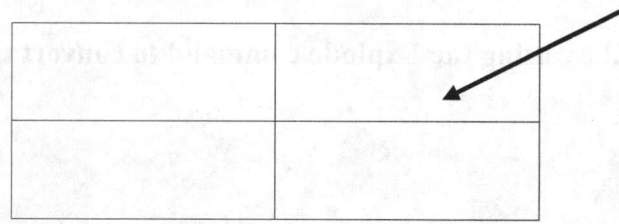

As you move your cursor around the first corner point, four locations are available to choose. Pick the upper right location for the rectangle.

Command: (AutoCAD® will automatically end the Rectangle command)

When done, you will be left with only one rectangle:

5. **Use the offset command to draw the outside walls:**

    (Pick Offset icon)
    Command: _offset
    Current settings: Erase source=No Layer=Source OFFSETGAPTYPE=0
    Specify offset distance or [Through] <Through>: **6** ↵

    Specify point on side to offset or [Exit/Multiple/Undo] <Exit>: **(Pick the rectangle)**
    Select object to offset or [Exit/Undo] <Exit>: **(Pick to the outside of the rectangle)**

    Since no more offset lines are required, pressing the ↵ Enter key will end the Offset command.

    Select object to offset or <exit>: ↵
    Command:

When completed, your drawing will look like this.

In Step 6b, we will erase this line

6. Draw the 9″ outside wall on the right side:

Our plan is to explode the rectangles first so that they become individual lines that we can work with. We will then be able to construct the thicker right wall.

6a. Prepare to draw the right outside wall by using the Explode command to convert the rectangles to lines:

(Pick the Explode icon)
Command: _explode

Select objects: (Pick one of the rectangles) 1 found:
Select objects: (Pick the other rectangle) 1 found, 2 total

Since no more objects are to be exploded, pressing the ↵ Enter key will end the Explode command.

Select objects: ↵
Command:

6b. Erase the furthest right vertical line:

(Pick the Erase icon)
Command: _erase
Select objects: (Pick the right vertical line) 1 found

Since no more objects are being erased, pressing the ↵ Enter key will end the Erase command.

Select objects: ↵
Command:

When completed,
your drawing will
look like this.

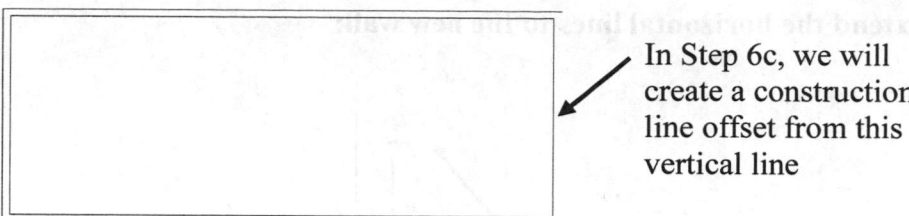

In Step 6c, we will
create a construction
line offset from this
vertical line

6c. Construct the new right outside wall line for the 9″ thick wall:

(Pick the Construction Line icon)
Command: _xline Specify a point or [Hor/Ver/Ang/Bisect/Offset]: **o** ⏎
Specify offset distance or [Through] <0'-6">: **9** ⏎
Select a line object: (Pick the right vertical line)
Specify side to offset: (Pick anywhere to the right of the line you just selected)

Since no more offset construction lines are required, pressing the ⏎ Enter key will end the
Offset command.

Select a line object: ⏎
Command:

When you are done, your drawing should now look like this:

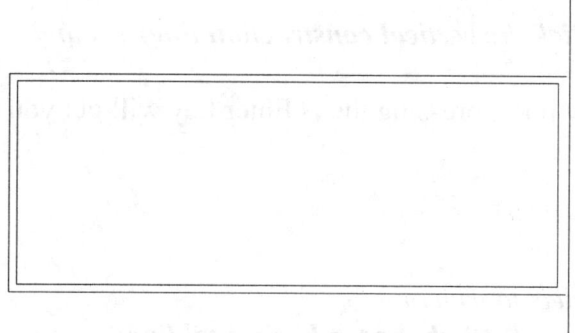

6d. Extend the horizontal lines to the new wall:

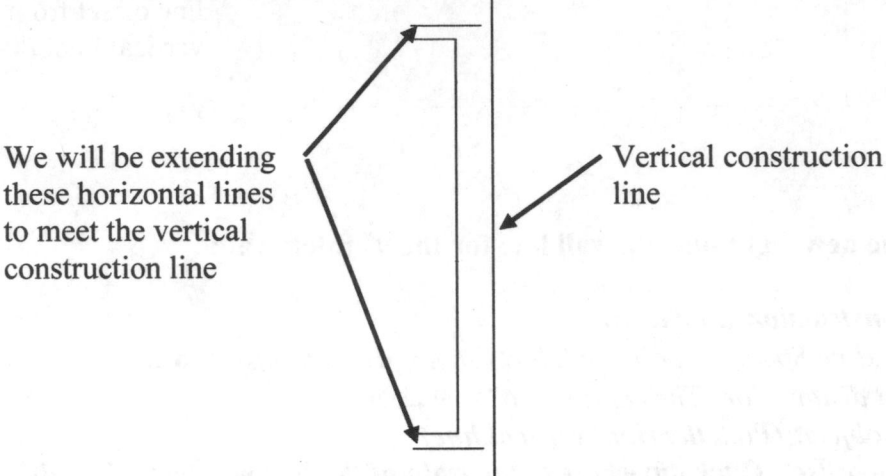

We will be extending
these horizontal lines
to meet the vertical
construction line

Vertical construction
line

Remember that the Extend command is a 2-part command; for the first part you pick the object (or objects) that you plan to extend to, for the second part you pick the objects to be extended.

(Pick the Extend icon)

Command: _extend
Current settings: Projection=UCS, Edge=Extend
Select boundary edges ...
Select objects or <select all>: (Pick the vertical construction line) 1 found

Since there are no more boundary lines, pressing the ↵ Enter key will get you to the second part of the command.

Select objects: ↵

Select object to extend or shift-select to trim or
[Fence/Crossing/Project/Edge/Undo]: (Pick the top horizontal line)

Select object to extend or shift-select to trim or
[Fence/Crossing/Project/Edge/Undo]: (Pick the bottom horizontal line)

Note: the order in which you pick the lines to extend does not matter.

Since there are no more lines that need to be extended, pressing the ↵ Enter key will end the Extend command.

Select object to extend or shift-select to trim or
[Fence/Crossing/Project/Edge/Undo]: ↵
Command:

When done, this portion of your drawing should look like this:

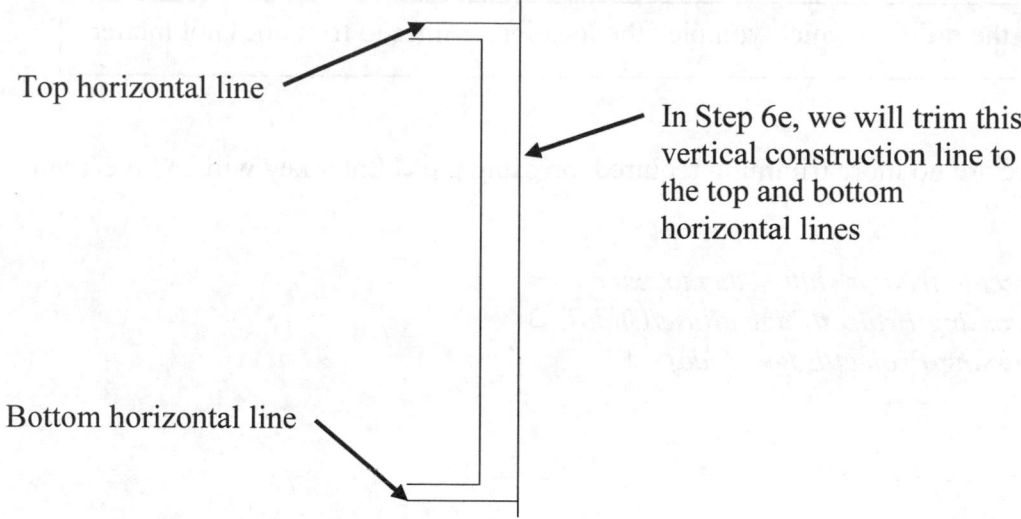

Top horizontal line

In Step 6e, we will trim this
vertical construction line to
the top and bottom
horizontal lines

Bottom horizontal line

6e. Trim the vertical construction line of the new wall to the top and bottom walls:

Remember that the Trim command is a 2-part command (just as it was for the Extend
command): for the first part you pick the object (or objects) that you plan to trim to (as if they
were cutting knives); for the second part you pick the objects to be extended.

(Pick the Trim icon)

Command: _trim
Current settings: Projection=UCS, Edge=Extend
Select cutting edges ...

Select objects or <select all>: **(Pick the top horizontal line)** *1 found*
Select objects: **(Pick the bottom horizontal line)** *1 found, 2 total*

Note: the order in which you pick the cutting edges does not matter.

Since there are no more cutting edges, pressing the ↵ Enter key will get you to the second part
of the command.

Select objects: ↵

Select object to trim or shift-select to extend or
[Fence/Crossing/Project/Edge/eRase/Undo]: **(Pick the construction line in a location above the top horizontal line)**

Select object to trim or shift-select to extend or
[Fence/Crossing/Project/Edge/eRase/Undo]: **(Pick the construction line in a location below the bottom horizontal line)**

> Note: the order in which you pick the location or lines to trim does not matter.

Since there are no more trimming required, pressing the ↵ Enter key will end the Trim command.

Select object to trim or shift-select to extend or
[Fence/Crossing/Project/Edge/eRase/Undo]: ↵
Fence/Crossing/Project/Edge/Undo]: ↵
Command:

When you are done, your drawing should look like this:

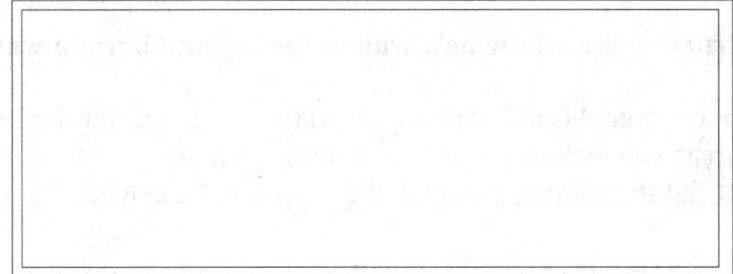

7. Create the window opening in the bedroom

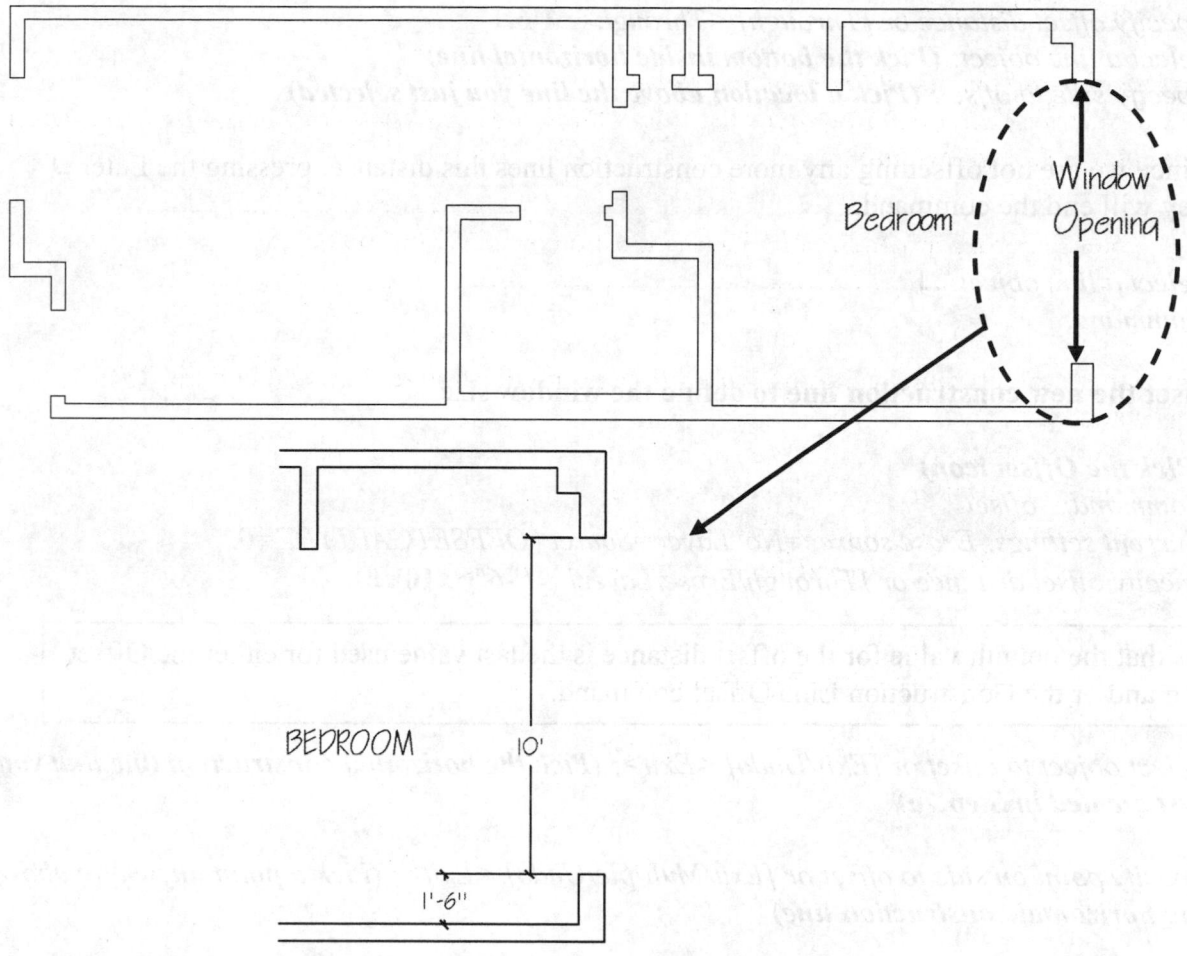

Our plan is to use both the **Construction Line – Offset** command and the **Offset** command to define the window opening. We will then trim the lines (and construction lines) to complete the window opening.

7a. Create a construction line offset from the bottom inside horizontal wall:

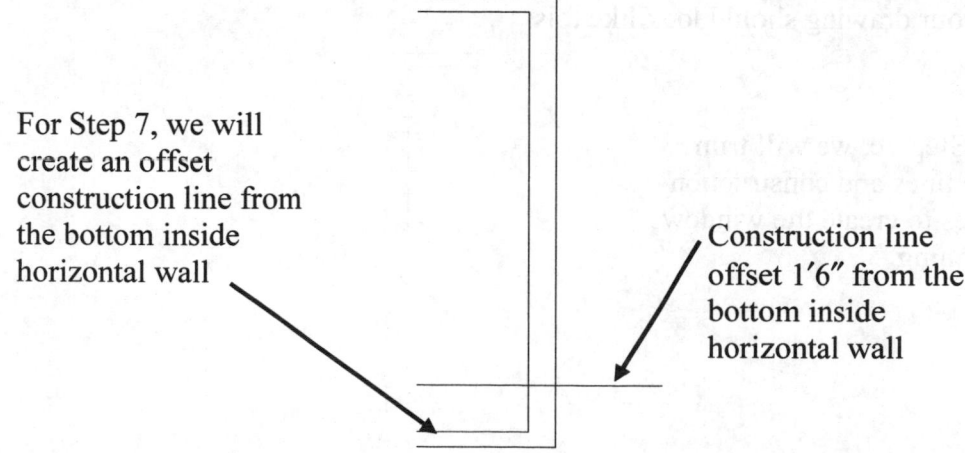

For Step 7, we will create an offset construction line from the bottom inside horizontal wall

Construction line offset 1'6" from the bottom inside horizontal wall

(Pick the Construction Line icon)
Command: _xline Specify a point or [Hor/Ver/Ang/Bisect/Offset]: **o↵**
Specify offset distance or [Through] <Through>: **1'6↵**
*Select a line object: **(Pick the bottom inside horizontal line)***
*Specify side to offset: **(Pick a location above the line you just selected)***

Since we are not offsetting any more construction lines this distance, pressing the Enter ↵ key will end the command.

Select a line object: ↵
Command:

7b. Offset the new construction line to define the window size

(Pick the Offset icon)
Command: _offset
Current settings: Erase source=No Layer=Source OFFSETGAPTYPE=0
Specify offset distance or [Through/Erase/Layer] <1'-6">: **10'↵**

Note that the default value for the offset distance is the last value used for either the Offset command or the Construction Line Offset command.

---

*Select object to offset or [Exit/Undo] <Exit>: **(Pick the horizontal construction line that you just created in Step 7a)***

*Specify point on side to offset or [Exit/Multiple/Undo] <Exit>: **(Pick a point anywhere above the horizontal construction line)***

Since there are no more objects that we plan to offset, pressing the ↵ Enter key will end the command.

Select object to offset or [Exit/Undo] <Exit>: ↵
Command:

When you are done, your drawing should look like this:

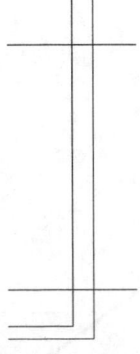

In Step 7c, we will trim
the lines and construction
lines to create the window
opening

7c. Use the Trim command to trim the lines and construction lines:

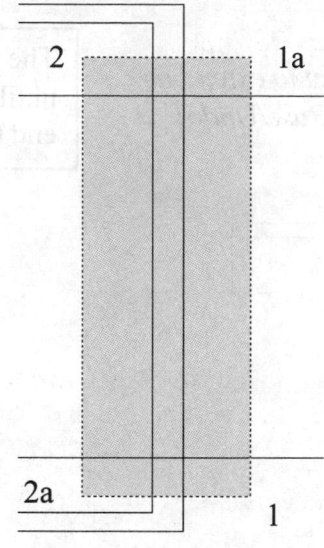

Using a crossing
window will allow us
to select multiple
cutting edges with
only two mouse clicks

Remember: a crossing
window goes from right to
left, and any object that
"crosses" that window, or
is completely inside that
window, is selected

(Pick the Trim icon)
Command: _trim
Current settings: Projection=UCS, Edge=Extend
Select cutting edges ...
Select objects or <select all>: **(Pick point at either location 1 or 1a)**
Specify opposite corner **(Pick a point at either location 2 or 2a)** *4 found*

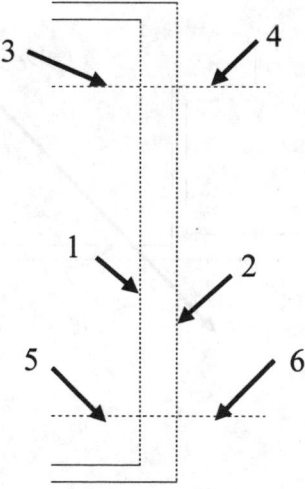

Since there are no more cutting edges, pressing the ↵ Enter key will get you to the second part
of the command.

In the second part of the command, select the objects to be trimmed in the approximate locations shown (1-6). Note that the order in which you select the objects to be trimmed does not matter.

Select object to trim or shift-select to extend or [Fence/Crossing/Project/Edge/eRase/Undo]: ↵
Command:

The select object prompt will repeat until you press the ↵ Enter key to end the command.

When your are done trimming, your window will be complete

8. Create the upper right corner of the bedroom

Bedroom

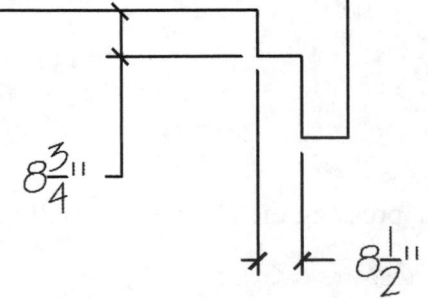

$8\frac{3}{4}"$

$8\frac{1}{2}"$

The upper right corner of the bedroom has a bump-out into the room because there is a structural column supporting the outside wall of the building. Our plan is to draw this bump-out by using the Offset and Trim commands.

Before beginning, you may want to use Zoom and Pan (using your mouse-wheel) to get a larger view of the upper right corner.

8a. Use the Offset command to offset the right inside wall line.

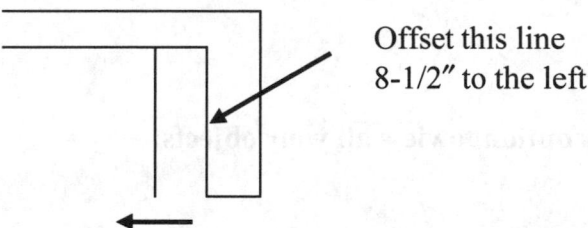

Offset this line
8-1/2″ to the left

8b. Press the ↵ Enter key to repeat the Offset command to offset the top inside wall line.

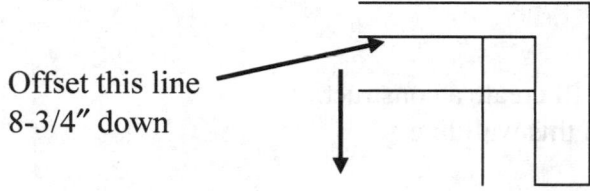

Offset this line
8-3/4″ down

8c. Use the trim command to complete the corner

Use a crossing window to select the cutting edges:

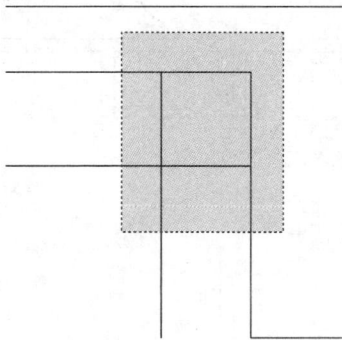

Select the lines to be trimmed at the locations shown:

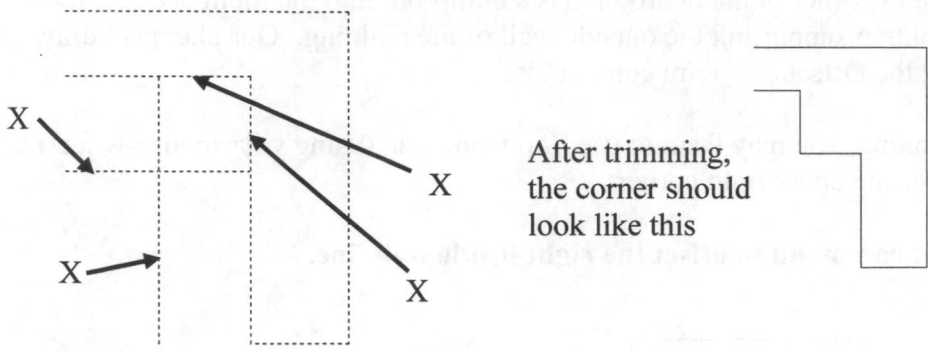

After trimming,
the corner should
look like this

8d. Use Zoom with the Extents option to view all your objects:

Command: **z** ↵
ZOOM
Specify corner of window, enter a scale factor (nX or nXP), or
[All/Center/Dynamic/Extents/Previous/Scale/Window/Object] <real time>: **e**↵

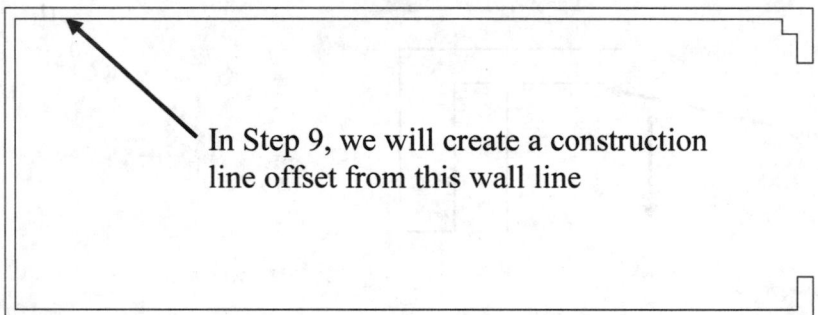

In Step 9, we will create a construction
line offset from this wall line

9. Create the window opening in the living room area

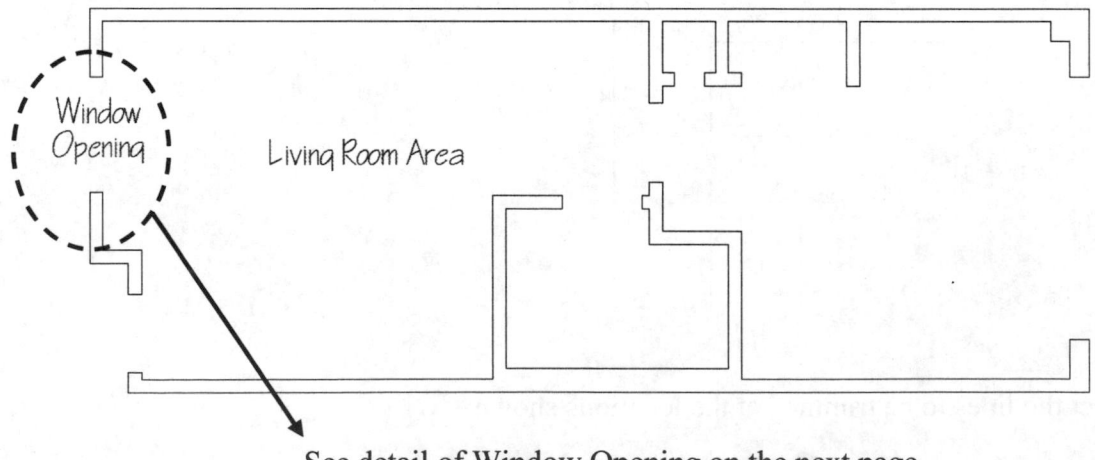

See detail of Window Opening on the next page

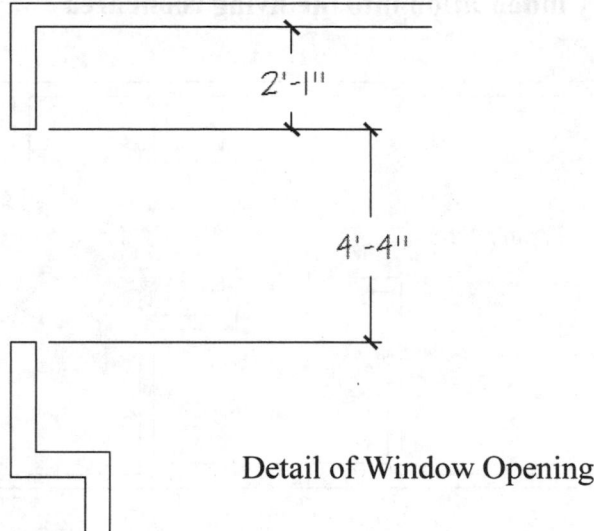

2'-1"

4'-4"

Detail of Window Opening

The steps required to create this window opening are very similar to the steps needed to create the bedroom window opening of Step 7.

Our plan is to use both the Construction Line – Offset command and the Offset command to define the window opening. We will then trim the lines (and construction lines) to complete the window opening.

Before beginning, use the wheel mouse to zoom and pan to get a closer view of the window opening area that we will be working on.

9a. Create a Construction Line Offset 2′1″ from the upper inside wall

9b. Offset the construction line of Step 9a 4′4″ down

9c. Use the Trim command to complete the window opening

Use the crossing window method to select the cutting edges, just like we did in Step 7.

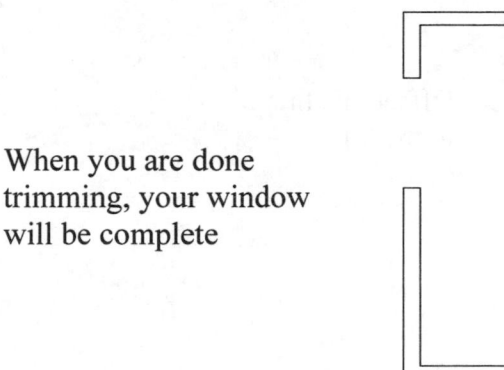

When you are done trimming, your window will be complete

10. Create the entryway indentation into the living room area

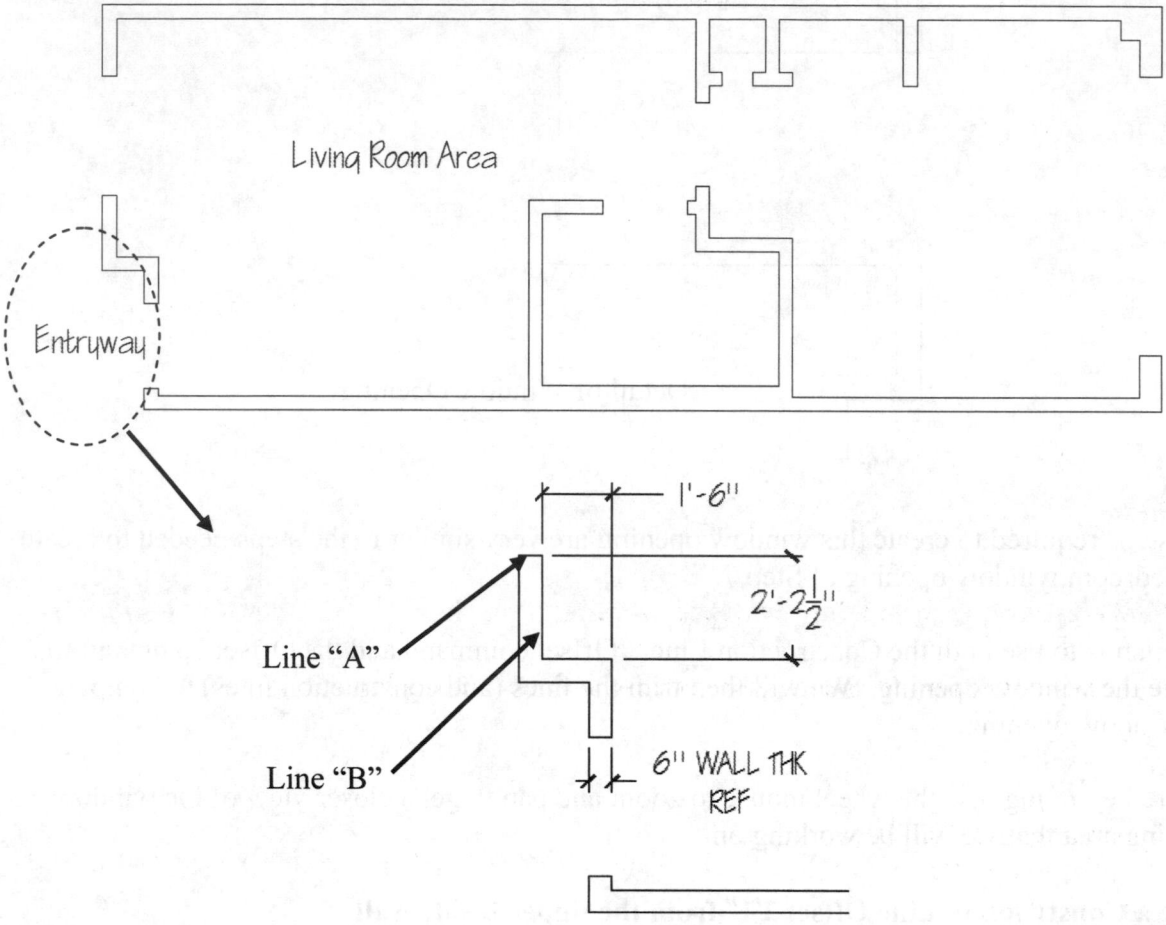

Living Room Area

Entryway

1'-6"

2'-2 1/2"

Line "A"

Line "B"

6" WALL THK
REF

10a. Create a Construction Line Offset 2'2-1/2" down from line "A"

10b. Create a Construction Line Offset 1'6" to the right of line "B"

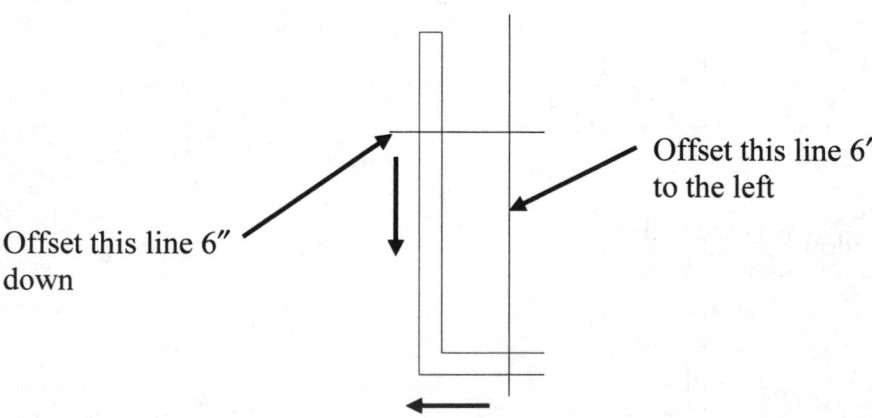

Offset this line 6"
to the left

Offset this line 6"
down

10c. Use the Offset command to Offset both construction lines

After this step, this part of your drawing should look like this:

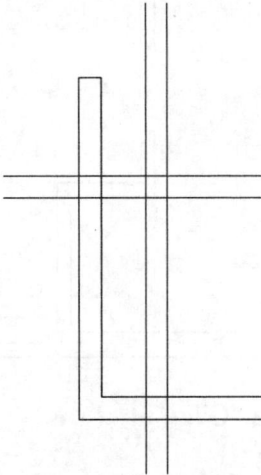

10d. Use the Trim command to trim construction lines

10e. Use the Erase command (if needed) to get eliminate any extra lines

Depending on the order and location of the lines you picked during trimming, you may have some extra lines left over. Use the Erase command to eliminate them.

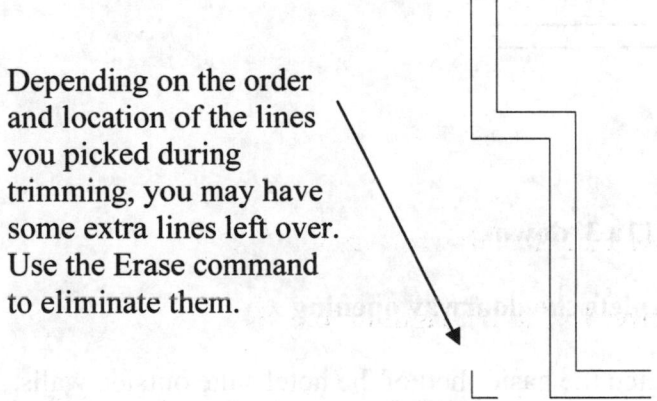

This is how much you have created so far! – Almost done!

11. Create the doorway opening into the living room area

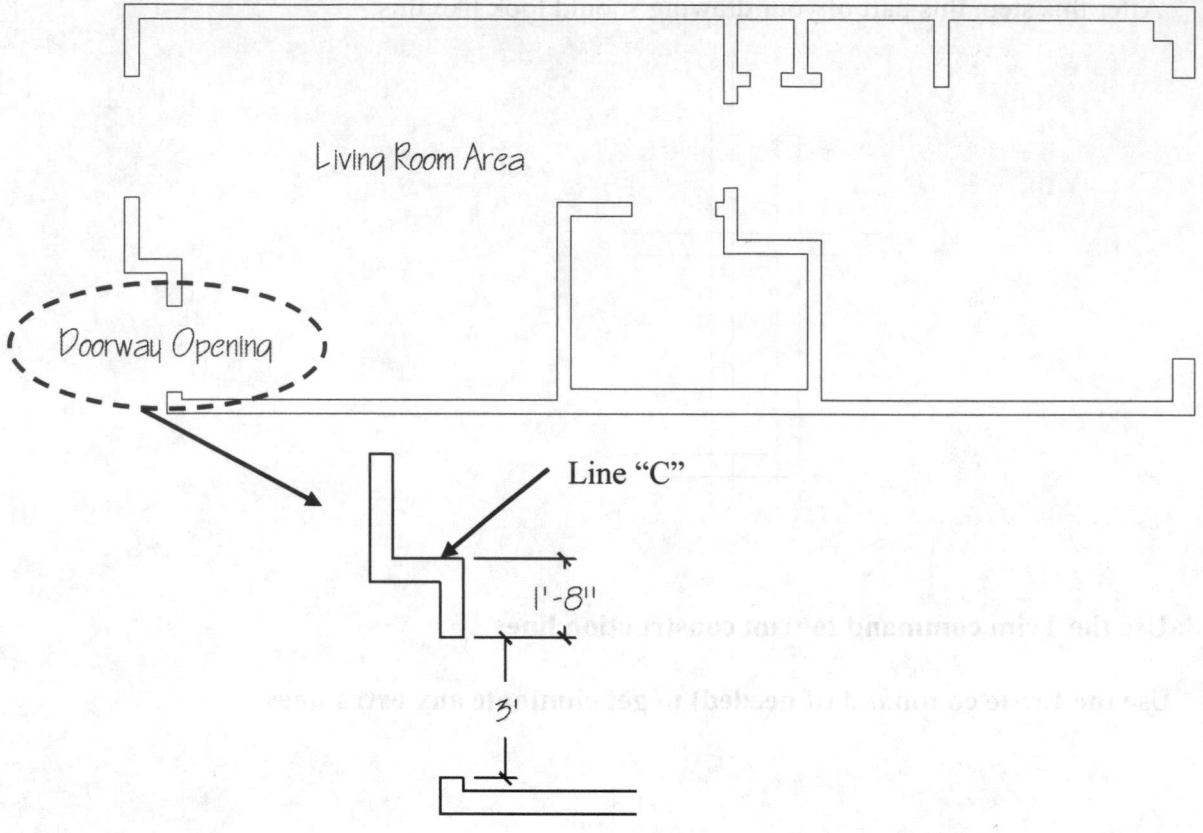

Living Room Area

Doorway Opening

Line "C"

1'-8"

3'

11a. Offset line "C" 1'8" down

11b. Offset the line created in Step 11a 3' down

11c. Use the Trim command to complete the doorway opening

Congratulations! You have now completed the basic shell of the hotel suite outside walls. Make sure to save your drawing so all that hard work won't be wasted!

12. Save the drawing

(Pick the Save icon)

After picking the Save icon, a dialog box will appear. If this is the first time saving, it will look similar to this:

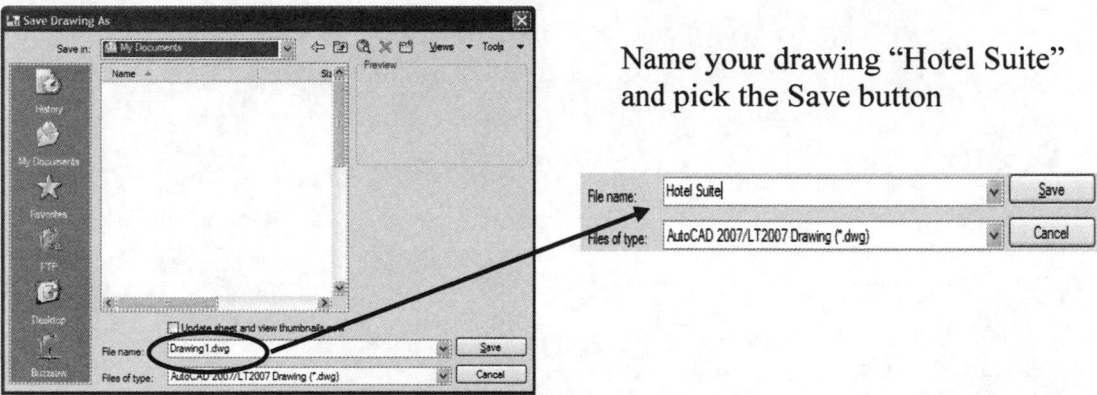

Name your drawing "Hotel Suite" and pick the Save button

Notes:

Chapter 5
Commands – Set 2: Working with Your Drawing

Learning Objectives:

- Measure distances and angles between objects
- Measure the radius of an arc or a circle
- Obtain information about an object
- Create round, beveled or sharp corners
- Move, copy, rotate, and make a mirror image of objects
- Use the Array command to perform a 2-direction Copy for a Rectangular Array
- Use the Array command to perform a simultaneous Rotate and Copy for a Polar Array

We are now able to draw basic objects very accurately. After you draw them, you may want to be able to verify that what you have drawn is as accurate as you believe you have drawn them. Fortunately, AutoCAD® has a tool for getting information about the objects on your drawing. That tool is Inquiry.

Inquiry – Getting Information from Your Drawing

The Inquiry toolbar has commands that allow you to interrogate information from your drawing. Two of those commands, Measure Geometry and List are covered in this write-up. If the Inquiry toolbar is not displayed on your screen, you can bring it up by right-clicking on any toolbar and selecting Inquiry from the list of choices.

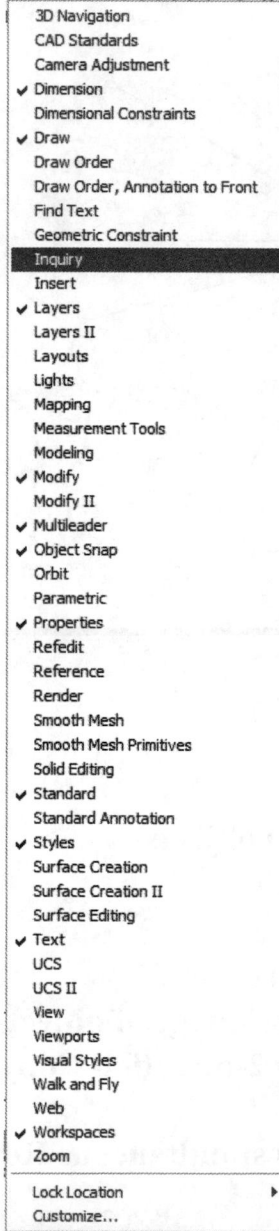

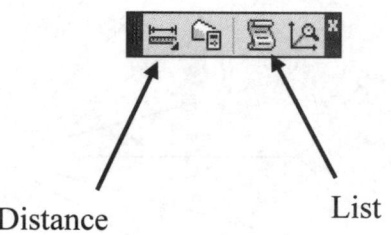

Distance   List

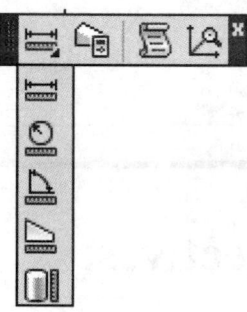

The Distance icon is a fly-out type of icon. You know this because of the black triangle in the lower right corner of the icon. Left-click and hold to get the icons beneath the Distance icon to appear. If you select one of these icons, then that icon will now be on the top of the fly-out list.

Measure Geometry

Under the Measure Geometry feature, AutoCAD® allows you to measure distance between points, the radius of a circular object, the angle between lines, and the area bounded by an object or shape defined by selected points. The icon is a fly-out type of icon, with distance as the default icon on top. If you select other than the distance icon on the fly-out, that icon will now be displayed instead.

Distance

The Distance command is used to find the distance between two points, such as the endpoints of lines, center point of circle, etc. For accurate measurements, make sure you have OSNAP turned on.

Procedure:

Pick (left click): **Distance icon** from the Inquiry toolbar.

The command line prompts you with the following:

Command: _MEASUREGEOM
Enter an option [Distance/Radius/Angle/ARea/Volume] <Distance>: _distance
Specify first point:

Select the first point of the two points you wish to find the distance between. For this example, pick point "A".

Example:

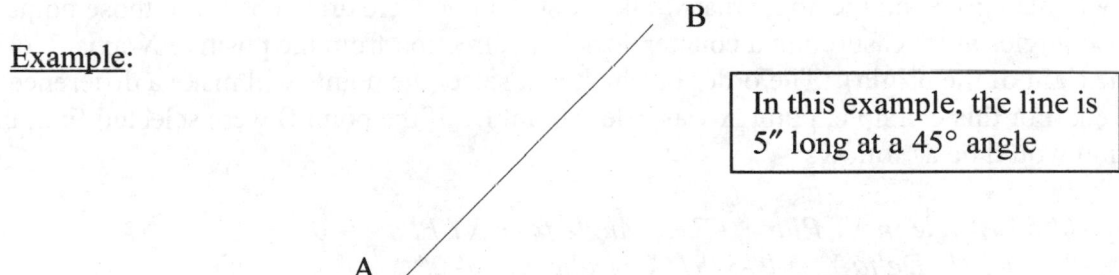

In this example, the line is 5″ long at a 45° angle

After you pick the first point, your command lines will look like the following:

Specify second point or [Multiple points]:

After you select the second point (point "B"), the command line will give the requested information:

Distance = 0'-5", Angle in XY Plane = 45, Angle from XY Plane = 0
Delta X = 0'-3 9/16", Delta Y = 0'-3 9/16",   Delta Z = 0'-0"

The command line will then prompt you to enter an option or continue to find distances:

*Enter an option [Distance/Radius/Angle/ARea/Volume/eXit] <Distance>: *Cancel**

The command line will continue to prompt for more distance measurements, and allows you to choose other Measure Geometry optons. If you have no more distances to measure, exit the command using the Escape key.

In addition to the command line, the information is also displayed on your screen:

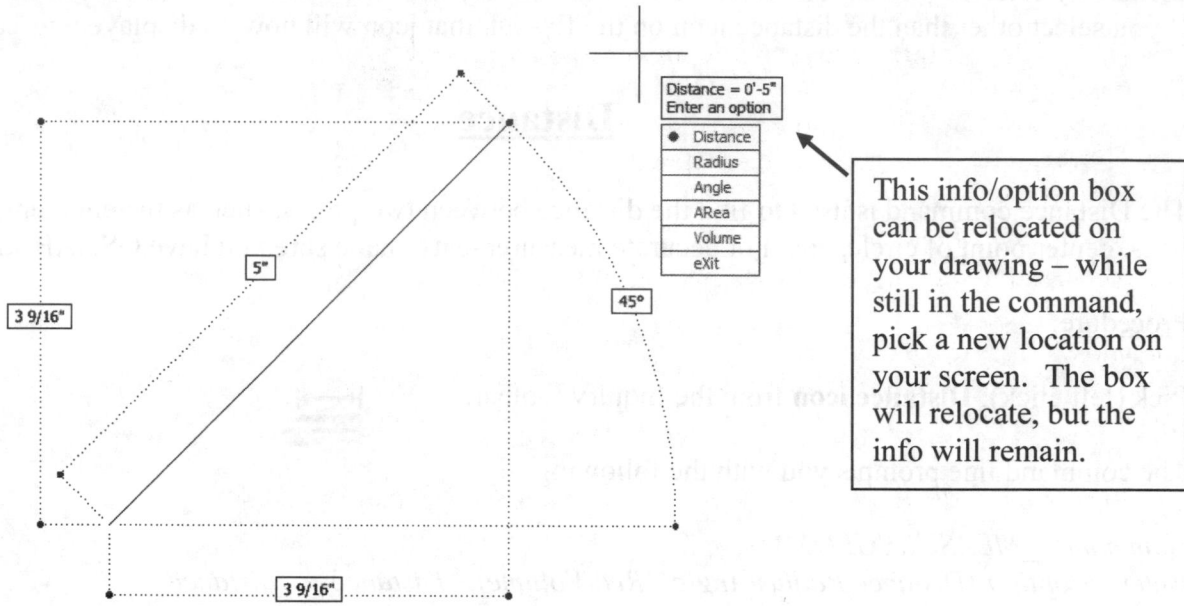

The information provided will give the distance between points, regardless of the angle between them. It will also give you the angle that would exist if a line were drawn between those points. Remember, angles are measured in a counterclockwise direction from the positive X-axis (Horizontal axis to the right of the origin). The order in which you select the points will make a difference in the angle given. For this example, point A was below point B. If the point B were selected first, the information would be as follows:

Distance = 0'-5", Angle in XY Plane = 225, Angle from XY Plane = 0
Delta X = -0'-3 9/16", Delta Y = -0'-3 9/16", Delta Z = 0'-0"
Command:

Notice that the angle of 225° is 180° more than 45° (45+180=225).

In addition to giving the direct distance between points, AutoCAD® also gives the distance from the first point to the second point in the X and Y (horizontal and vertical) directions (known as Delta X and Delta Y). Ignore the Z distance; this will always remain 0'-0" since we are drawing in 2-D.

Note that the first example (with the 45° angle) the X & Y values are positive because the direction from the first point to the second was to the right (+X) and up (+Y). For the second example (with the 225° angle) the X & Y values are negative because the direction from the first point to the second was to the left (-X) and down (-Y).

Radius

The Radius option allows you to measure the radius and diameter of an arc or circle.

Procedure:

Pick (left click): **Radius icon** from the Inquiry toolbar.

Note that if the icon is not on the top of the Fly-out list,
Pick and hold the top icon, then move down the icon
list to select the Radius icon.

The command line prompts you with the following:

Command: _MEASUREGEOM
Enter an option [Distance/Radius/Angle/ARea/Volume] <Distance>: _radius
Select arc or circle:

Pick the arc or circle you are interested in. For this example, pick the arc:

Example:

Radius = 0'-3 9/16"
Diameter = 0'-7 3/16"

Both the radius and diameter of the selected object are displayed on the command line and on the
screen:

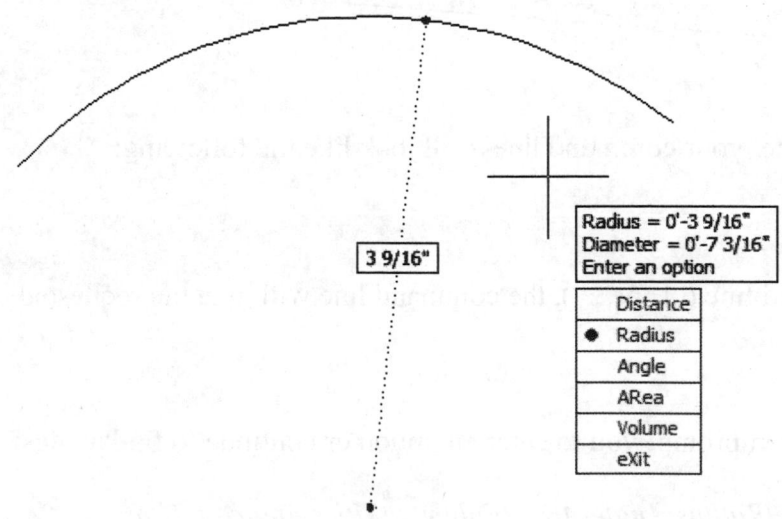

The command line will continue to prompt for more radial measurements, and allows you to choose other Measure Geometry optons. If you have no more radii to measure, exit the command using the Escape key.

*Enter an option [Distance/Radius/Angle/ARea/Volume/eXit] <Radius>: *Cancel**

Angle

The Angle option allows you to measure the angle between lines, and between arc endpoints.

Procedure:

Pick (left click): **Angle icon** from the Inquiry toolbar.

Note that if the icon is not on the top of the Fly-out list, Pick and hold the top icon, then move down the icon list to select the Radius icon.

The command line prompts you with the following:

Command: _MEASUREGEOM
Enter an option [Distance/Radius/Angle/ARea/Volume] <Distance>: _angle
Select arc, circle, line, or <Specify vertex>:

Select the first line of the two lines you wish to find the angle between. For this example, pick "Line 1".

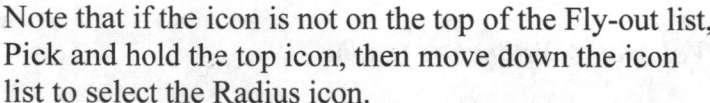

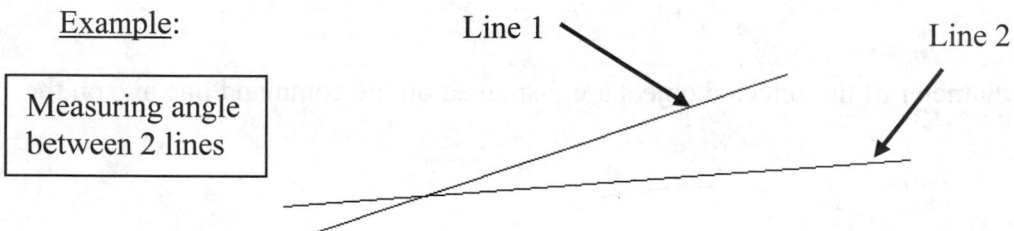

Example:

Line 1   Line 2

Measuring angle
between 2 lines

After you pick the first line, your command lines will look like the following:

Select second line:

After you select the second line ("Line 2"), the command line will give the requested information:

Angle = 14°

The command line will then prompt you to enter an option or continue to find angles:

*Enter an option [Distance/Radius/Angle/ARea/Volume/eXit] <Angle>: *Cancel**

The command line will continue to prompt for more distance measurements, and allows you to choose other Measure Geometry optons. If you have no more distances to measure, exit the command using the Escape key.

In addition to the command line, the information is also displayed on your screen:

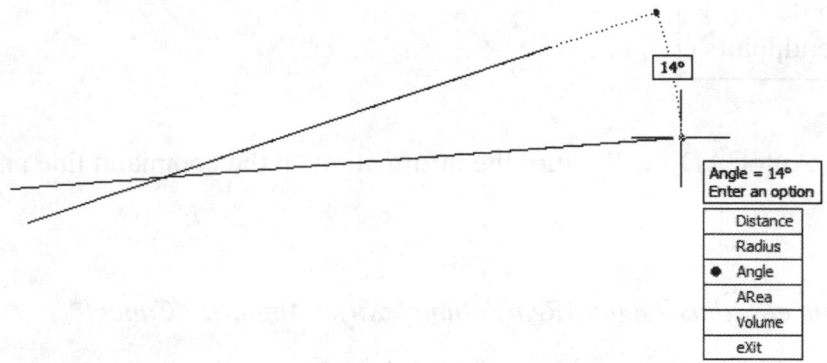

The angle that is measured may not have been the angle you desired. If you wanted the larger angle between the two, you could subtract the angle found from 180°. Alternatively, you could use the Vertex option. The vertex of an angle is the point where the two lines intersect.

Notice in the command line prompt, the vertex option is available:

Select arc, circle, line, or <Specify vertex>:

Simply press the ↵ Enter key to select this option. AutoCAD® will then prompt you with the following:

Specify angle vertex: (Pick the intersection of the two lines)
Specify first angle endpoint: (Pick the endpoint of Line 1)
Specify second angle endpoint: (Pick the endpoint of Line 2)
Angle = 166°
*Enter an option [Distance/Radius/Angle/ARea/Volume/eXit] <Angle>: *Cancel**

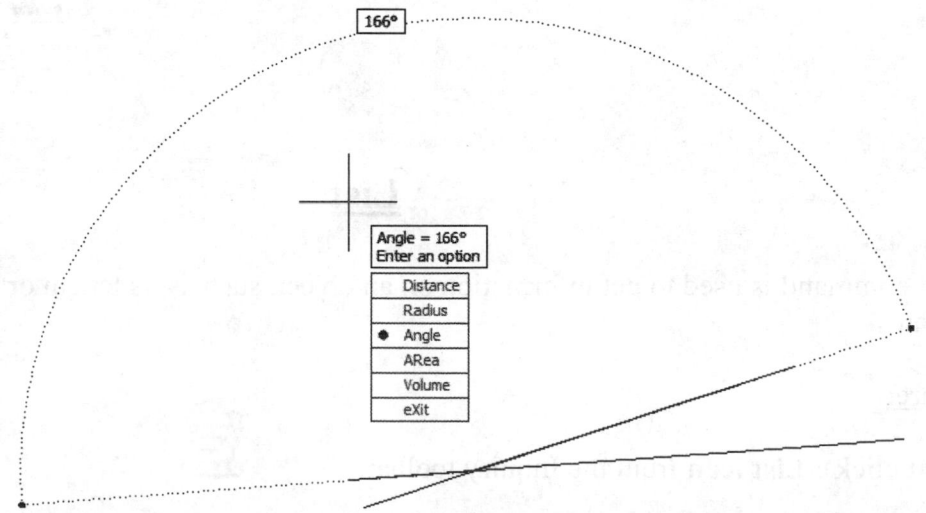

You can also measure the angle between arc endpoints. When prompted to select the object to measure the angle, simply pick the arc.

Example:

| Measuring angle between arc endpoints |

After selecting the arc, AutoCAD® will return the information on the command line and on your screen:

Angle = 104°
*Enter an option [Distance/Radius/Angle/ARea/Volume/eXit] <Angle>: *Cancel**

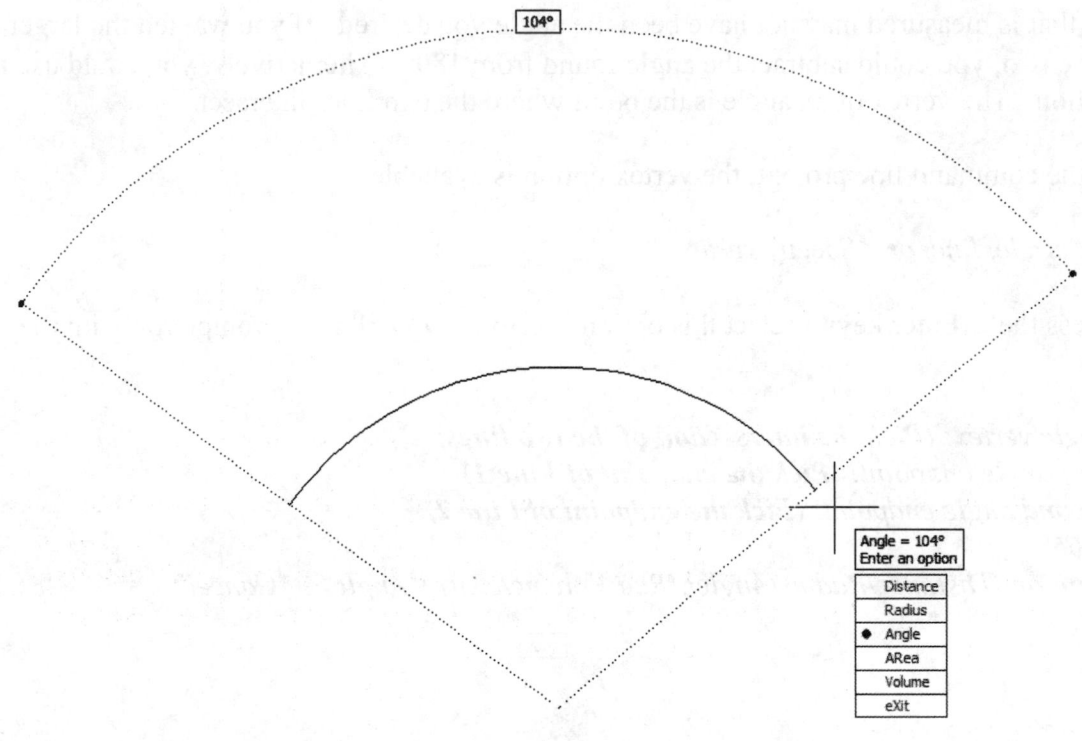

List

The List command is used to get information on an object, such as its length or location in the X-Y coordinates.

Procedure:

Pick (left click): **List icon** from the Inquiry toolbar.

Command: _list
Select objects:

Pick the object you are interested in. The command line will continue to prompt for more objects until you press the ↵ Enter key:

Select objects:1 found
Select objects:

After you press the ↵ Enter key, a Text Window will appear. This Text Window provides you with the information about that object:

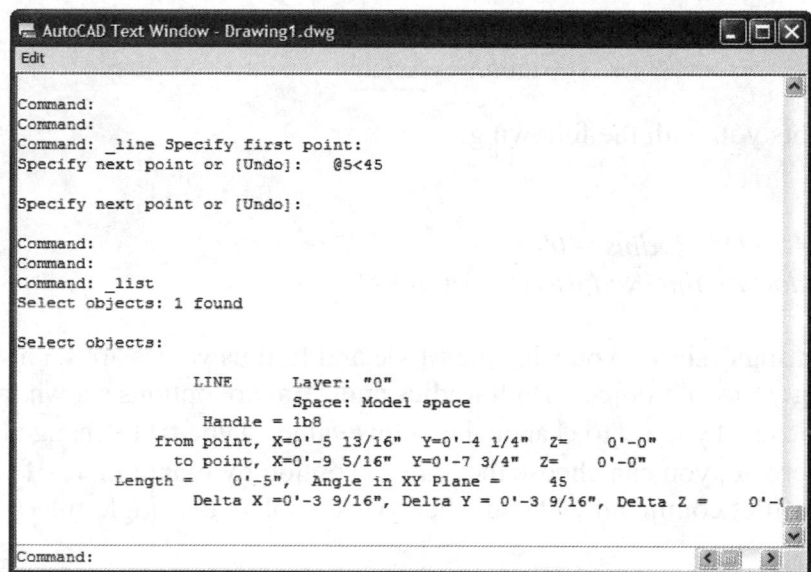

The information provided includes the type of object, (in this example, a line was selected), the layer that object is on, the start and end point in X & Y coordinates, the length, the angle it makes relative to the positive X-axis and the X & Y (Horizontal & Vertical) distance between the endpoints. For each object there is different information provided, depending on the type of object selected. Try this on your own and you will discover how useful this can be.

To close out the Text Window, pick the X in the upper right corner. This will return you to the command line.

We have been able to make circles, lines, and construction lines. When we trim intersecting lines or construction lines, we end up with a sharp corner. There are many times that we want to make rounded corners. AutoCAD® has a command just for that and it is called Fillet.

But, in addition to making rounded corners, Fillet can also make square corners. This doesn't seem logical at first, but it can really come in handy. The square-corner Fillet is created by using a radius value of 0″. One major advantage of using the Fillet command for a square corner is to trim or extend lines simultaneously to complete an intersection.

Fillet – Creating Round or Square Corners

The Fillet command allows you to connect two objects with an arc of a specified radius. The icon is on the Modify toolbar.

Procedure:

Pick (left click): **Fillet icon** from the Modify toolbar.

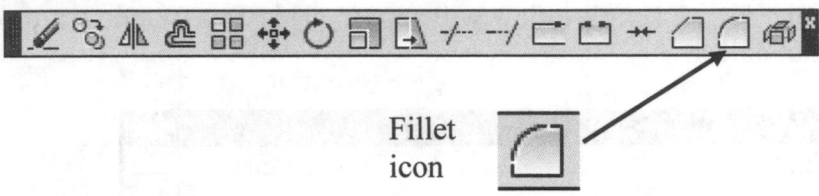

Fillet
icon

The command line prompts you with the following:

Command: _fillet
Current settings: Mode = TRIM, Radius = 0'-0"
Select first object or [Undo/Polyline/Radius/Trim/Multiple]:

Note that the "Current settings" shows you what the Mode and Radius values are set at. These can be changed prior to selecting your first object. Both Radius and Trim are options shown in the square brackets that you can choose. Type **r⏎** to change the radius value. Type **t⏎** to change trim value. If you have many fillets to create, you can choose the multiple option by typing **m⏎** . If you do not choose multiple, then the fillet command will end when you complete the single fillet.

Setting the Fillet Radius

The fillet radius is the radius of the arc that connects the two objects. If you set the fillet radius to 0", filleted objects are trimmed or extended until they intersect, but no arc is created. Whatever value you choose for the fillet radius will be the default radius value the next time you select the fillet command.

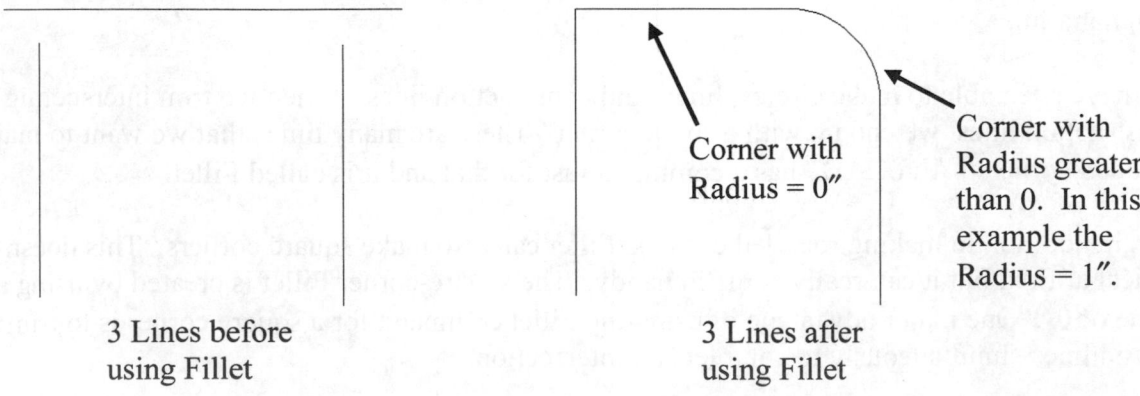

Corner with
Radius = 0"

Corner with
Radius greater
than 0. In this
example the
Radius = 1".

3 Lines before
using Fillet

3 Lines after
using Fillet

Trim Option

You can use the Trim option to specify whether the selected objects are trimmed or extended to the endpoints of the resulting arc or left unchanged. By default, all objects except circles, full ellipses, closed polylines, and splines (ellipses, polylines and splines will be discussed in a later chapter) are trimmed or extended when filleted.

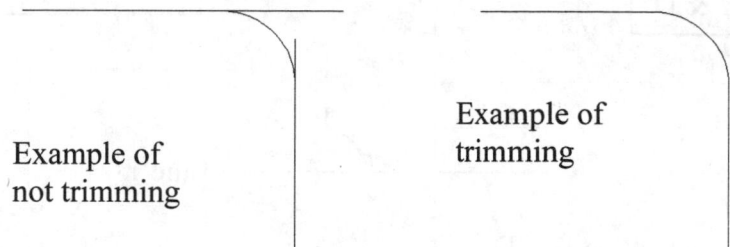

Example of
not trimming

Example of
trimming

Selecting Objects to Fillet

Select the first of two objects required to define a fillet, then, select the second object. The following will result (with *Mode = TRIM*):

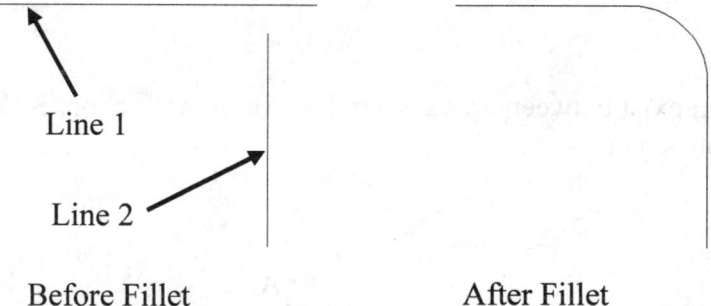

Line 1

Line 2

Before Fillet   After Fillet

Note that although the lines are labeled as "1" and "2", the order selected does not matter. As you will see later, what does matter is where you pick the objects to fillet.

If you select lines, arcs, or polylines, AutoCAD® extends or trims them until they intersect. Circles do not extend or trim with the fillet command.

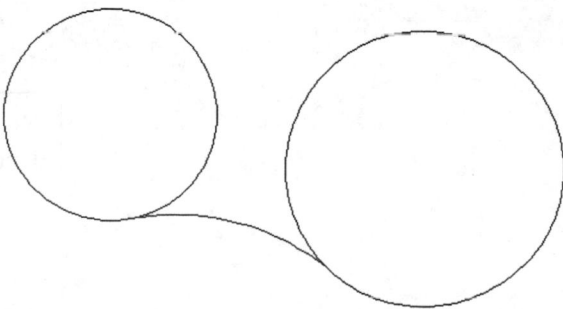

Importance of Pick Location

Depending on the locations you specify, more than one possible fillet can exist between the selected objects. Compare the selection points and resulting fillets for Lines "1" & "2":

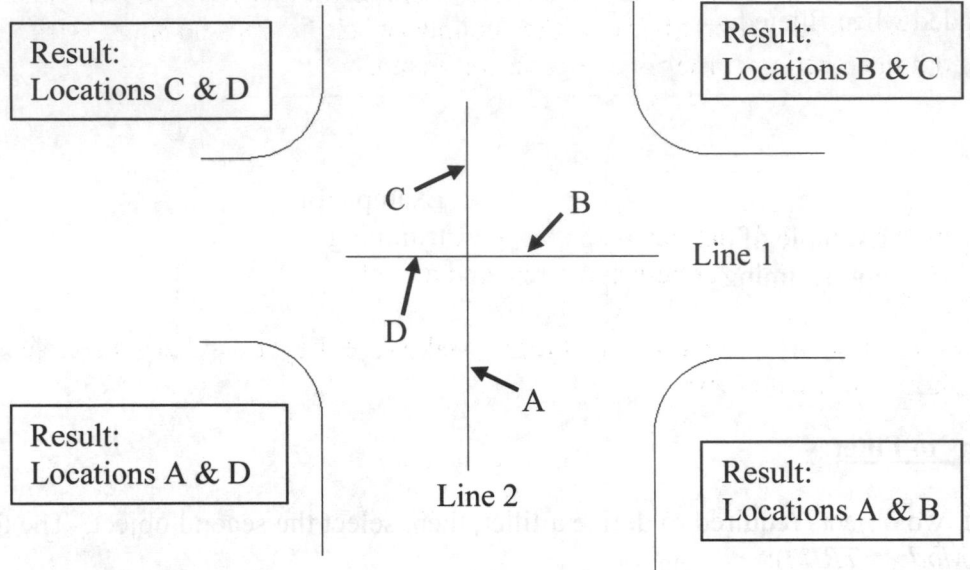

More than one fillet can exist between arcs and circles. AutoCAD® chooses the fillet with endpoints closest to the points you select.

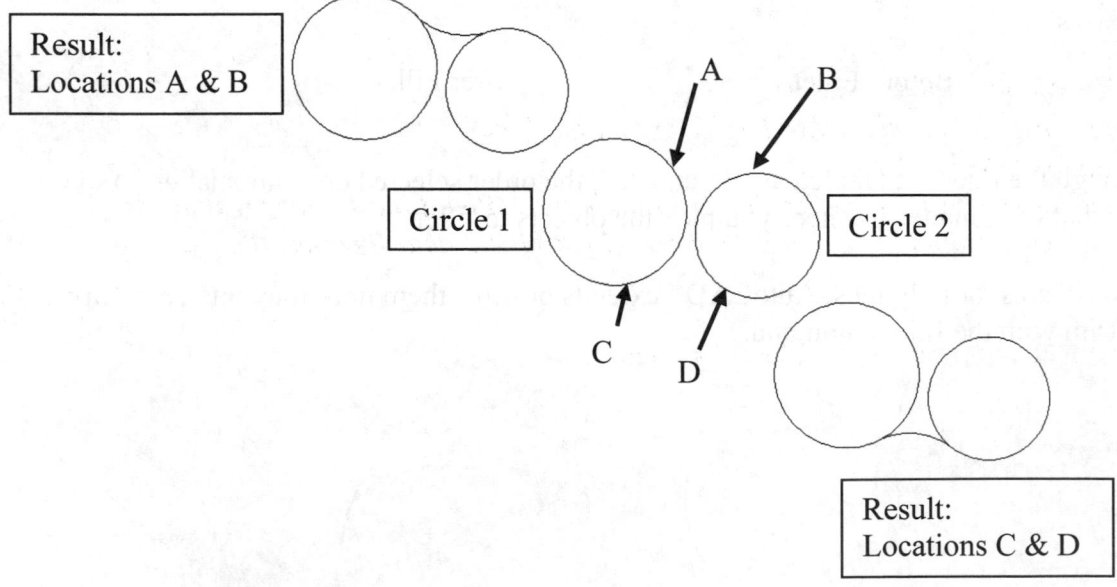

Recommendation:

Fillets are very useful for rounding inside or outside corners. With a radius value set to 0″, Fillets are extremely handy for closing a gap between two lines you want to have intersect with each other. For example, if you offset the inside wall line to the outside to create the outside wall line, this will come up short. Extending would be difficult because the "boundary" also comes up short. Using Fillet will extend and trim both intersecting corner lines in one command.

Try it:

Let's try two examples: 1. Fillet between two lines
                                       2. Fillet between a line and a circle

Example 1. Draw two lines anywhere on your screen. Make sure they are at least a couple inches long and are not parallel to each other:

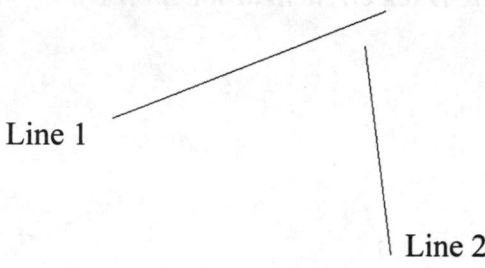

Line 1

Line 2

Now use the Fillet command to draw a 1″ Radius arc between them. Make sure that the Trim mode is on.
(Pick the Fillet icon)

Command: _fillet
Current settings: Mode = TRIM, Radius = 0'-0"
Select first object or [Undo/Polyline/Radius/Trim/Multiple]: r↵
Specify fillet radius <0'-0">: 1↵
*Select first object or [Undo/Polyline/Radius/Trim/Multiple]: **(Pick Line 1 near location A)***
*Select second object or shift-select to apply corner: **(Pick Line 2 near location B)***
Command:

When you are done, your drawing will look like this:

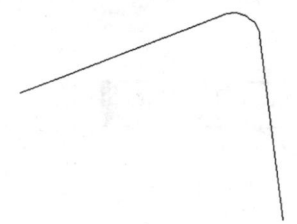

Example 2: Draw a 2″ radius circle. Draw a line from the center of the circle to several inches beyond the circle:

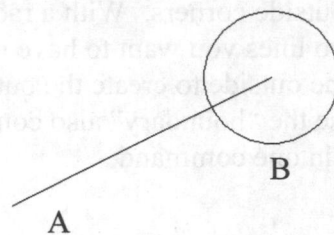

(Pick the Fillet icon)

Command: _fillet
Current settings: Mode = TRIM, Radius = 0'-1"
*Select first object or [Undo/Polyline/Radius/Trim/Multiple]: **(Pick the line near location A)***
*Select second object or shift-select to apply corner: **(Pick circle near location B)***
Command:

When you are done, your drawing will look like this:

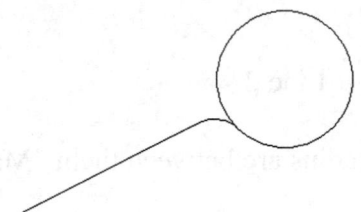

Chamfer – Creating Beveled Edges

The Chamfer command allows you create a beveled edge of a specified angle or distance between two non-parallel lines. The icon is on the Modify toolbar. This command works very similar to the Fillet command.

Procedure:

Pick (left click): **Chamfer icon** from the Modify toolbar.

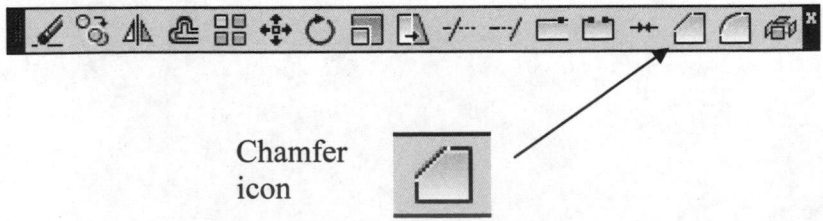

Chamfer
icon

The command line prompts you with the following:

Command: _chamfer
(TRIM mode) Current chamfer Dist1 = 0'-0", Dist2 = 0'-0"
Select first line or [Undo/Polyline/Distance/Angle/Trim/mEthod/Multiple]:

Note that the "Current chamfer" shows you what the Mode and Distance values are set at. These can be changed prior to selecting your first object. Both Distance and Trim are options shown in the square brackets that you can choose. Type **d↵** to change the distance value. Type **t↵** to change trim value. Type **a↵** to change the angle value. If you have many chamfers to create, you can choose the multiple option by typing **m↵**. If you do not choose multiple, then the chamfer command will end when you complete the single chamfer.

Setting the Chamfer Distance

The chamfer distance is the starting and ending distance from the intersection of the two lines. If you set the chamfer distance to 0", chamfered lines are trimmed or extended until they intersect, but no chamfer is created. Whatever value you choose for the chamfer distance will be the default distance values the next time you select the chamfer command. You can also specify the chamfer angle. This option will require you to specify the distance to the first line and then the angle value.

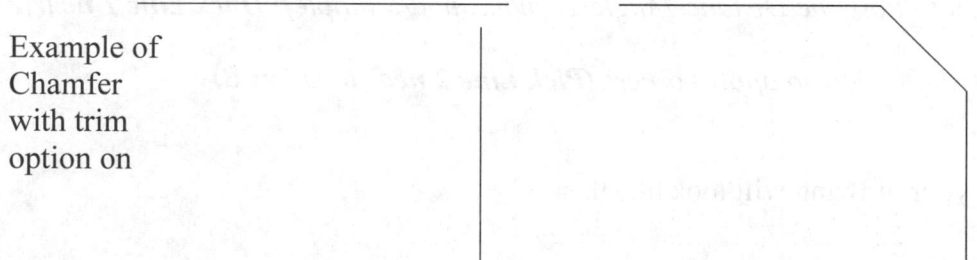

Example of
Chamfer
with trim
option on

Other than the fact that this command creates angled corners (as opposed to rounded corners) it is very similar to the Fillet command. The trim option can be turned on and off, and the pick location is important. It is recommended that you understand the Fillet commands first and then explore the Chamfer command on your own.

Recommendation:

Chamfers are very useful for beveling corners. With a distance value set to 0", chamfers are extremely handy for closing a gap between two lines you want to have intersect with each other. For example, if you offset the inside wall line to the outside to create the outside wall line, this will come up short. Extending would be difficult because the "boundary" also comes up short. Using Chamfer, with a distance value of 0", will extend and trim both intersecting corner lines in one command.

Try it:

Usually (but not always) when you want to bevel an edge, it is between two perpendicular lines. For this example, let's draw a 45° beveled edge that begins 1″ from the corner.

Draw two perpendicular lines, each at least a few inches long, anywhere on your screen:

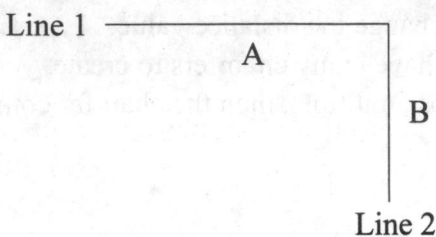

Line 1

A

B

Line 2

(Pick the Chamfer icon)

Command: _chamfer
(TRIM mode) Current chamfer Dist1 = 0'-0", Dist2 = 0'-0"
Select first line or [Undo/Polyline/Distance/Angle/Trim/mEthod/Multiple]: **a↵**
Specify chamfer length on the first line <0'-0">: **1↵**
Specify chamfer angle from the first line <0>: **45↵**
Select first line or [Undo/Polyline/Distance/Angle/Trim/mEthod/Multiple]: **(Pick Line 1 near location A)**
Select second line or shift-select to apply corner: **(Pick Line 2 near location B)**
Command:

When you are done, your drawing will look like this:

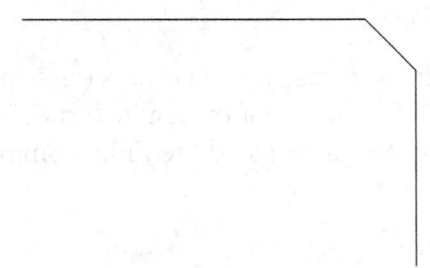

Manipulating Existing Objects

You can manipulate existing objects in the following ways:

- Move objects using the Move command.
- Make a copy of the objects to a new location using the Copy command
- Rotate objects using the Rotate command.
- Make a mirror image of objects using the Mirror command.
- Make a rectangular or polar array – combines Move with Copy, and Rotate with Copy

These commands are two part commands. The first part of the command requires you to select the objects. After the objects are selected, press the ↲ Enter key to get to the second part of the command. The second part of the command is further explained for each command in this document. The command icons are located on the Modify toolbar.

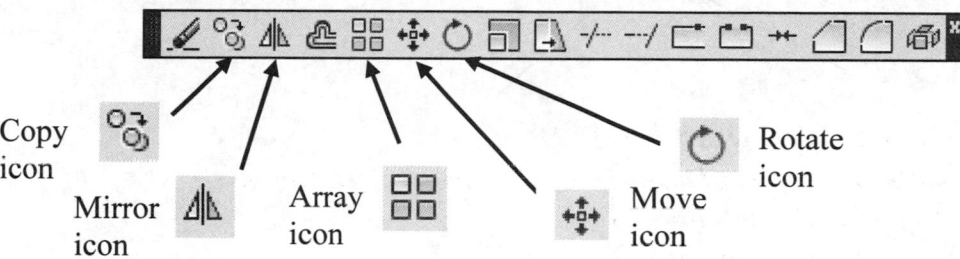

Move

Procedure:

Pick (left click): **Move icon** from the Modify toolbar.

AutoCAD® will prompt you to select objects, and will continue to do so until you press the ↲ Enter key.

Command: _move
Select objects: (Pick the objects you wish to move)
Select objects: 1 found   (You can continue selecting as many objects you desire to move)
Select objects: ↲   (Pressing the ↲ Enter key will get you to the second part of the command)
Specify base point or displacement: (Pick a point to move "From")
Specify base point or displacement: Specify second point of displacement or
<use first point as displacement>: (Pick a point to move "To")
Command: (AutoCAD® ends the command)

Try it:

Let's move an object to a specific location on the screen. For this example, let's move a circle to the intersection of two lines.

Before beginning this example, make sure that you have Object Snap (OSNAP) turned on with Center and Intersection selected.

Draw two intersecting lines anywhere on your screen. Draw a circle off to the side of these two lines. Now use the Move command to relocate the center of the circle to the intersection of the two lines:

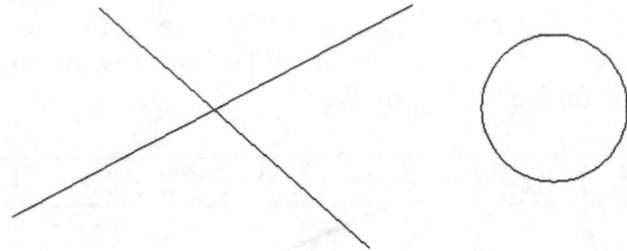

(Pick the Move icon)

Command: _move
*Select objects: **(Pick the circle)** 1 found*
Select objects: ↵
*Specify base point or [Displacement] <Displacement>: **(Pick the center of the circle – ensure that the AutoSnap marker shows that the center of the circle was found)***
*Specify second point or <use first point as displacement>: **(Pick the intersection of the lines – ensure that the AutoSnap marker shows that the intersection was found)***
Command:

When you are done, your drawing will look like this:

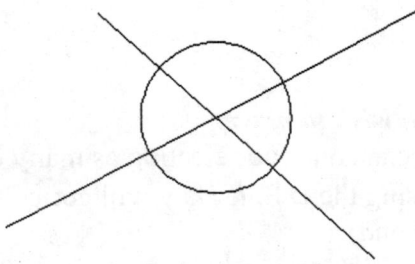

Copy

Procedure:

Pick (left click): **Copy icon** from the Modify toolbar.

AutoCAD® will prompt you to select objects, and will continue to do so until you press the ↵ Enter key.

Command: _copy
Select objects: **(Pick the objects you wish to copy)**
Select objects: 1 found   (You can continue selecting as many objects you desire to copy)
Select objects: ↵   (Pressing the ↵ Enter key will get you to the second part of the command)
Specify base point or displacement: **(Pick a point to copy "From")**
Specify base point or displacement: Specify second point of displacement or
<use first point as displacement>: **(Pick a point to copy "To")**
Specify second point of displacement:
          (AutoCAD® allows you to continue to make multiple copies)
Specify second point of displacement: ↵
          (Pressing the ↵ Enter key will end the command)
Command:

Try it:

Starting with the example from the Move command, add two more intersecting lines on your drawing:
(Make sure Object Snap is turned on with Center and Intersection selected)

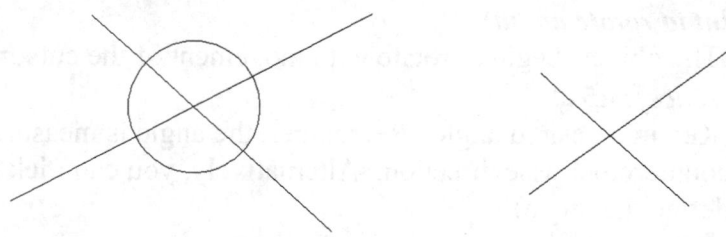

(Pick the Copy icon)

Command: _copy
Select objects: **(Pick the circle)** *1 found*
Select objects: ↵
Current settings: Copy mode = Multiple
Specify base point or [Displacement/mOde] <Displacement>: **(Pick the center of the circle)**

Specify second point or <use first point as displacement>: **(Pick the intersection of the 2 new lines)**
Specify second point or [Exit/Undo] <Exit>:⏎
Command:

When you are done, your drawing will look like this:

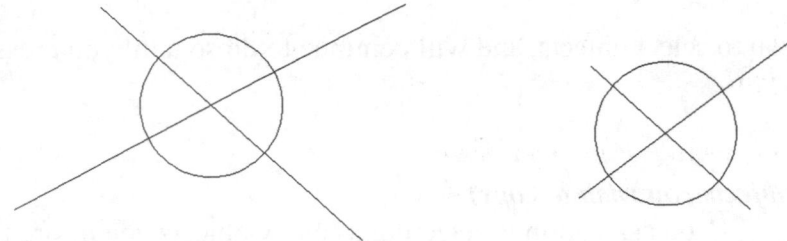

Rotate

Procedure:

Pick (left click): **Rotate icon** from the Modify toolbar.

AutoCAD® will prompt you to select objects, and will continue to do so until you press the ⏎ Enter key.

Command: _rotate
Current positive angle in UCS: ANGDIR=counterclockwise ANGBASE=0
Select objects: **(Pick the objects you wish to rotate)**
Select objects: 1 found   (You can continue selecting as many objects you desire to rotate)

Select objects: ⏎   (Pressing the ⏎ Enter key will get you to the second part of the command)
Specify base point: **(Pick a point to rotate about)**
          (The objects begin to rotate with movement of the cursor)
Specify rotation angle or [Reference]: **45** ⏎
          (Key in a desired angle. Remember, the angle is measured in a counterclockwise direction. Alternatively, you can Pick a point to define the angle)
Command: (AutoCAD® ends the command)

Try it:

Starting with the example of the Copy command, let's rotate the right circle 90° about the left circle.

(Pick the Rotate icon)
Command: _rotate
Current positive angle in UCS: ANGDIR=counterclockwise ANGBASE=0
Select objects: (Pick the right circle) 1 found
Select objects: ↵
Specify base point: (Pick the center of the left circle)
Specify rotation angle or [Copy/Reference] <0>: **90**↵
Command:

When you are done, your drawing will look like this:

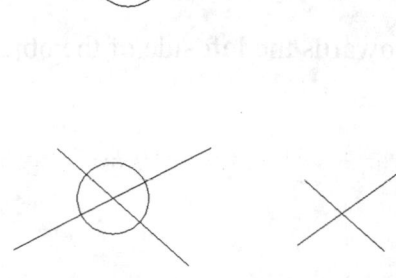

Mirror

Procedure:

Prior to using the Mirror command, it is a good idea to have a pre-defined line to mirror about.
AutoCAD® looks for two points that define a mirror line.

Pick (left click): **Mirror icon** from the Modify toolbar.

AutoCAD® will prompt you to select objects, and will continue to do so until you press the Enter ↵
key.

Command: _mirror
Select objects: [Pick the objects you wish to mirror]
Select objects: 1 found   (You can continue selecting as many objects you desire to mirror)
Select objects: ↵   (Pressing the Enter ↵ key will get you to the second part of the
    command)

Specify first point of mirror line:

> (If you have a pre-determined line you want to mirror about, then select the first endpoint of that line. A mirror image of the objects will follow your cursor until the second mirror line is defined)

Specify first point of mirror line: Specify second point of mirror line: **(Select the second endpoint of the pre-defined line)** (The mirror image will temporarily disappear)

Delete source objects? [Yes/No] <N>:

> (Type "**y**" if you wish to delete the original objects. Otherwise, accept the default value of "**n**" by pressing the ↵ Enter key. This will leave the original objects in place and you will have a mirrored-copy of your objects)

Command: (AutoCAD® ends the command)

Try it:

Starting with the example from the Rotate command, let's make a mirror image of what we have drawn.

Start by drawing a line that is nearly vertical towards the left side of the objects on the screen:

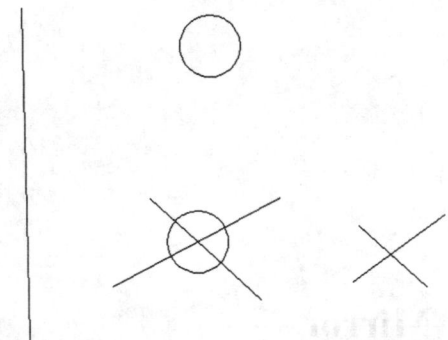

(Pick the Mirror icon)

Command: _mirror
Select objects: **(Pick the objects that are to the right of the line using a selection window)**
 Specify opposite corner: 6 found
Select objects: ↵
Specify first point of mirror line: **(Pick the endpoint of the nearly-vertical line)**
Specify second point of mirror line: **(Pick the other endpoint of the nearly-vertical line)**
Erase source objects? [Yes/No] <N>: ↵
Command:

When you are done, your drawing will look like this:

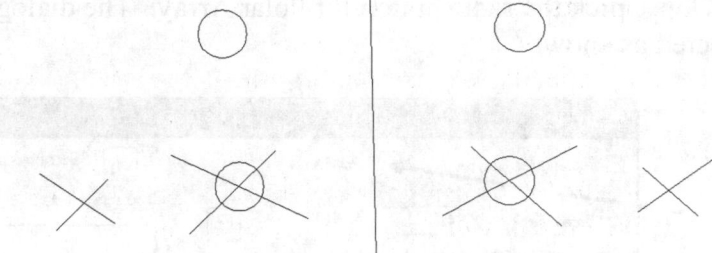

Recommendation:

These commands are very powerful and allow you to complete a drawing much faster than doing it by hand. There are additional options for these commands that are not covered here. It is left to the student to learn more about these options by exploring or using the online help. To rotate while copying, or move while copying, use the Array command.

Array

The Array command allows you to copy while rotating or moving. The Array command icon is located on the Modify toolbar.

Using the Array command

Pick (left click): **Array icon** from the Modify toolbar.

The Array dialog box appears:

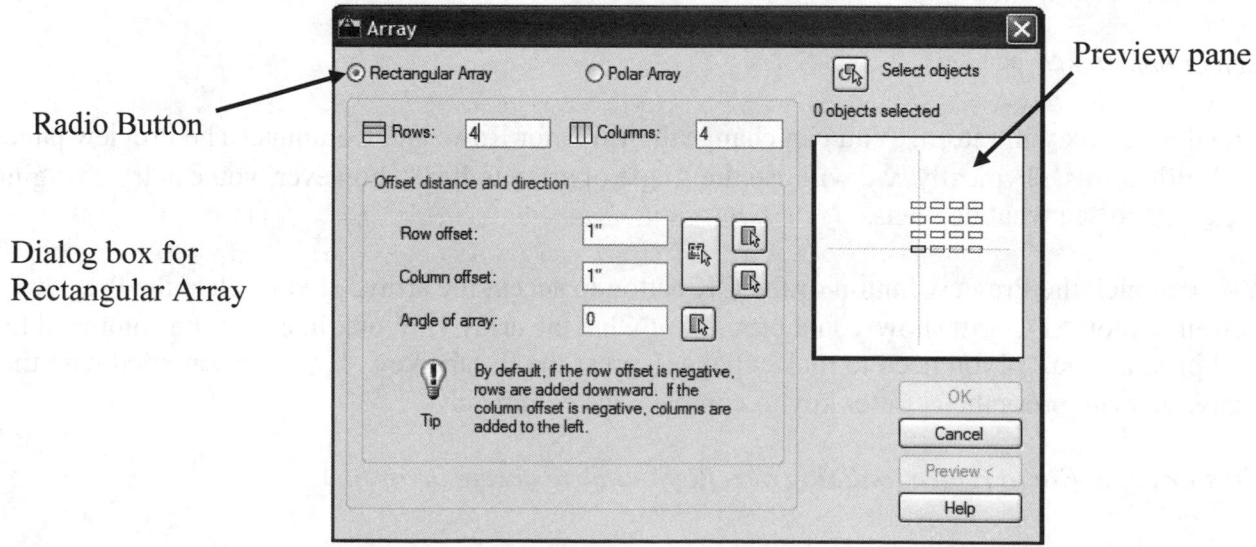

This dialog box shows the Rectangular Array selected. This would be good for a Move & Copy.

If you wish to Rotate & Copy, pick the radio button for Polar Array. The dialog box will change when Polar Array is selected as shown:

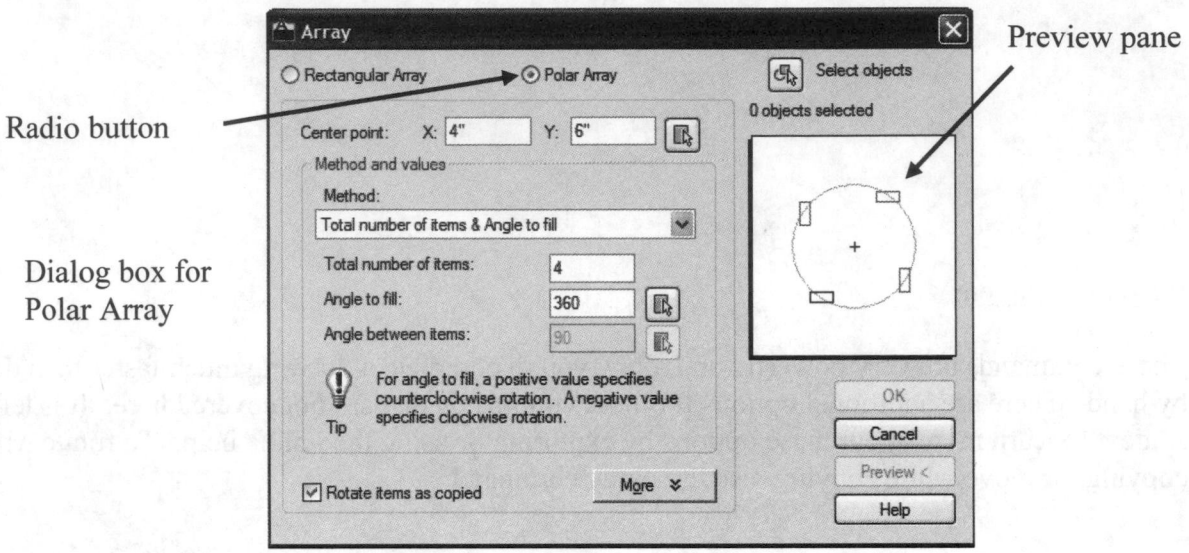

Radio button

Dialog box for Polar Array

Preview pane

Rectangular Array

The Rectangular Array will allow you to make copies of the original object in rows and columns. To pick the original objects, pick the Select objects button in the upper right-hand part of the Array dialog box. AutoCAD® will return you to the drawing screen so that you can select objects. In addition, the following will appear in the command line:

Command: _array
*Select objects: **[Pick the objects that will be used for the array]***
Select objects: 1 found   (AutoCAD® will allow you to continue picking objects until you press
                    the ↵ Enter key)
Select objects: ↵

The dialog box will return. You can change the value for Rows and Columns. The Preview pane will reflect this. Typically, we will use the Angle of array to be 0°, however, you can try changing the angle to see what happens.

You can pick the Preview button or the OK button to accept the array. If you select the Preview button, AutoCAD® will show you a preview of what the array will look like, and the command line will prompt you. If you need to make changes, press the Escape key. If you are satisfied with the array, you can press the ↵ Enter key to complete the command.

Pick or press Esc to return to dialog or <Right-click to accept array>:↵

Try it:

Let's draw a 6x6 pattern of 1″ squares that are 1-1/8″ apart (this will put a 1/8″ gap between the squares):

First, draw the 1″ square anywhere on the screen (use the Rectangle command):

(Pick the Array command)

Command: _array

The Array dialog box will appear. *(Pick the Select Objects button at the top right of the dialog box)*

The dialog box will disappear and the command line will prompt you to select objects.

Select objects: (Pick the square) 1 found
Select objects: ↵

The dialog box will re-appear.

Type 1-1/8 in both the Row offset and the Column offset sections

Type 6 for the value in both the Rows and Columns sections

(Pick the OK button)

When you are done, your drawing will look like this:

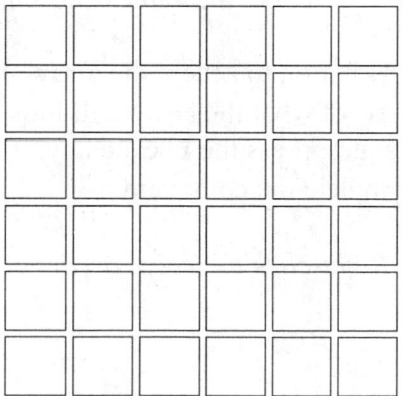

Polar Array

The Polar Array will allow you to make copies of the original object rotated about a point. To pick the original objects, pick the Select objects button in the upper right-hand part of the Array dialog box. AutoCAD® will return you to the drawing screen so that you can select objects. In addition, the following will appear in the command line:

Command: _array
Select objects: **(Pick the objects that will be used for the array)**
Select objects: 1 found　　　　　(AutoCAD® will allow you to continue picking objects until you press the ↵ Enter key)

Select objects: ↵

The dialog box will return. You can change the value for Center point, which is the point you will rotate the copies about, by keying an X & Y value, or by picking the Pick Center Point button. Picking this button will return you to the drawing screen so that you can pick the point. In addition the following will appear in the command line:

Specify center point of array: **(Pick a point that the selected objects will rotate about)**

The dialog box will return. You have 3 methods to choose from for the Polar Array. Use the pull-down arrow to make your choice.

- Total number of items & Angle to fill
- Total number of items & Angle between items
- Angle to fill & Angle between items

The three boxes below the method choices show the values of two of the three that can be changed. The third item is grayed-out (you cannot change the value) and will change according to the values you choose for other two selections. Which of the three items that is grayed-out depends on the method chosen.

A check-box in the lower left part of the dialog box will allow you to rotate the items as they are copied if it is checked. If it is not checked, the orientation of the copied objects will remain the same as the original objects. The Preview pane will reflect the values chosen.

You can pick the Preview button or the OK button to accept the array. If you select the Preview button, AutoCAD® will show you a preview of what the array will look like, and the command line will prompt you. If you need to make changes, press the Escape key. If you are satisfied with the array, you can press the ↵ Enter key to complete the command.

Pick or press Esc to return to dialog or <Right-click to accept array>: ↵

Try it:

Let's draw the 4 flower petals shown:

First we will draw a single flower petal, and then we will rotate and copy that petal by using the Array command. The petal is a 1″ radius circle drawn at the intersection of a line and a 2″ radius circle.

Start by drawing a 2″ radius circle anywhere on your screen. Now draw a horizontal construction line through the center of the circle. At the right intersection of the construction line and the 2″ radius circle, draw a 1″ radius circle.

At this point, your drawing will look like this:

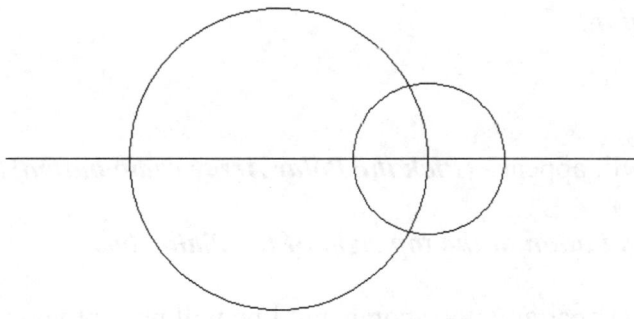

Now draw two lines that start from the center of the 2″ radius circle and ending tangent to the 1″ radius circle:

(If you do not have OSNAP set to Tangent, you can use the Object Snap toolbar to snap to the tangent of the circle when the Line command is prompting for the second endpoint

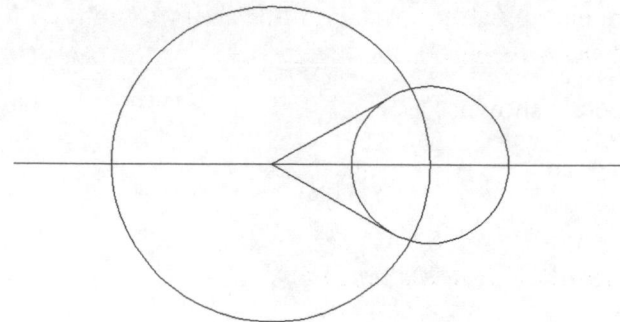

Use the Trim command to trim away the small portion of the 1″ radius circle:

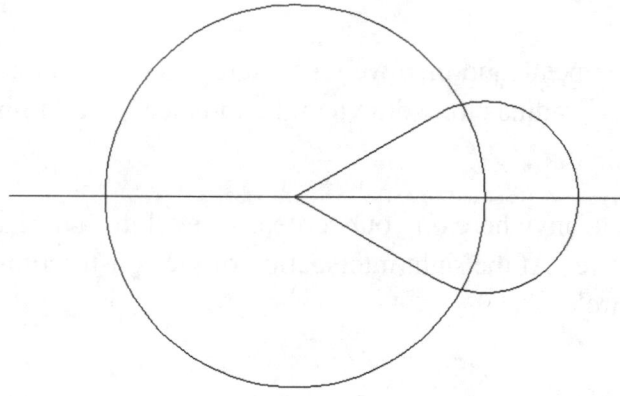

Now that we have the first petal drawn, we can use the Array command to copy it around the center of the 2″ radius circle.

(Pick the Array command)

Command: _array

The Array dialog box will appear. ***(Pick the Polar Array radio button)***

(Pick the Select Objects button at the top right of the dialog box)

The dialog box will disappear and your command line will prompt you to select objects.

(Pick the two lines and the semi-circle)

Select objects: 1 found
Select objects: 1 found, 2 total
Select objects: 1 found, 3 total
Select objects: ↵

The dialog box will re-appear.

(Pick the Center Point button in the dialog box)

The dialog box will disappear and your command line will prompt you to choose a center point.
(Pick the Center of the 2″ radius circle)

Specify center point of array: ↵

The dialog box will re-appear.

Type "4" for the Total number of items section.

Make sure that the Angle to fill is 360.

(Pick the OK button)

When you are done, your drawing will look like this:

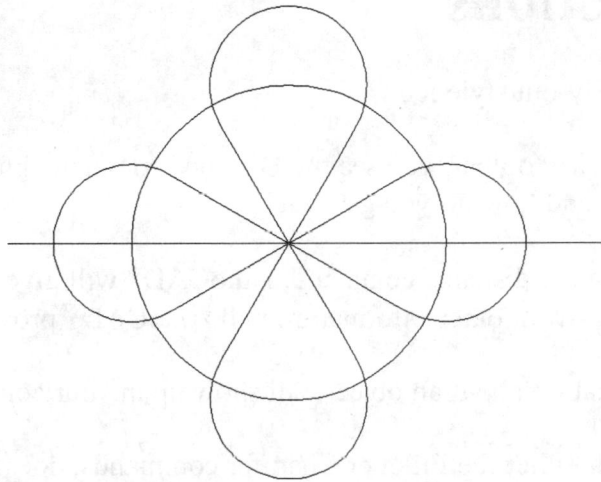

You can erase the 2″ radius circle and the construction line to get the final drawing of the flower:

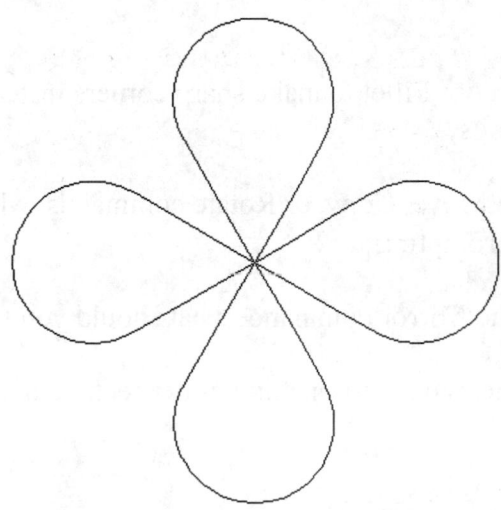

Summary

In this chapter you have learned to:

- Recognize and understand a Fly-out icon
- Measure distances between points
- Measure the radius and diameter of an arc or circle
- Measure the angle between lines
- Obtain all the information available about an object
- Move, copy, rotate, and mirror objects
- Create a rectangular pattern of objects
- Create a circular pattern of objects

Review Questions

1. What is a Fly-out style icon?

2. On the Inquiry toolbar, you see the Distance command but not the Angle command. Where is it and how do you get to it?

3. When using the distance command, AutoCAD® will give you the distance between two points. What other information will AutoCAD® provide?

4. The information about an object will show up in your command line and where else?

5. When using either the Fillet or Chamfer commands, does the order in which you pick the objects matter? Does the location matter?

6. If Fillets are used to make rounded corners, how can you use it to make a sharp corner?

7. Why would you use Fillet to make sharp corners instead of using either the Trim or Extend commands?

8. When using the Move, Copy, or Rotate commands, what is a base point that AutoCAD® is prompting for?

9. Prior to using the Mirror command, what should you have prepared in advance?

10. Which command is used for making either rectangular or circular patterns?

Exercises

1. Draw the conference room.

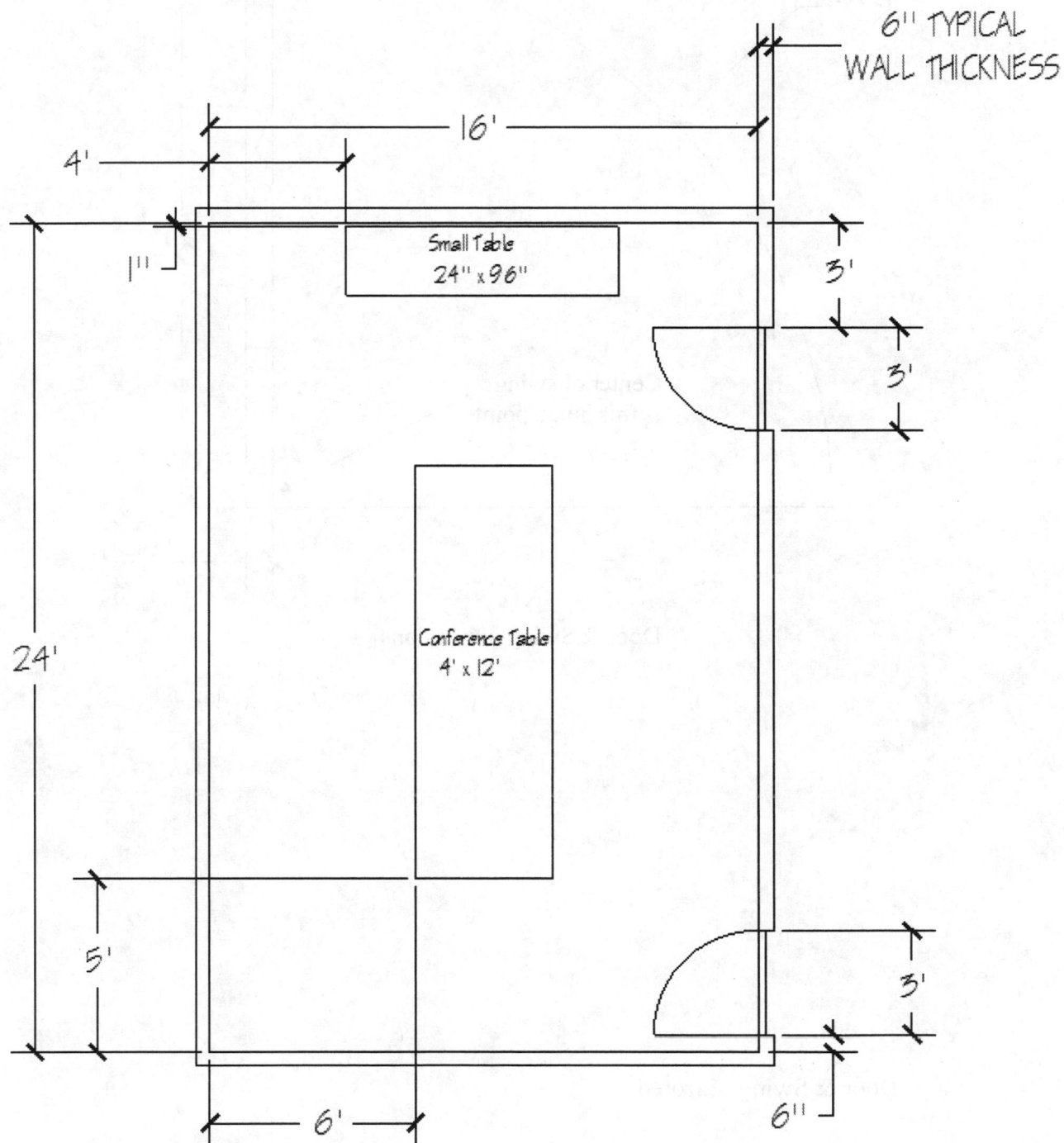

2. Draw the 3'x1-3/4" door and door swing. Make mirrored-copies of the door. Copy and rotate the mirrored-copies 90°.

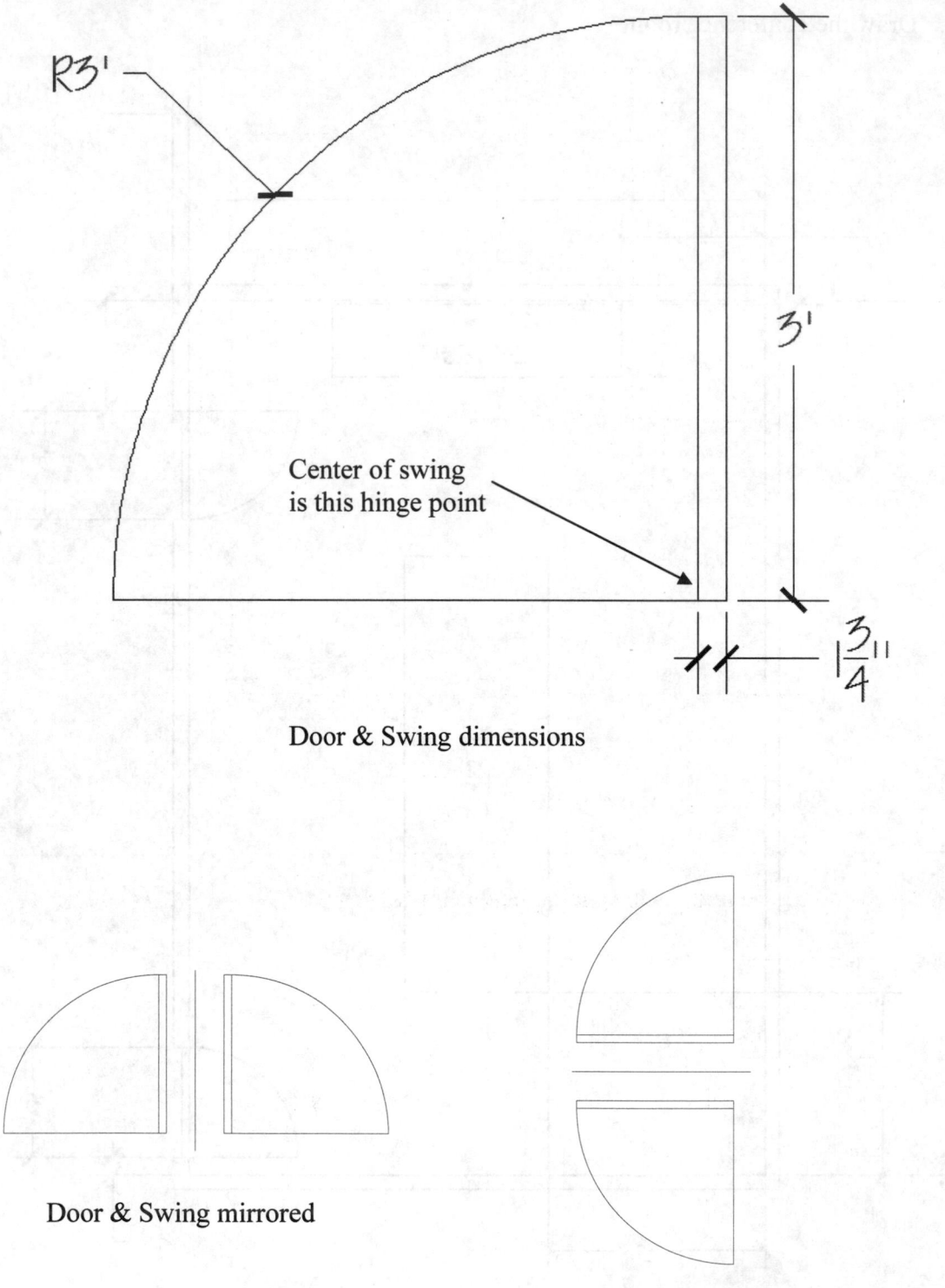

R3'

3'

Center of swing
is this hinge point

$1\frac{3}{4}$"

Door & Swing dimensions

Door & Swing mirrored

Door & Swing rotated 90° after mirroring

3. Draw the Conference Chair.

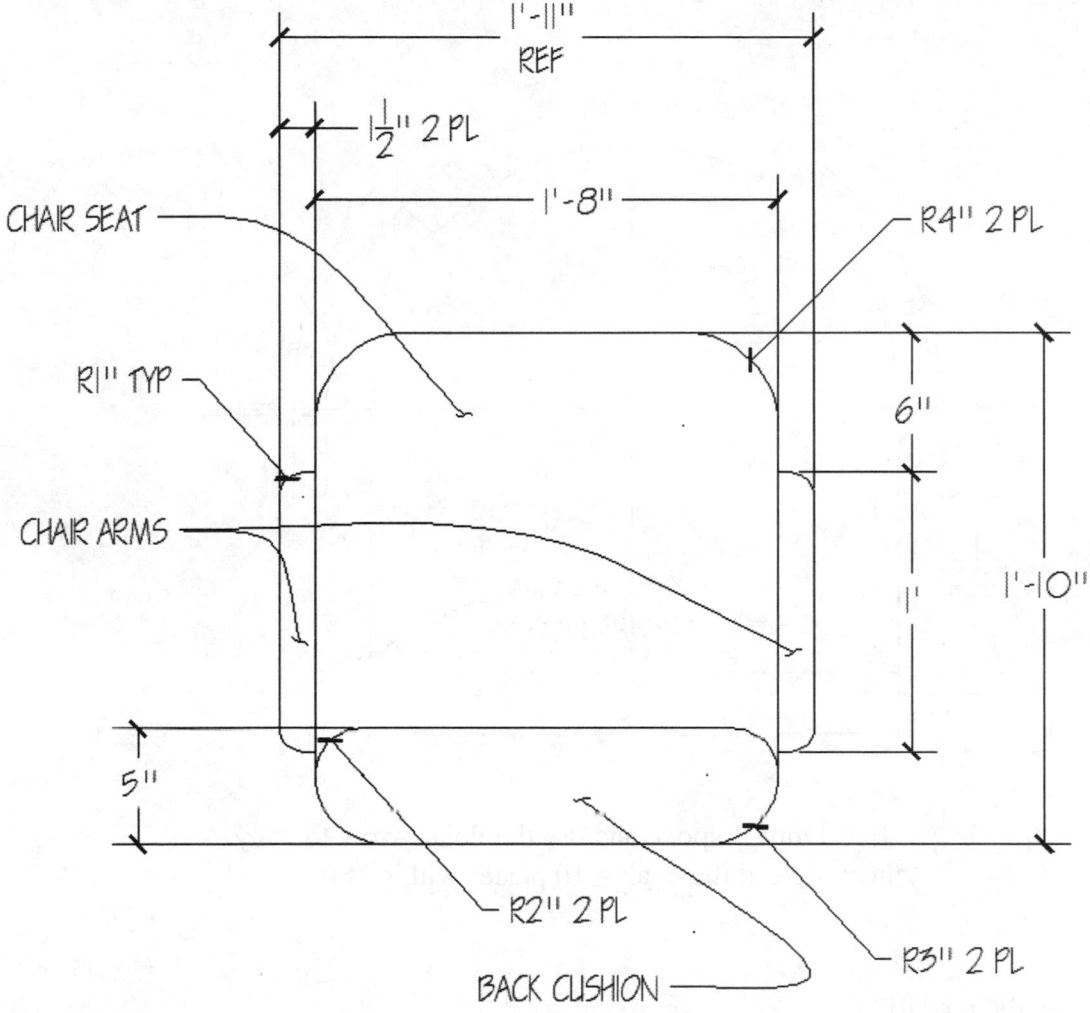

4. Draw the tile pattern. The spacing between tiles is 1/16″.

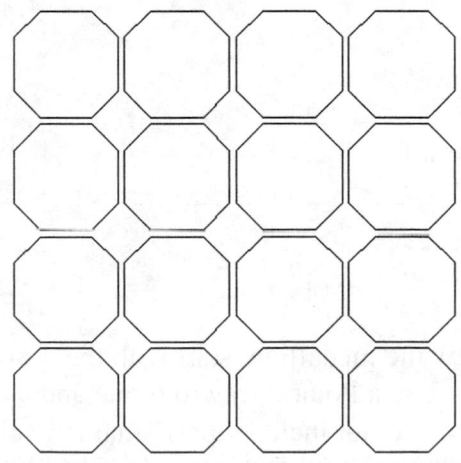

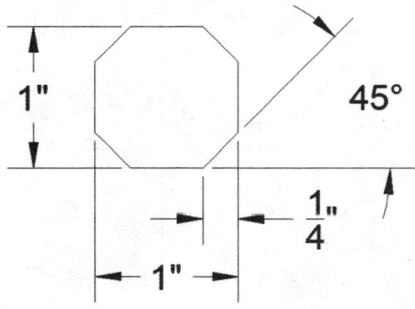

Draw the single tile shown and use a Rectangular Array with spacing set to 1-1/16″ for both columns and rows

5. Draw the Spoke Chair

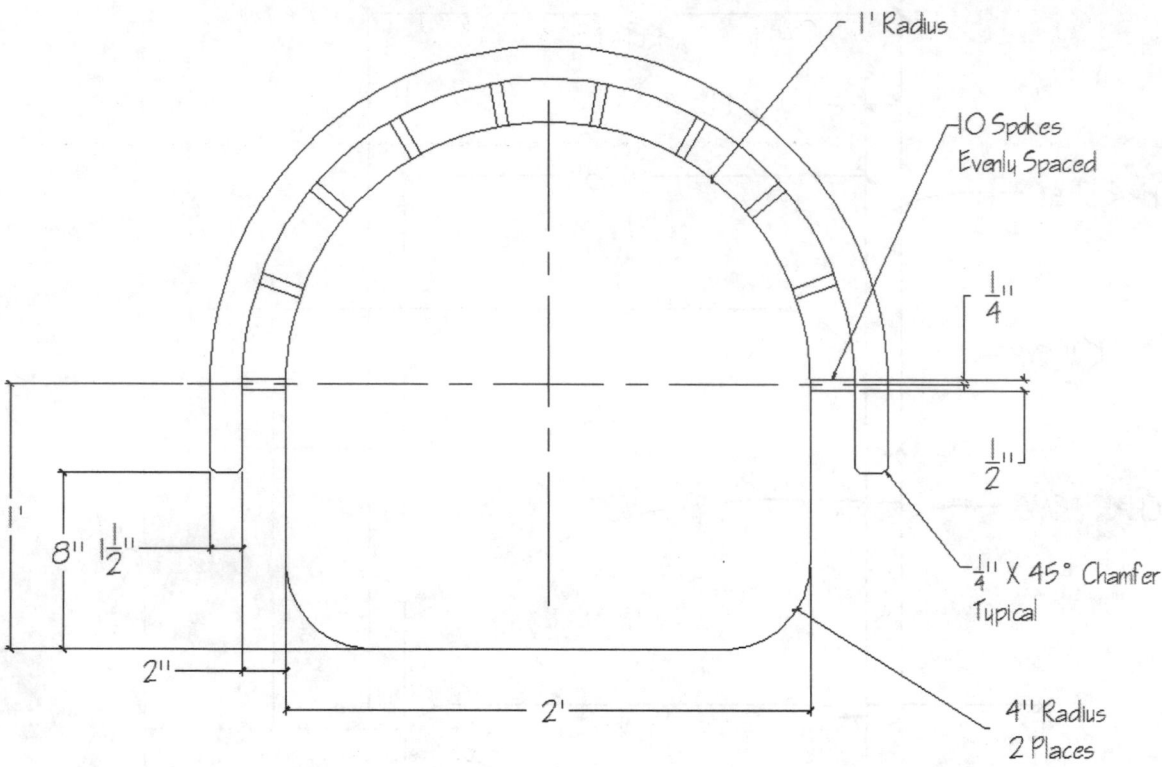

Hint: Draw 1 spoke and use the Polar Array to copy
them around the chair – 10 places within 180°

6. Draw the medallion.

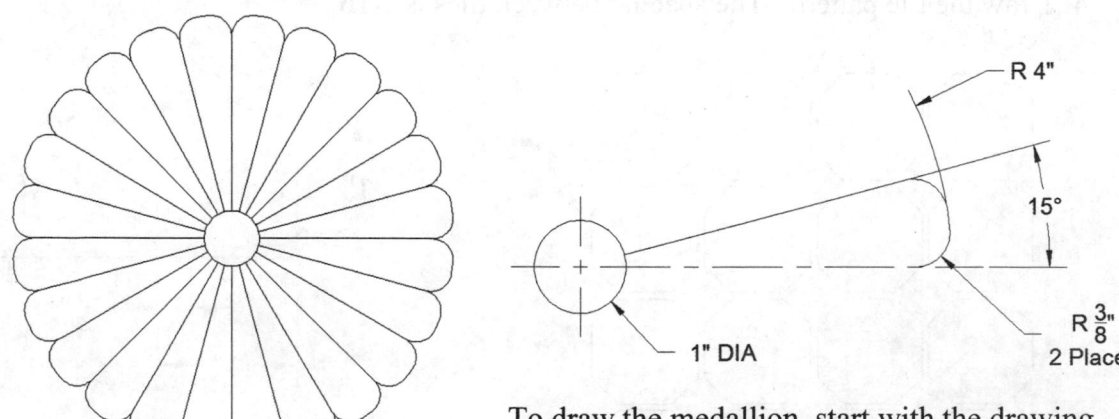

To draw the medallion, start with the drawing
above. Use a Polar Array to rotate and copy the
objects. Do not include the 1″ diameter circle
or the centerlines when you select the objects
for the array.

Chapter 6
Hotel Suite Project – Tutorial 2

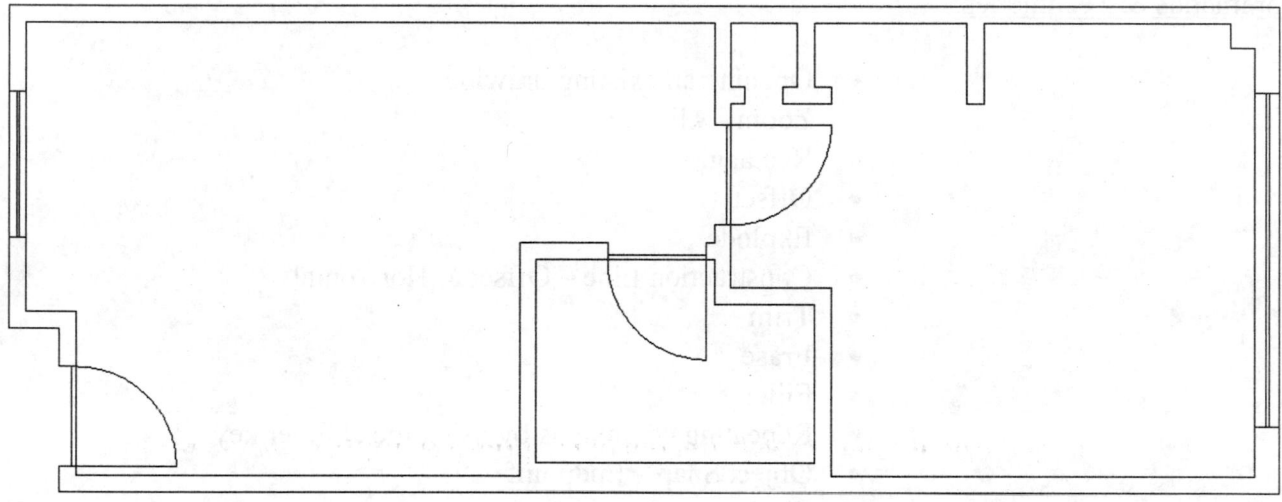

Learning Objectives:

- **To continue creating a drawing of a real-world application of AutoCAD®**
  - o **Create the plan view of the bathroom and closet walls of the hotel suite**
  - o **Create the doors and windows of the suite**
- **To utilize and reinforce the use of the AutoCAD® commands learned in the previous chapters**

This tutorial builds on Tutorial 1 found in Chapter 4. We will create the bathroom and closet walls of the hotel suite. When you are finished with this tutorial, all the walls of the plan view of the hotel suite will be completed.

The drawing methods used to complete the walls are very similar to those used for Tutorial 1.

Commands & Techniques:

- Opening an existing drawing
- Zoom - All
- Rectangle
- Offset
- Explode
- Construction Line – Offset & Horizontal
- Trim
- Erase
- Fillet
- Repeating commands by using the ↵ Enter key
- Object Snap – Endpoint
- Distance
- Copy
- Rotate
- Mirror
- Move
- Save

<u>Create the Bathroom Walls</u>

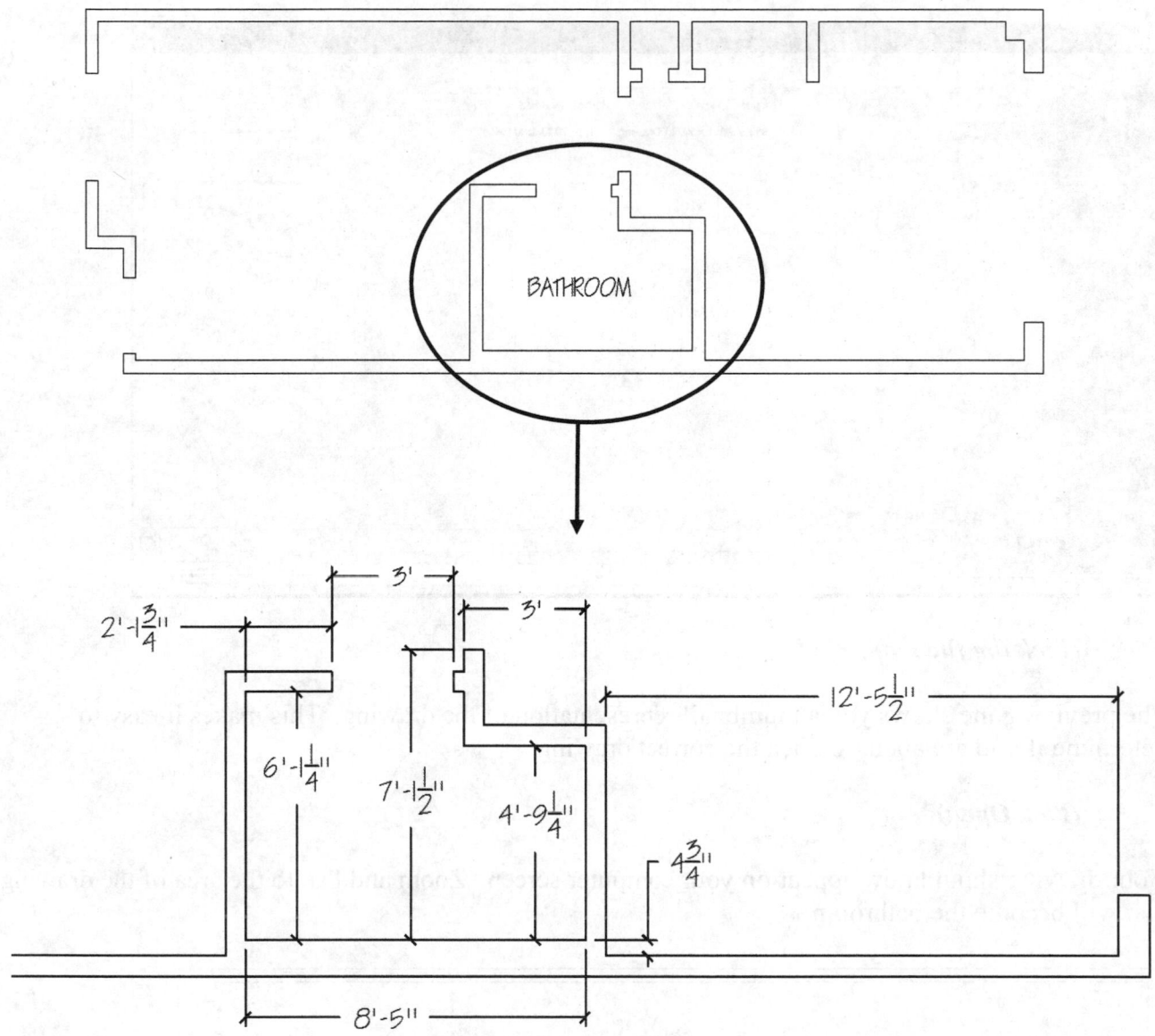

Bathroom Dimensions

- To begin, we will call up the drawing that you created in Tutorial 1.

1.   **Use the Open icon to open the Hotel Suite drawing.**

   (Pick the Open icon)

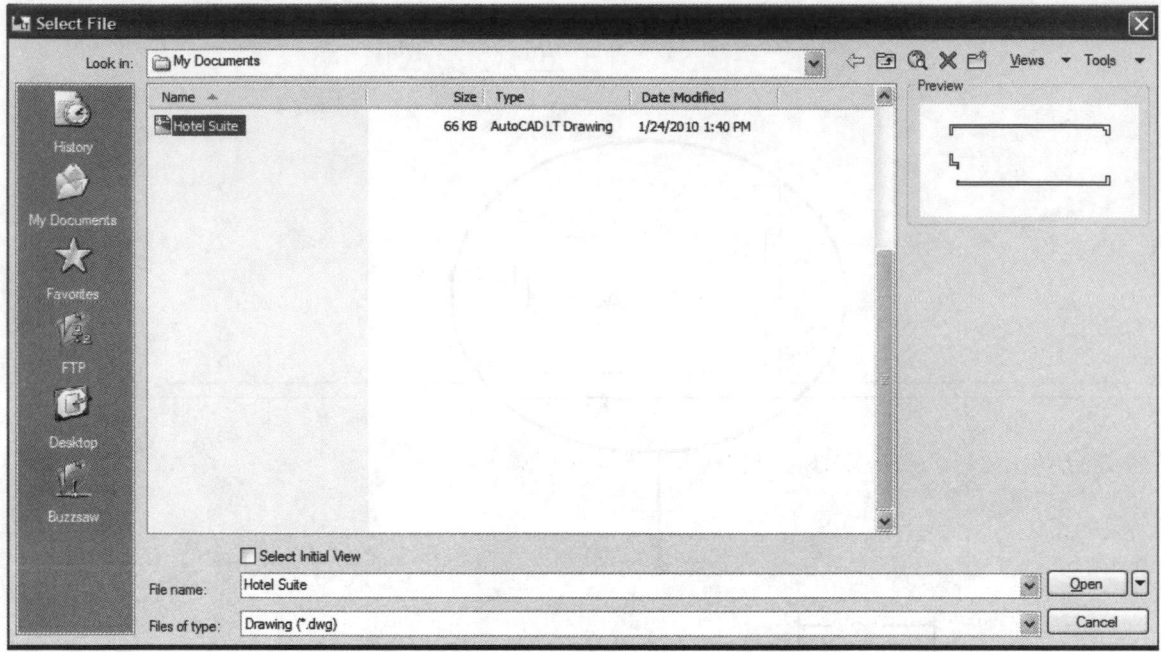

   (Pick the file icon)

The preview pane shows you a thumbnail representation of the drawing. This makes it easy to determine if you are about to open the correct drawing.

   (Pick Open)

Your drawing should now appear on your computer screen. Zoom and Pan to the area of the drawing that will become the bathroom.

2. Create construction lines for the right and left vertical walls

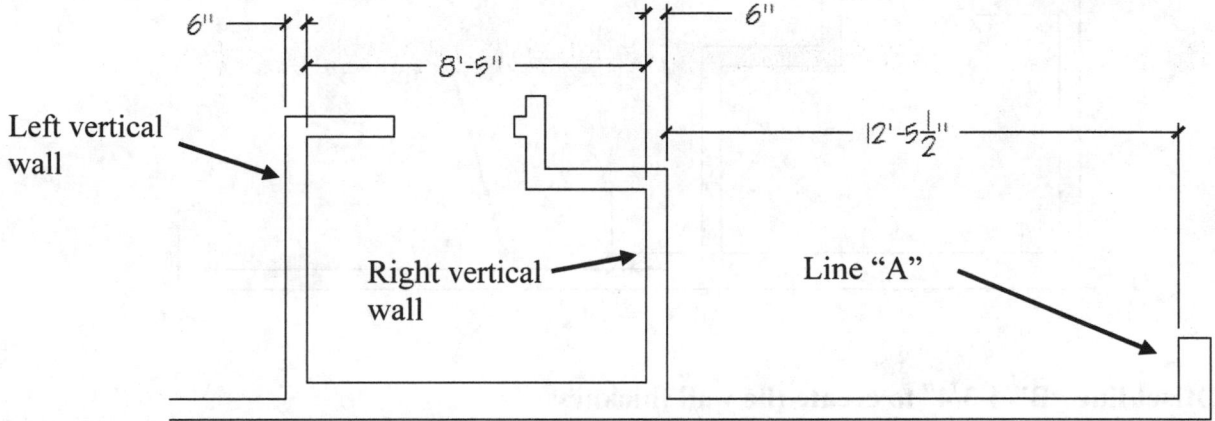

2a. Create a Construction Line Offset 12'5-1/2" from line "A"

Use the **Construction Line** command with the **Offset** option

2b. Offset the construction line of Step 2a 6" to create the wall thickness

Use the **Offset** command.

2c. Offset the construction line of Step 2b 8'5" to create the inside left vertical wall line

Press the ↵ Enter key to repeat the **Offset** command

2d. Offset the construction line of Step 2c 6" to create the wall thickness

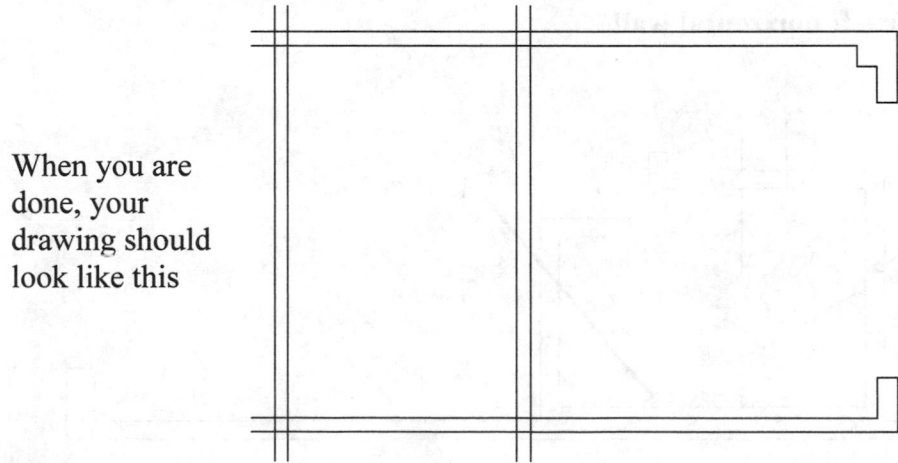

When you are
done, your
drawing should
look like this

3.   Create the lower horizontal wall

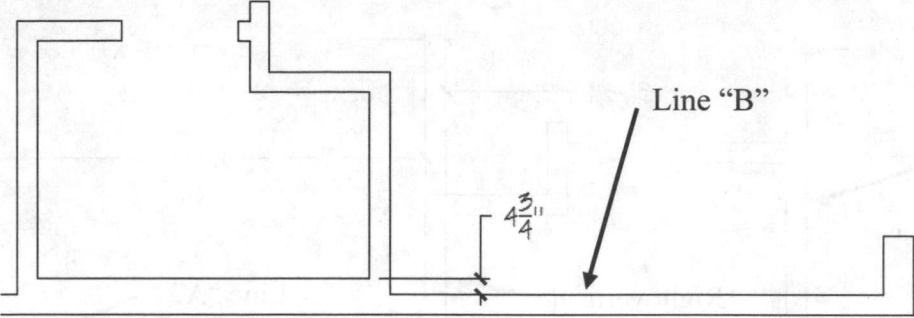

Line "B"

$4\frac{3}{4}$"

3a. Offset line "B" 4-3/4″ to create the wall thickness

3b. Use the Trim command to complete the lower horizontal wall

Take advantage of using a crossing window to select your cutting edges.

Remember, if during trimming you have extra lines as a result of the location and order in which you picked the lines to trim, use the Erase command to eliminate them.

When you are done, your drawing should look like this:

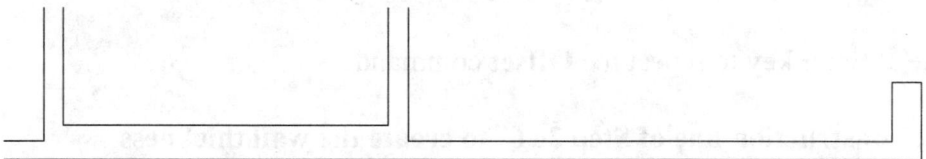

4.   Create the upper left horizontal wall

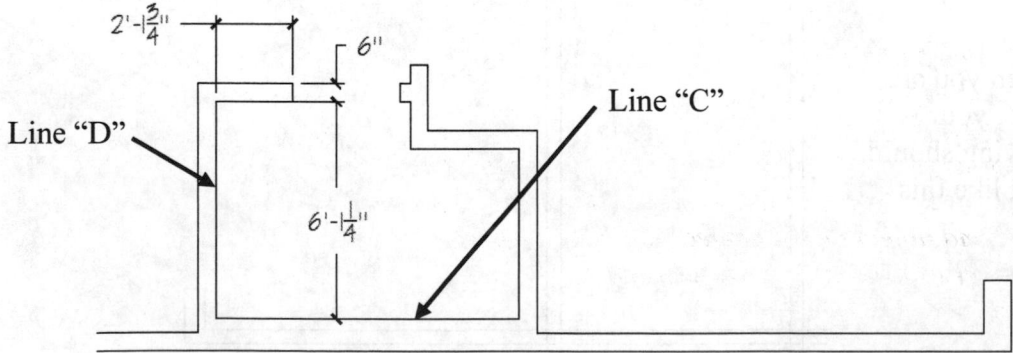

$2'-1\frac{3}{4}$"

6"

Line "C"

Line "D"

$6'-1\frac{1}{4}$"

4a. Offset line "C" 6′1-1/4″ up to create the inside line of the upper left horizontal wall

4b. Offset the line created in Step 4a 6″ up to create the wall thickness

4c. Offset line "D" 2′1-3/4″ to the right

So far, your drawing should look like this:

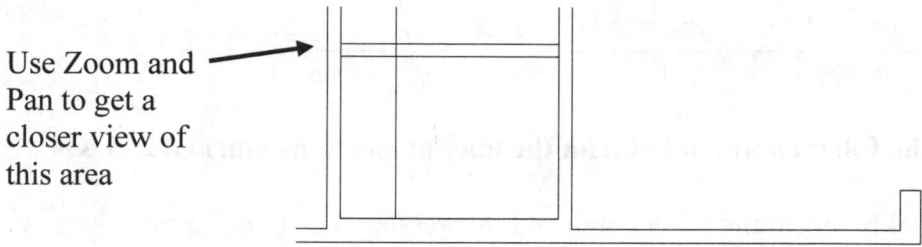

Use Zoom and
Pan to get a
closer view of
this area

To continue on, it may be easier to complete the wall by getting a closer view. Use the wheel mouse to Zoom and Pan to do this.

A close-up view
of the upper left
wall area

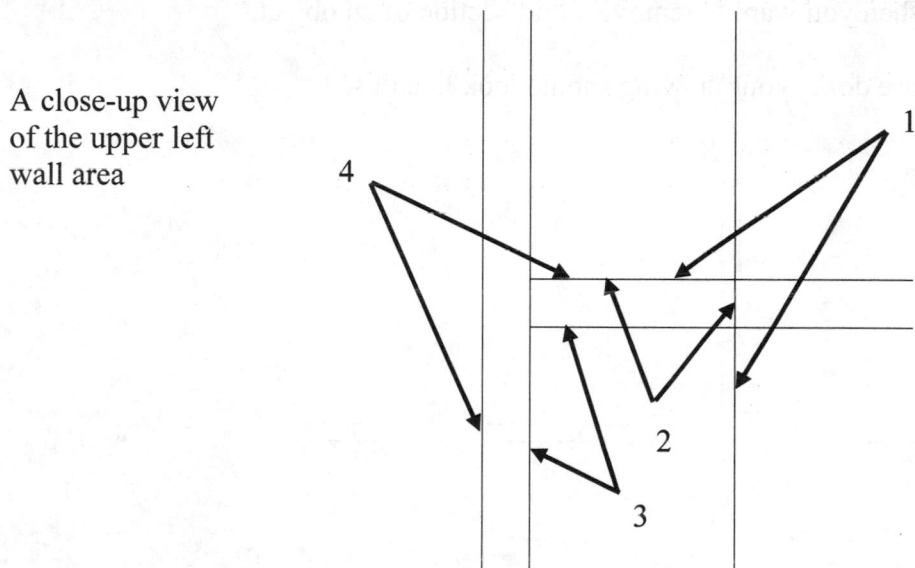

4d. Use the Fillet command to close out the wall lines

(Pick the Fillet icon)
Command: _fillet
Current settings: Mode = TRIM, Radius = 0'-0″
Select first object or [Undo/Polyline/Radius/Trim/Multiple]:
(Pick one of the lines at location marked 1)
Select second object or shift-select to apply corner:
(Pick the other line at location marked 1)
Command:

> If the Radius is not
> set to 0′-0″ press **r**↵
> and change the
> value by keying **0**↵

The Fillet command will end after the second line is picked and it will trim both lines.

Both lines are trimmed and the corner is square

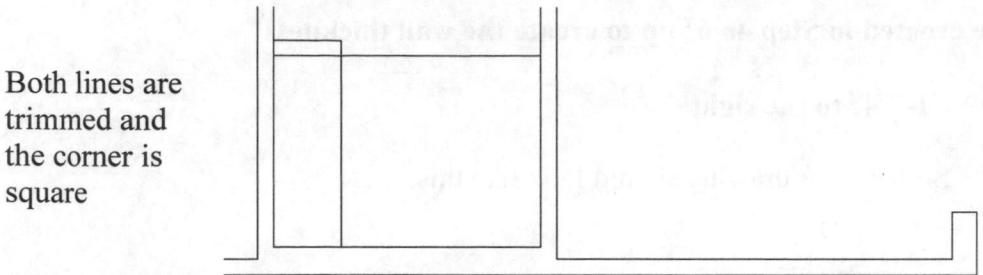

4e. Continue using the Fillet command to trim the lines at locations marked 2, 3 & 4

Remember, you can quickly repeat the Fillet command by pressing the ↵ Enter key.

Now that you have used the Trim and/or Extend commands and the Fillet command, you may notice that the Fillet command comes in very handy. I find the Fillet command to be fewer steps. The Trim command is still needed when you want to remove a mid-section of an object.

When you are done, your drawing should look like this:

5.   Create the upper right horizontal and vertical walls

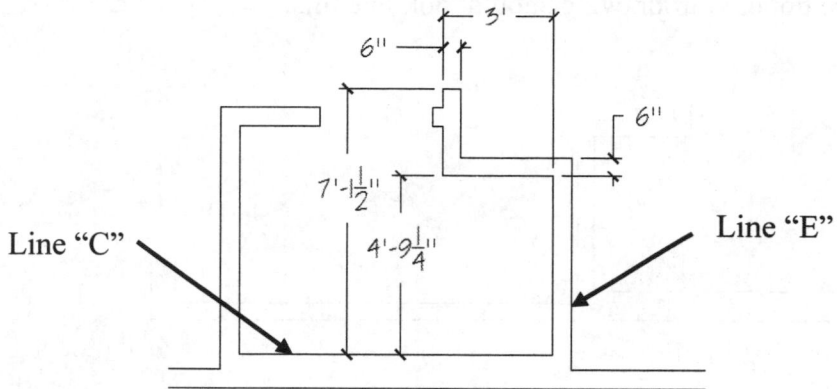

Line "C"   Line "E"

5a. Offset line "C" 4′9-1/4″ up to create the inside wall line

5b. Offset the line you created in Step 5a 6″ up to create the wall thickness

5c. Offset line "E" 3′ to the left

5d. Offset the line you created in Step 5c 6″ to the right to create the wall thickness

So far, your drawing should look like this:

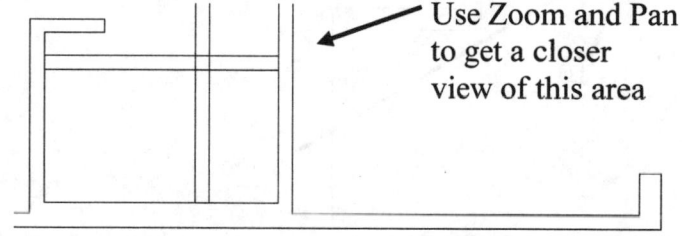

Use Zoom and Pan
to get a closer
view of this area

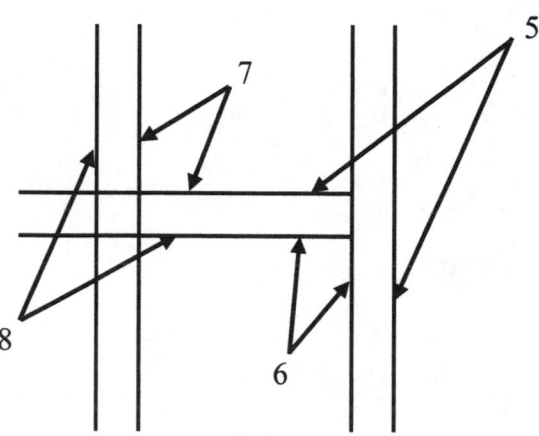

5e. Use the Fillet command to trim the lines at locations marked 5, 6, 7, & 8

When you are done, your drawing should look like this:

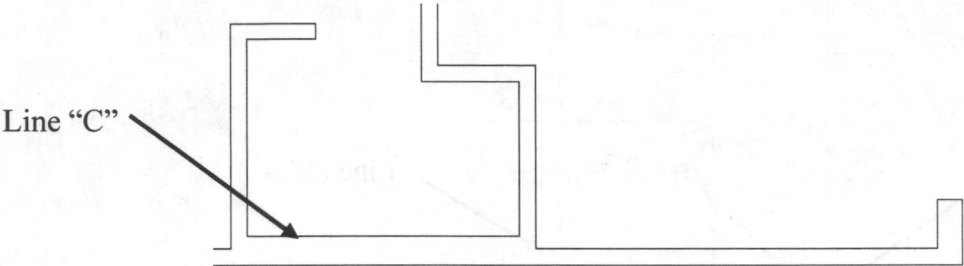

Line "C"

5f. Offset line "C" 7′ 1-1/2″ up

5g. Use the Fillet command to close out the corners of the wall

6. Create the door opening

For the door opening, a small piece of horizontal wall needs to be added. This is in-line with the left horizontal wall.

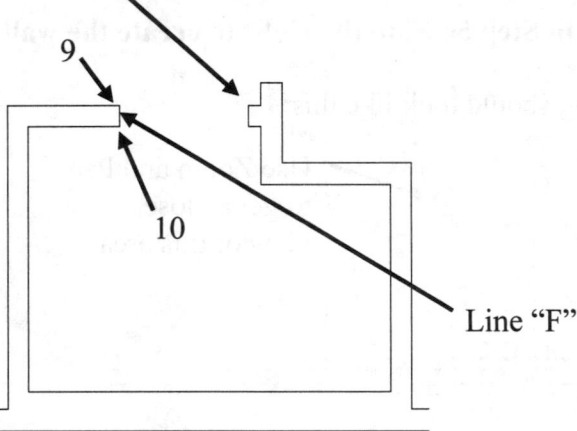

9

10

Line "F"

6a. Turn on Object Snap Endpoint

Right-Click on the
Object Snap switch

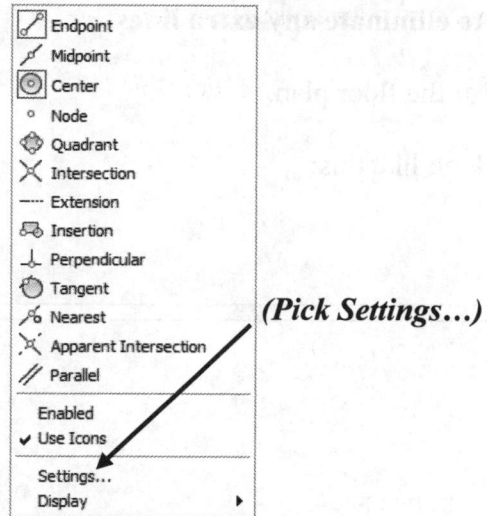

(Pick Settings...)

When the Drafting Settings dialog box appears, left-click the check-box next to Endpoint and Object Snap On if they are not already checked off. Pick OK to close the dialog box.

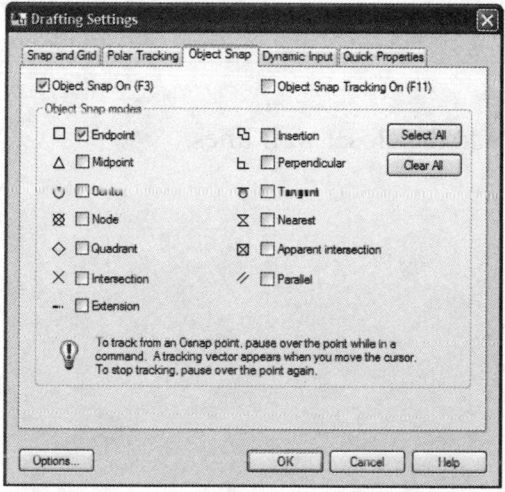

6b. Create Horizontal Construction Lines to define the right side of the door opening

(Pick the Construction Line icon)
Command: _xline Specify a point or [Hor/Ver/Ang/Bisect/Offset]: **h** ↵
Specify through point: (Pick the endpoint at location marked 9)
Specify through point: (Pick the endpoint at location marked 10)
Specify through point: ↵
Command:

6c. Offset line "F" 3′ to the right to define the door opening

6d. Use the Trim command to complete the opening

6e. Use the Erase command if needed to eliminate any extra lines

This now completes the bathroom portion of the floor plan.

When you are done, your drawing should look like this:

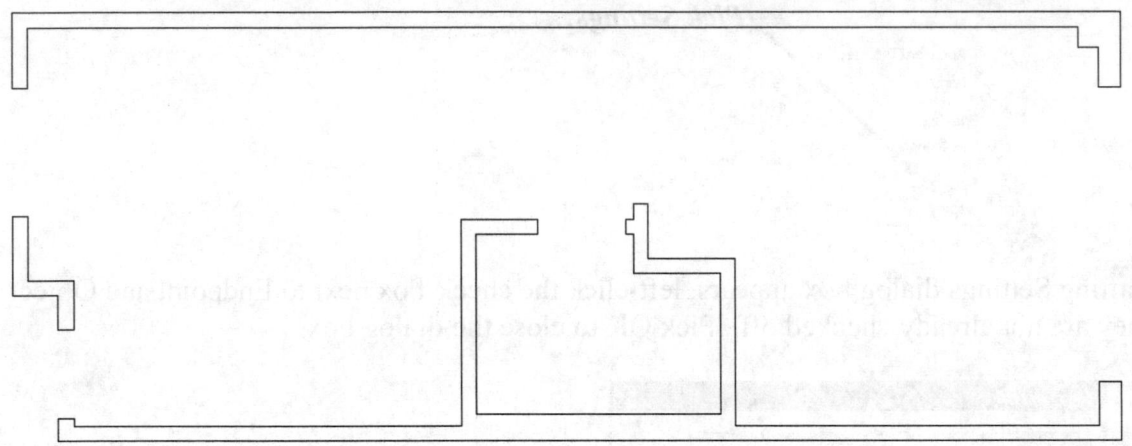

Make sure to save your drawing. Next, we will add the closet wall lines.

Create the Closet Walls

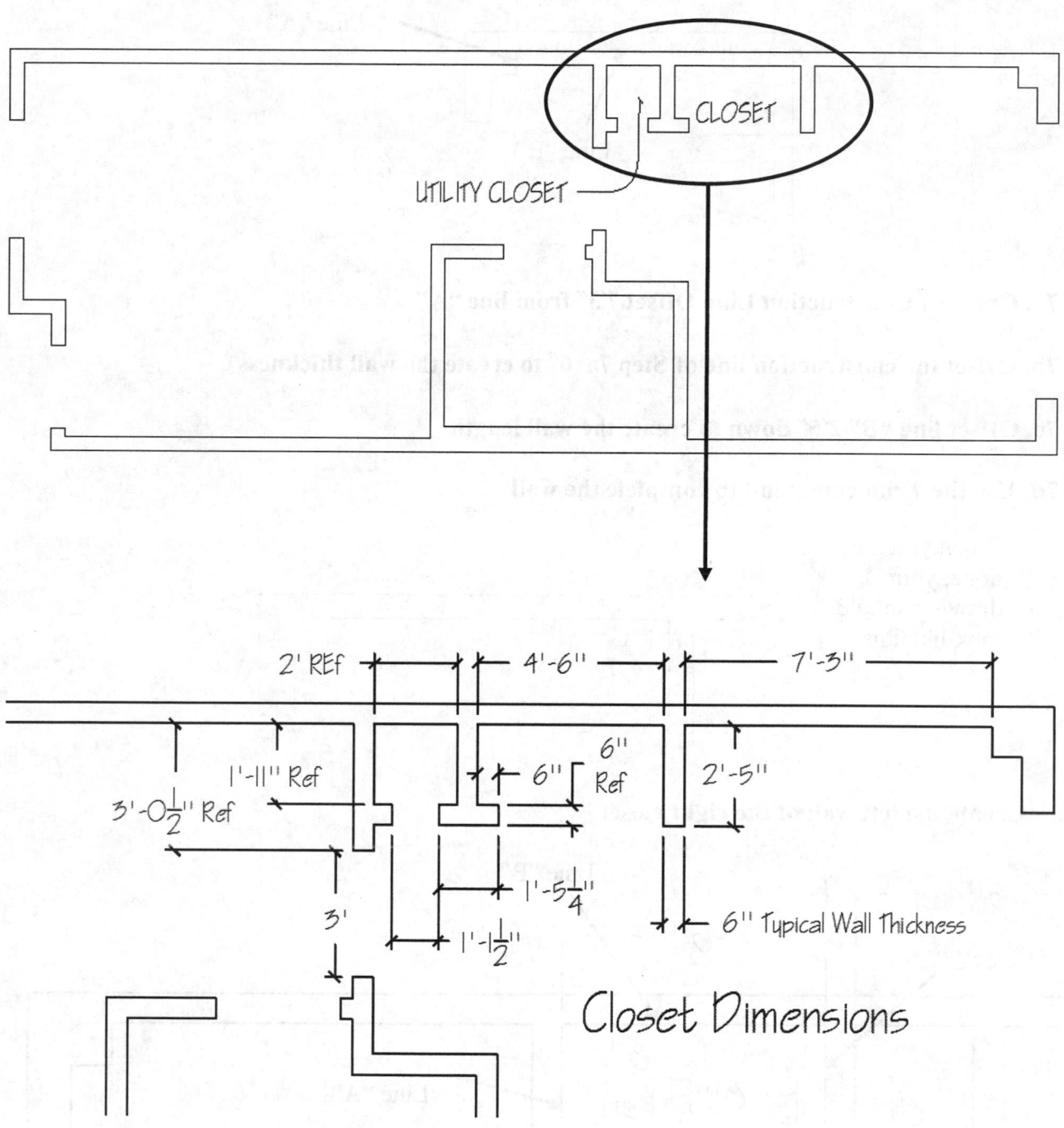

UTILITY CLOSET

CLOSET

2' REf 4'-6" 7'-3"

1'-11" Ref

3'-0½" Ref

6"
6"
Ref
2'-5"

1'-5¼"

3'

1'-1½"

6" Typical Wall Thickness

Closet Dimensions

7. Create the right vertical wall of the right closet

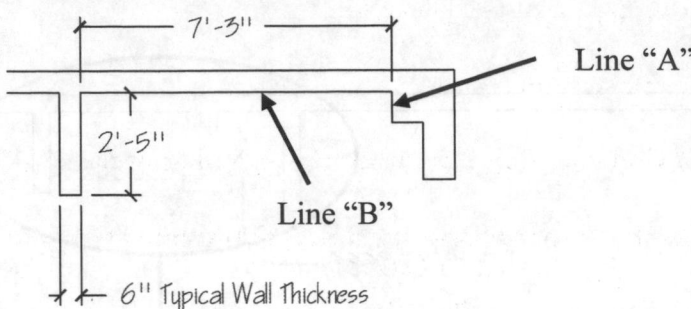

Line "A"

2'-5"

Line "B"

6" Typical Wall Thickness

7'-3"

7a. Create a Construction Line Offset 7'3" from line "A"

7b. Offset the construction line of Step 7a 6" to create the wall thickness

7c. Offset line "B" 2'5" down to create the wall length

7d. Use the Trim command to complete the wall

When you are done, your drawing should look like this

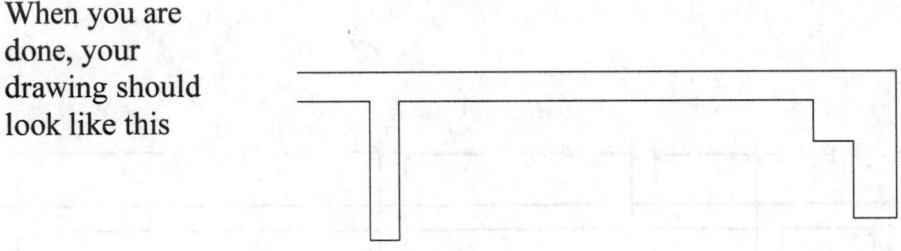

8. Create the left wall of the right closet

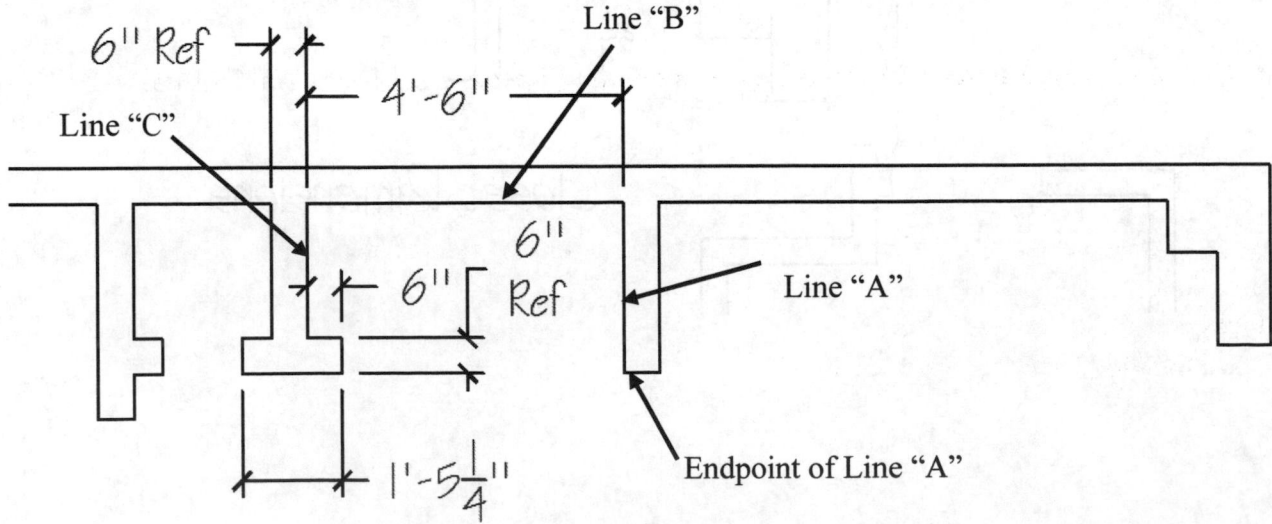

6" Ref

Line "C"

Line "B"

4'-6"

6" Ref

6"

Line "A"

Endpoint of Line "A"

$1'-5\frac{1}{4}"$

8a. Offset line "A" 4′6″ to the left

8b. Offset the line created in Step 8a 6″ to the left

8c. Use the Trim command to trim line "B"

8d. Create a Horizontal Construction Line from the endpoint of line "A"

8e. Offset 6″ - the horizontal construction line upward and line "C" to the right

8f. Repeat the Offset command and Offset the vertical line created in Step 8 1′5-1/4″ to the left

8g. Use the Fillet command with a 0″ radius to finish the corners shown

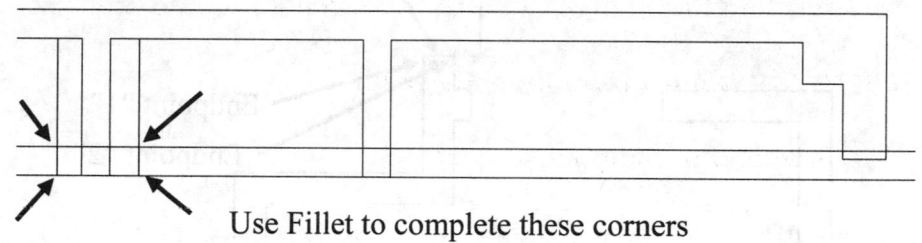

Use Fillet to complete these corners

When you are
done, your
drawing should
look like this

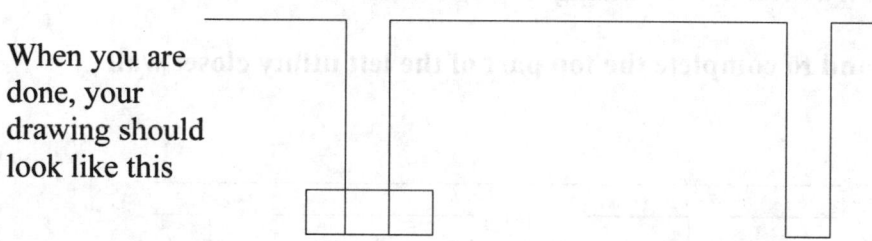

8h. Use the Trim command to clean up the remaining lines

When you are
done, your
drawing should
look like this

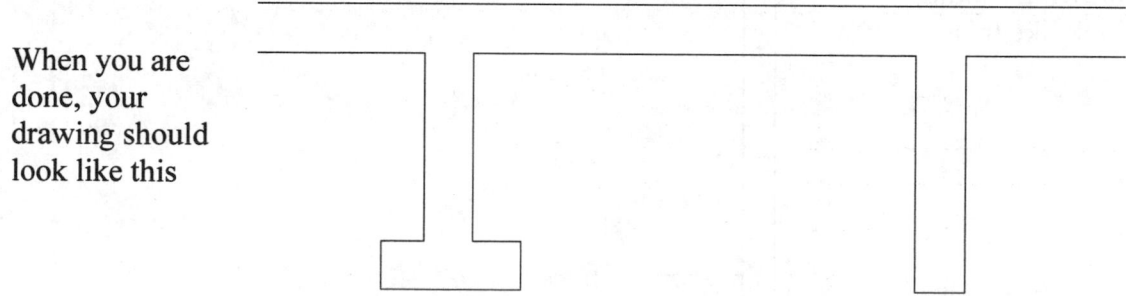

9. Create the left wall of the utility closet

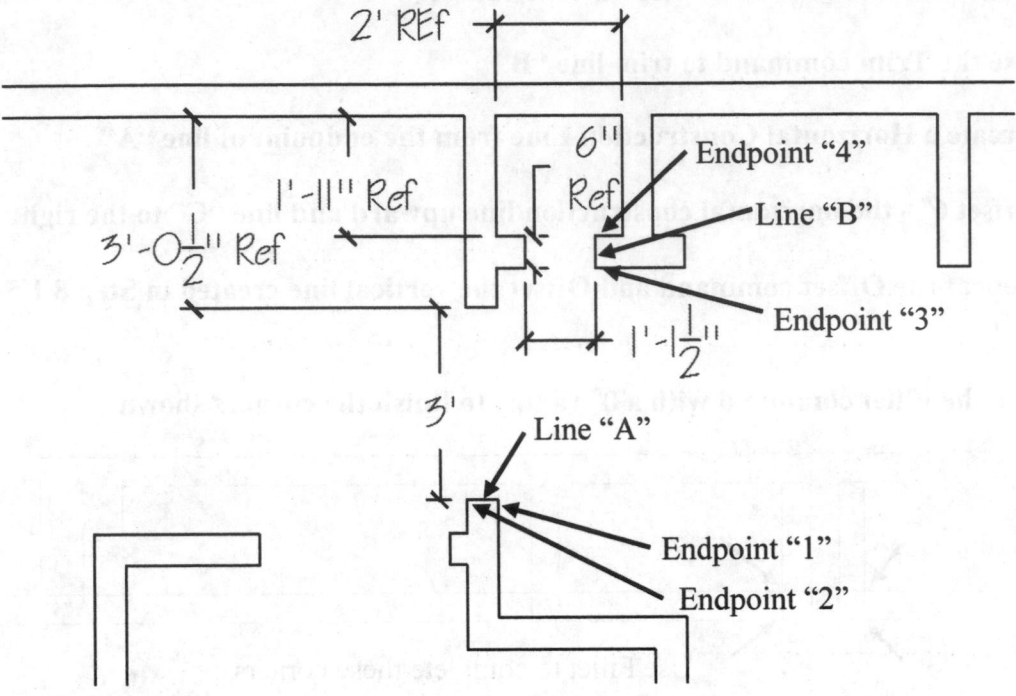

9a. Create Vertical Construction Lines passing through endpoints "1" and "2"

9b. Use the Trim command to complete the top part of the left utility closet wall

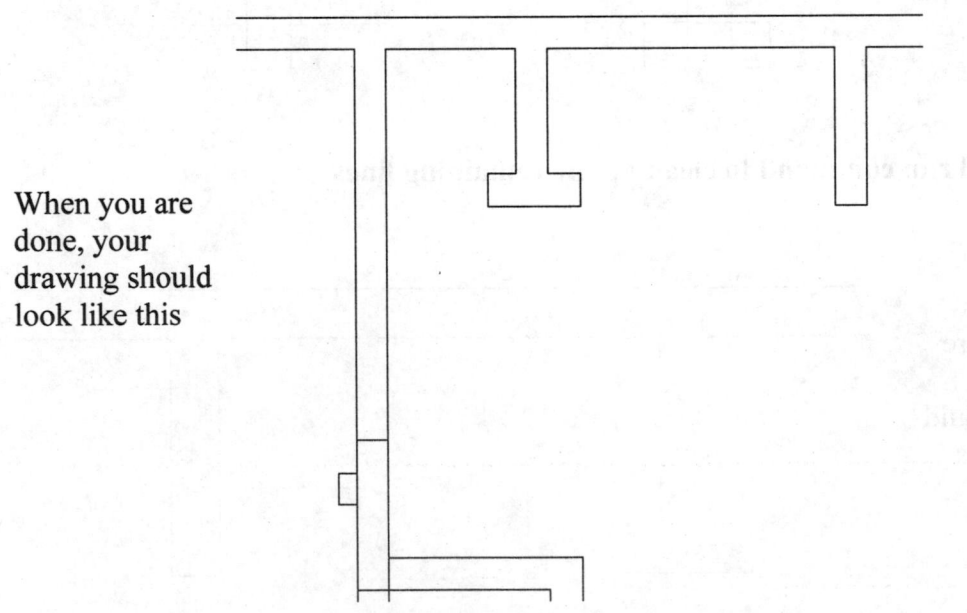

When you are done, your drawing should look like this

10. Create the door opening for the bedroom

10a. Offset line "A" 3′ up

10b. Use the Trim command to complete the door opening

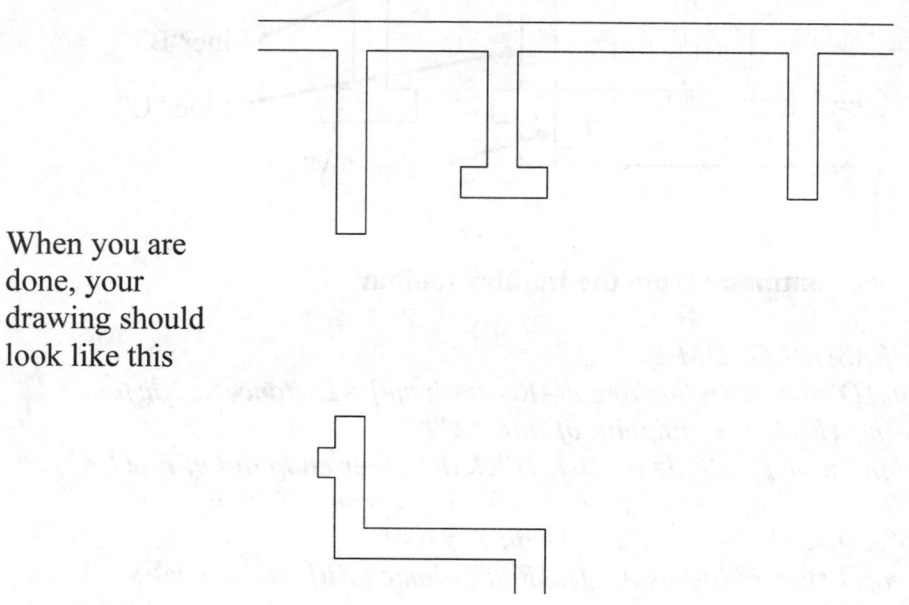

When you are
done, your
drawing should
look like this

11. Finish the utility closet structure

11a. Create Horizontal Construction Lines through endpoints "3" and "4"

11b. Offset line "B" 1′1-1/2″ to the left

11c. Use the Trim command to complete the structure

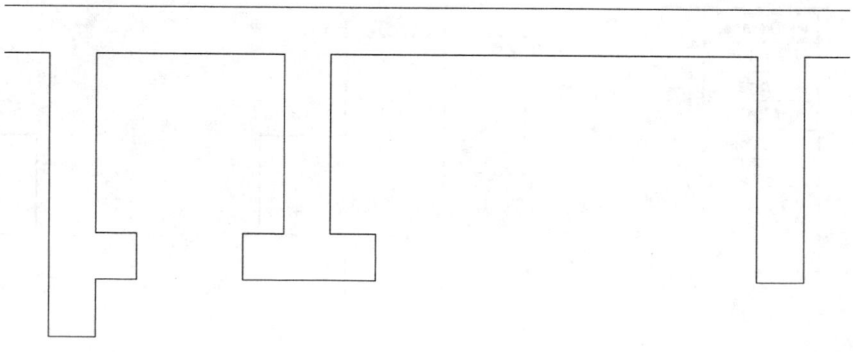

When you are
done, your
drawing should
look like this

12. Confirm the reference dimensions for lines "A", "B", and "C"

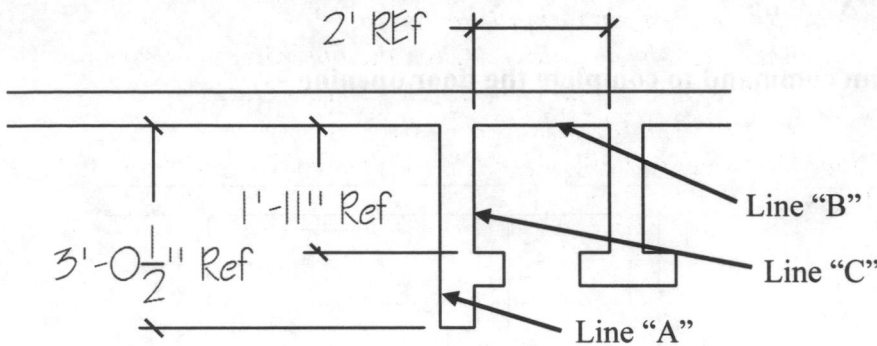

12a. Pick the Distance command from the Inquiry toolbar

Command: _MEASUREGEOM
Enter an option [Distance/Radius/Angle/ARea/Volume] <Distance>: _distance
Specify first point: **(Pick one endpoint of line "A")**
Specify second point or [Multiple points]: **(Pick the other endpoint of line "A")**
Distance = 3'-0 1/2", Angle in XY Plane = 90, Angle from XY Plane = 0
Delta X = 0'-0", Delta Y = -3'-0 1/2",   Delta Z = 0'-0"
Enter an option [Distance/Radius/Angle/ARea/Volume/eXit] <Distance>:

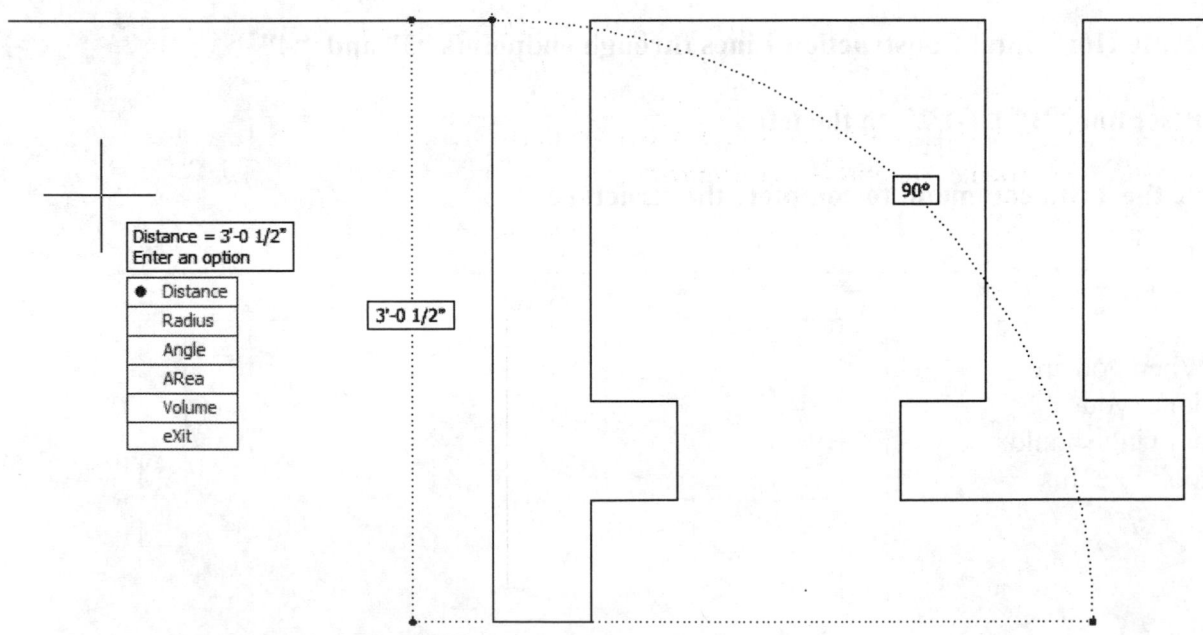

12b. Press the ↵ Enter key to repeat the Distance command

*Specify first point: **(Pick an endpoint of line "B")***
*Specify second point or [Multiple points]: **(Pick the other endpoint of line "B")***
Distance = 2'-0", Angle in XY Plane = 0, Angle from XY Plane = 0
Delta X = 2'-0", Delta Y = 0'-0",   Delta Z = 0'-0"
Enter an option [Distance/Radius/Angle/ARea/Volume/eXit] <Distance>:

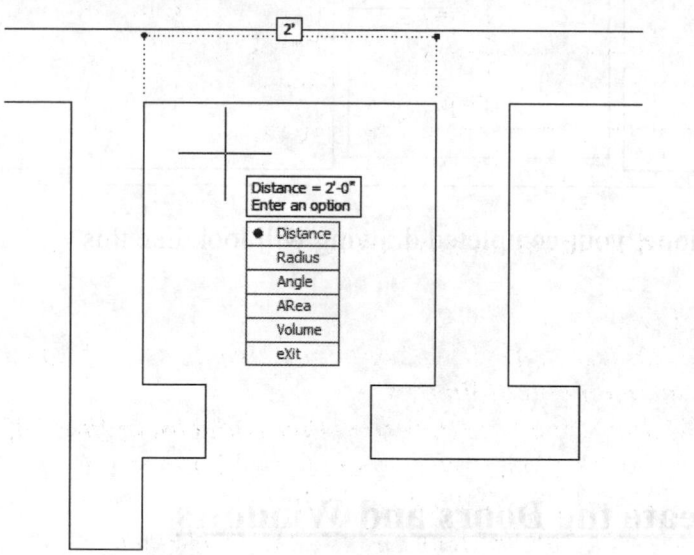

12c. Press the ↵ Enter key to repeat the Distance command

*Specify first point: **(Pick and endpoint of line "C")***
*Specify second point or [Multiple points]: **(Pick the other endpoint of line "C")***
Distance = 1'-11", Angle in XY Plane = 90, Angle from XY Plane = 0
Delta X = 0'-0", Delta Y = -1'-11",   Delta Z = 0'-0"
Enter an option [Distance/Radius/Angle/ARea/Volume/eXit] <Distance>: *Cancel*
Press the Escape key to end the command

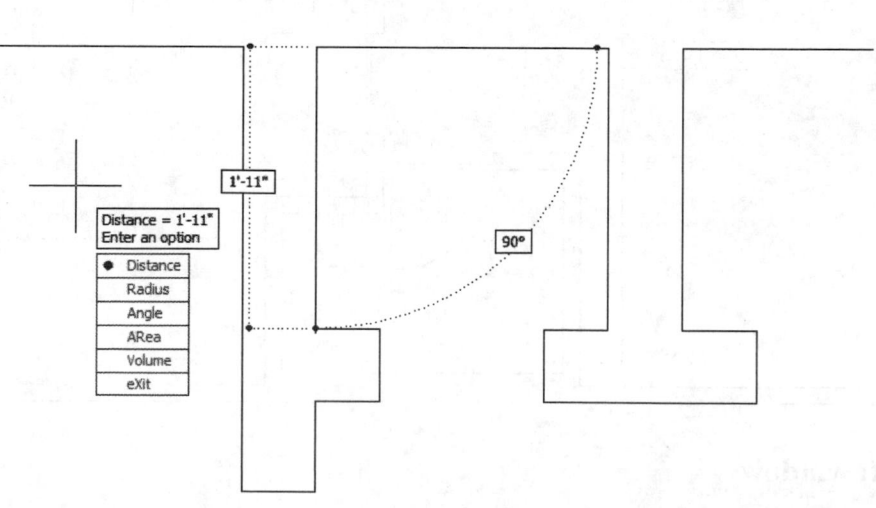

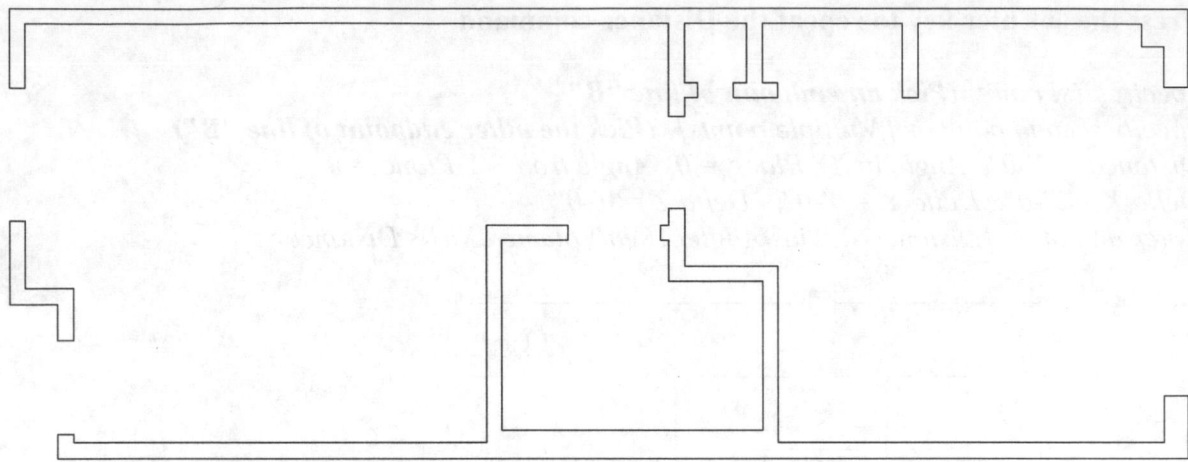

When you are done, your completed drawing will look like this

Create the Doors and Windows

The doors for this room are 1-3/4″ thick. There are three doors to the suite. We could create each door individually, but instead, we will take advantage of the Copy, Move, and Mirror commands.

The window glass is 1″ thick, and is centered in the window opening. Let's complete the windows first since that is easier to do.

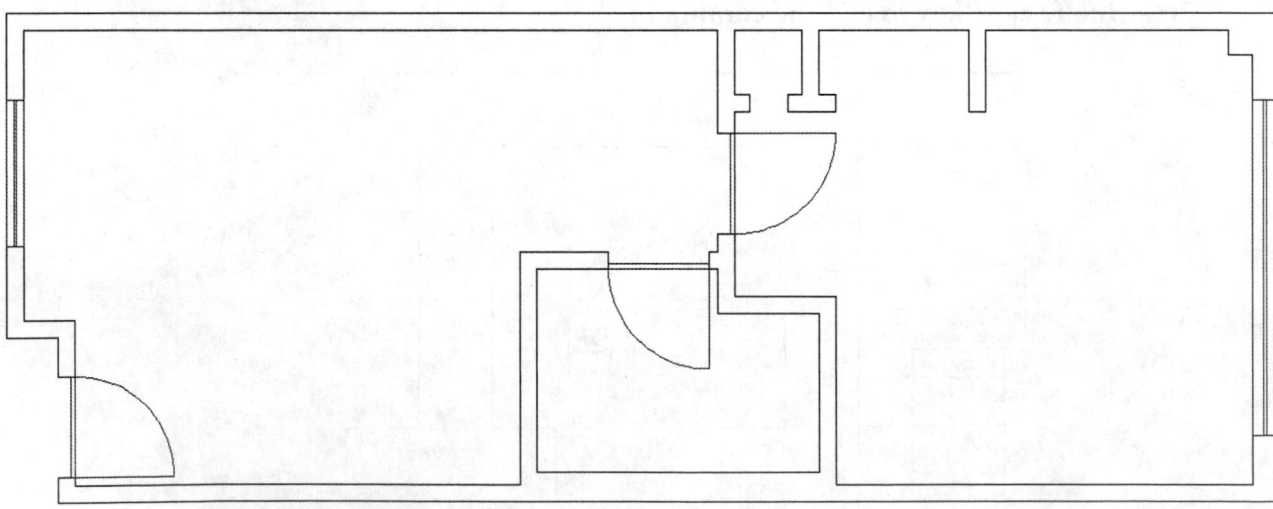

13. Create the left window

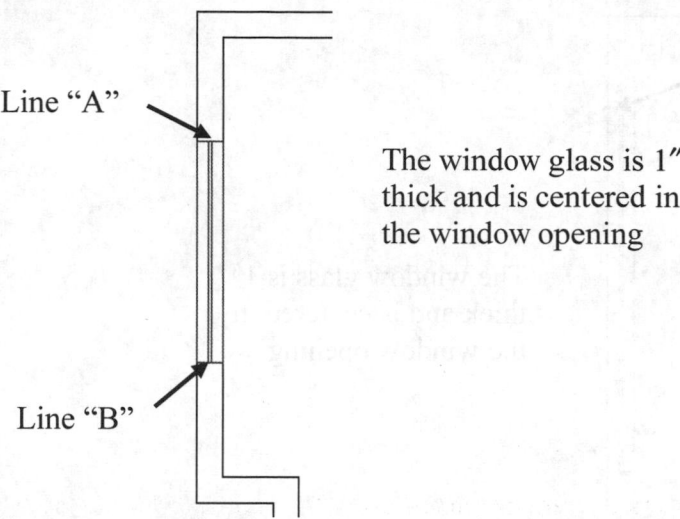

Line "A"

The window glass is 1″ thick and is centered in the window opening

Line "B"

13a. Change the Object Snap setting to ensure Midpoint is selected

13b. Use the Line command to create a line from the Midpoint of line "A" to the Midpoint of line "B"

13c. Offset the line created in Step 13b 1/2″ in each direction

The window glass is 1″ thick centered in the opening. Offsetting half the thickness of the glass (in this case it is 1/2″) from the center of the window (which is what we created in Step 13b) will give us the full thickness of the glass (1″).

13d. Erase the line created in Step 13b

13e. Use the Line command to create 2 vertical lines – one at each endpoint of lines "A" and "B"

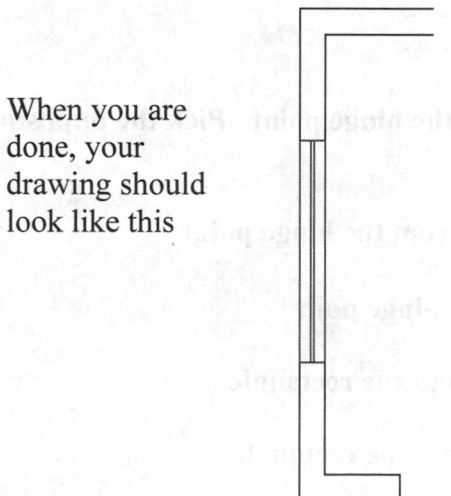

When you are done, your drawing should look like this

14. Create the right window

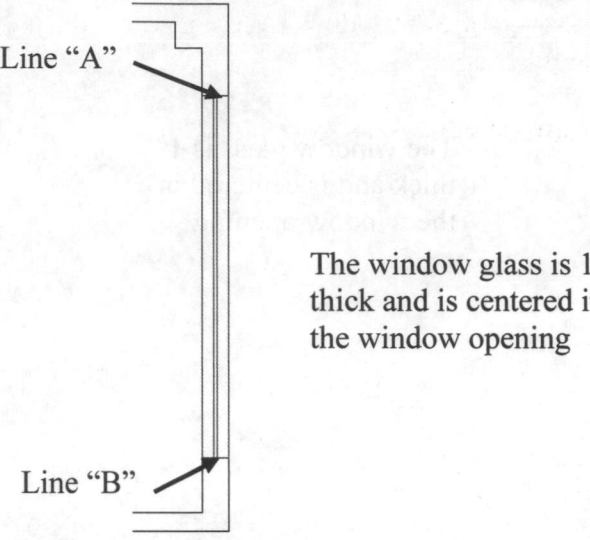

Line "A"

The window glass is 1″ thick and is centered in the window opening

Line "B"

Creating this window is identical to creating the left window. Follow the steps used to create the left window to create this window.

15. Create the Entry Door

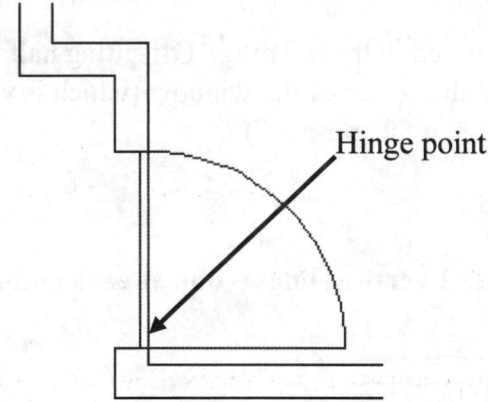

Hinge point

15a. Draw a 1-3/4″ x 3′ Rectangle starting at the hinge point. Pick the opposite corner to be towards the outside of the room

15b. Create a Horizontal Construction Line from the hinge point

15c. Create a 3′ radius Circle centered on the hinge point

15d. Trim the circle to the construction line and the rectangle

15e. Trim the construction line to the circle and the rectangle

You have now completed the entry door. We will use this same door in the two remaining locations. Notice that the orientation is not identical to the entry door. We will use the Copy, Rotate, Mirror, and Move commands to complete the other doors.

16. Copy the entry door off to the side of your drawing

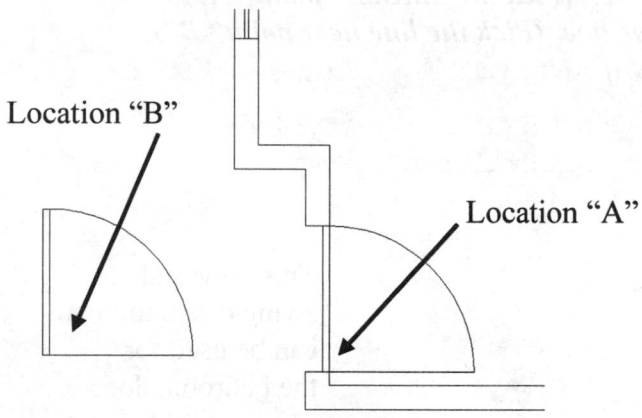

Location "B"

Location "A"

(Pick the Copy command)
Command: _copy
*Select objects: **(Pick the arc)** 1 found*
*Select objects: **(Pick the rectangle)** 1 found, 2 total*
*Select objects: **(Pick the line that connects the arc to the rectangle)** 1 found, 3 total*
Select objects: ⏎
Current settings: Copy mode = Multiple
*Specify base point or [Displacement/mOde] <Displacement>: **(Pick a point near location "A")** Specify second point or <use first point as displacement>: **(Pick a point near location "B")***
Specify second point or [Exit/Undo] <Exit>: ⏎
Command:

17. Create a Mirror image of the copy you just made of the door and swing

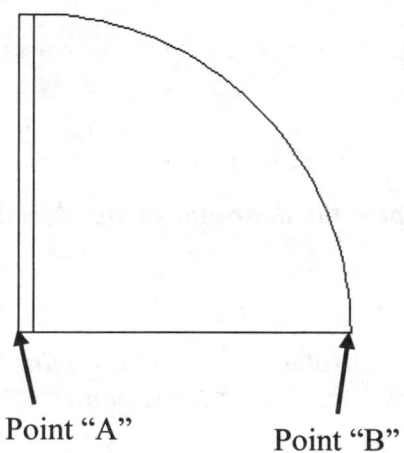

Point "A"   Point "B"

(Pick the Mirror command)
Command: _mirror
*Select objects: **(Use a Selection Window to pick the door and swing objects)***
Specify opposite corner: 3 found
Select objects: ↵
Specify first point of mirror line: ***(Pick the line near point "A")***
*Specify second point of mirror line: **(Pick the line near point "B")***
Erase source objects? [Yes/No] <N>: **y**↵
Command:

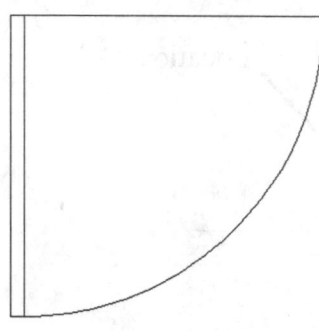

When you are done, your drawing should look like this

This door and swing orientation can be used for the bedroom door

18. Copy the new door and swing from Step 17 to the bedroom location

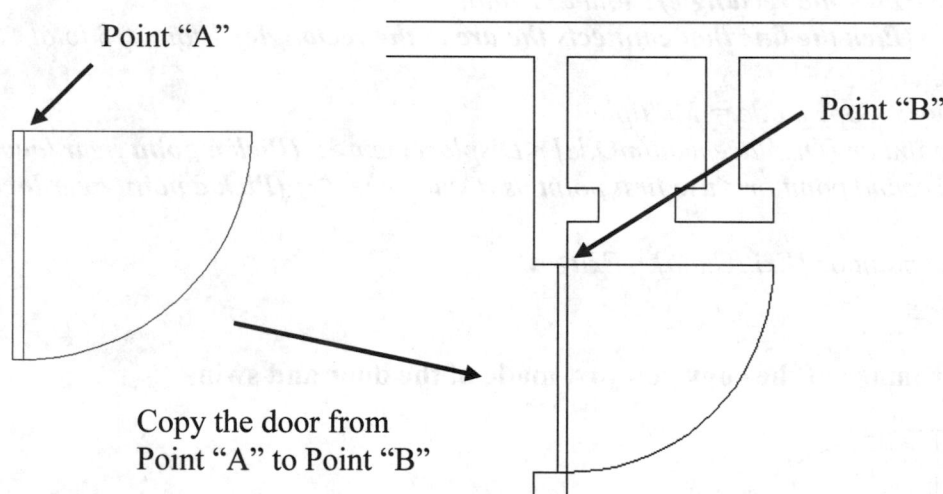

Point "A"

Point "B"

Copy the door from Point "A" to Point "B"

(Pick the Copy icon)
Command: _copy
*Select objects: **(Use a Selection Window to pick the door and swing objects)***
Specify opposite corner: 3 found
Select objects: ↵
Current settings: Copy mode = Multiple
*Specify base point or [Displacement/mOde] <Displacement>: **(Pick point "A")***
*Specify second point or <use first point as displacement>: **(Pick point "B")***
Specify second point or [Exit/Undo] <Exit>: ↵
Command:

Because we used the Copy command, we still have the door and swing off to the side of our drawing. We will now change the orientation so that it can be used for the bathroom.

19. Rotate the door and swing to get it in the correct orientation for the bathroom

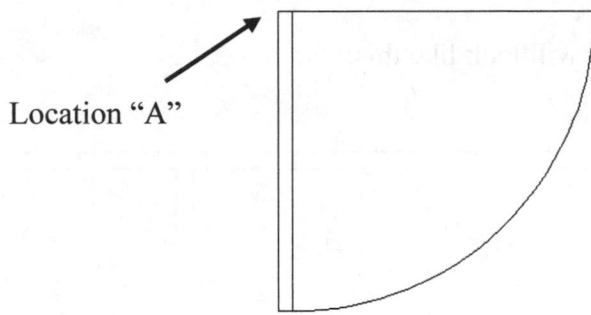

Location "A"

> *(Pick the Rotate icon)*
> *Command: _rotate*
> *Current positive angle in UCS: ANGDIR=counterclockwise ANGBASE=0*
> *Select objects: (Use a Selection Window to pick the door and swing objects)*
> *Specify opposite corner: 3 found*
> *Select objects: ⤶*
> *Specify base point: (Pick a point near location "A")*
> *Specify rotation angle or [Copy/Reference] <0>: -90⤶*
> *Command:*

When you are done, your drawing should look like this

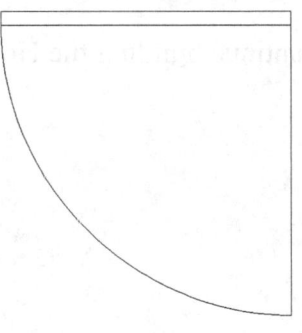

This door and swing orientation can be used for the bathroom door

20. Move the door and swing to the bathroom location

Move the door from Point "A" to Point "B"

Point "B"

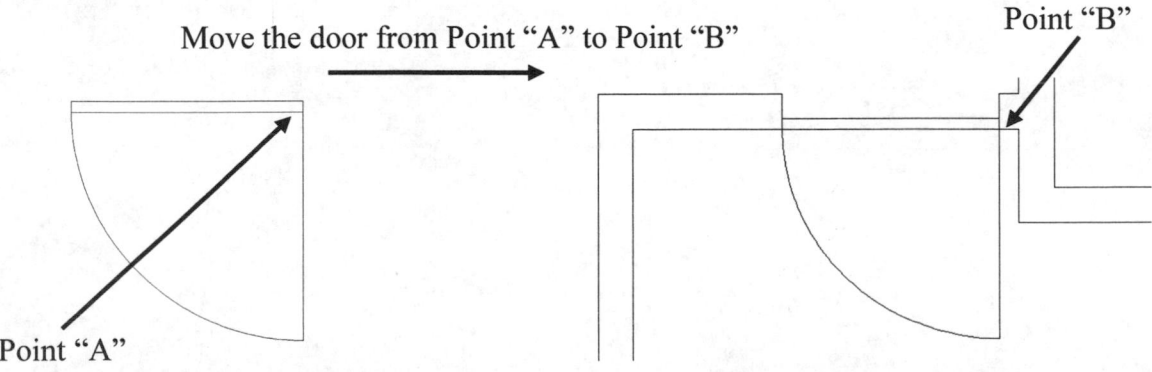

Point "A"

Congratulations! You have now completed the floor plan walls, doors, and windows for the hotel suite.

When you are done, your completed drawing will look like this:

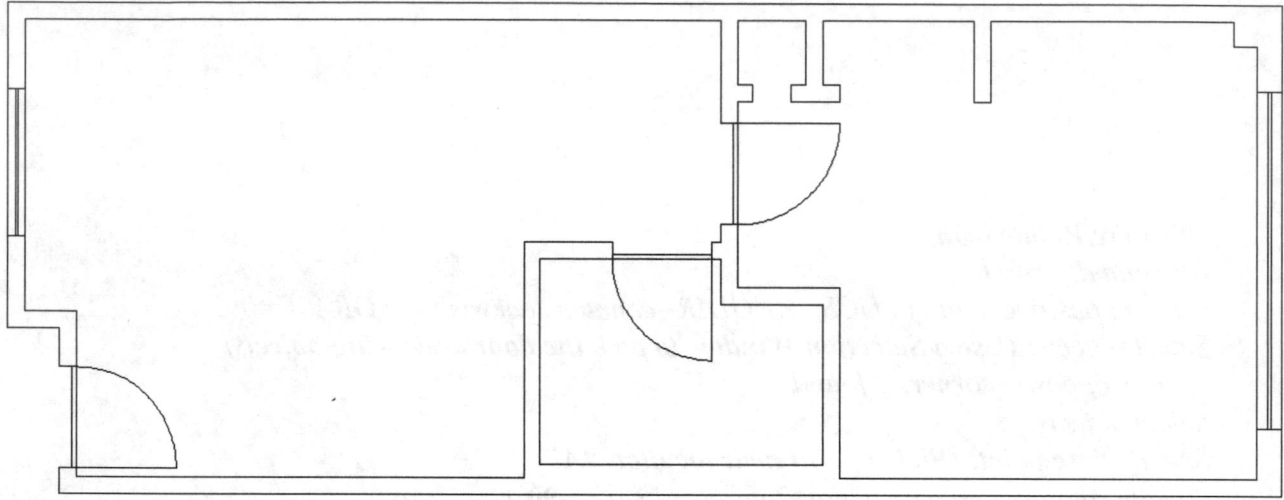

Remember to Save your drawing. We will continue building the Hotel Suite in the next tutorial.

Chapter 7
Commands – Set 3: Laying-out Your Drawing for Printing

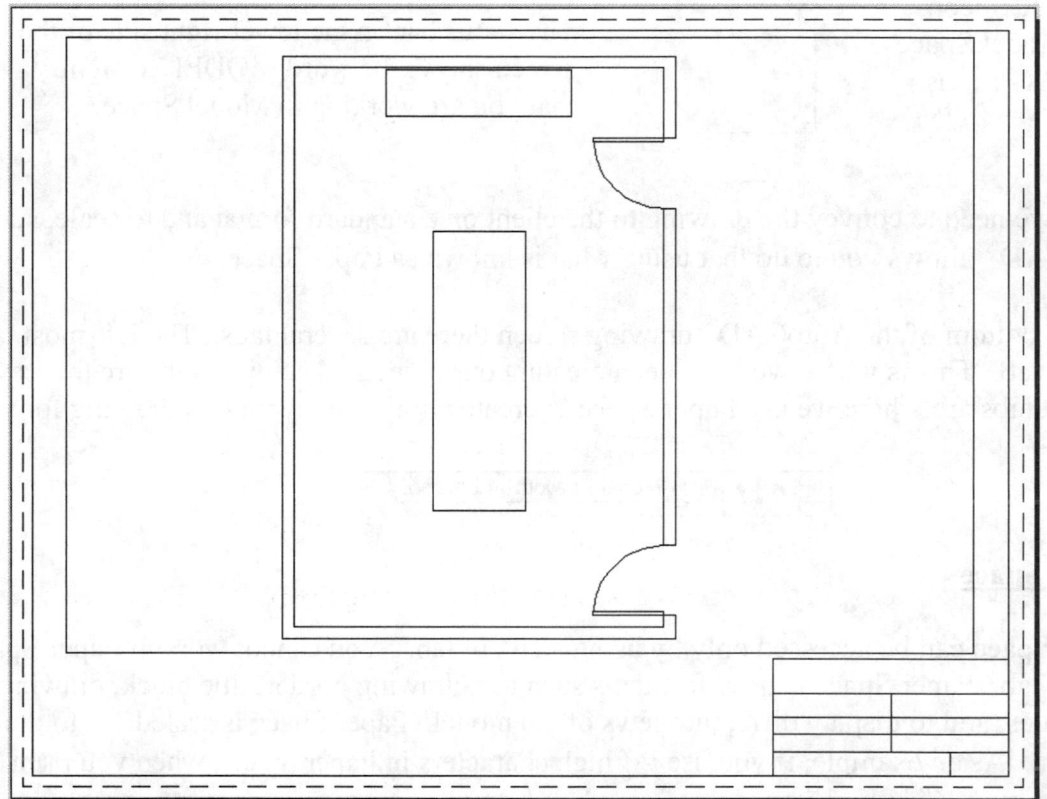

Learning Objectives:

- Understand the difference between Model Space and Paper Space
- Creating Viewports on your Layout to see your Model Space objects
- Changing the size and location of the Viewport on your Layout
- Setting and Locking the Scale of the Viewport
- Setting up and Plotting from Paper Space
- Renaming, adding, and deleting Layout tabs

Model Space & Paper Space

Model Space

All the drawing work we have been doing so far has been in the Model tab and the space we have been drawing in is called Model Space. In Model Space, the designer creates the objects full scale.

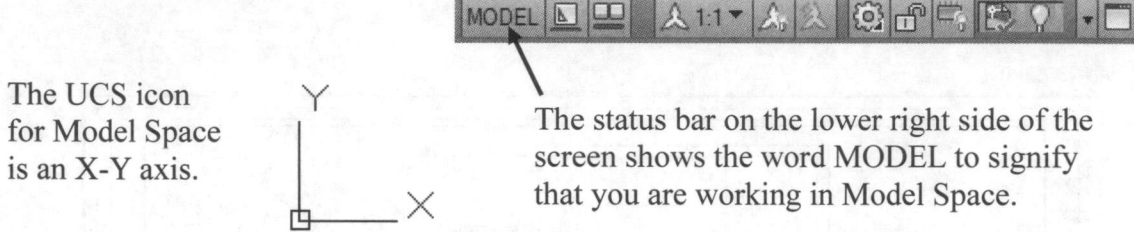

The UCS icon for Model Space is an X-Y axis.

The status bar on the lower right side of the screen shows the word MODEL to signify that you are working in Model Space.

Since we need to convey the drawing to the client on a standard format and to scale, such as ¼″ =1′, AutoCAD® allows you to do that using what is known as Paper Space.

On the bottom of the AutoCAD® drawing screen there are several tabs. The left-most tab is the Model tab. This is where we have been creating our objects. The other tabs are the Layout tabs. The Layout tabs are where we use Paper Space to create a finished layout of a drawing for printing.

Paper Space

Paper Space can be accessed only by using a layout tab. You cannot work in Paper Space on the Model tab. Paper Space is used for items such as a drawing border, title block, drawing notes, schedules, and to display different views of the model. Paper Space is scaled 1:1 to the paper you print on. As an example, if you use ¼″ high characters in Paper Space, when you print it out, they will measure ¼″ in height.

The UCS icon for Paper Space is a triangle.

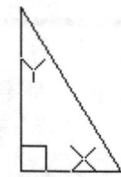

The status bar shows the word PAPER to signify that you are working in Paper Space.

Viewports

Viewports are used to view specific areas of the model. You can think of viewports as windows that show different views of the model. Viewports can be different sizes and shapes. The default shape is rectangular. The shape of the viewport on some of the drawing templates is a polygon (AutoCAD® calls this a Polyline).

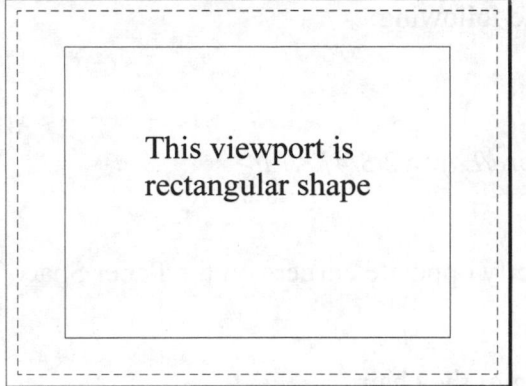

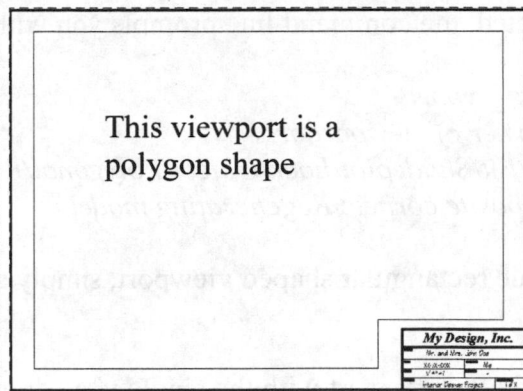

The border that defines the viewport is a Paper Space object, and can be on its own layer, have its own color, and it can be erased, re-sized, or moved just like any rectangle or polygon can.

A Layout can have more than one viewport. As an example the following shows two viewports: one showing the chair, and the other showing the plant. The objects were created in Model Space in different locations on the drawing. The viewports allow you to look at the model objects – which can be located in the viewport using Pan and Zoom.

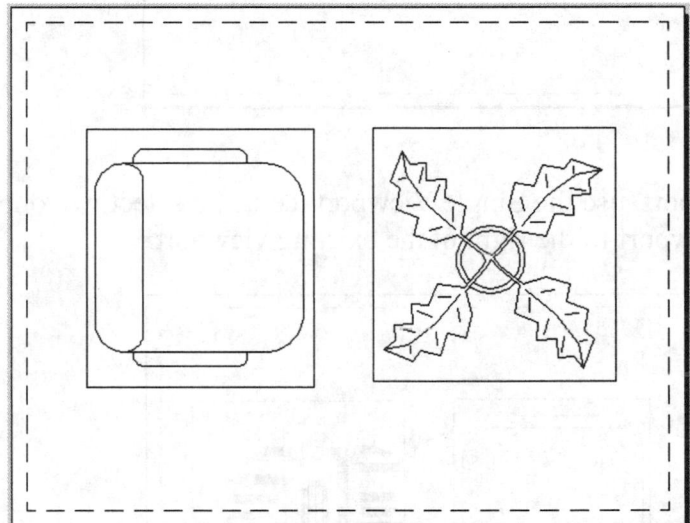

Viewports Toolbar

You can bring up the Viewports toolbar by right-clicking on any toolbar and selecting Viewports. The Viewports toolbar allows you to easily create additional viewports.

You can create a single viewport by selecting the Single Viewport icon on the Viewports toolbar.

Single Viewport icon

Once selected, the command line prompts you with the following:

Command: _-vports
Specify corner of viewport or
[ON/OFF/Fit/Shadeplot/Lock/Object/Polygonal/Restore/Layer/2/3/4] <Fit>:
Specify opposite corner: Regenerating model.

For a simple rectangular shaped viewport, simply specify opposite corners on the Paper Space drawing.

As an example, let's start with the single view drawing of the chair:

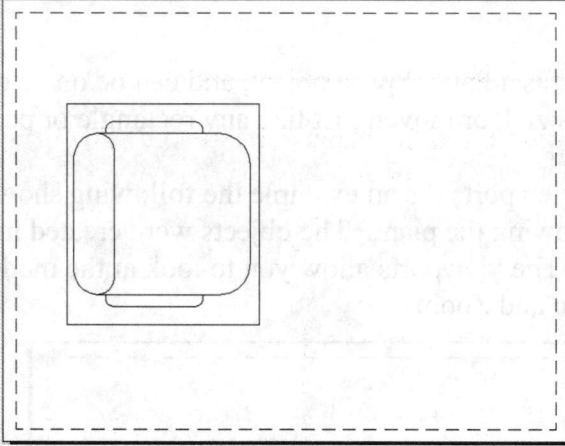

To create a second viewport, use the Single Viewport icon, and select two opposite corners to define a second rectangular viewport to the right of the existing viewport:

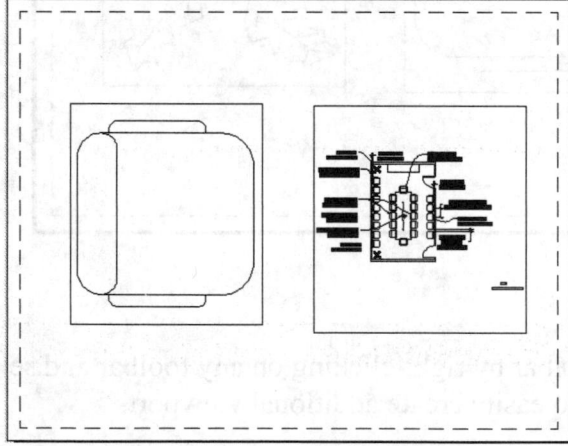

Notice that the new viewport does not show the objects of the model the way that we want it. We can now switch to Model Space by selecting the PAPER button on the status bar, so that it becomes a MODEL button. This will activate the viewport. If the active viewport is not the new viewport, you can use Ctrl-R to toggle the active viewport.

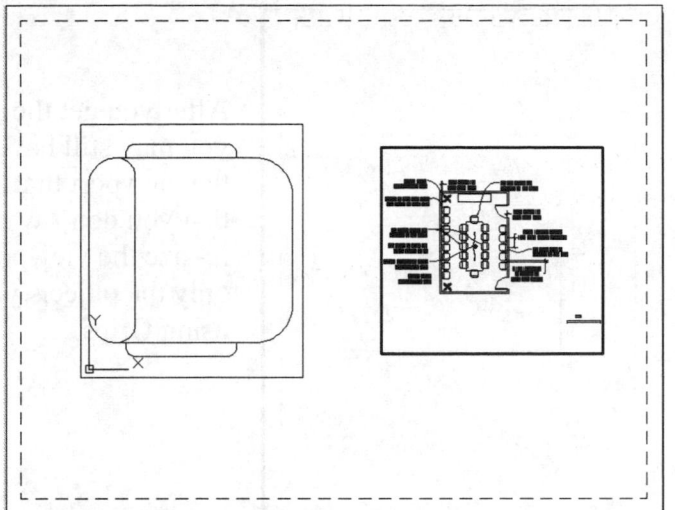

> To make a viewport active, use Ctrl-R to toggle between viewports.

Use the wheel mouse to Pan and Zoom to find the plant. Change the scale using the pull-down arrow on the Viewports toolbar to select a suitable scale. I used 1-1/2″ = 1′. An alternative is to use the scale on the status bar:

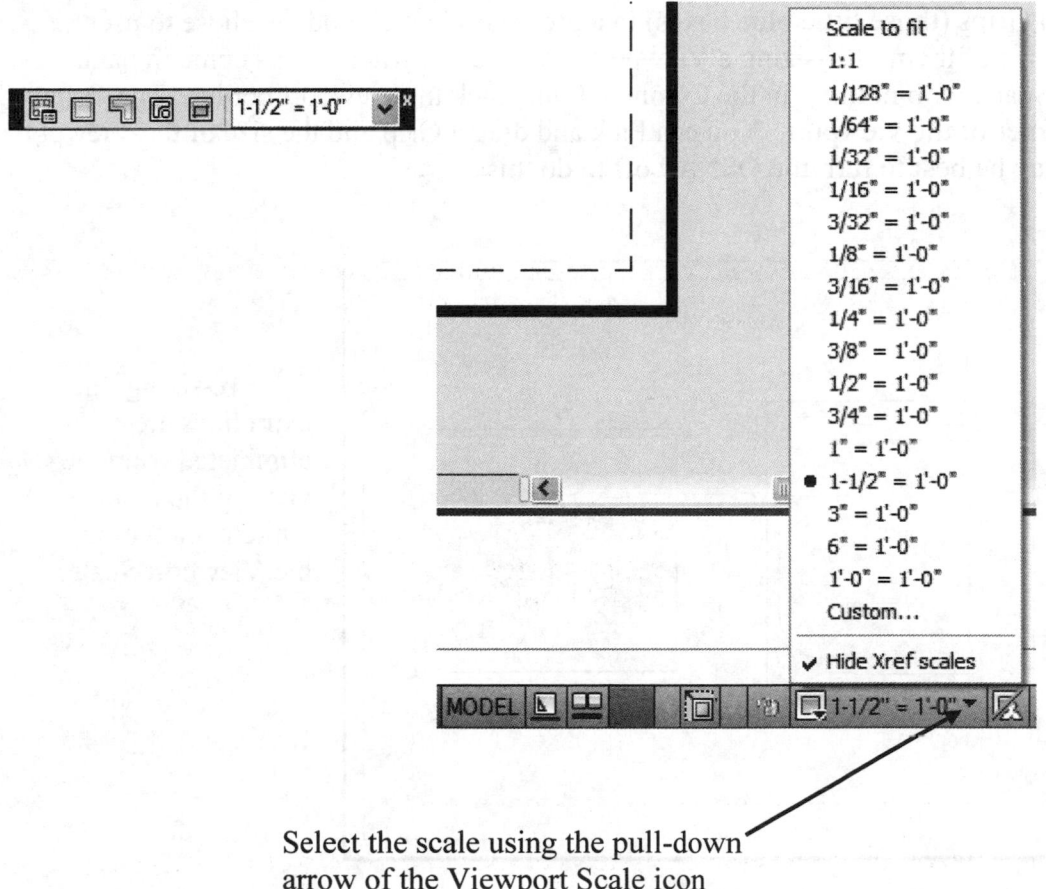

Select the scale using the pull-down arrow of the Viewport Scale icon

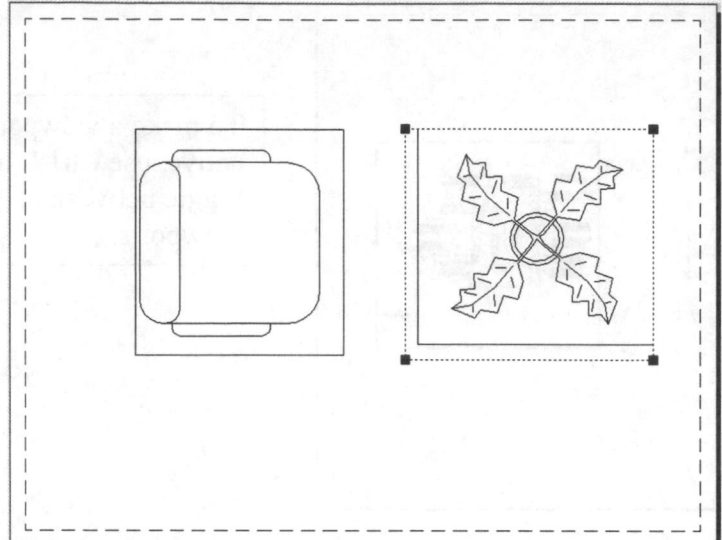

After you get the scale set, you may still have objects in the viewport that are visible that you don't want. You can re-size the viewport to show only the objects you want by using Grips.

Re-Sizing a Viewport

We had discussed Grips (those little blue boxes) in a previous chapter, and we chose to use the Escape key to get rid of them. Re-sizing a Viewport is a situation where Grips come in handy. When you are in Paper Space with nothing in the Command line, pick the viewport border. The Grips will appear at each corner of the viewport. You can Pick and drag a Grip and the size of the Viewport will change. It may be best to turn the OSNAP off to do this.

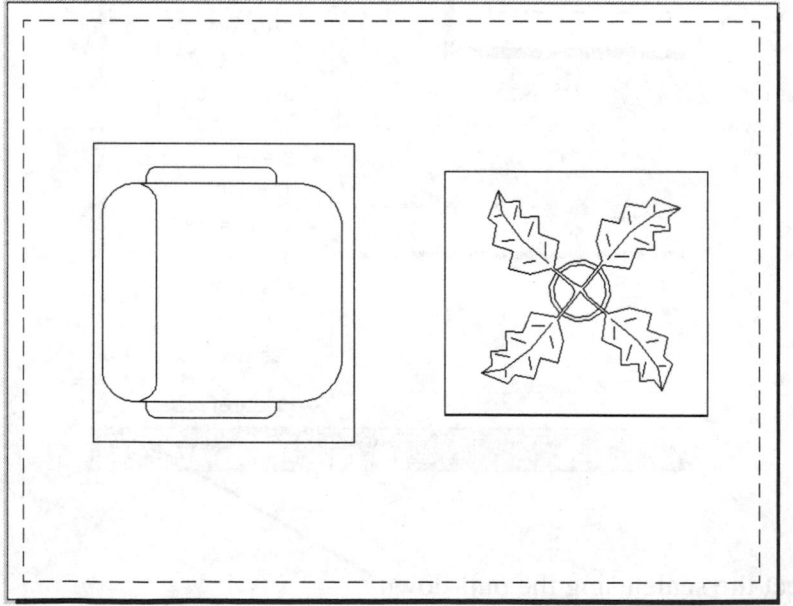

After re-sizing, the extra lines are eliminated from the view of the plant while maintaining the Viewport Scale.

Access Model Space in Layout tab

Although we have been working on our model using the Model tab, we can also work on our model in the Layout tab, as long as at least one viewport is created. While in the Layout tab, pick the PAPER button on the status bar. The text on the button will become MODEL, the UCS icon will change from a triangle to an X-Y axis, the cursor crosshairs are only visible in the active viewport, and the viewport border will thicken or highlight.

If you have more than one viewport, only one viewport border will thicken/highlight. This signifies that it is the active or current viewport. You can make a different viewport active/current by clicking in it or by holding the Ctrl key and the letter R simultaneously (Ctrl-R). Using Ctrl-R allows you to toggle between viewports.

Once the viewport is active, you can create or modify the Model Space objects, and you can Pan or Zoom to make the objects fit the viewport better.

Create and Modify Objects in a Layout Viewport

Creating or modifying Model Space objects in the Layout tab is best done by using the Maximize Viewport button on the status bar. The maximized layout viewport expands to fill the drawing area. The center point and the layer visibility settings of the viewport are retained, and the surrounding objects are displayed.

Maximize Viewport button

Once you maximize the viewport, the button changes to a Minimize Viewport button, and the toggle arrows are active.

Maximize Previous Viewport ⟶ 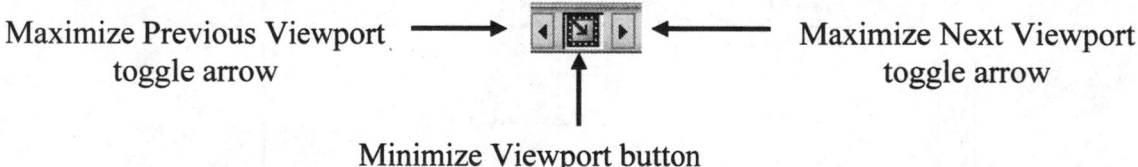 ⟵ Maximize Next Viewport
toggle arrow   toggle arrow

Minimize Viewport button

You can pan and zoom while you are working in Model Space, but when you restore the viewport (using the Minimize Viewport button) to return to Paper Space, the position and scale of the objects in the layout viewport are restored.

Adjust the View in a Layout Viewport

If you plan to pan the view and change the visibility of layers (Layers will be discuss later), double-click inside a layout viewport to access model space. The viewport border becomes thicker, and the crosshair cursor is visible in the current viewport only. All active viewports in the layout remain visible while you work. You can freeze and thaw layers in the current viewport in the Layer Properties Manager, and you can pan the view. To return to paper space, double-click an empty area on the layout outside a viewport. The changes you made are displayed in the viewport.

If you set the scale in the layout viewport before you access model space, you can lock the scale to prevent changes. When the scale is locked, you cannot use ZOOM while you work in model space.

To accurately and consistently scale each displayed view in the plotted drawing, set the scale of each view relative to paper space. You can change the view scale of the viewport using the Properties palette, the XP option of the ZOOM command, the Viewports toolbar, or the Viewport Scale button on the Status bar. I have found that using the Viewport Scale button is the easiest to use.

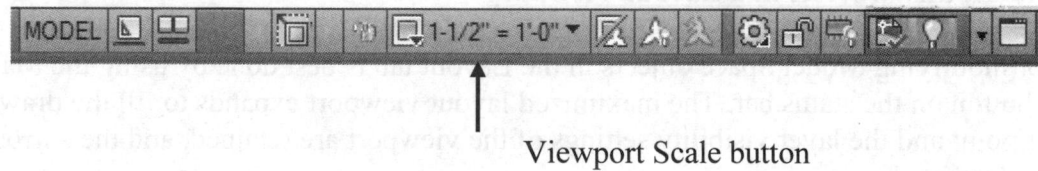

Viewport Scale button

When you work in a layout, the scale factor represents a ratio between the actual size of the model displayed in the viewports and the size of the layout. Changing the scale factor can be done while in Model Space by using the pull-down arrow of the Viewport Scale button. As an example, the Conference Room drawing is scaled at ¼″ =1′. This is a standard scale that was set by using the pull-down arrow on the Viewport Scale button.

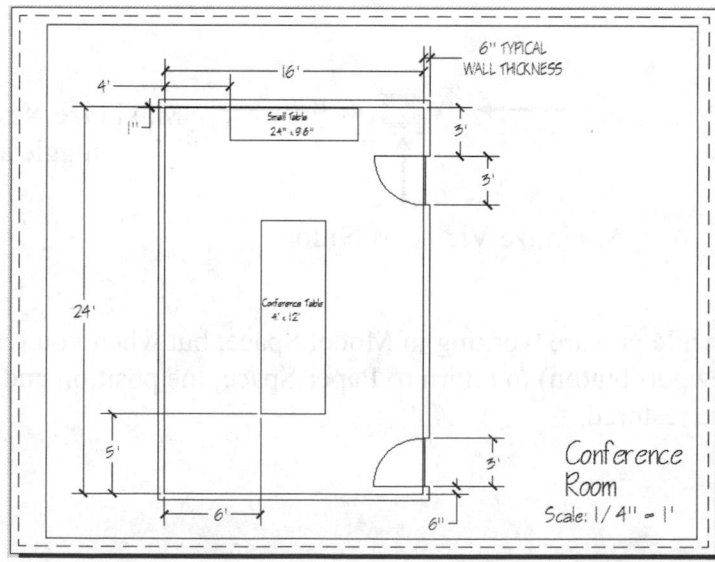

Note that scaling or stretching the layout viewport border, while in Paper Space, does not change the scale of the view of the model within the viewport.

Lock the Scale of Layout Viewports

Once you've set the viewport scale, if you zoom in within the viewport, you change the viewport scale at the same time. By locking the viewport scale first, you can zoom in to view different levels of detail in your viewport without altering the viewport scale.

Scale locking locks the scale that you set for the selected viewport. Once the scale is locked, you can continue to modify the objects in the viewport without affecting the viewport.

To lock the Viewport scale, pick the Lock/Unlock Viewport icon on the lower status bar:

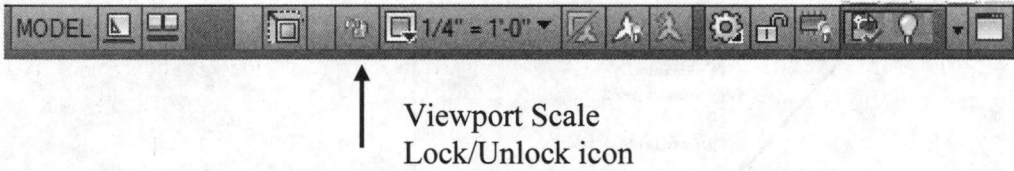

Viewport Scale
Lock/Unlock icon

Once selected, the icon now appears as a closed padlock:

Viewport Scale
Lock/Unlock icon –
shown locked

The current viewport's scale is locked. If you change the zoom factor in the viewport, only paper space objects are affected.

Plotting from Paper Space

Paper Space was created to allow you to set up your drawing, which was done in real world size, for printing on select size paper. The paper size can be chosen from multiple standard sizes.

If a printer/plotter is not selected for the layout, selecting Plot Preview from the File pull-down menu will result in the following message on the command line:

Command: _preview No plotter is assigned. Use Page Setup to assign a plotter to the current Layout.

Both paper size and assigning a printer/plotter are chosen from the Page Setup Manager.

Page Setup Manager

Use the File pull-down menu from the Standard toolbar to select the Page Setup Manager.

Pick Page Setup Manager

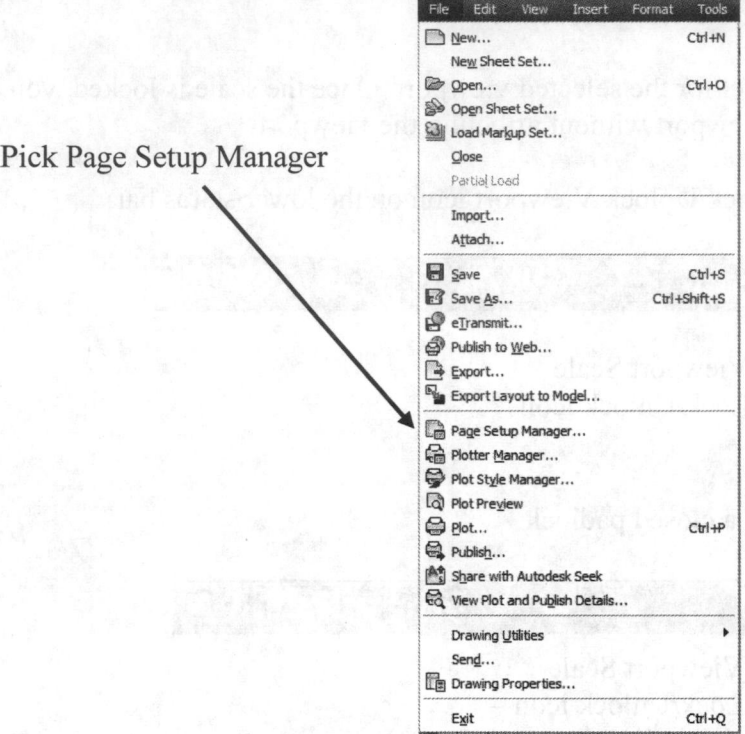

The Page Setup Manager dialog box appears. Pick the Modify button.

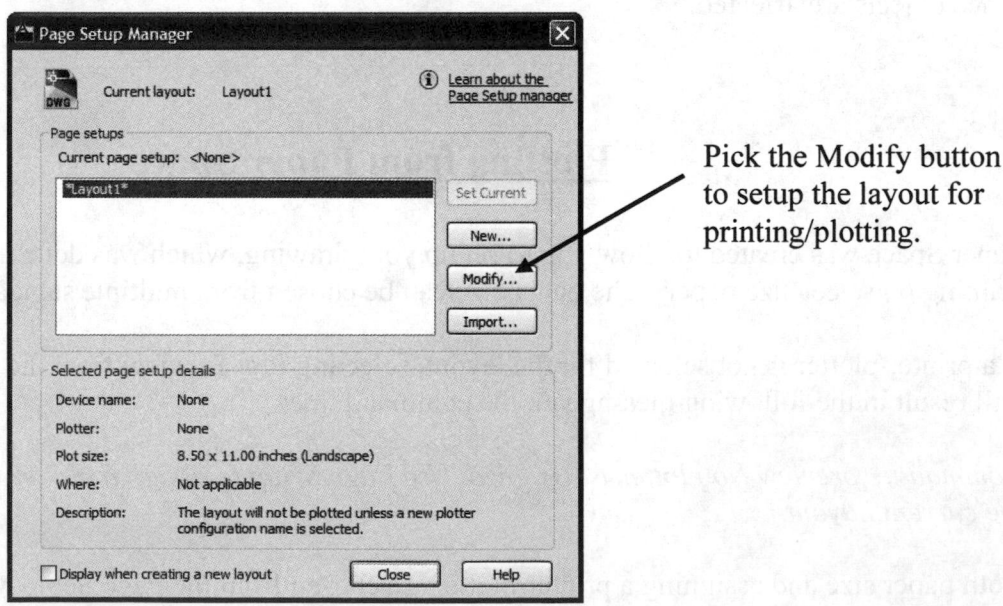

Pick the Modify button
to setup the layout for
printing/plotting.

The Page Setup dialog box for the current layout will appear.

Select the
Printer/plotter
here

Select the
paper size
here

Choose the
orientation
here

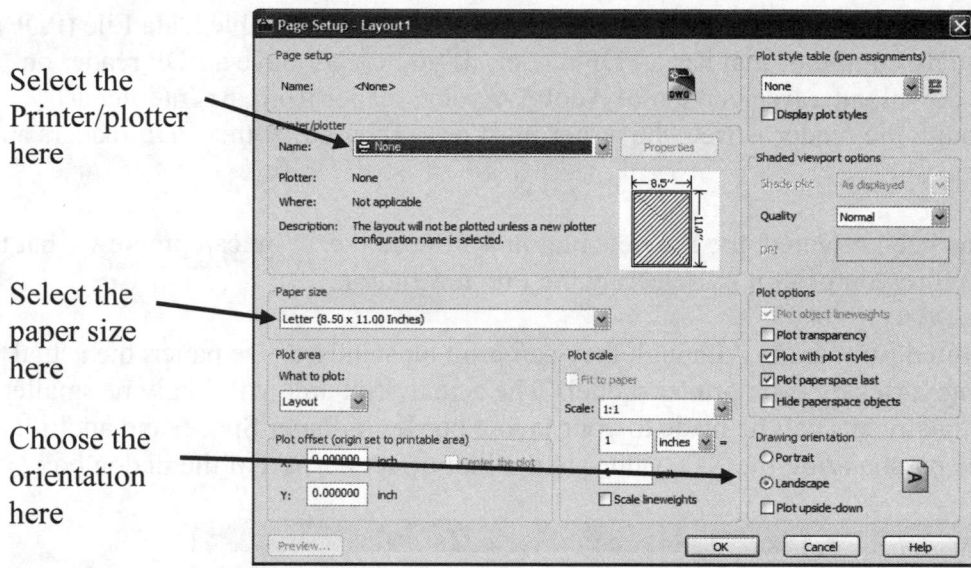

Use the pull-down arrow in the Paper size section of the dialog box to select the size of the paper to print. This will also change the size of the Layout drawing area to match.

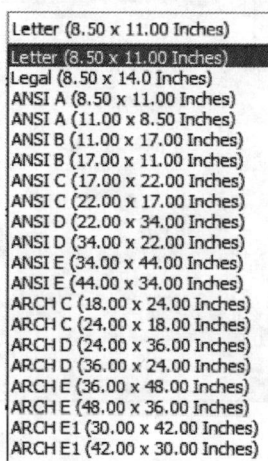

This is a partial listing of the sizes available. Only the Inch sizes available are shown.

Use the pull down arrow to select the printer you plan to use.

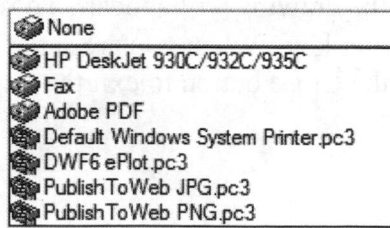

The choices of Printers/plotters available is dependant on what is loaded on your computer.

For this example, I have chosen to print to Adobe PDF. This will create a Portable Data File (PDF) which can be viewed on any computer that has a PDF reader. If you do not have a PDF reader on your computer, you can download a free version of Adobe Acrobat reader from the Internet at www.adobe.com. Although the reader is free, the writer must be purchased. Other PDF readers and writers are also available.

Once a Printer/plotter has been selected, the Preview button is now active. You can preview what the drawing will look like before you print it by selecting the Preview button.

Some printers have a limited print area. Although they can print on standard size paper, the actual area available for printing varies by each printer model. The actual print area will likely be smaller than the entire sheet. Adjustments can be made to your layout border in Paper Space, and additional adjustments can be made by changing the X-Y values in the Plot offset portion of the dialog box.

Additional adjustments can be made to fit your Plotter/printer by changing the X-Y values here

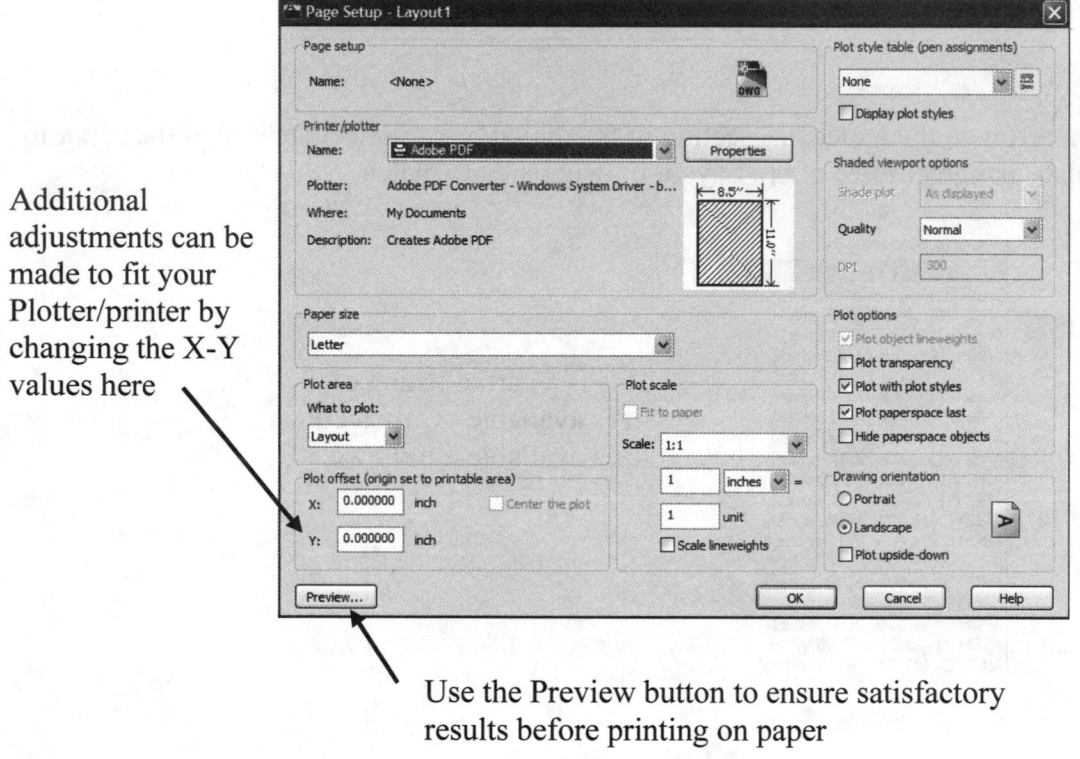

Use the Preview button to ensure satisfactory results before printing on paper

Once you select the Preview button, a preview of the drawing will appear. To return to the Page Setup dialog box, press the Escape key or the ↵ Enter key. When you are satisfied with the setup, press the OK button to exit the dialog box. Press the Close button to exit the Page Setup Manager dialog box.

Plotting/Printing Your Drawing

Use the File pull-down menu to select the Plot command.

Pick Plot

A Plot dialog box will appear. Additional plotting changes can be made here prior to Printing/plotting. Many choices are similar to the Plot Manager dialog box.

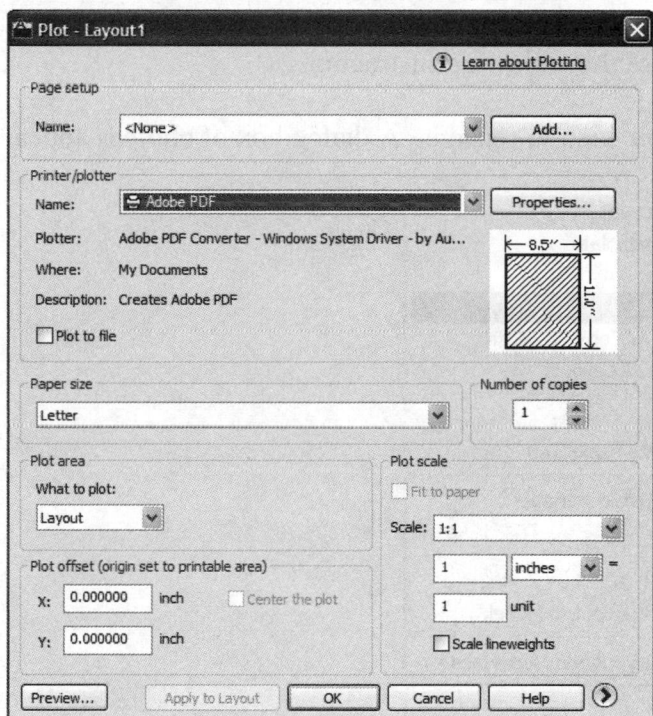

Pick the OK button to send the drawing to the Printer/plotter. A balloon will appear on the lower right side of the screen that indicates that plotting was successful.

Model & Layout Tabs

Initial AutoCAD® drawings have three tabs displayed at the bottom of the Classic screen as follows:

The Model tab is the one that AutoCAD® defaults to. It is for Model Space objects, and is the one that we have been doing all of our drawing work in. The Layout tabs display the Paper Space.

The Layout tabs can be renamed for your convenience. A typical name that you may find would be Sheet 1 or Sheet 2, etc. Or, you could name them Floor Plan, Elevation, etc. It is up to you. The Model tab cannot be renamed.

Renaming Layout Tabs

To rename the Layout tabs, use the following instructions:

Right-Click on the tab that you wish to rename. A dialog box of choices appears. Select Rename.

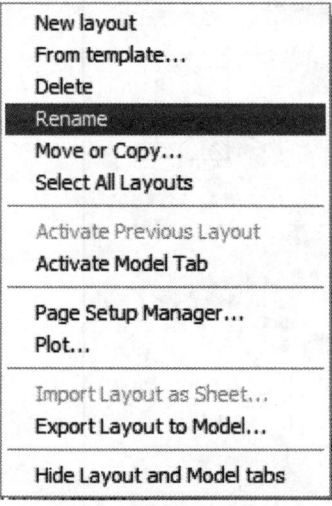

A current layout name highlights and is ready for editing. For this example, let's assume you wish to name this Sheet 1. Type Sheet 1 for the new name.

Notice that the tab has been renamed to the new name that you typed in.

Adding a Layout Tab

Let's assume that you already have Sheet 1 and Sheet 2 for named layout tabs:

If you have a drawing that requires more than two sheets, you may wish to add another tab. To do that, use the following instructions:

Right-Click on the Sheet 2 tab to bring up the dialog box. Pick Move or Copy... from the choices you are given.

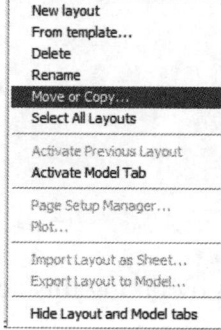

The Move or Copy dialog box appears. Pick the (move to end) choice and put a check mark in the Create a copy check-box.

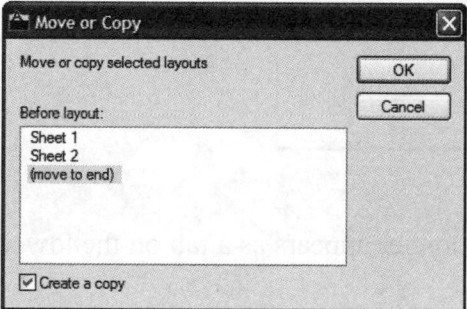

A copy of Sheet 2 is created and added to the end of the layout tab listing. AutoCAD® automatically assigns the name of Sheet 2 (2) for this new layout tab.

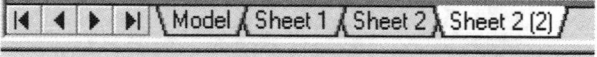

Rename this new tab to Sheet 3 using the same technique as describe above for renaming layout tabs.

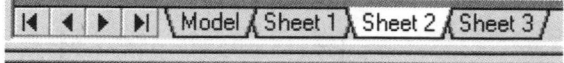

Deleting Layout Tabs

To delete a layout tab, use the following instructions:

Right-Click on the Layout tab you wish to delete. A dialog box appears. Pick Delete from your given choices.

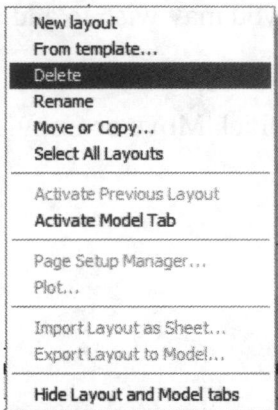

A warning dialog box appears. This dialog box warns you that by taking this action, the layout will be permanently deleted. Pick the OK button.

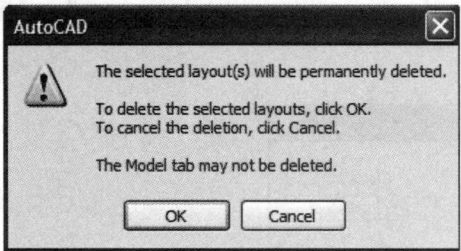

Your selected layout is now deleted and no longer appears as a tab on the lower part of your screen.

Summary

In this chapter you have learned to:

- Understand the concept of Model Space and Paper Space
- Create a viewport using the Viewport toolbar
- Re-size a viewport
- Set and lock the scale of the viewport
- Set up for plotting using Page Setup Manager
- Plot your drawing from Paper Space
- Rename Layout tabs
- Add or delete Layout tabs

Review Questions

1. Why does AutoCAD® have both Model Space and Paper Space?

2. What is the difference between Model Space and Paper Space?

3. What is a Layout?

4. What is an easy way to change the size/shape of a Viewport?

5. What is the advantage of using Paper Space?

6. Does changing the scale of the Viewport change the size of the objects themselves?

7. To print your drawing, what do you need to do first to set it up for printing?

8. The AutoCAD® default template provides two Layout tabs named Layout 1 and Layout 2. How can you add more Layout tabs and rename them?

9. Why can't you delete the Model tab?

10. Why can't you access Paper Space from the Model tab?

Exercises

1. Starting with the Conference Room of Chapter 5 Exercise 1 (or a different drawing you have created already), create a Title Block on Layout 1 Tab in Paper Space. You may need to Zoom and Pan the view of the conference room off to the side to improve your visibility.

While in Model Space, Pan and Zoom your view of the conference room to the side so that you can draw the Title Block with better visibility. After you do this, make sure to switch to Paper Space before drawing the Title Block

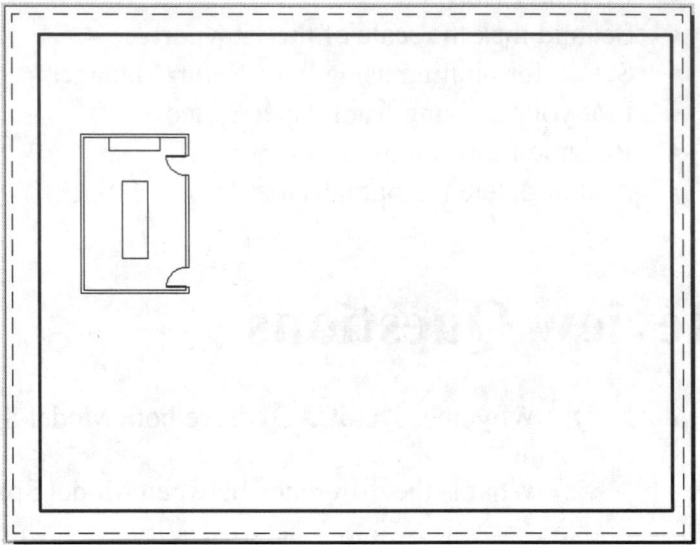

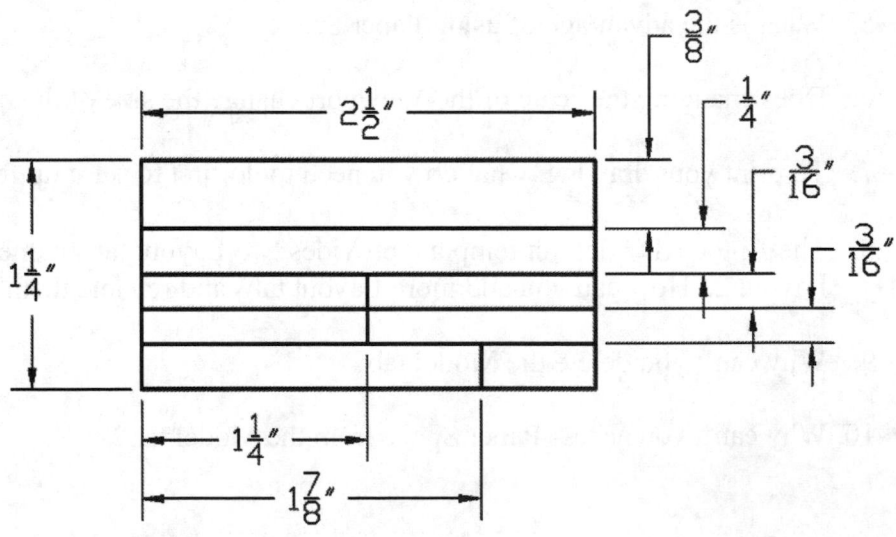

Title Block Dimensions

2. In Paper Space, add to Exercise 1 by drawing a 10-1/2″ x 8″ border. Position the border so that it fits well on the layout. Move the Title Block to the lower right-hand corner. Use Grips to re-size the Viewport so it does not cross the Title Block. Rename the Layout Tab as "Sheet 1".

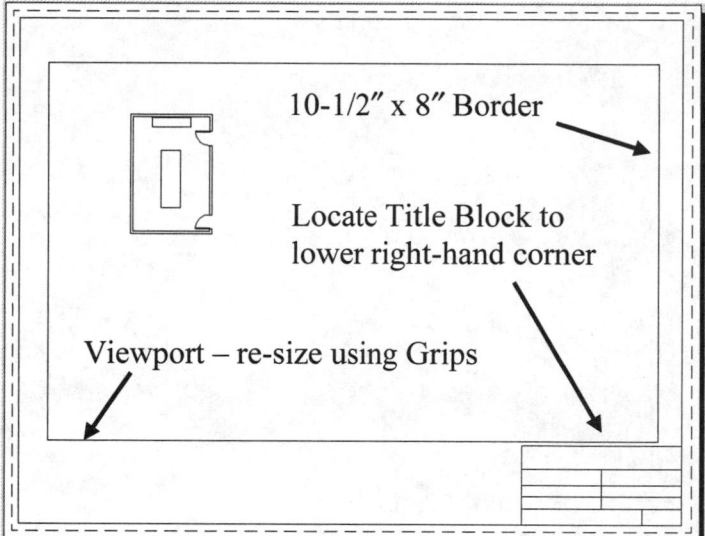

3. After you complete Exercise 2, switch back to Model Space to set the scale and place the view of the conference room properly on the drawing format. Set and Lock the Viewport Scale to ¼″ = 1′. You may have to re-size the viewport again to make sure the entire conference room is in the viewport.

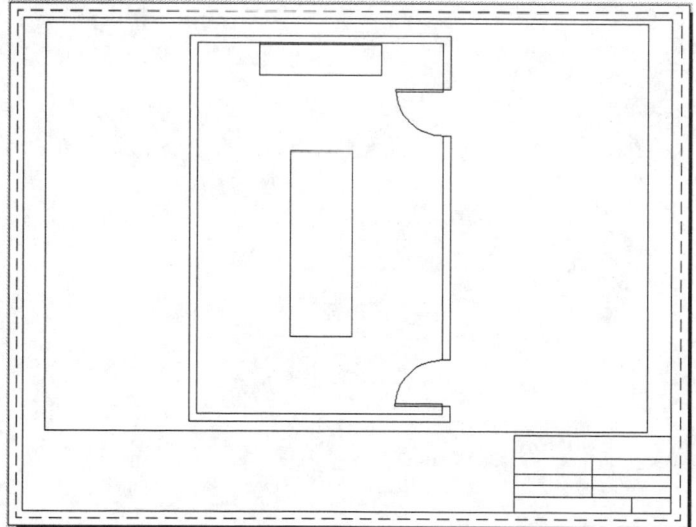

4. After completing Exercise 3, set up and plot the conference room drawing. Use the Page Setup Manager to select the proper paper size for your printer. Use the Preview button to ensure that your drawing will plot correctly for your printer. Make size adjustments using plot offset and make a print of your drawing.

Notes:

Chapter 8
Hotel Suite Project – Tutorial 3

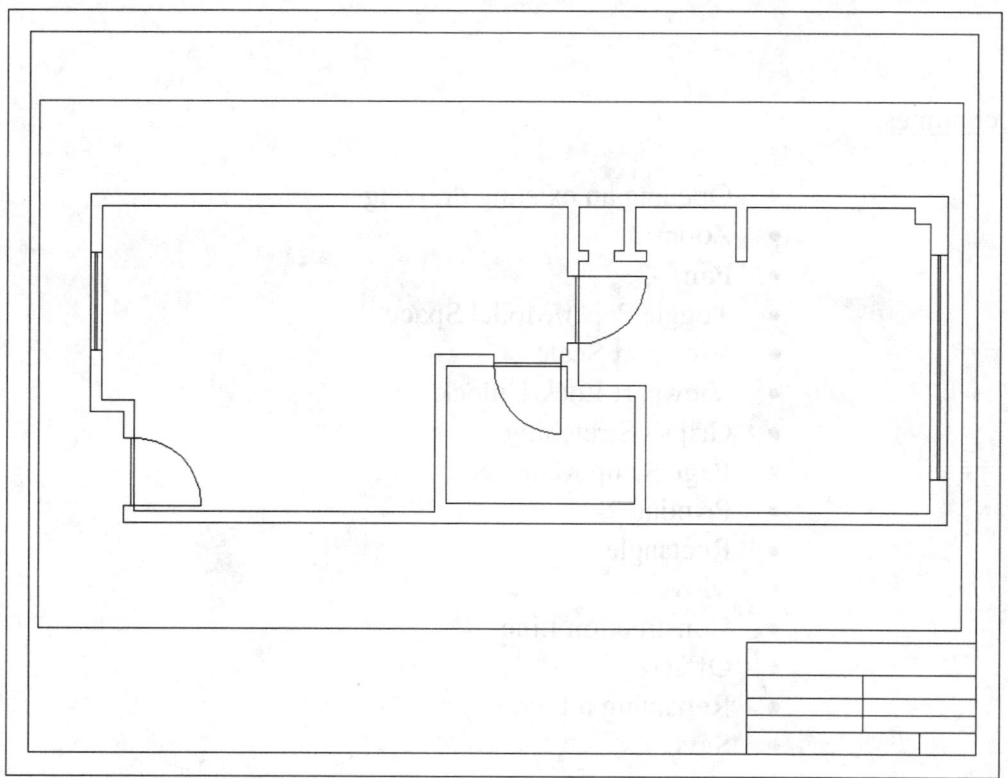

Learning Objectives:

- **To continue creating a drawing of a real-world application of AutoCAD®**
  - o **Create a layout for plotting the plan view of the hotel suite at a standard scale**
  - o **Create a drawing border and titleblock for the layout**
  - o **Set up and plot the layout**
- **To utilize and reinforce the use of the AutoCAD® commands learned in the previous chapters**

This tutorial builds on Tutorial 2 found in Chapter 6. We will use Paper Space for a layout of the model created; set and lock the scale of the drawing; create a drawing border and titleblock; and set up and plot the layout. When you are finished with this tutorial, you will have a scaled printout of the floor plan.

The following commands and techniques will be used:

Commands & Techniques:

- Opening an existing drawing
- Zoom
- Pan
- Toggle Paper/Model Space
- Viewport Scale
- Viewport Lock/Unlock
- Grips - Stretching
- Page Setup Manager
- Printing
- Rectangle
- Move
- Construction Line
- Offset
- Renaming a Layout Tab
- Save

Create a Layout for Plotting

Before beginning, open the Hotel Suite drawing that you updated in Tutorial 2.

1. Use the Layout tab to see how your drawing will look when printed:

Pick the Layout1 tab at the bottom of the drawing screen:

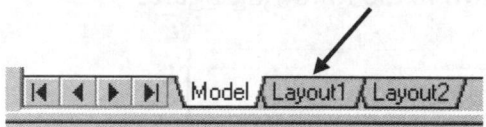

AutoCAD® will bring you to the Paper Space of Layout1.

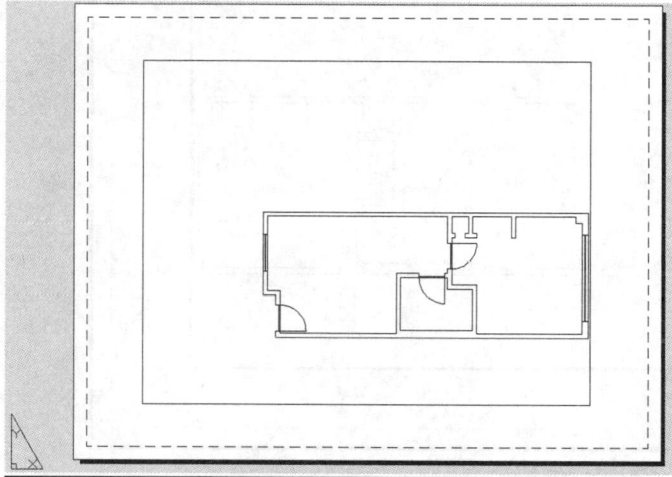

When in the Paper Space mode of Layout1, your drawing screen will look similar to that shown above. Notice the UCS icon is a triangle shape. This is how it appears when you are in the Paper Space mode.

Depending on where you drew the hotel suite relative to the drawing area, the hotel suite may not appear exactly as shown here.

2. Switch from Paper Space mode to Model Space mode:

(Pick the PAPER toggle) near the bottom of your screen:

Once you pick the toggle, it will switch from Paper Space mode to Model Space mode, and the toggle will display the word MODEL.

In addition, the outline of the Viewport becomes highlighted, and the Model Space UCS icon and the Navigation Cube appear inside the Viewport. This is shown in the following figure.

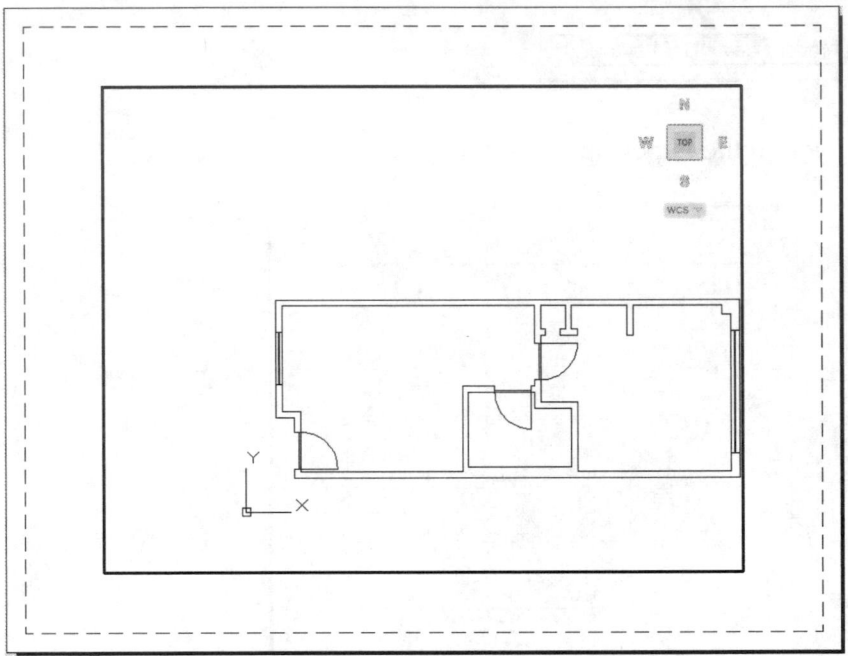

3.   **Pan and Zoom the model to fit on the layout:**

Using your mouse wheel, relocate and size the model so that it fits on the layout. Note that the default layout size is 8-1/2″ x 11″ for a standard paper printer.

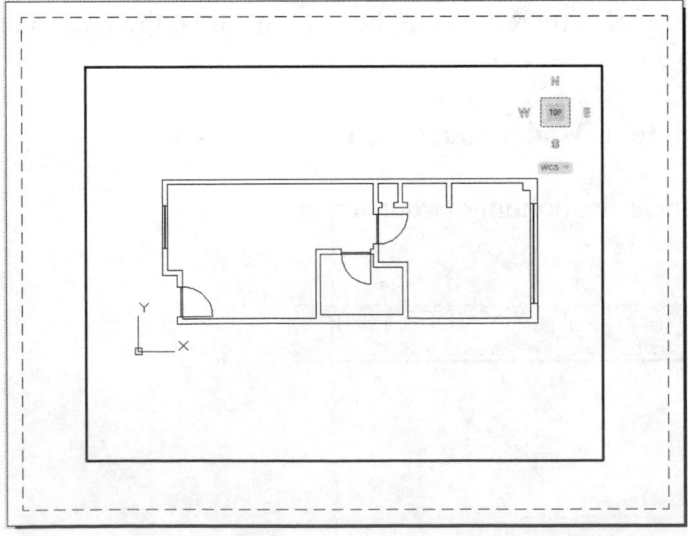

When you print your drawing, you want to be able to print it at a standard scale. When we used the zoom and pan commands to change the way the model was displayed on the layout, we did not set it to any specific scale factor. Let's try the scale factor of ¼″ = 1′, which is typical for Interior Design. Sometimes, another standard scale may be required. This would depend on the size of the room, and the size of the paper you want to plot it on.

4.   Set and lock the scale of the drawing relative to the paper:

(Pick the Viewport Scale icon) at the bottom right side of the screen. Then select the 1/4″=1′ scale:

Pick ¼″=1′ ➡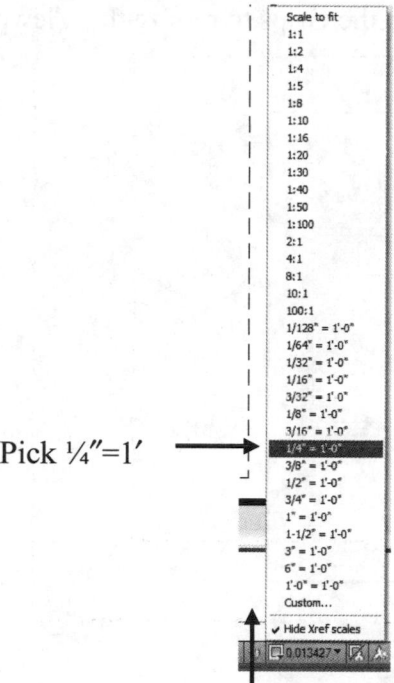

Lock the Viewport

The scale of your drawing should now be ¼″=1′ relative to the paper. You may have noticed a slight change in the size of the drawing on your layout.

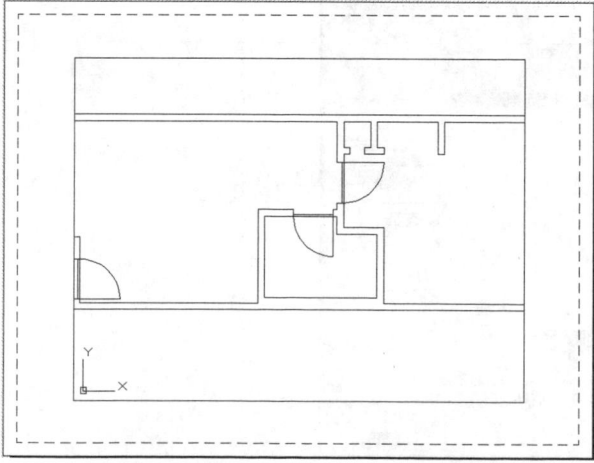

(Pick the Lock/Unlock Viewport icon) to lock the display.

Anytime that you attempt to zoom when the viewport scale is locked, the following message will appear on the command line:

Viewport is view-locked. Switching to Paper space.
Switching back to Model space.

(Pick the Model toggle) to switch back to Paper Space.

(Pick the Viewport border) to get Grips. Use the Grips to re-size the Viewport and fit the entire floor plan on the paper.

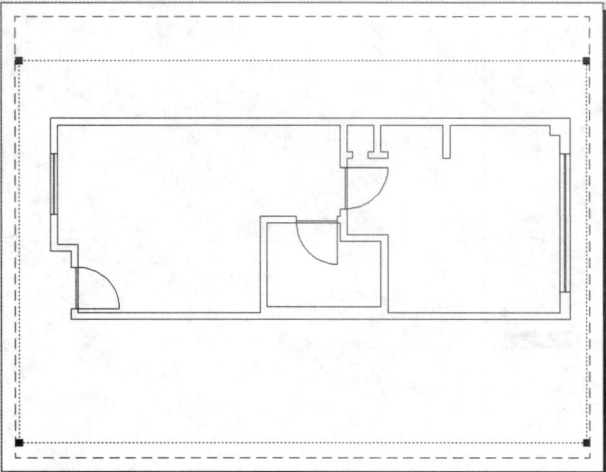

5.   **Select the printer and plot:**

(Pick pull-down menu File and select Page Setup Manager...)

The Page Setup Manager dialog box will appear.

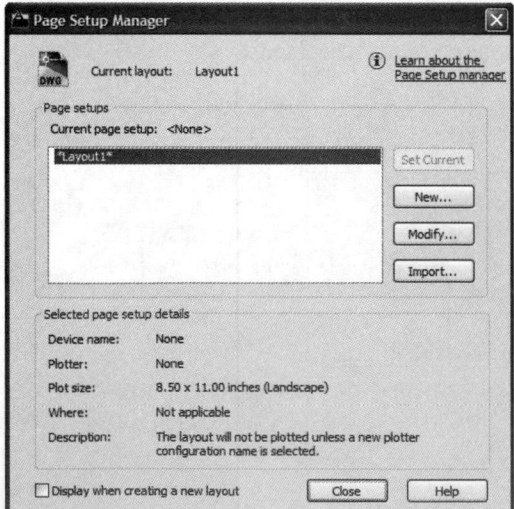

(Pick the Modify… button)

The Page Setup dialog box will appear.

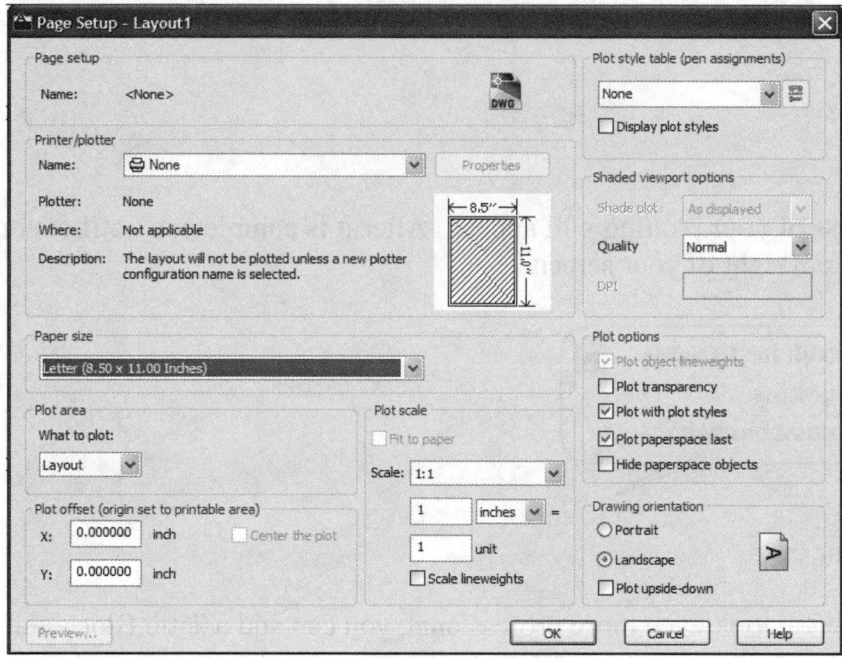

(Use the pull-down arrow to select the printer)

You must have a printer connected to print. It may have defaulted to "None". Use the pull-down arrow to select a printer.

Once a printer is selected, several items that were grayed-out are now available. In this example, a PDF writer was chosen as the printer:

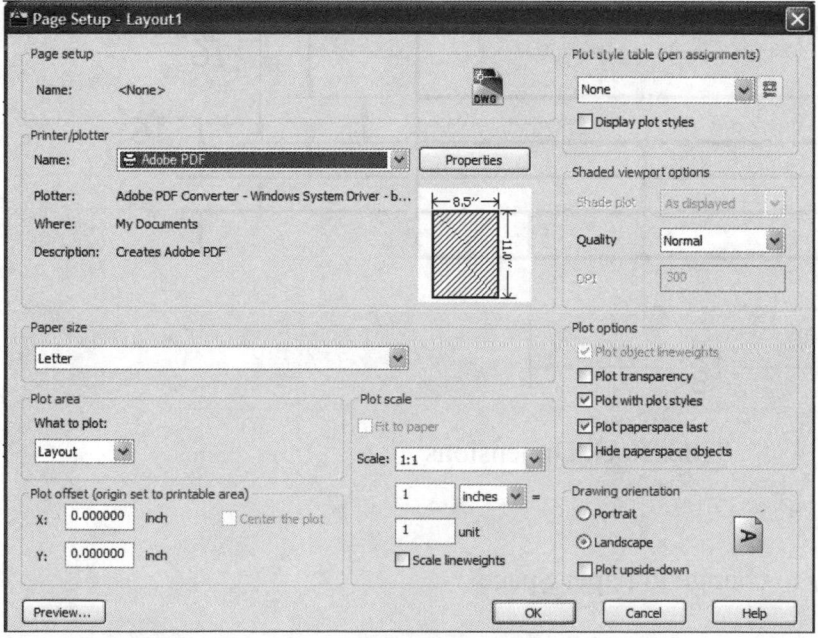

- The pull-down for Paper size is all the available sizes for your chosen printer.
- The Plot scale section will allow you to fit your print to the size of the paper or select a specific scale.
- You can preview your plot by selecting the preview button

If you are satisfied….

(Pick OK to print)

A display showing the progress of your plotting will appear. After it is complete, a notification balloon will appear at the bottom right of your screen.

6. Create a drawing format

If you want to make your drawing look even more professional, you can add a Title Block and Border to create a drawing Format. Remember, these are drawn as Paper Space objects.

For the 8-1/2″ x 11″ paper, let's create the same Title Block and Border that was done for one of the Exercises of Chapter 7. The dimensions of the border are 8″ x 10-1/2″ and the dimensions for the Title Block are shown below:

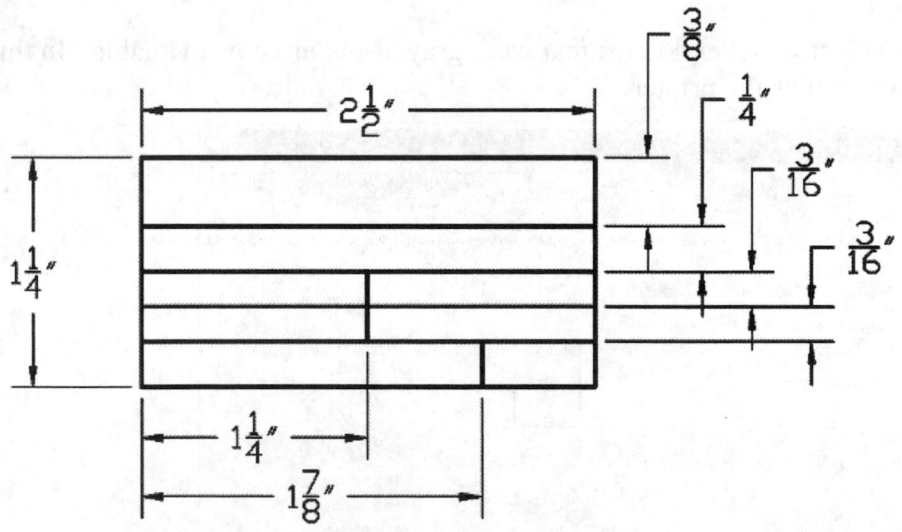

Title Block Dimensions

(Pick the Model toggle) to change to Paper Space

6a. Draw a rectangle 10-1/2″ in the Horizontal direction and 8″ in the Vertical direction to create the border

6b. Use the Move command to locate the rectangle for best fit on the layout

6c. Draw the 2-1/2″ x 1-1/4″ rectangle in the lower right corner of the border

6d. Use Grips to adjust the size of the Viewport to clear the Title Block

6e. Use Construction Line Offset to offset the top horizontal line of the Title Block 3/8″ down

6f. Offset the construction line 1/4″ down

6g. Offset the line from Step 6e 3/16″ down

6h. Offset the line from Step 6f 3/16″ down

6i. Trim the construction lines using the rectangle as a cutting edge

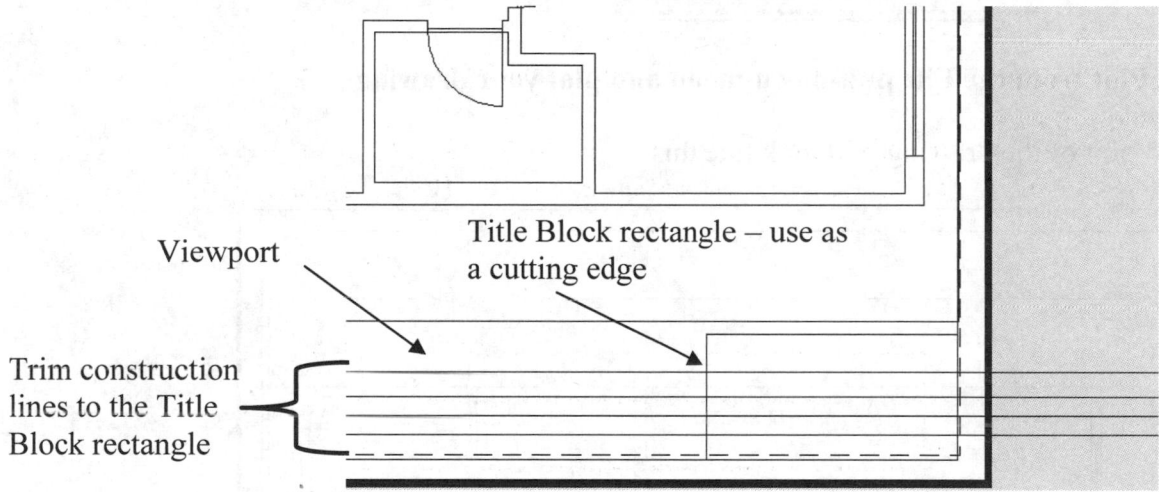

6j. Use Construction Line Offset to offset the left vertical line of the Title Block 1-1/4″ to the right

6k. Use Construction Line Offset to offset the left vertical line of the Title Block 1-7/8″ to the right

6l. Trim the vertical construction lines as shown in the Title Block dimensions

7.   Rename the Layout Tab

Let's rename our Layout tab from "Layout 1" to "Plan View".

7a. Right-click on the Layout 1 tab and pick Rename from the list of choices

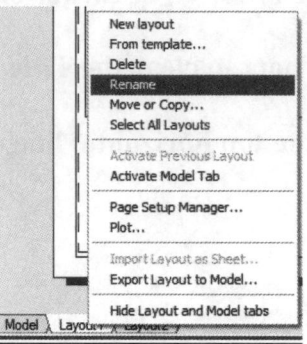

7b. Type the words "Plan View" in place of the Layout 1

8.   Pick Plot from the File pull-down menu and plot your drawing

Your final plot of the drawing will look like this:

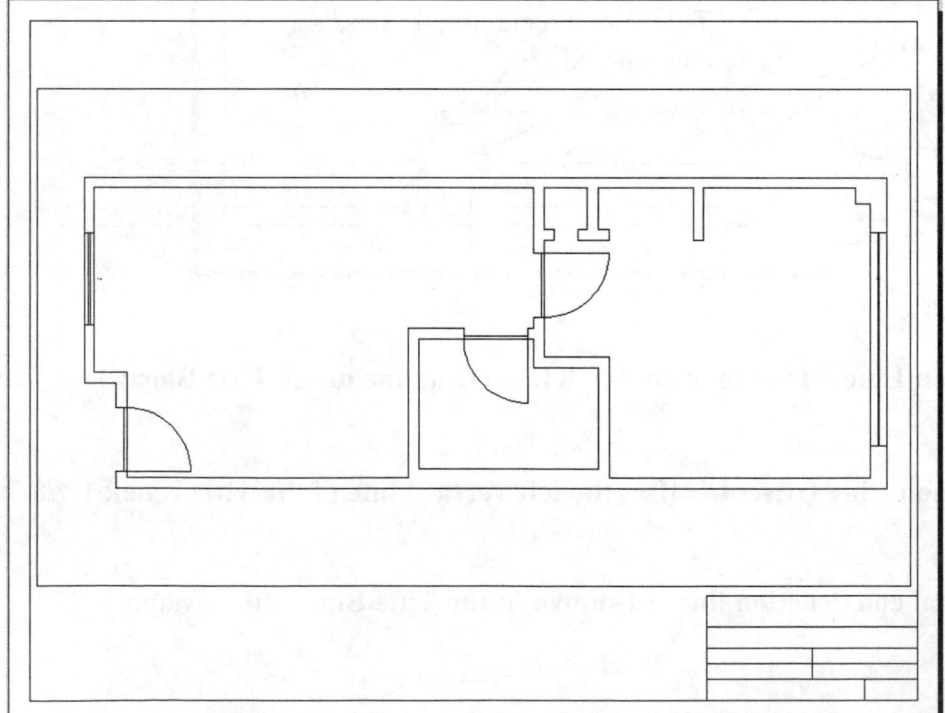

You have now completed Tutorial 3. Make sure to save your drawing.

Chapter 9
Commands – Set 4: Re-Using Objects and Getting Organized

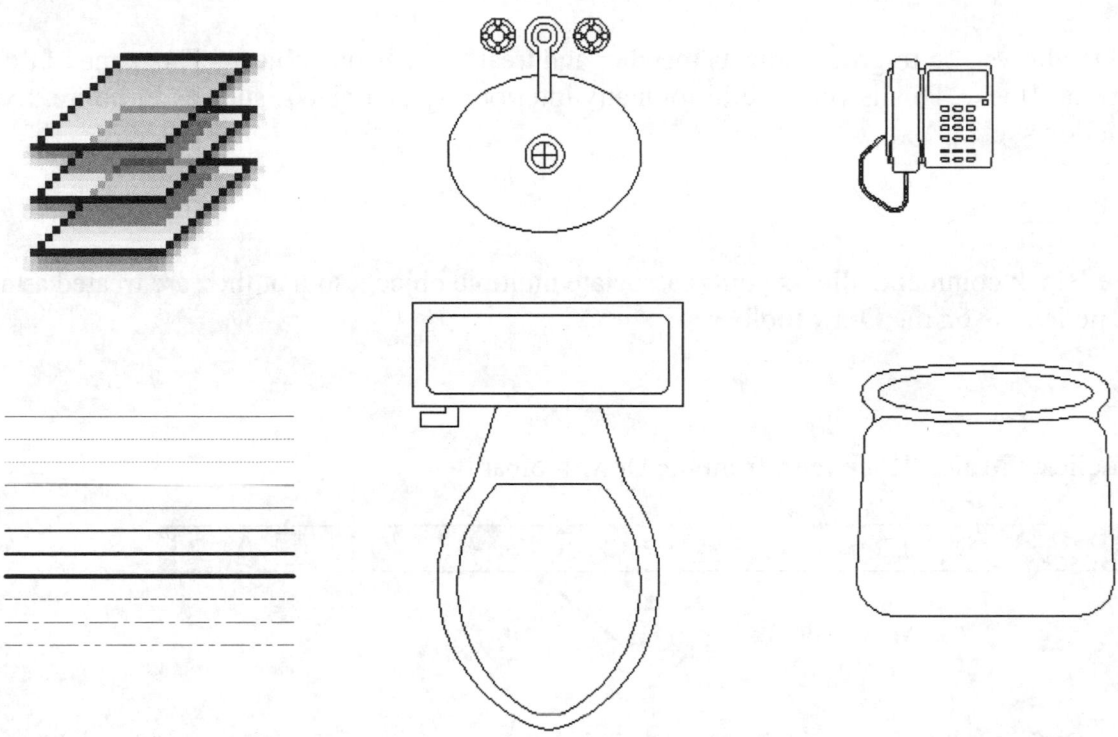

Learning Objectives:

- **Creating and Using Blocks**
- **Using Design Center to bring Blocks in from other drawings**
- **Creating and using Layers**
- **Changing Properties**
- **Setting Color, Line Type, and Lineweights**

Everything we have done so far, we have had to create ourselves. A big advantage of using AutoCAD® is that you only have to create something once. You can then use what you created multiple times throughout your drawing, and for other drawings as well. In fact, you can use groups of objects (Blocks) that someone else created, which can save you time. In this chapter we will see the major advantage that this has over drawing by hand.

Blocks – Treating Multiple Objects as One

AutoCAD® allows you to group objects together and treat them as one object. The name of this grouping is a Block. This is very useful for many Interior Design objects, such as furniture, fixtures, doors, windows, etc.

Making Blocks

The Make Block command allows you to associate multiple objects so that they are treated as a single object. The icon is on the Draw toolbar.

Procedure:

Pick (left click): **Make Block icon** from the Draw toolbar.

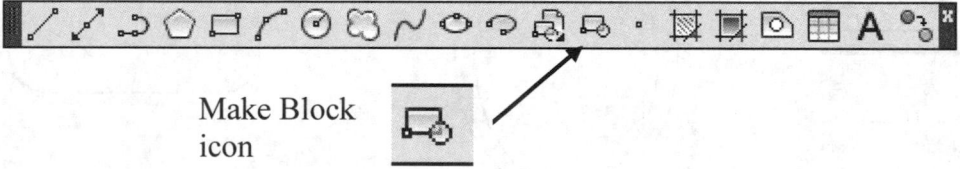

Make Block icon

The Block Definition dialog box will appear. This is where you specify the name of your block and the objects that make it up:

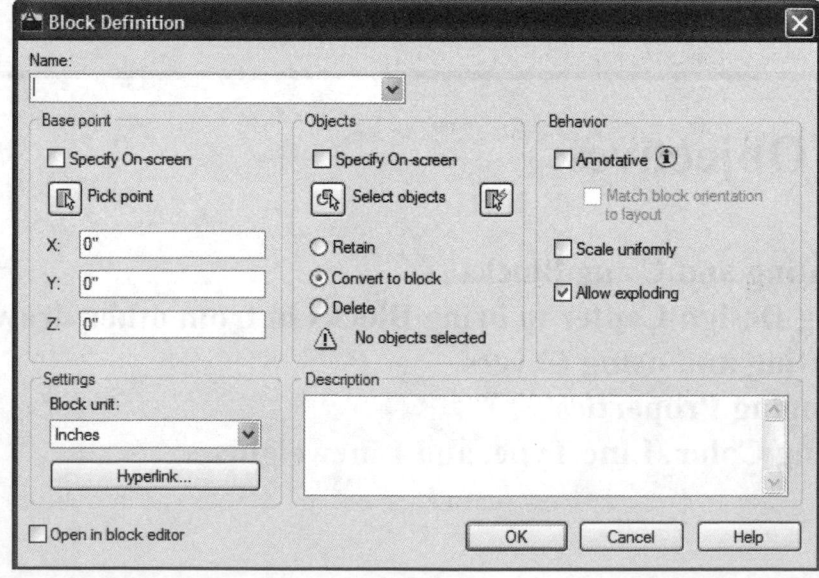

As an example, download the file *Telephone.dwg* from the publisher website and open the drawing. This is an example of multiple objects that should be treated as a single item on your drawing.

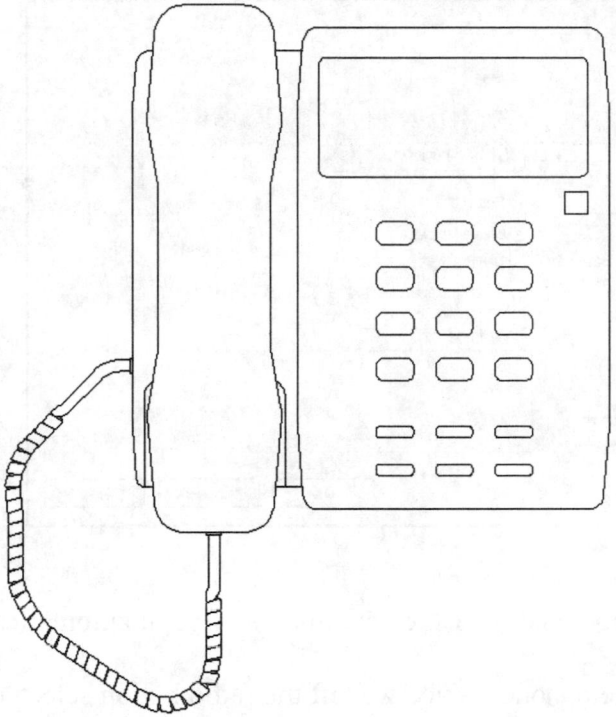

We will type in the name "Telephone" for the name of the block.

We need to select the objects that make up the block. Pick the Select Objects button in the dialog box. The dialog box will disappear and the command line will prompt you to select the objects. Use a Selection Window to select all the objects that make up the telephone.

Command: _block
Select objects: Specify opposite corner: 747 found

Once all the objects are selected, press the ⏎ Enter key.

Select objects: ⏎

The dialog box will reappear on your screen.

We need to select the Base Point of the block. This is the point that will become the origin of the block. Select the Pick point button in the dialog box. The command line will prompt you to select the insertion base point.

Specify insertion base point: Specify insertion base point:

Pick any object on the telephone as your base point. As soon as you pick the point, the dialog box will reappear.

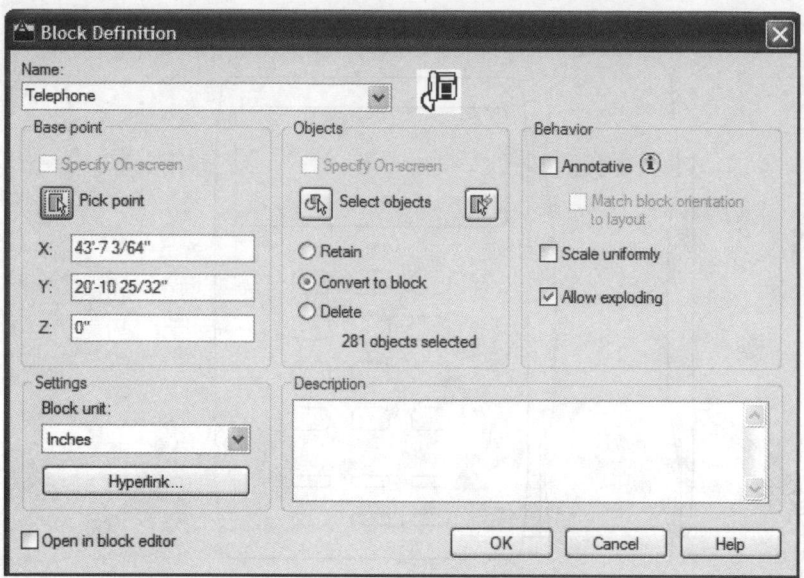

Pick the OK button to exit the dialog box, and the Block command will exit automatically.

You have now created a Block of the telephone. Since we left the radio button selected to "Convert to block", the existing objects that make up the telephone are now joined as a block. You can confirm this with the List command.

Command: _list
Select objects: 1 found

Select objects: ↵

        BLOCK REFERENCE Layer: "0"
            Space: Model space
        Handle = 734
     Block Name: "Telephone"
       at point, X=43'-7 1/16" Y=20'-10 3/4" Z=   0'-0"
X scale factor: 1.0000
Y scale factor: 1.0000
rotation angle: 0
Z scale factor: 1.0000
   InsUnits: Inches
Unit conversion: 1.0000
Scale uniformly: No
Allow exploding: Yes

Inserting Blocks

The Insert Block command allows you to insert Blocks into your drawing. These can be Blocks that were created within the drawing, or the complete insertion of an external drawing. The icon is on the Draw toolbar.

Procedure:

Pick (left click): **Insert Block icon** from the Draw toolbar.

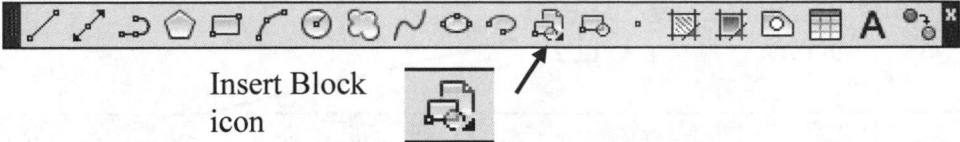

Insert Block
icon

The Insert dialog box will appear. This is where you select the block to insert into your drawing.

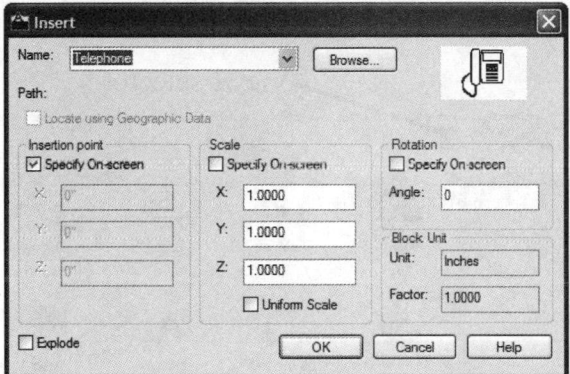

Use the pull-down arrow to select from the list of blocks that are currently in the drawing. Otherwise, you can select the Browse button. If you select the Browse button, the Select Drawing File dialog box will appear. This is very similar to an Open File dialog box. Using the Browse button method will insert the entire drawing into your current drawing. It will not limit it to just a specific Block from that drawing. In order to select a specific Block from a drawing other than the current drawing, AutoCAD® has the Design Center feature. This feature is described next.

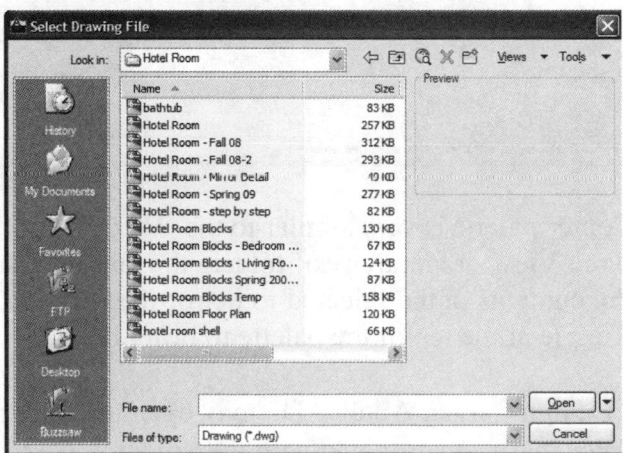

Design Center

The Design Center feature of AutoCAD® allows you to use items that were created on other drawings, and bring them into your current drawings. It is especially useful for Blocks, but can also be used for other things such as Dimension Styles, Layers, Text Styles, Layouts, etc.

You can bring up the Design Center palette by selecting the Design Center icon, located on the Standard toolbar.

Design Center
icon

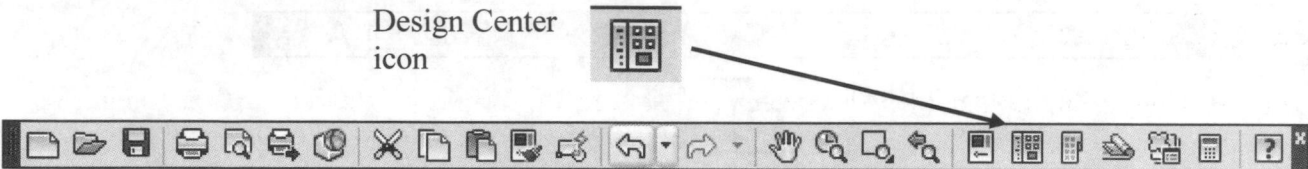

Once you select the icon, the Design Center palette will appear on your screen:

Tree View Toggle ⟍ ⟋ Views selector

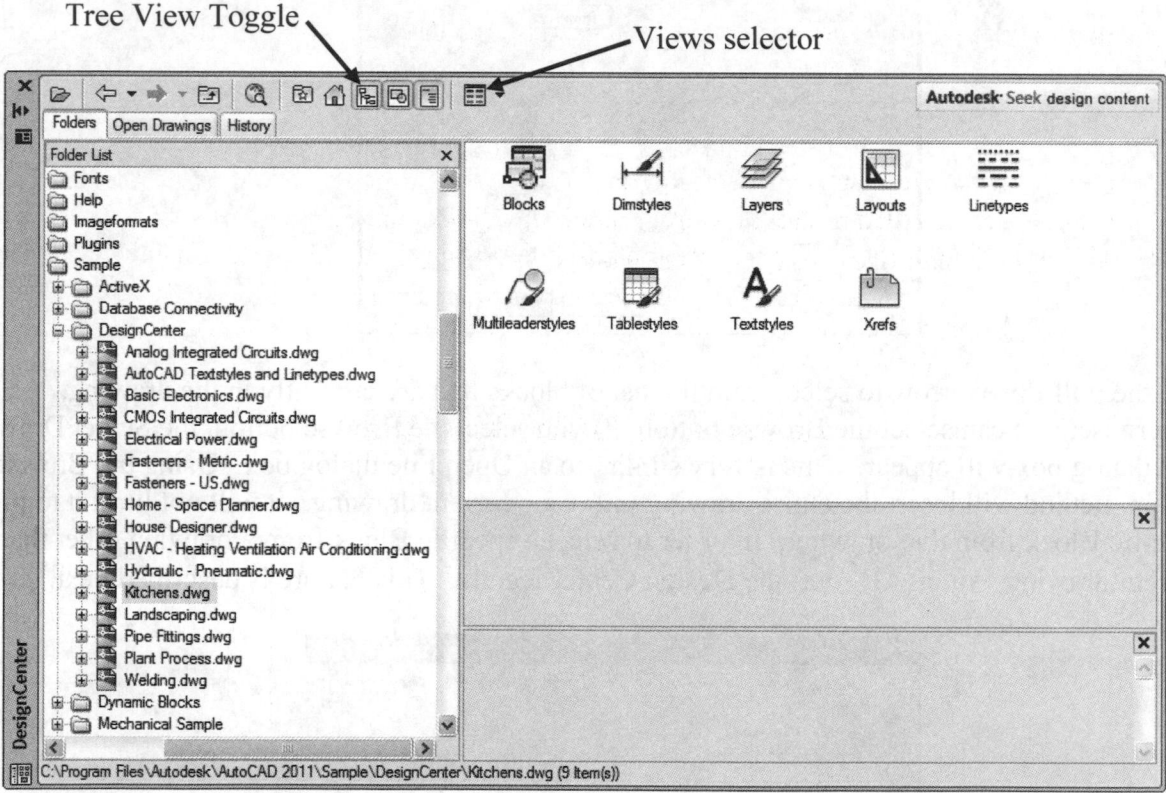

The appearance of the Design Center palette is very similar to the Windows tool My Computer. The left side of the palette shows a Tree View or hierarchy of folders that are on your computer. The right side of the palette shows the contents of the selected folder or file. If the Tree View is not displayed, pick the Tree View Toggle at the top of the palette to bring it up.

When you initially bring up the Design Center, AutoCAD® may open the folder within the AutoCAD® program to the samples that were provided with the program. Use the Tree on the left side to select the folder you want.   Using the Views selector icon can control the method by which the contents are displayed. In this example, the display is using Large icons.

If you always want the Design Center to open a specific folder when you first bring it up, you can right-click on that folder and select "Set as Home" from the shortcut menu. In addition, if there are multiple folders that you want to access frequently, you can right click on each folder (one at a time) and select "Add to Favorites" from the shortcut menu.

Using Design Center

The following examples assume that you currently have a drawing open and you wish to bring in items from existing drawings. It also assumes that you have already opened the Design Center palette and selected the drawing of your choice.

Bring Blocks into your drawing:

Blocks that were previously created, other than those in the drawing you are currently working on, are easy to bring into your drawing by using the Design Center.

1. Double-click the Blocks icon on the right side of the Design Center palette. The alternative is to expand the drawing by picking on the "+" in front of that drawing on the left side of the Design Center palette, and then single-click the Blocks icon.
2. The right side of the Design Center palette now displays all the blocks contained in the drawing. Click on the Block of your choice and drag it into your drawing. An alternate method is to double-click on the Block of your choice and follow the instructions of the Insert dialog box that appears.

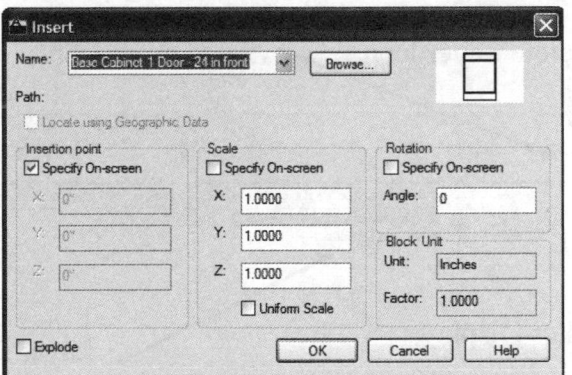

Double-clicking the Block will bring up the Insert dialog box

Bring Styles, etc. into Your Drawing

Bringing other items, such as Dimension Styles, Text Styles, Layers, Layouts, etc. are done in the same manner as bringing Blocks into your drawing. The only difference is that it may not be as obvious that it was brought into the drawing. You can use the Styles toolbar to verify that the Dimension Styles, Text Styles, and Table Styles were brought in. Use the Layers Manager to verify that Layers were brought in, etc.

Layers

Layers are available in AutoCAD®. Layers can be thought of as see-through sheets that are stacked on top of each other. You can use layers to organize and manage your objects. You can turn specific layers off, and they are no longer visible. You can lock any layer so that any objects on that layer cannot be changed. Some design teams require you to follow specific naming conventions for your layers, and other teams do not. If you are working independently, as the designer, it is your choice how you use and name layers. You can add any number of layers. Once layers are created, and you no longer need them, they can also be deleted. You cannot delete Layer 0. It is the default layer for AutoCAD® drawings. If you bring items in using Design Center, AutoCAD® will create a layer named Defpoints. You cannot delete this layer either – just ignore it.

The AutoCAD® Classic screen set-up includes the Layers toolbar at the top of the screen. If it is not on yours, you can right-click on any toolbar and select Layers to bring it up. The toolbar is as shown:

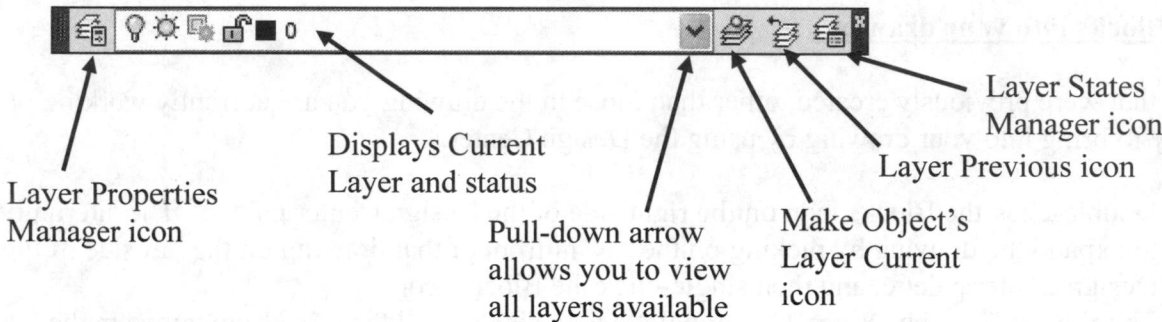

Layer Properties Manager icon

Displays Current Layer and status

Pull-down arrow allows you to view all layers available

Make Object's Layer Current icon

Layer Previous icon

Layer States Manager icon

Layer Properties Manager

When you select the Layer Properties Manager icon, a dialog box will appear:

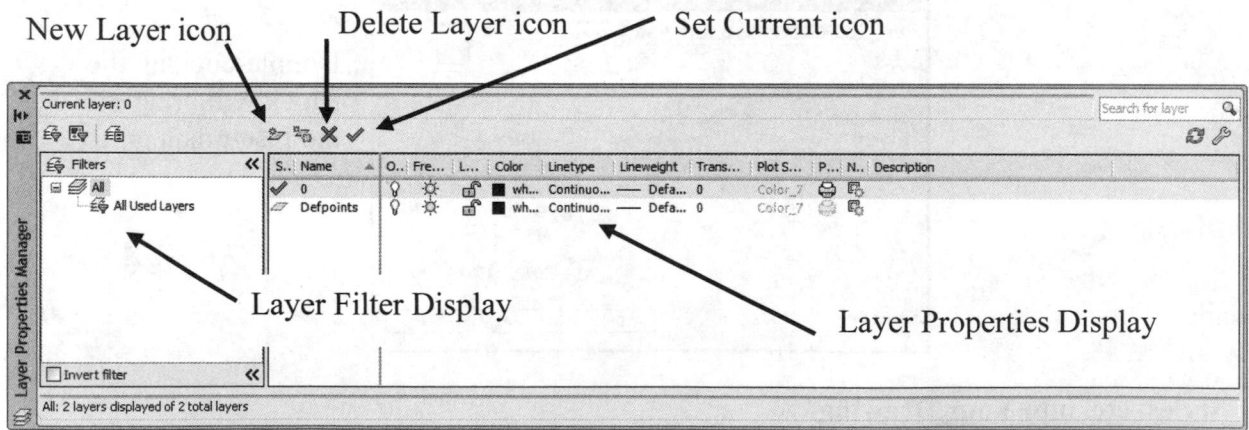

New Layer icon

Delete Layer icon

Set Current icon

Layer Filter Display

Layer Properties Display

Notice that the dialog box has two sides, the Layer Filter and the Layer Property displays. We will not be using Filters, so, these instructions will be limited to Layer Properties.

The dialog box shown has Layers 0 and Defpoints. We will use this dialog box to create new layers, and define properties for those layers.

Creating a New Layer

Pick the New Layer icon. A new row appears on the list. This represents the new layer and is automatically given a default name of Layer1, which is highlighted and ready for editing. As an example, let's name this layer Existing Structure. Simply type that in place of Layer1.

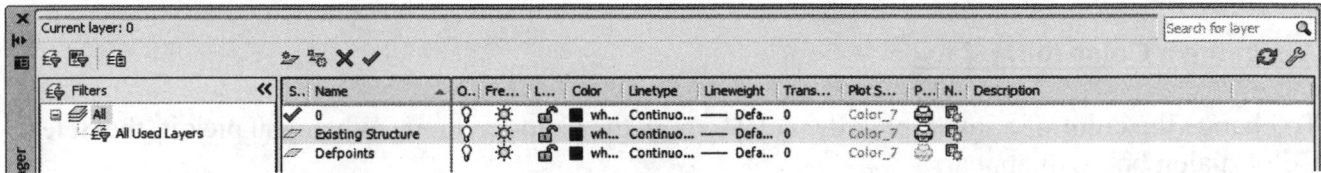

There are several columns in the Layer Properties display. The width of the columns can be adjusted by moving your cursor to the line separating the column names and dragging. Double-clicking will adjust the column to minimum width and still allow the word to fit.

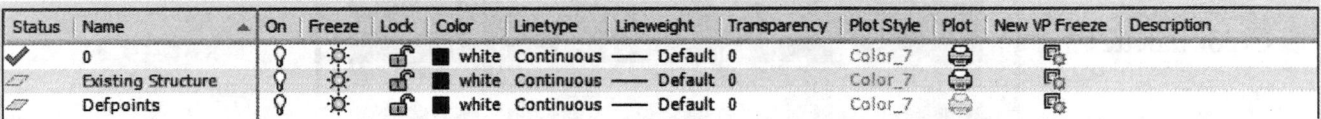

Visibility of Layers

Layers can be turned on or off, frozen or thawed, and locked or unlocked, by picking the relative icon in each column. These icons change as each option is selected:

Icon	Meaning
On, Thawed, Unlocked
Off, Frozen, Locked

When a layer is turned off or frozen, the objects on that layer become invisible. The difference between the two is subtle – the drawing is regenerated when you thaw a frozen layer, but it is not when you turn a layer that was off back on. The typical designer doesn't care about this subtlety. These differences are not important.

What is important is this: when in a Layout, freezing a layer in the "current viewport" is the best way to control visibility – especially for printing. If you turn a layer off, it is invisible in all viewports; this is usually not what is desired. This difference comes in handy when you have multiple viewports or multiple Layouts.

When a layer is Locked, it remains visible, but you cannot change or delete any of the objects that reside on that layer. This is a good tool for preserving objects, such as those on layers provided by the architect. You use this feature when you don't want to risk changing objects that were provided by others on your design team.

For the new layer we just created, we will leave the icons On, Thawed, and Unlocked.

Assigning a Color to the Layer

To change the color of a layer, pick the color icon in the Color column. When you pick it, the Select Color dialog box will appear.

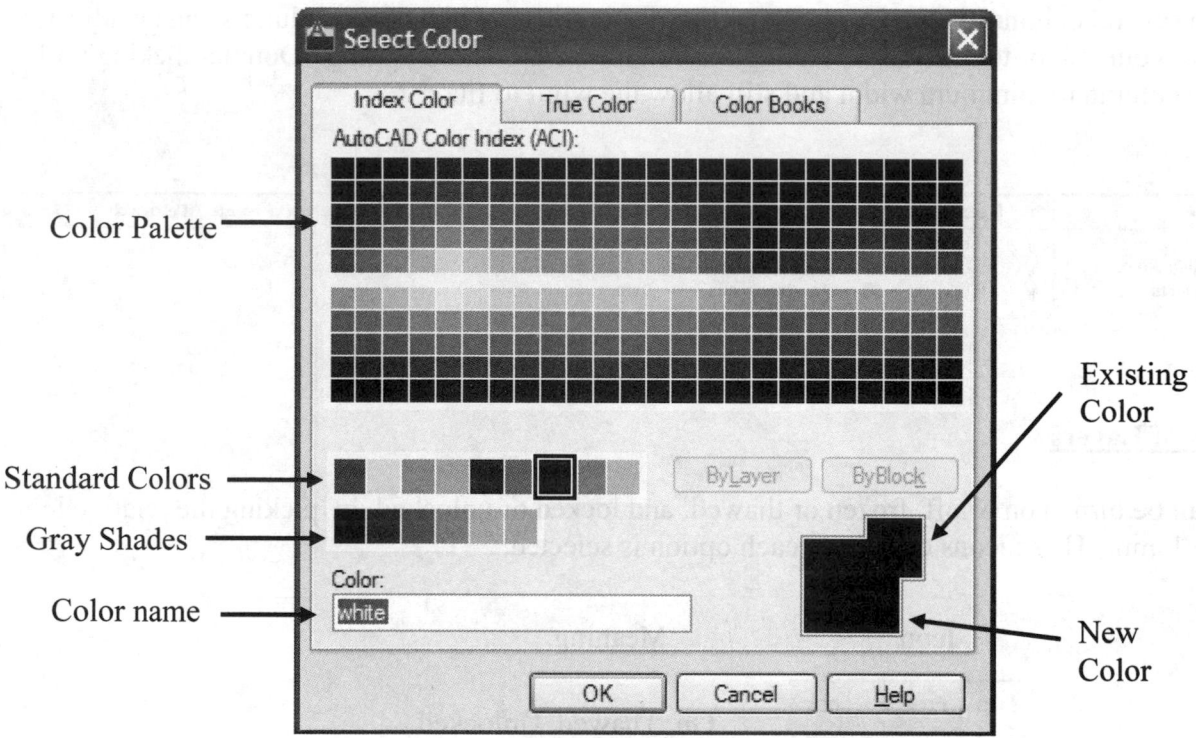

There are three tabs to choose your color: Index Color, True Color, and Color Books. The index color is shown above and has pre-defined standard colors and numbered colors. The other tabs are illustrated below:

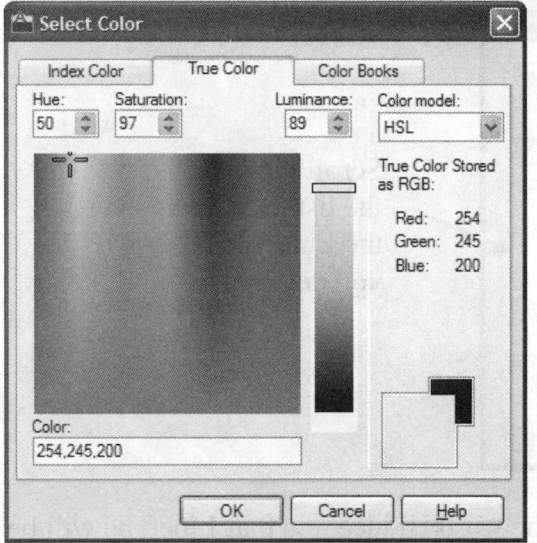 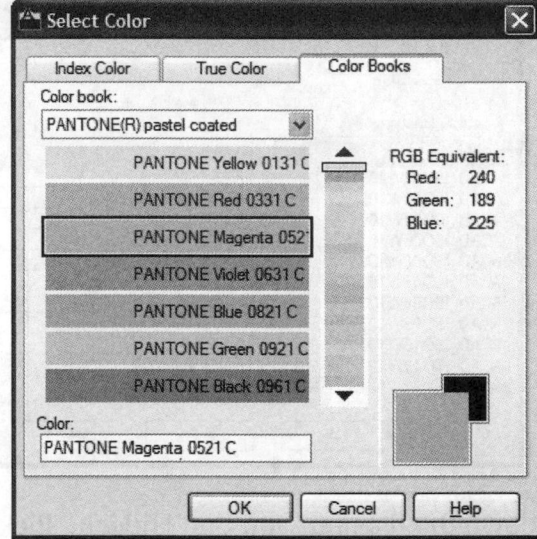

Under the Color Books tab, there is a pull-down arrow that you can use to select from a variety of available color books, including Pantone colors.

Choose the color you desire for your layer then pick the OK button to exit the dialog box.

Assigning a Linetype to the Layer

To change the linetype of a layer, pick the word in the Linetype column (in this case the word is Continuous). When you pick it, the Select Linetype dialog box will appear.

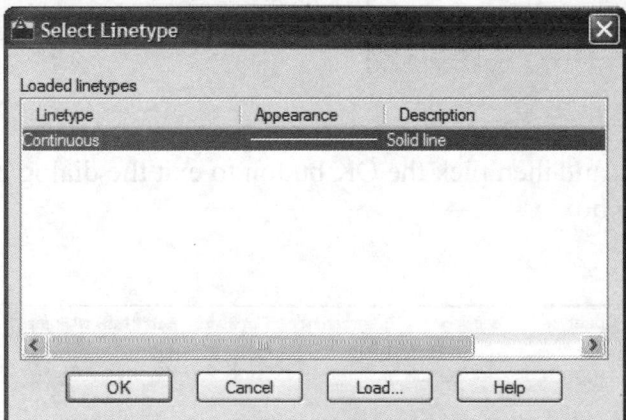

There are a number of different line types to choose from in AutoCAD®, however, they may not be loaded in your drawing yet. These are stored in a common AutoCAD® program file in order to minimize the amount of memory each drawing will require.

As an example, suppose we wish to change the Linetype to a hidden line. Since that is not available in the Select Linetype dialog box, we will have to load it. Pick the Load... button. The Load or Reload Linetypes dialog box will appear.

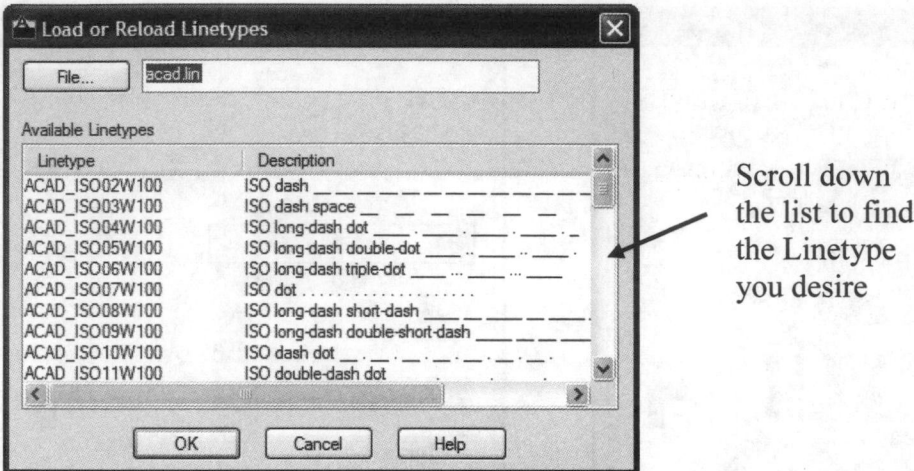

Scroll down the list to find the Linetype you desire

Scroll down the list until you find Hidden. Pick on the word Hidden and that Linetype will be highlighted. Then pick the OK button to exit the dialog box and return to Select Linetype dialog box. In that dialog box, the Hidden Linetype is now available as a Linetype choice.

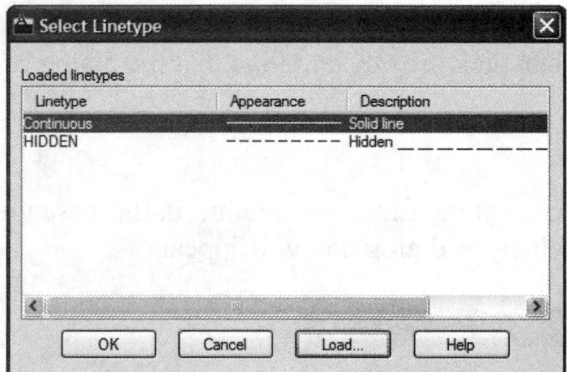

Pick the HIDDEN Linetype to select it, and then pick the OK button to exit the dialog box and return to the Layer Properties Manager dialog box.

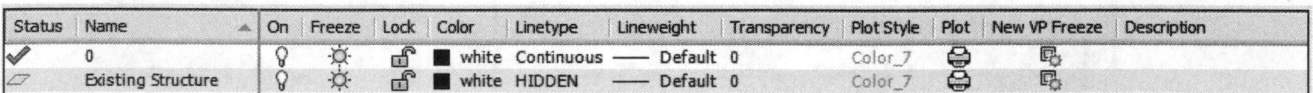

Status	Name		On	Freeze	Lock	Color	Linetype	Lineweight	Transparency	Plot Style	Plot	New VP Freeze	Description
✓	0	▲	♀	☼	🔓	■ white	Continuous	—— Default	0	Color_7	🖨	🖫	
◿	Existing Structure		♀	☼	🔓	■ white	HIDDEN	—— Default	0	Color_7	🖨	🖫	

Linetype Scale

Each linetype is defined as a specific size. For a hidden line, AutoCAD defines the length of the dash, and the length of the space between dashes. With large drawings used in interior design, the hidden line may actually appear as a solid line. To correct the visibility of the hidden line, you can change the linetype scale. To change the scale of all linetypes in your drawing, you need to type in the command "ltscale" on the command line:

Example:

Shown here is a countertop with two cabinets underneath. The lines of the cabinets should be dashed because they are hidden lines. We can create those lines on a layer with the linetype of hidden. However, because of the size of the object, it is difficult to distinguish that these are dashed lines.

We can correct this by typing the LTSCALE command. The value of the scale factor can be determined by trial and error.

Command: **ltscale⏎**
Enter new linetype scale factor <1.0000>: **10⏎**
Regenerating model.
Command:

The following shows the results of using the scale factor of 10:

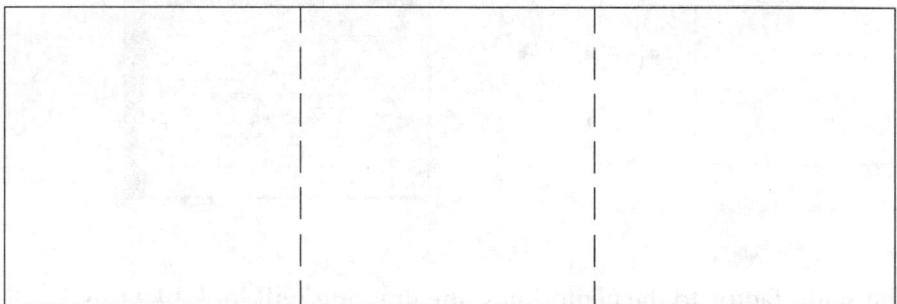

As you can see, the appearance of the hidden lines is much better.

Using the LTSCALE command globally changes the scale factor of all linetypes on your drawing. This may not always be desirable. If you also have centerlines on your drawing, applying the same scale factor may not be desired. In that case, you can use the Properties pallet to change the linetype scale of an individual object selected

Example:

Suppose we had a circle located on the center of the countertop of the previous example, with lines drawn and the linetypes of the lines are set to "center". With the current LTSCALE factor of 10, the centerlines of the circle will appear as follows:

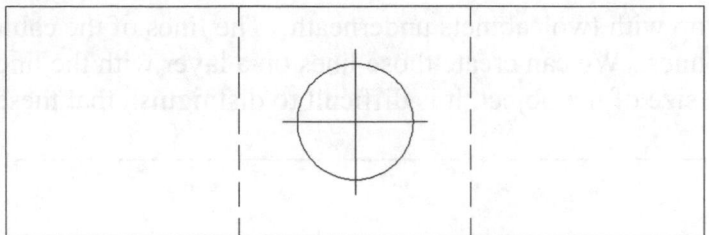

As you can see, they do not properly appear as centerlines. Since we like the scale factor we have chosen for the hidden lines, we do not want to globally change that factor by using the LTSCALE command. Instead, we can use the Properties pallet, select the centerlines, and change the Lintype scale factor for those lines.

Here we can see that the two centerlines were selected and the Properties pallet Linetype scale portion was also selected. We can simply type in a new scale factor for the centerlines. In this case, a scale factor of .5 seems to work best. Choosing .5 would have been the same as a global scale factor of 5 since a global scale factor of 10 is already applied (.5 x 10 = 5).

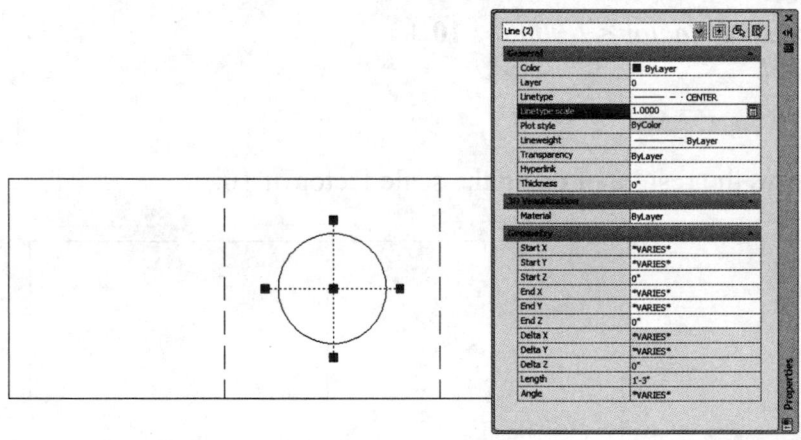

After you apply the scale factor to the centerlines, the drawing will look like this:

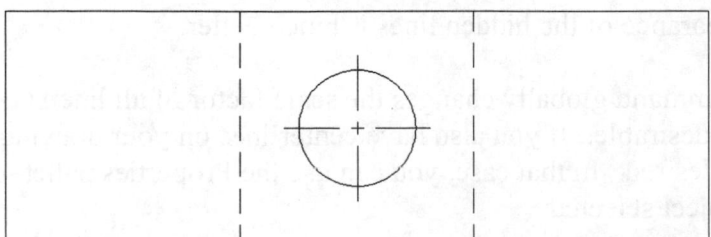

Current Layer

The Current Layer is the layer that objects will reside on as you draw. There are a number of ways to make a layer the Current Layer. While still in the Layer Properties Manager, you can highlight the layer and pick the Set Current icon. When a layer is the current layer, the green check mark is shown in the Status column for that layer.

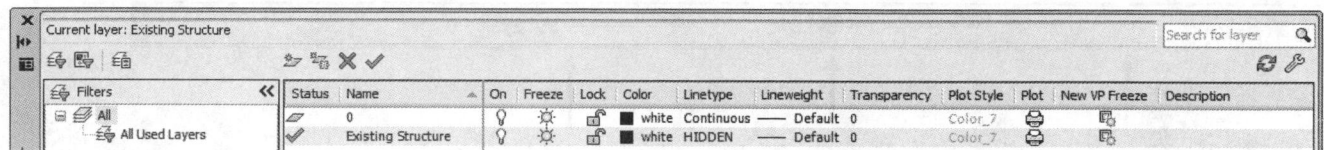

Picking the X on the upper left corner of the dialog box will exit the Layer Properties Manager dialog box and return you to the drawing screen.

The Layers toolbar will now show the layer you selected as the Current Layer.

Using the Layers toolbar, you can change the Current Layer by using the pull-down arrow and picking the layer. As an example, lets make layer 0 the Current Layer:

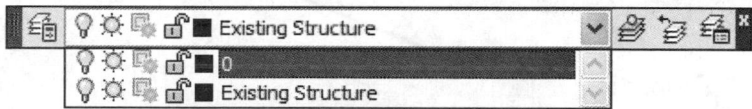

Layer 0 is now displayed as the Current Layer:

You can also use the Make Objects Layer Current icon. With nothing in the command line, select an object. The blue grips will display, and the Layers toolbar will show the name of the layer that the object is on.
As an example, suppose there are two circles on the drawing. One circle is on layer 0, and the other is on layer Existing Structure. Regardless of the current layer displayed, when an object is selected, the name of the layer that it resides on will be displayed in the Layer toolbar:

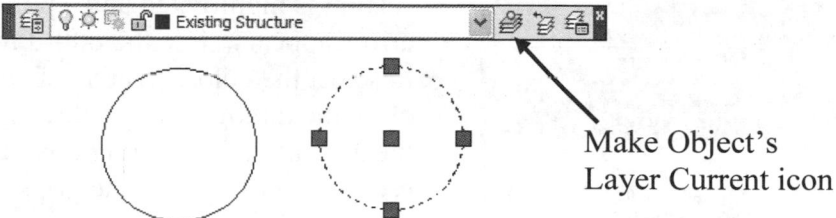

Make Object's
Layer Current icon

Pick the Make Object's Layer Current icon. This now makes the Layer that the selected object is on the Current Layer.

Properties

The AutoCAD® default screen set-up includes the Properties toolbar at the top of the screen. If it is not on yours, you can right-click on any toolbar and select Properties to bring it up. The toolbar is as shown:

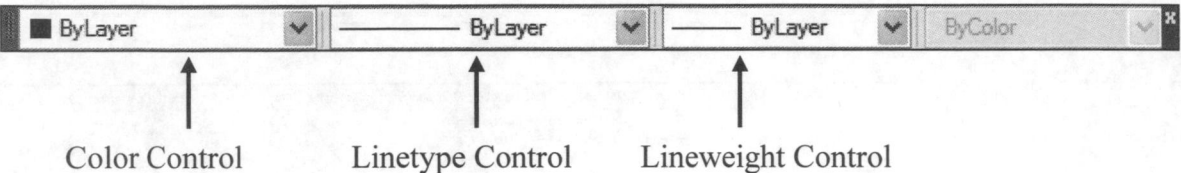

Color Control   Linetype Control   Lineweight Control

All three controls have ByLayer and ByBlock as selection options. The default is ByLayer, which means that the values that were set for that Layer will be used for the objects drawn. ByBlock allows you to retain the properties of the Blocks inserted.

Changing Object Properties

You can change properties of objects using the Properties icon. The Properties icon is located on the Standard toolbar:

Properties
icon

When you select this icon, the Properties palette will appear:

Object Selection
Display

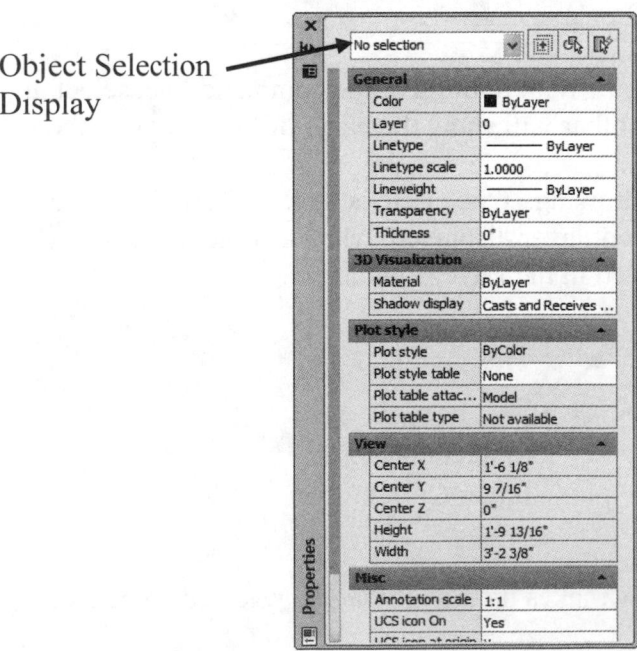

Using the Properties dialog box allows you to change properties for selected objects. You can change any of the items that are shown in the dialog box. For example, if you want to change the color of an item, pick on Color, and the entire section is highlighted and a pull-down arrow appears. Use the pull-down arrow to select the color. When you are done, close the dialog box by selecting the X in the gray bar of the dialog box. Use the escape key to remove the grips from the selected objects.

Lineweight

Typically, the object lines for your designs should have a thicker line than the dimension lines. That makes it easier to distinguish the items of interest. AutoCAD® has a feature that allows you to control and view the lineweight. This can be done for individual objects or for any object drawn on a layer that has the lineweight defined. This is very similar to assigning colors or linetype.

Before setting the lineweight, make sure the units that you select for lineweight is Inches and not Millimeters. To ensure that you have the correct units, use the pull-down menu item Format, and select Lineweight.

The Lineweight Settings dialog box will appear. Ensure that the radio button in front of Inches is selected and the check box for Display Lineweight is checked. When you are done, pick the OK button to close the dialog box.

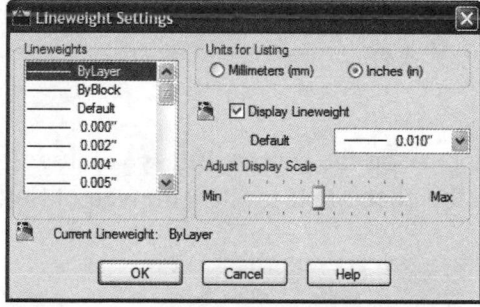

To change the lineweight of all objects on a specific layer, use the Layer Properties icon to bring up the Layer Properties Manager dialog box.

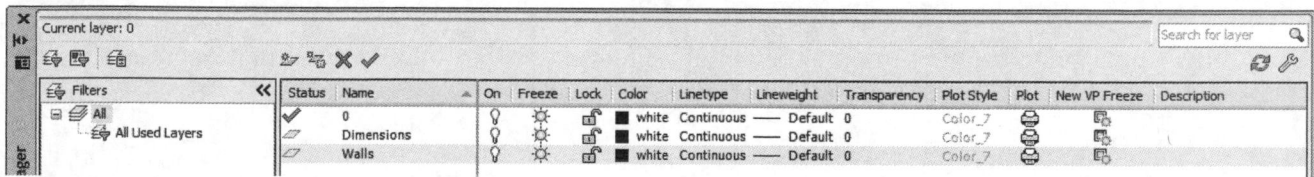

In this example, we will change the Lineweight of layer Walls to a thicker value than the default value. The default value of Lineweight is set at .25 mm (which is approximately .010 inches). We will choose .020″ to make the lines twice as thick.

In the dialog box, pick on the word Default under the Lineweight column of the layer Walls. A Lineweight dialog box will appear. Scroll down the list of available Lineweights and pick .020″. When you are done, pick the OK button to close the dialog box.

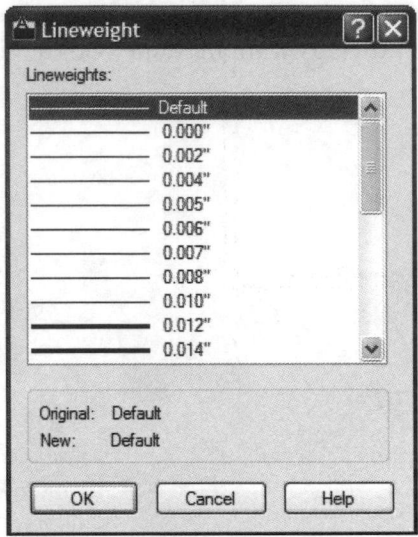 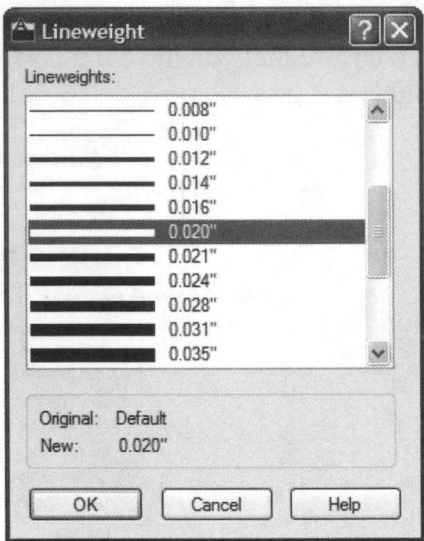

Notice that the new value of the Lineweight for the layer Walls is displayed in the Layer Properties Manager dialog box. Pick the X in the upper left corner to close the dialog box.

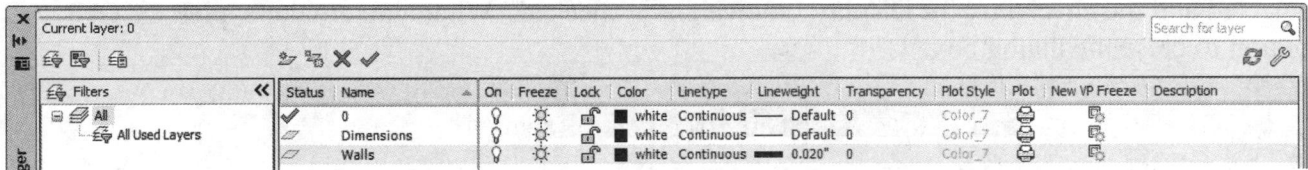

The visibility of the thicker lines will not appear on the screen unless you toggle the Show/Hide Lineweight switch on the status bar (or use the check box in the Lineweight Settings dialog box).

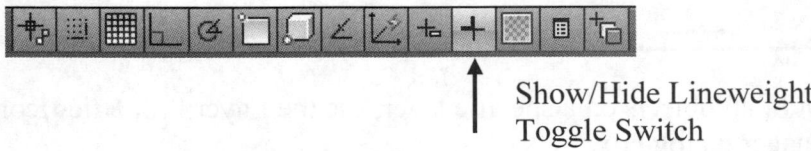

Show/Hide Lineweight
Toggle Switch

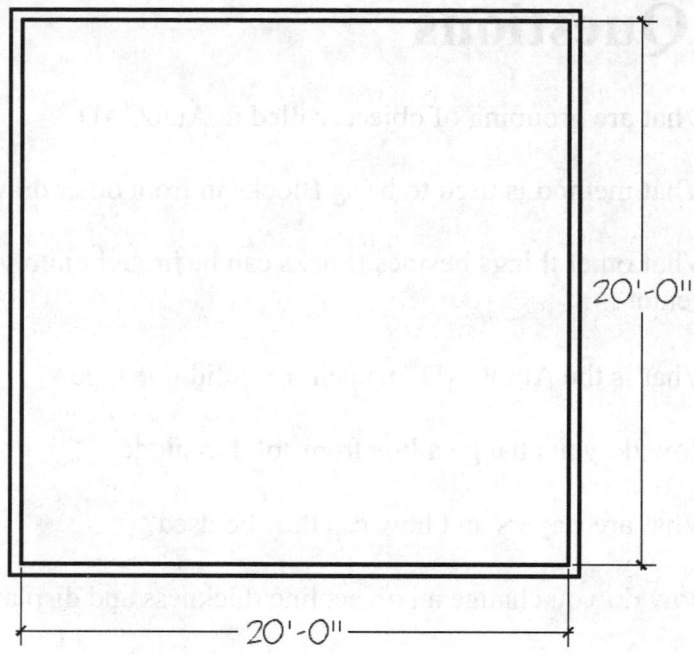

This is an example of
the visibility of the
lineweight. The object
lines are twice as thick
as the dimension lines

Summary

In this chapter you have learned to:

- Group objects together to become a block
- Insert blocks that exist within the drawing and entire files from outside the drawing
- Use Design Center to bring blocks in from other drawings
- Create new layers
- Load new linetypes
- Rename and define properties – color, linetype, lineweight – for layers
- Change properties of individual objects

Review Questions

1. What are grouping of objects called in AutoCAD®?

2. What method is used to bring Blocks in from other drawings?

3. What other things besides Blocks can be brought into your drawing using Design Center?

4. What is the AutoCAD® name for a solid line type?

5. How do you change a line from solid to hidden?

6. What are Layers and how can they be used?

7. How do you change an object line thickness and display it on your screen?

8. What are object properties and how can they be changed?

9. How do you correct the visibility of a hidden line if it still appears solid?

10. Why freezing a layer in the "current viewport" more useful than turning a layer off?

Exercises

1. Open the Conference Room from Exercise 1 of Chapter 5. Use the Insert Block command to import the Conference Chair you created from Exercise 3 of Chapter 5. Use the copy and move commands to locate the chairs in the conference room.

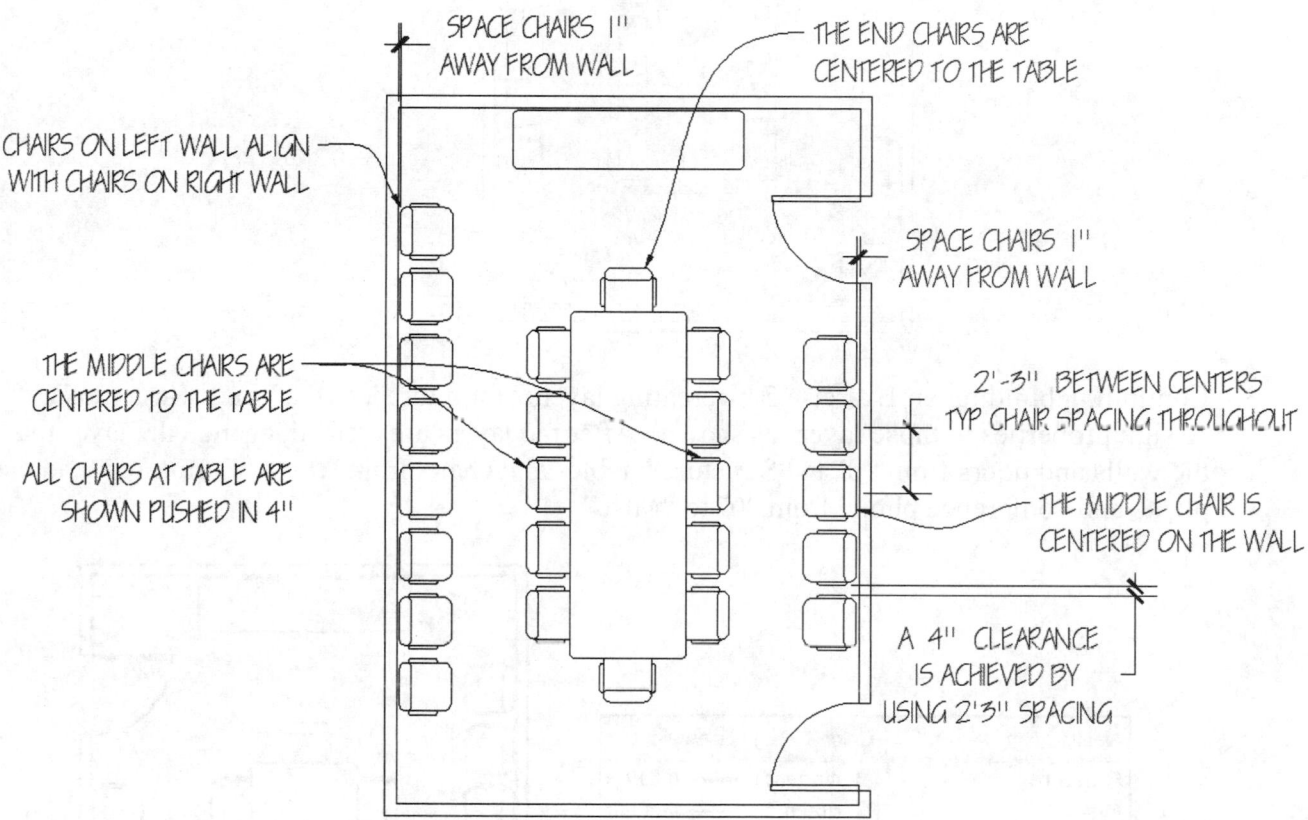

SPACE CHAIRS 1"
AWAY FROM WALL

THE END CHAIRS ARE
CENTERED TO THE TABLE

CHAIRS ON LEFT WALL ALIGN
WITH CHAIRS ON RIGHT WALL

SPACE CHAIRS 1"
AWAY FROM WALL

THE MIDDLE CHAIRS ARE
CENTERED TO THE TABLE

2'-3" BETWEEN CENTERS
TYP CHAIR SPACING THROUGHOUT

ALL CHAIRS AT TABLE ARE
SHOWN PUSHED IN 4"

THE MIDDLE CHAIR IS
CENTERED ON THE WALL

A 4" CLEARANCE
IS ACHIEVED BY
USING 2'3" SPACING

2. Download the Plant and Conference Phone drawings from the publishers web site. Use Design Center to put two plants and the conference phone into the conference room drawing as shown:

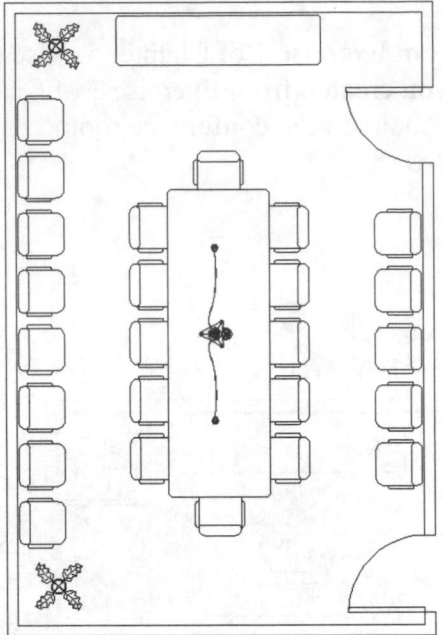

3. Continuing building on Exercise 2 by creating layers "Furniture", "Misc" and "Structure". Assign properties to those layers as shown. After the layers are created, change the layer that the walls and doors from "0" to "Structure"; tables and chairs from "0" to "Furniture"; and the plants and conference phone from "0" to "Misc".

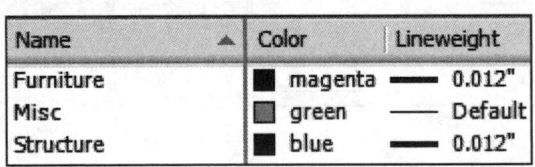

Name	▲	Color	Lineweight
Furniture		magenta	—— 0.012"
Misc		green	—— Default
Structure		blue	—— 0.012"

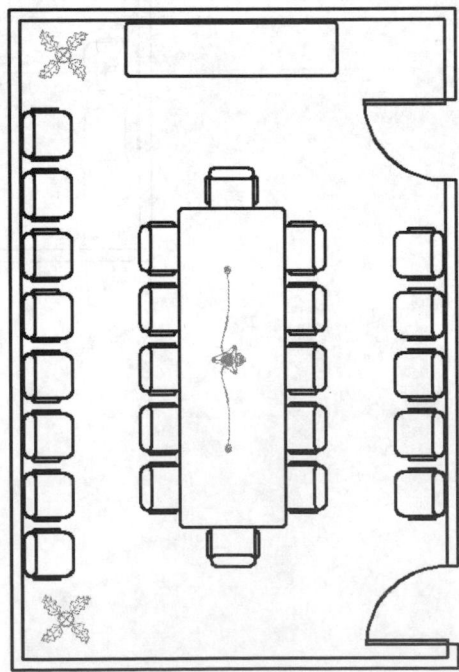

4. Draw the Galley Kitchen. Use Design Center to insert the Range, Refrigerator, and Sink. These are provided with the AutoCAD® program, and are also available on the publisher's web site.

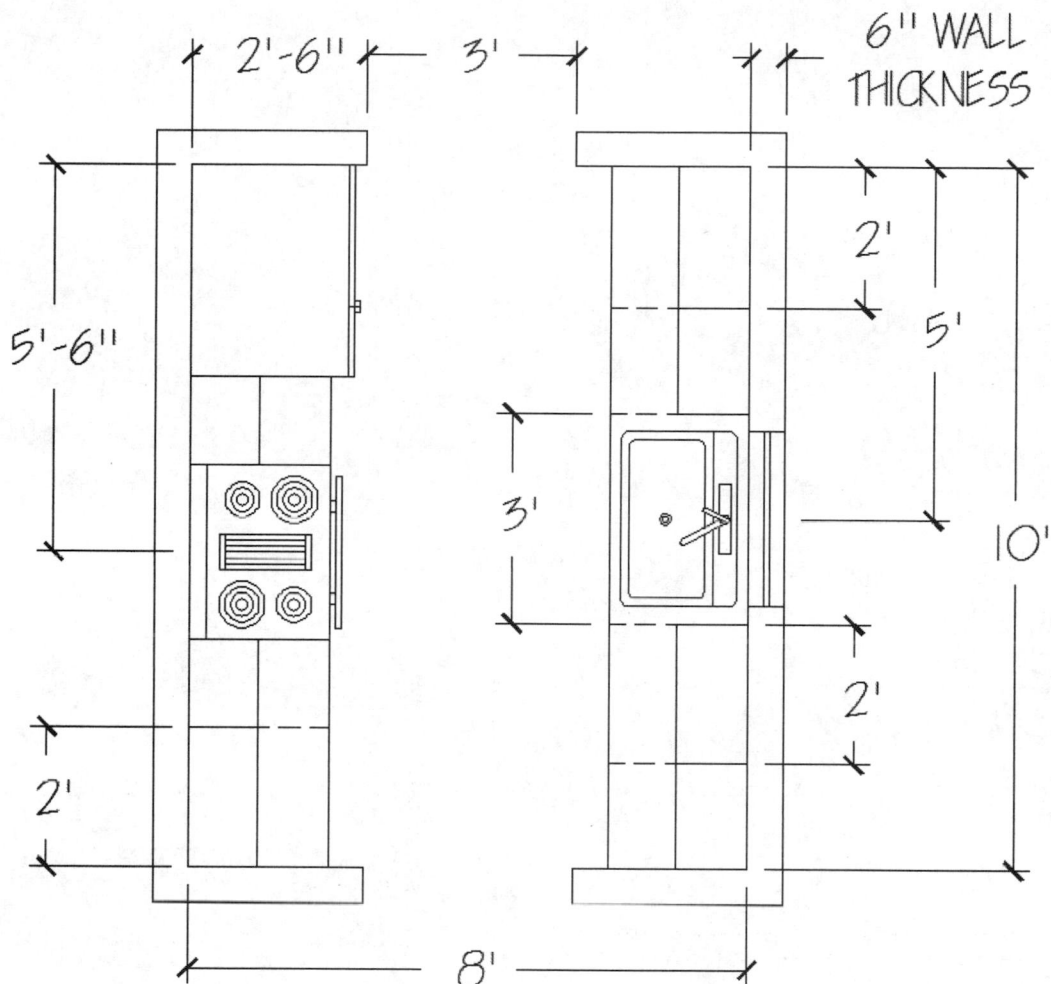

Notes:

Chapter 10
Hotel Suite Project – Tutorial 4

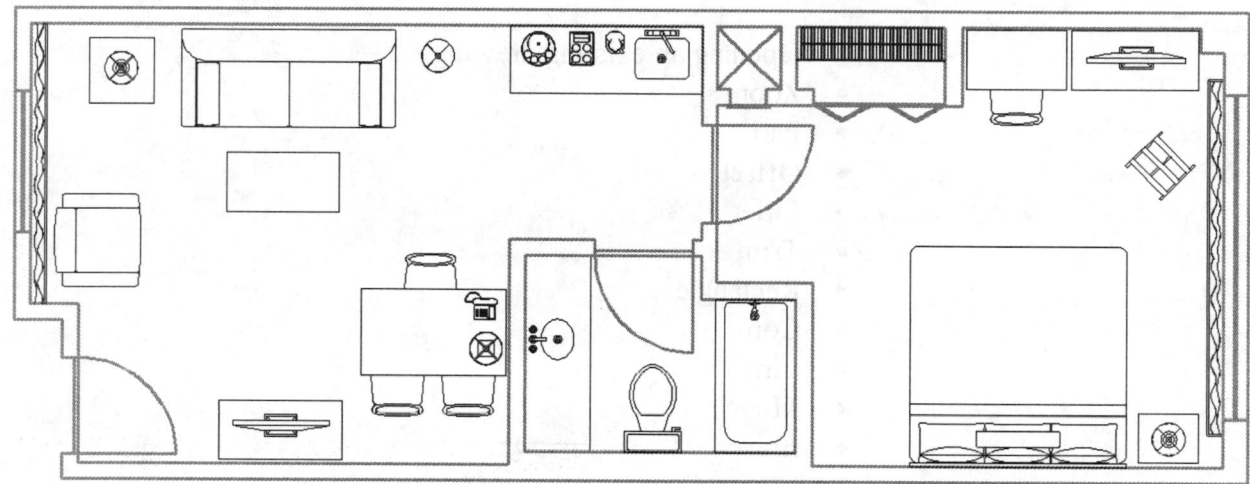

Learning Objectives:

- **To continue creating a drawing of a real-world application of AutoCAD®**
  - o **Use Design Center to insert furniture Blocks into the plan view**
  - o **Create and use Layers**
  - o **Change object Properties**
- **To utilize and reinforce the use of the AutoCAD® commands learned in the previous chapters**

This tutorial builds on Tutorial 3 found in Chapter 8. In this tutorial, we will put the furniture into our floor plan of the Hotel Suite. In addition, we will create and use layers. We will start with the simple rectangular shapes first. Rather than bring these in as Blocks, we will create them. When you are finished with this tutorial, all the furniture in the plan view of the hotel suite will be completed.

Commands & Techniques:

- Opening an existing drawing
- Zoom
- Pan
- Offset
- Fillet
- Trim
- Rectangle
- Copy
- Line
- Move
- Erase
- Design Center
- Rotate
- Explode
- Move
- Layers
- Properties
- Save

Placing Furniture/Fixtures on the Floor Plan

Before beginning, open the Hotel Suite drawing that you updated in Tutorial 3.

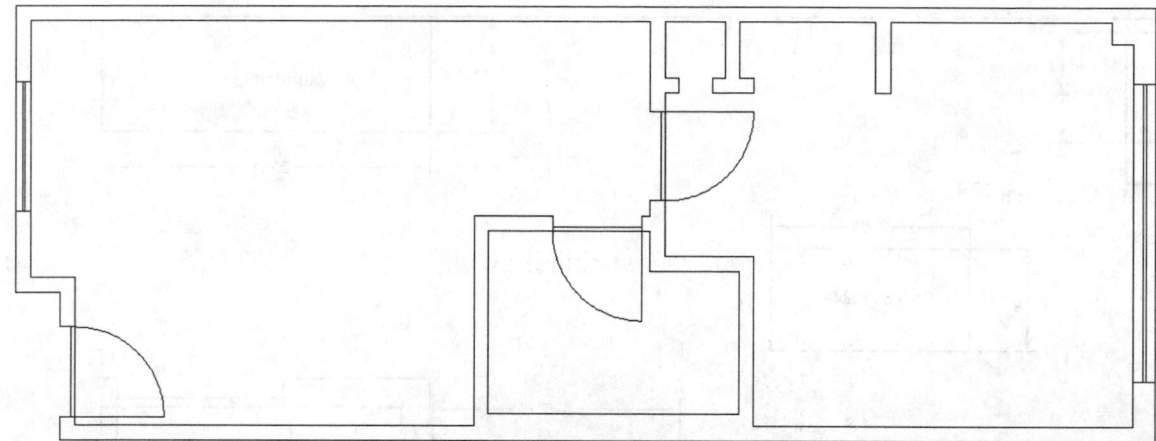

Many of the items of furniture, fixtures, etc. are already pre-drawn and have been provided for you in the form of Blocks. However, for the simple items that are rectangular shaped, we will draw those ourselves. The following drawing shows all the rectangular shapes we will draw.

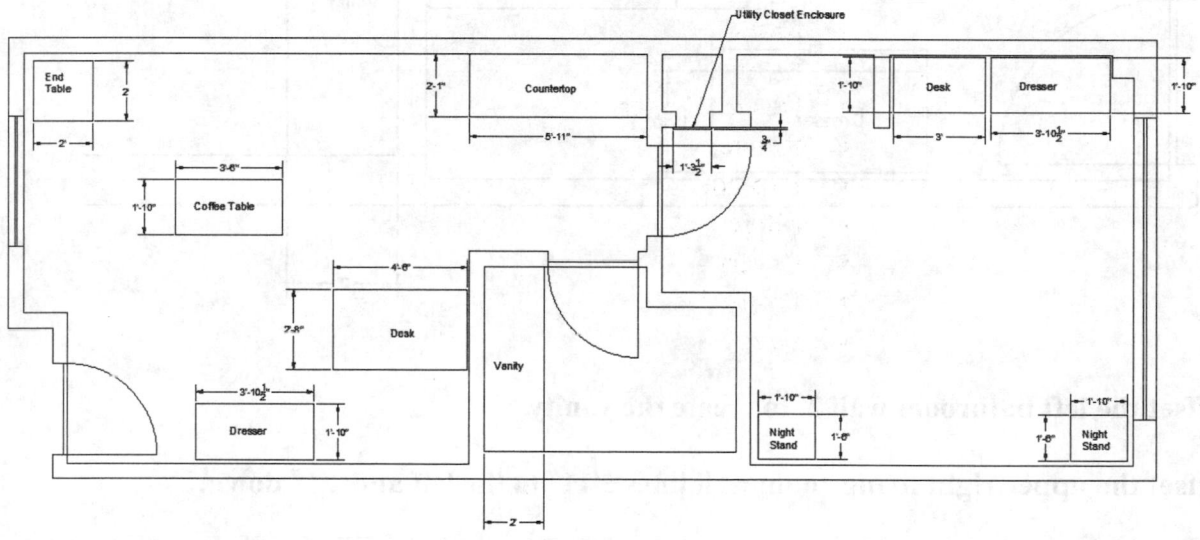

Let's start with the Living Room area and Bathroom. Although a drawing is provided, a listing of items and their sizes are as follows:

End Table:	2′ x 2′
Coffee Table:	3′6″ x 1′10″
Countertop:	5′11″ x 2′1″
Desk:	4′6″ x 2′ 8″
Dresser:	3′10-1/2″ x 1′10″
Vanity:	2′ x wall-to-wall

The vanity in the bathroom is the full length between the walls. The countertop is nestled in the corner of the living room. Both of these pieces are permanently located in place. Since these are movable, all other pieces are located approximately as shown.

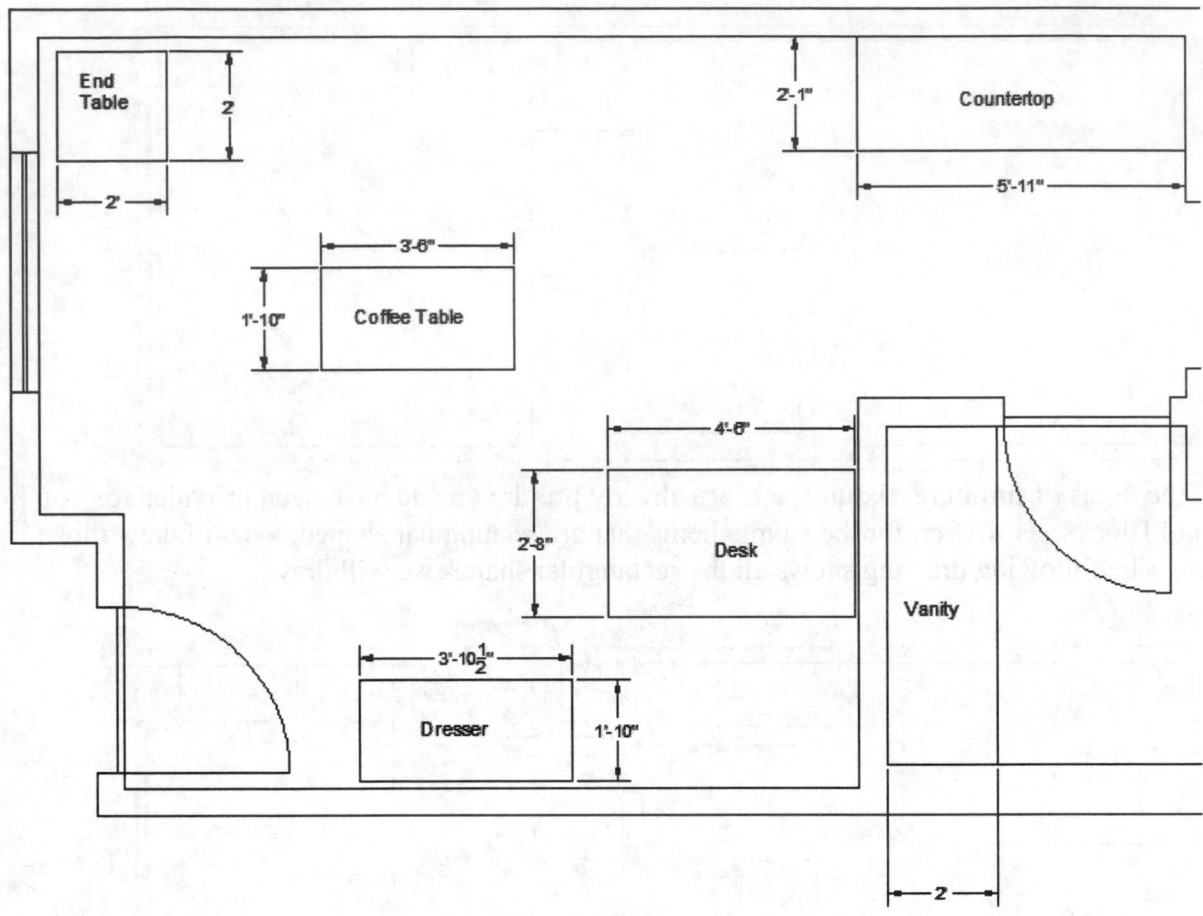

1. **Offset the left bathroom wall 2′ to create the vanity.**

2. **Offset the upper right living room wall lines 5′11″ to the left and 2′1″ down.**

3. **Use either the Fillet or Trim command to complete the countertop.**

4. **Use the Rectangle command to create the End Table, Coffee Table, Desk, and Dresser.**

    -   Use the dimensions and drawing to create and locate these items on the plan view.

Now we will create the rectangular shapes in the Bedroom. Although a drawing is provided, a listing of items and their sizes are as follows:

Night Stand:	1'10″ x 1'6″
Desk:	3' x 1'10″
Dresser:	3'10-1/2″ x 1'10″ (Same as the one in the living room)
Utility Enclosure:	1'3-1/2″ x 3/4″

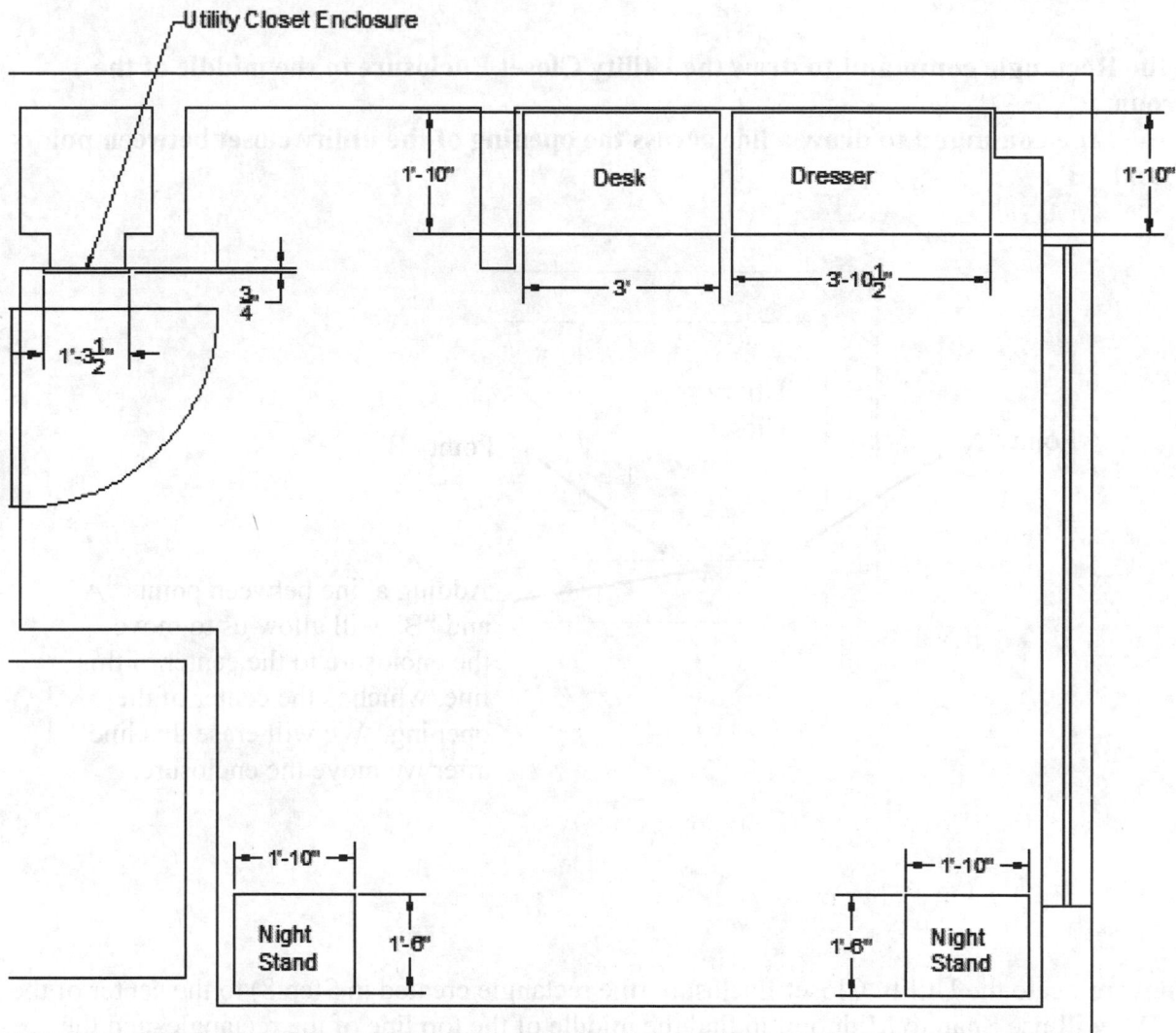

5. **Use the Rectangle command to create the Desk and one Night Stand.**

- Use the dimensions and drawing to create and locate these items on the plan view.

6. **Use the Copy command to create a second Night Stand.**

7. **Use the Copy command to duplicate the dresser created for the living room and locate it in the bedroom to the approximate location shown.**

The Utility Closet Enclosure is centered in the opening. In order to get the enclosure located where we want it, we will first create it in the middle of the room, then move it to the center of the opening. To find the center of the opening, we will draw a line across the opening.

8. **Use the Rectangle command to draw the Utility Closet Enclosure in the middle of the bedroom.**
9. **Use the Line command to draw a line across the opening of the utility closet between points "A" and "B".**

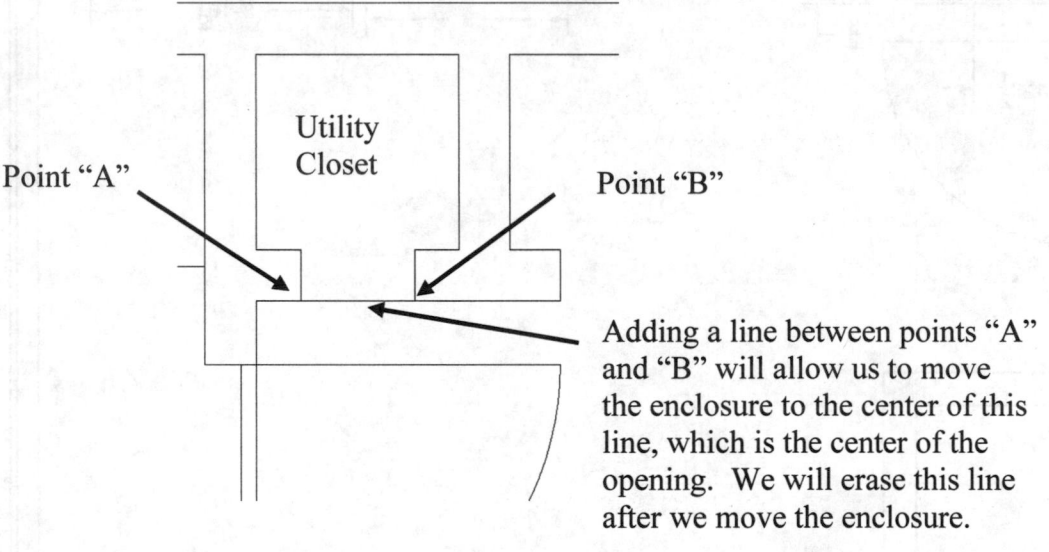

Point "A"

Utility Closet

Point "B"

Adding a line between points "A" and "B" will allow us to move the enclosure to the center of this line, which is the center of the opening. We will erase this line after we move the enclosure.

We will now relocate the Utility Closet Enclosure (the rectangle created in Step 8) to the center of the opening. We will use Snap to Midpoint to find the middle of the top line of the rectangle, and the middle of the line created in Step 9. Prior to moving on to Step 10, make sure Object Snap (OSNAP) is turned on and Midpoint is selected. As an alternative, you can use the Snap to Midpoint icon of the Object Snap toolbar twice during the Move command.

10. **Use the Move command to relocate the rectangle created in Step 8 to the center of the line created in Step 9.**

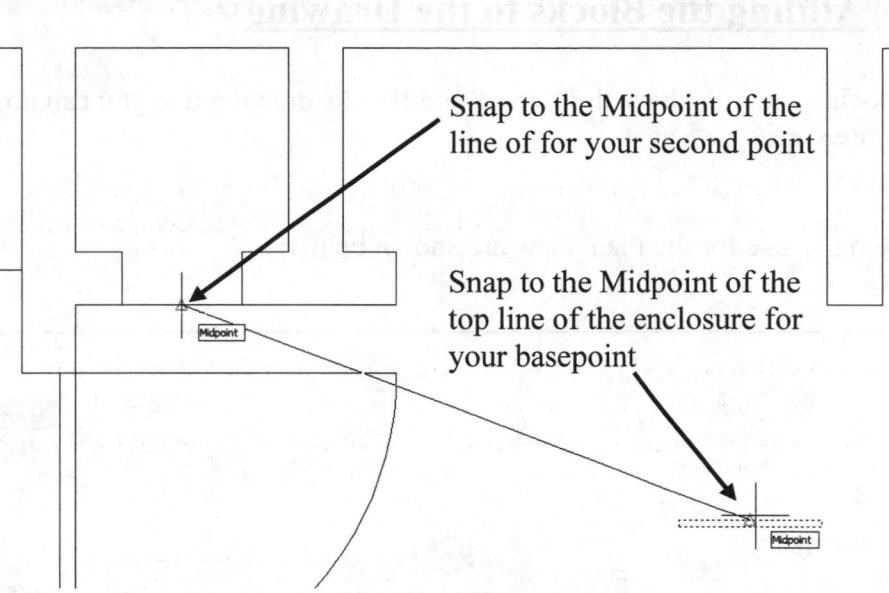

Snap to the Midpoint of the line of for your second point

Snap to the Midpoint of the top line of the enclosure for your basepoint

11. Erase the line that was created in Step 9. Use a Selection Window (Left-to-Right) to pick just the line and not the rectangle.

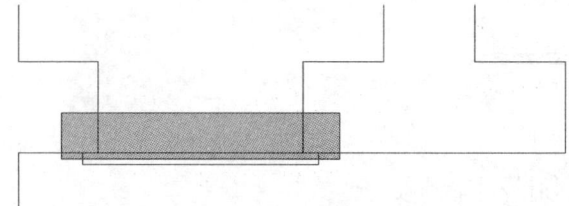

When you are done, your completed drawing will look like this:

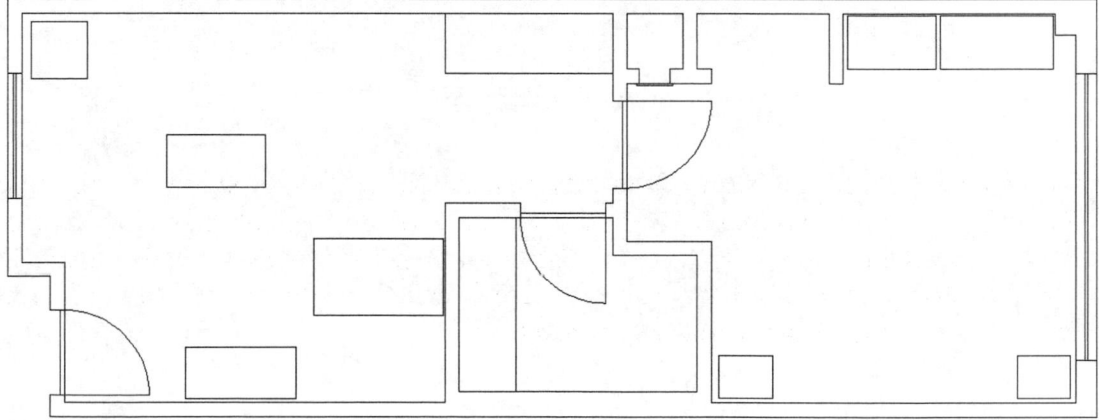

Now that we have all the rectangular shapes created, we will use Design Center to bring in the blocks for the furniture, fixtures, etc.

Adding the Blocks to the Drawing

Prior to bringing the blocks in, you must have the Hotel Suite Blocks drawing that you can download from the publisher's web site.

The Blocks that we are going to use for the Plan View are shown below:

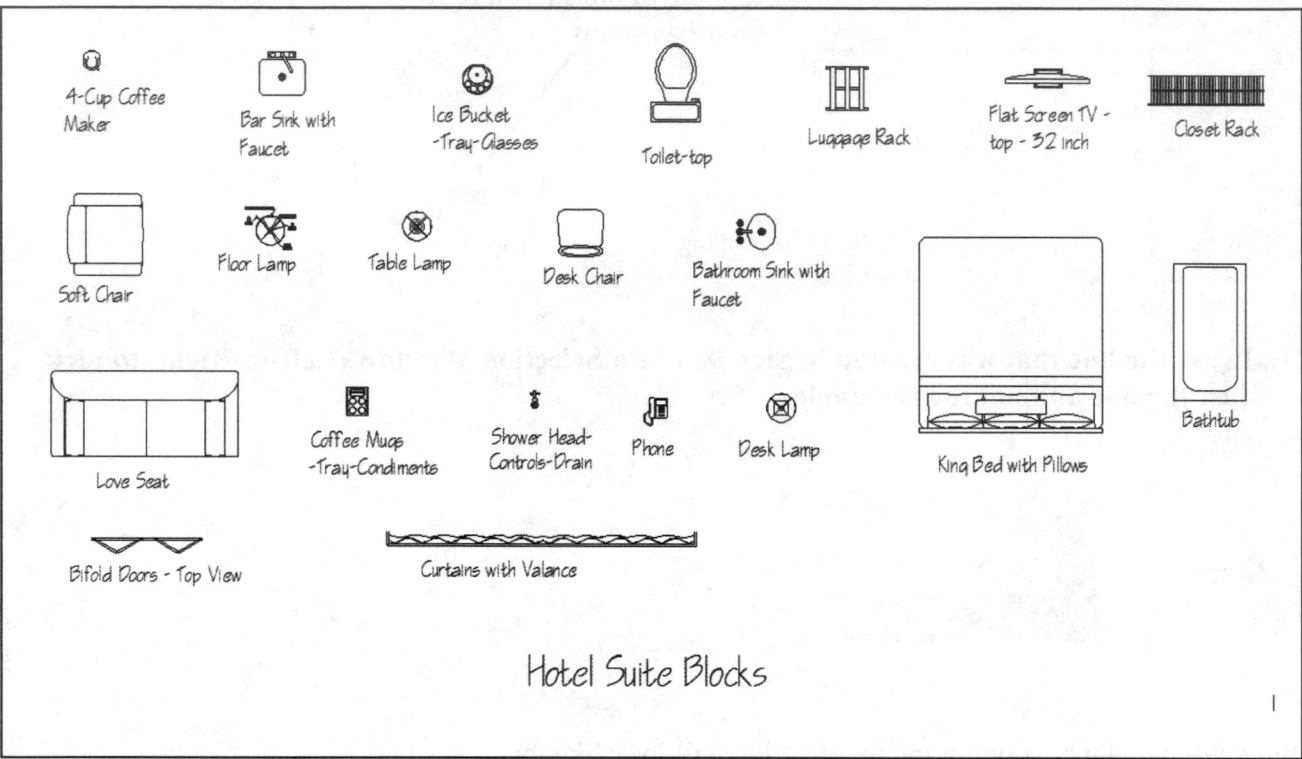

Adding Blocks to the Bedroom

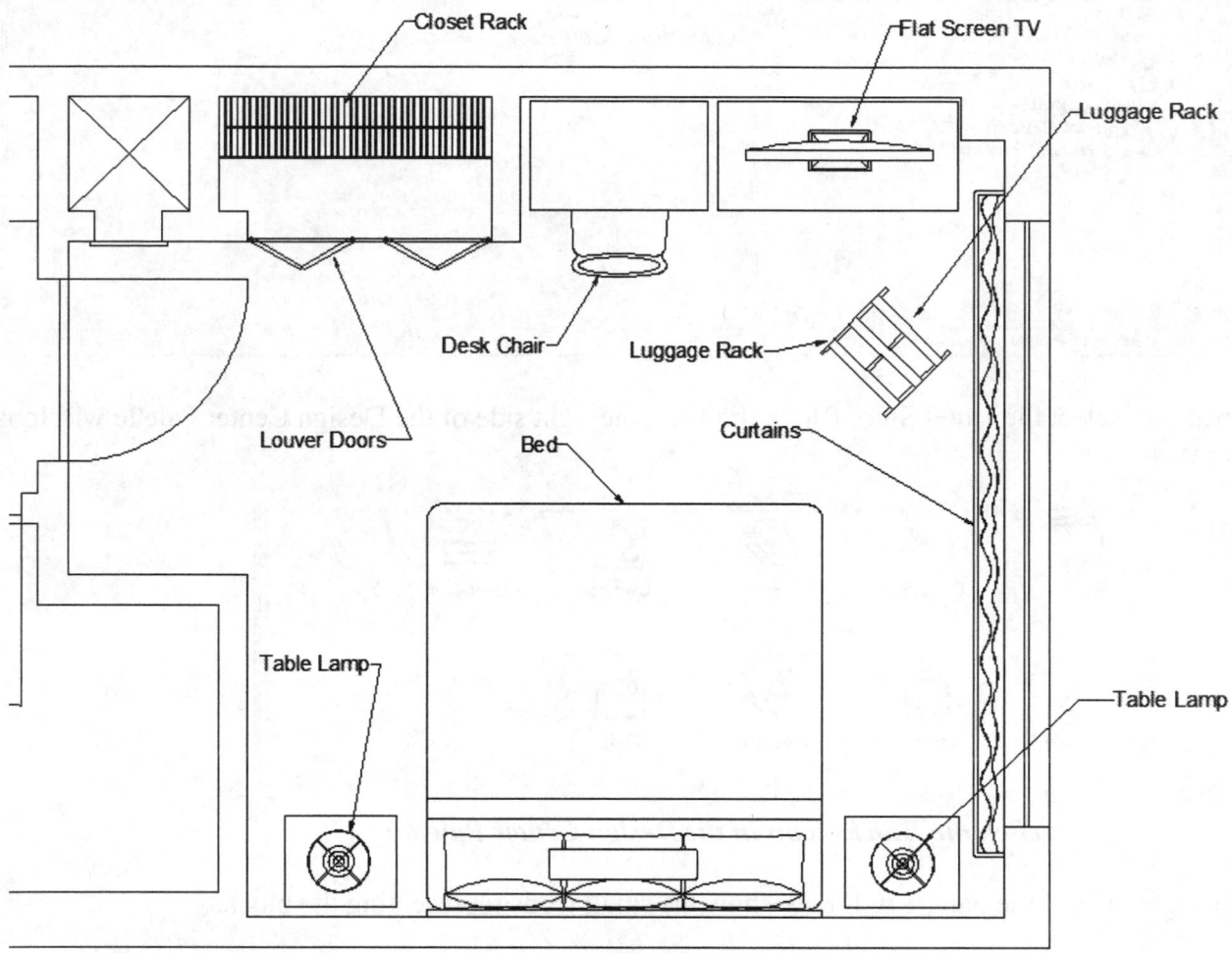

12. **Use Design Center to bring in the Blocks for the Bedroom.**

    (Pick the Design Center icon)

    The Design Center Palette will appear on your screen. Using the Tree View on the left side of the Design Center Palette, find the Hotel Suite Blocks drawing.

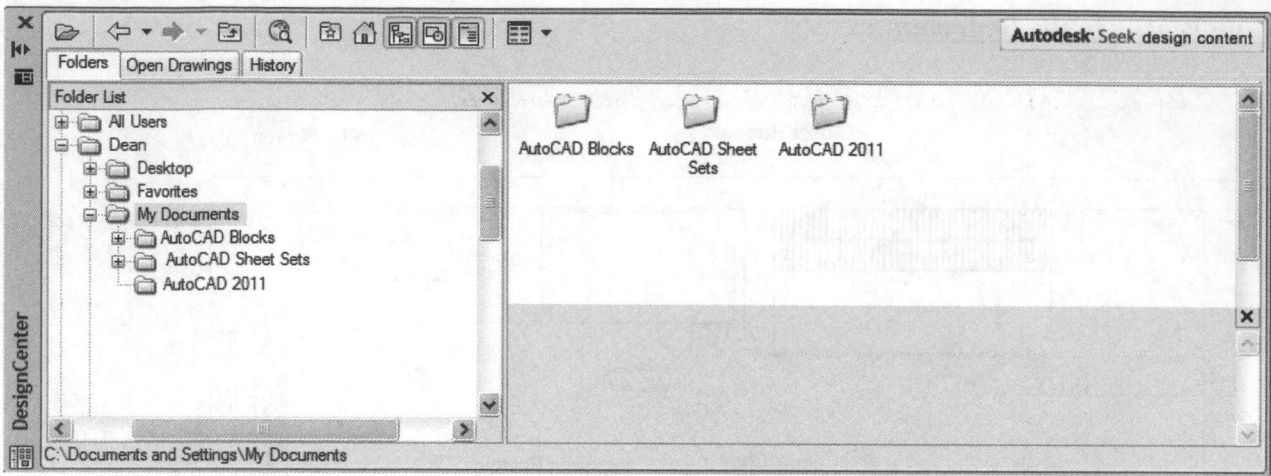

Once you select the Hotel Suite Block drawing, the right side of the Design Center Palette will look like this:

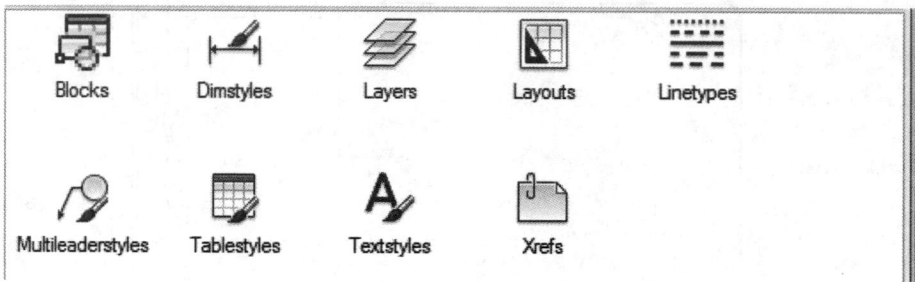

(Double-click the Blocks icon in the Design Center Palette)

The right side of the palette will now show the small icons representing the blocks.

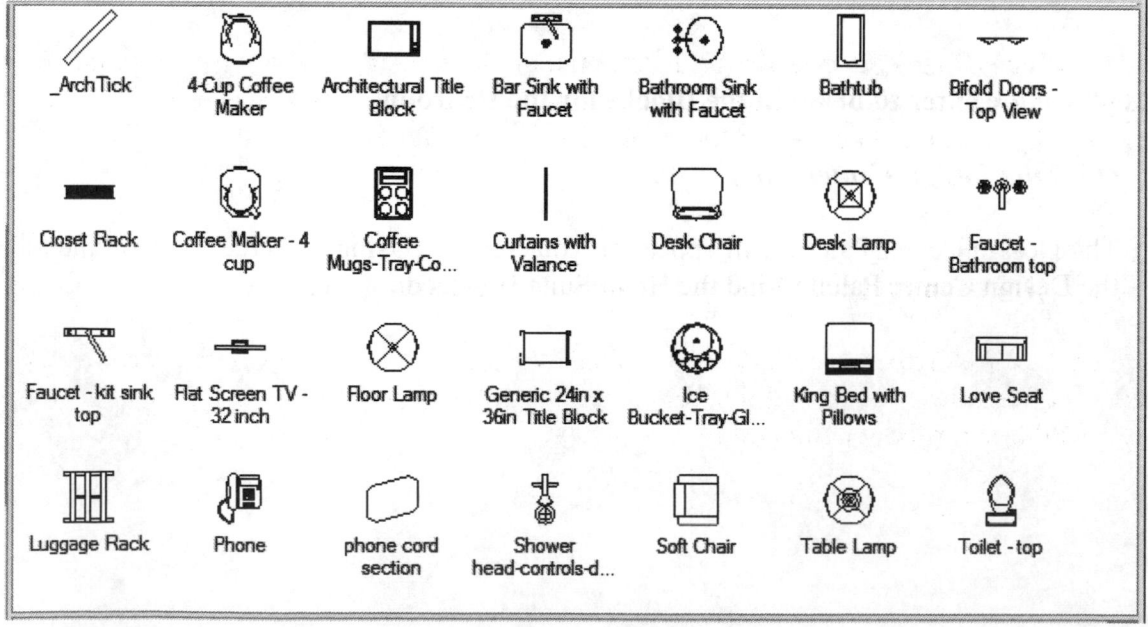

Let's move the bed into the drawing:

(Pick & Drag the icon of the King Bed with Pillows into the Bedroom)

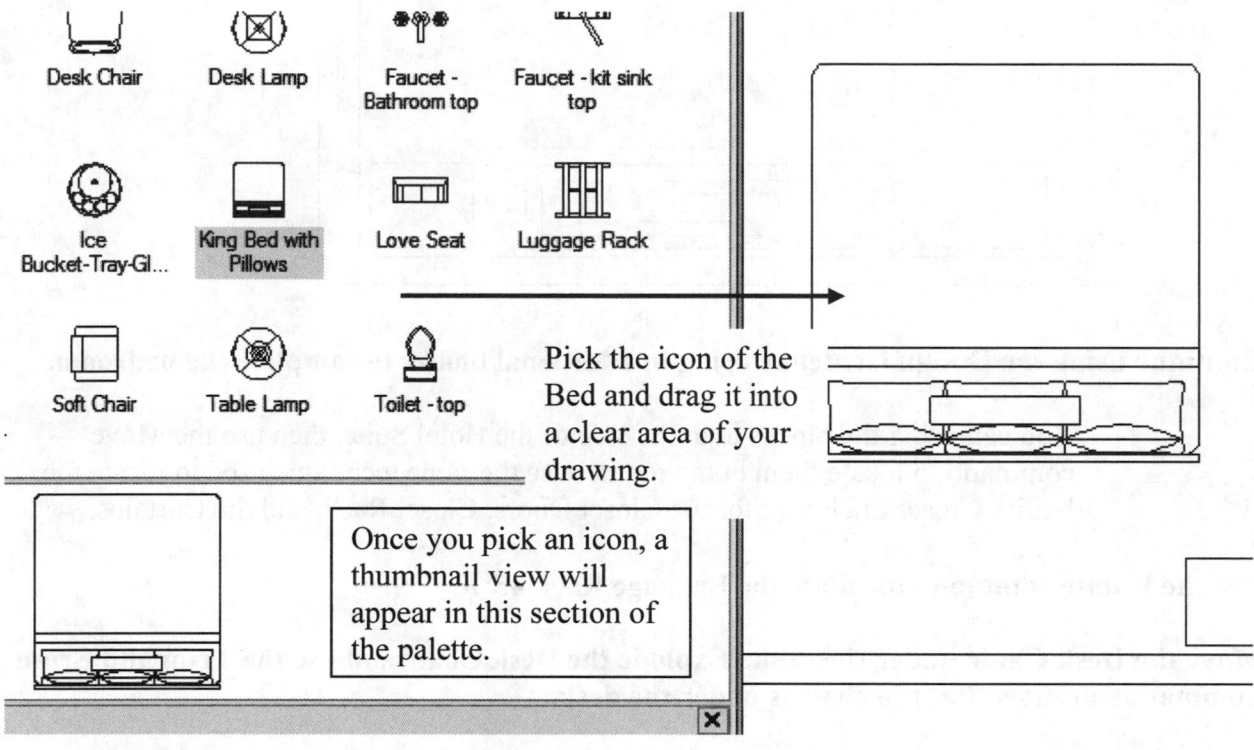

Pick the icon of the Bed and drag it into a clear area of your drawing.

Once you pick an icon, a thumbnail view will appear in this section of the palette.

(Pick the X in the upper corner of the palette to close it)

We will now locate the bed to the correct location in the room using the Move command. We want the bed to be located so that it is centered and against the wall. This will be easy to do since we can use Snap to Midpoint just like we did for the Utility Closet Enclosure.

13. Use the Move command and move the block of the bed.

Remember, because the bed is a block, it is treated as a single object. However, we can still use Snap to Midpoint of the lower horizontal line of the bed as the basepoint. We will then use the midpoint of the lower wall line for the second point.

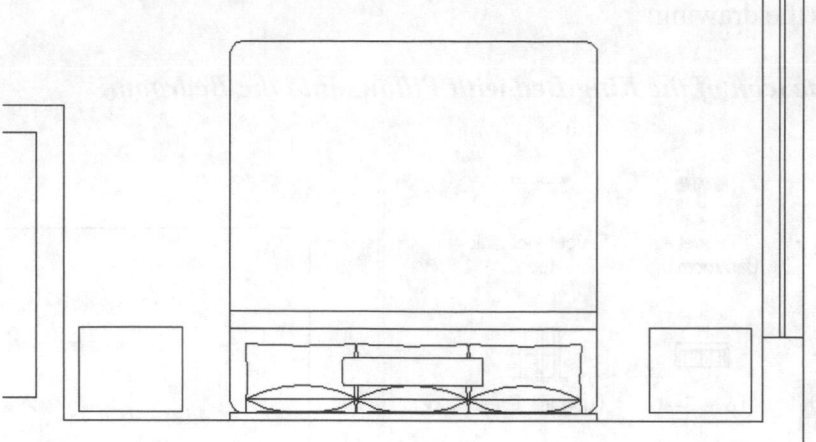

14. **Continue using the Design Center to bring in additional blocks to complete the bedroom.**

    - You can bring the blocks in to the side of the Hotel Suite, then use the Move command to locate them in the room. Use the same technique used to locate the Utility Closet Enclosure for the Closet Doors, Closet Rack, and the Curtains.

15. **Use the Rotate command to rotate the Luggage Rack 45°.**

16. **Move the Desk Chair under the desk. Explode the Desk Chair and use the Trim and Erase commands to show that the chair is under the desk.**

17. **Use the Line command to draw lines corner-to-corner inside the Utility Closet.**

When you are done, your drawing will look like this:

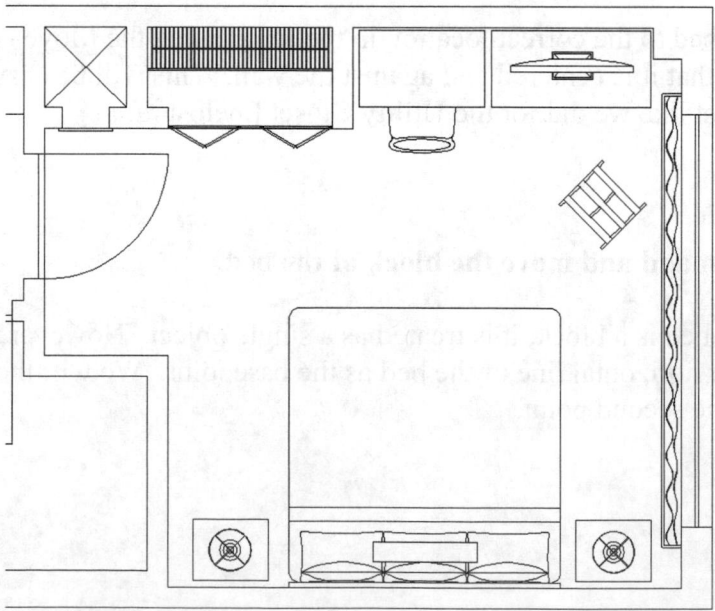

Adding Blocks to the Bathroom

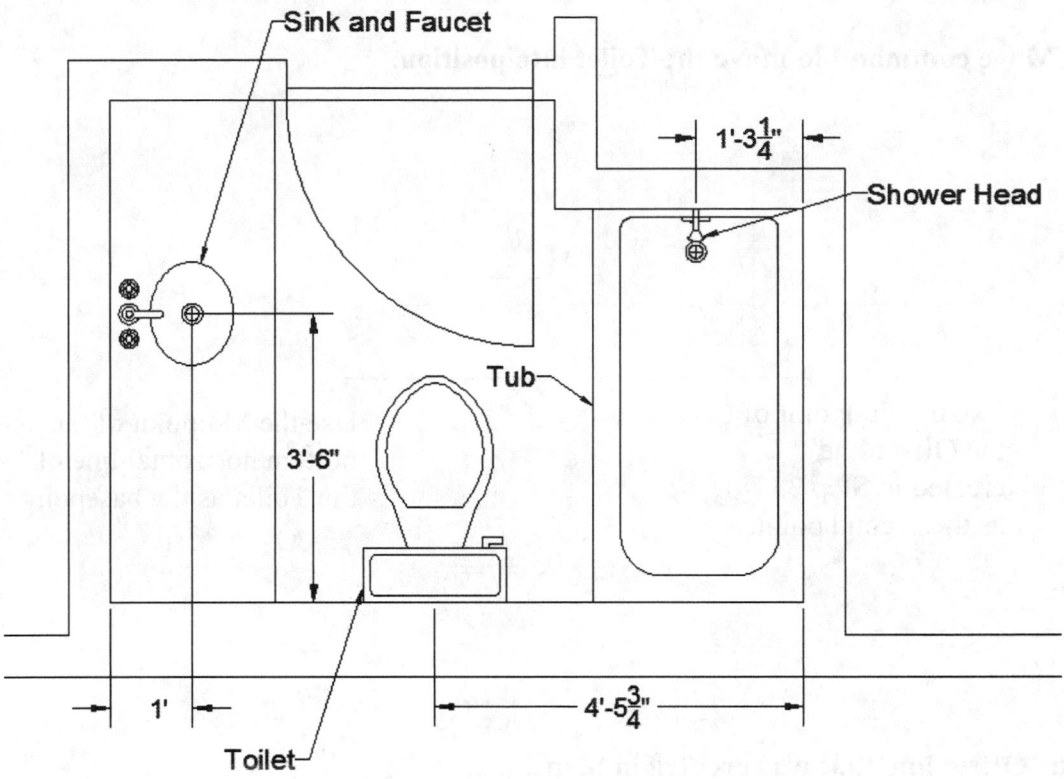

Sink and Faucet

1'-3$\frac{1}{4}$"

Shower Head

Tub

3'-6"

1'

4'-5$\frac{3}{4}$"

Toilet

18. **Use Design Center to bring in the Blocks for the Bathroom.**

19. **Use the Move command to move the Tub to the lower right hand corner.**

20. **Offset the right wall 1'3-1/4" to the left.**

21. **Use the Move command to move the Shower Head into position.**

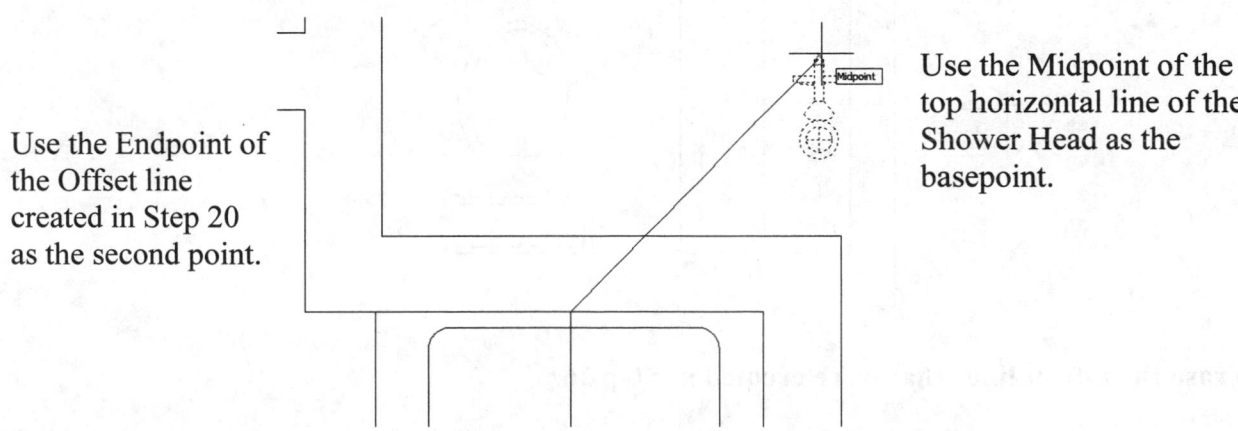

Use the Endpoint of the Offset line created in Step 20 as the second point.

Use the Midpoint of the top horizontal line of the Shower Head as the basepoint.

22. **Erase the Offset line that was created in Step 20.**

23. **Offset the right wall 4′5-3/4″ to the left.**

24. **Use the Move command to move the Toilet into position.**

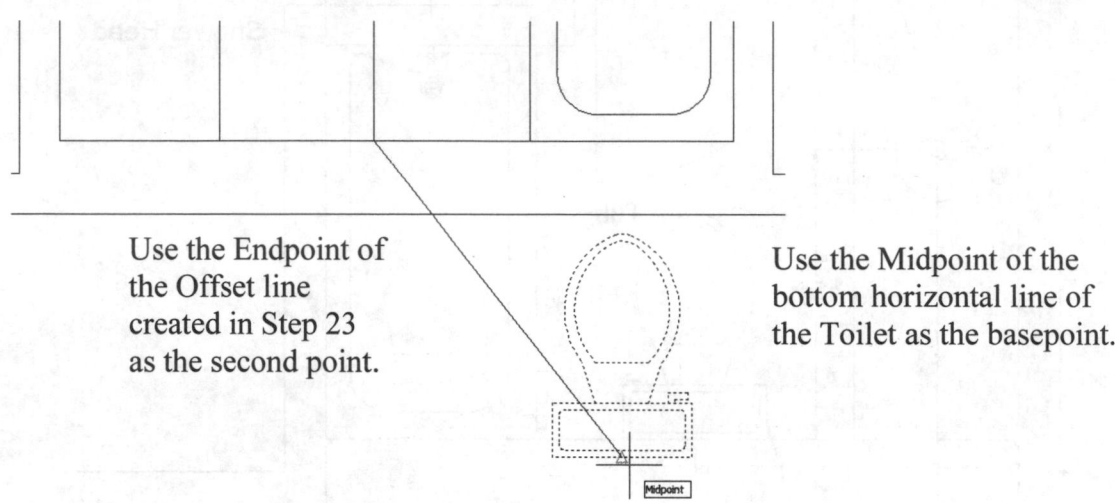

Use the Endpoint of
the Offset line
created in Step 23
as the second point.

Use the Midpoint of the
bottom horizontal line of
the Toilet as the basepoint.

25. **Erase the Offset line that was created in Step 23.**

26. **Offset the left wall 1′ to the right and the lower wall 3′6″ up.**

27. **Use the Move command to move the Sink into position.**

Use the Center of the
Sink as the basepoint.

Use the Intersection
of the offset lines
created in Step 26 as
the second point.

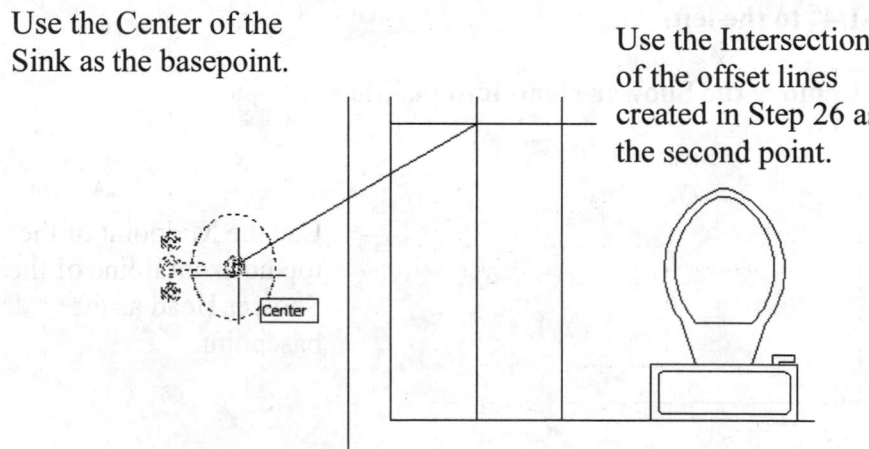

28. **Erase the Offset lines that were created in Step 26.**

When you are done, your drawing will look like this:

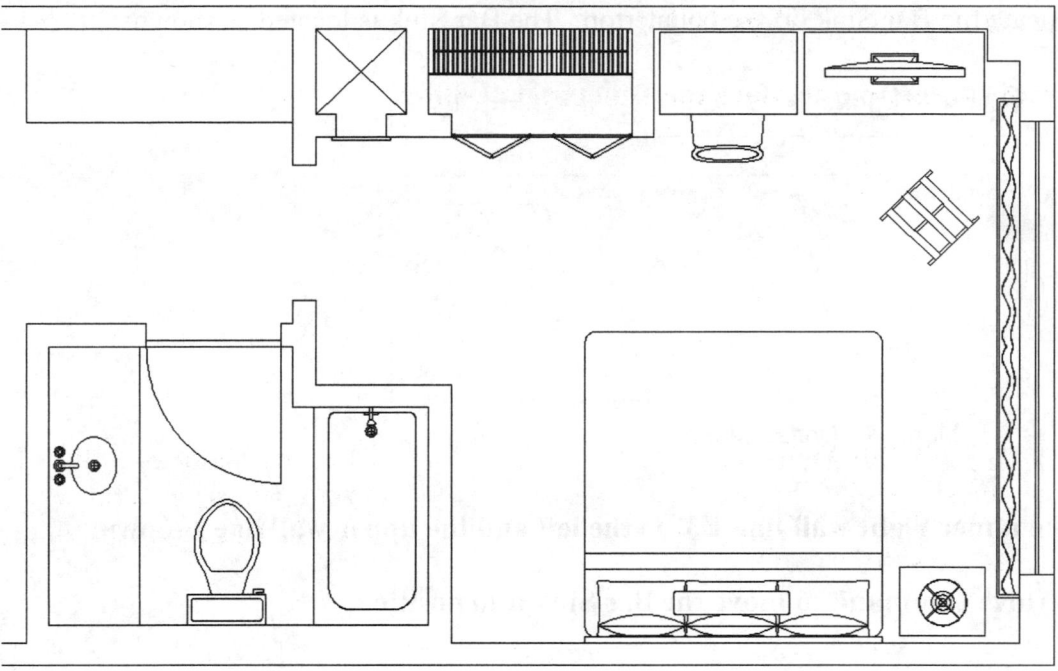

Adding Blocks to the Living Room

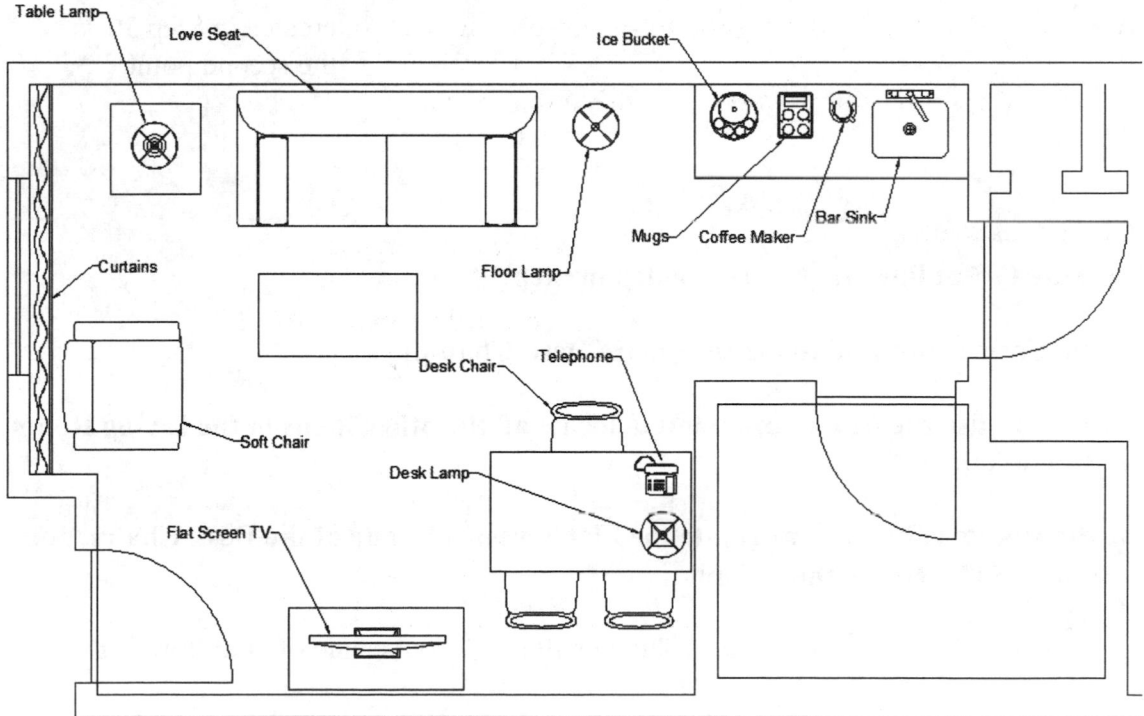

29. Use Design Center to bring in the Blocks for the Bathroom.

We need to locate the Bar Sink on the countertop. The Bar Sink is located as shown:

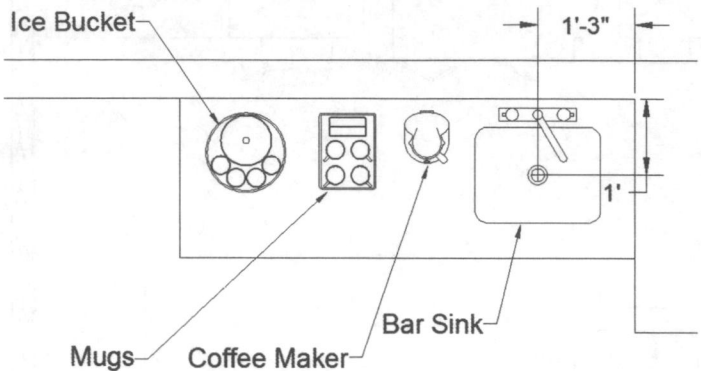

30. Offset the upper right wall line 1'3" to the left and the upper wall line 1' down.

31. Use the Move command to move the Bar Sink into position.

Use the Center of the Bar Sink as the basepoint.

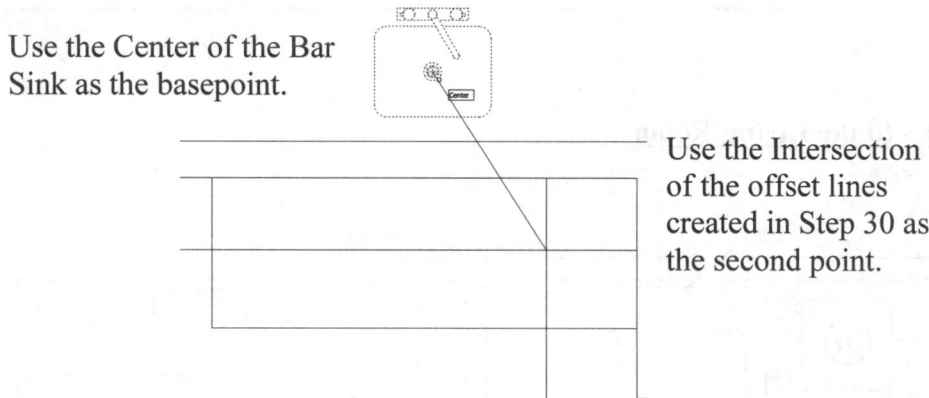

Use the Intersection of the offset lines created in Step 30 as the second point.

32. Erase the Offset lines that were created in Step 30.

33. Use the Copy command to create 2 more Desk Chairs.

34. Continue to use the Move command to locate all the other items in the Living Room except for the Curtain.

35. Use the Rotate command to rotate the Flat Screen TV, one of the Desk Chairs, and the Curtains 180°. Rotate the Telephone -90°.

- Note that the Curtains should still be off to the side of your drawing.

36. Use the Move command to move the Curtains into position.

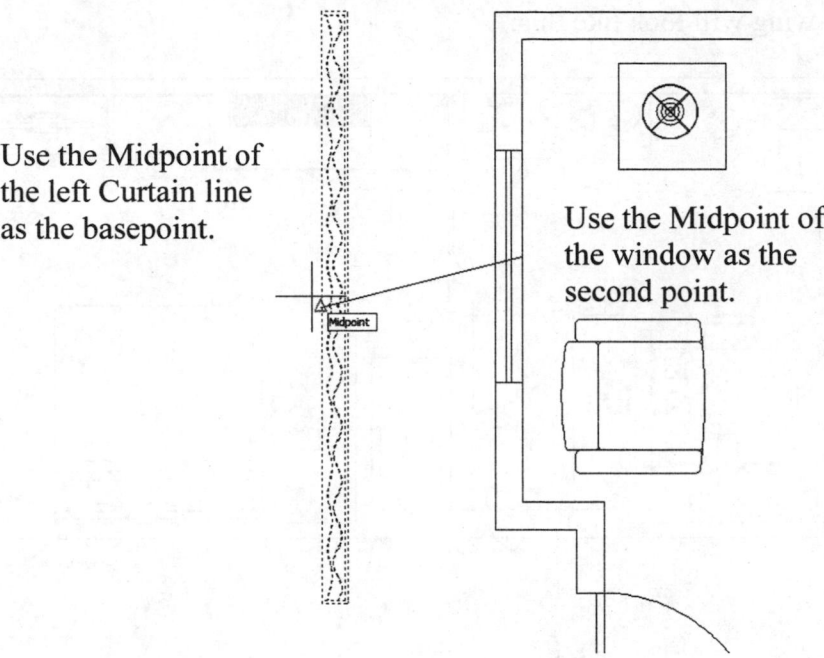

Use the Midpoint of
the left Curtain line
as the basepoint.

Use the Midpoint of
the window as the
second point.

37. Explode the Curtain block and use the Trim and Erase commands to complete the Living Room window treatment.

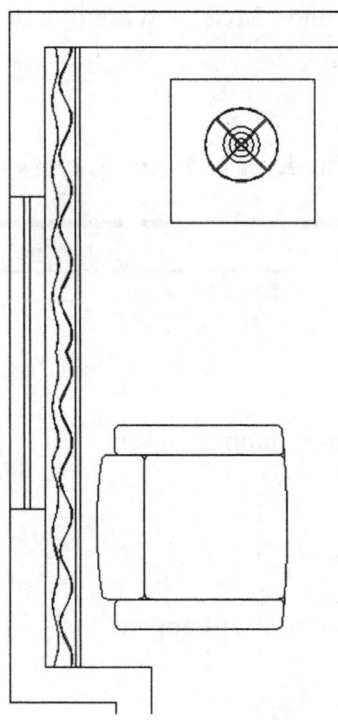

You are now done inserting all the Blocks onto the Plan View. Save your drawing.

When you are done, your drawing will look like this:

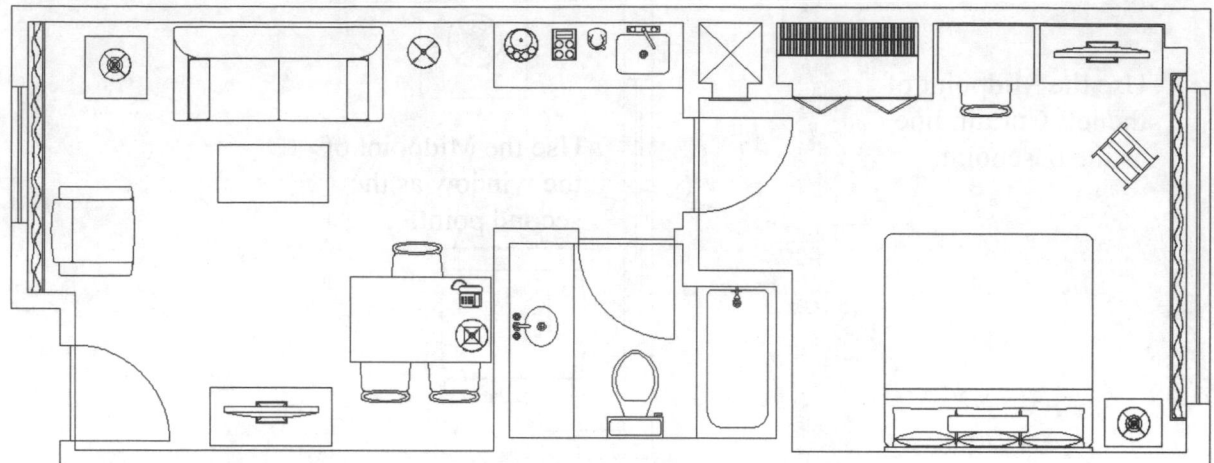

Creating Layers

Now that we have the Floor Plan completed, we can create layers and move the objects to the new layers. This will allow us to show only the items that we want to see. For this tutorial, we will create layers "Structure", "Furniture", "Fixtures", and "Misc". We will assign colors and lineweights to each layer.

38. Bring up the Properties Manager. The icon is on the Layers toolbar.

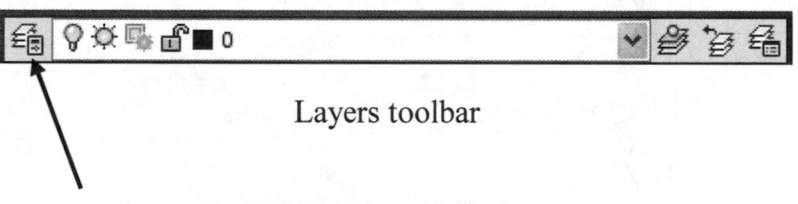

Layers toolbar

Layer Properties Manager icon

(Pick Layer Properties Manager icon)

The Layer Properties Manager dialog box will appear.

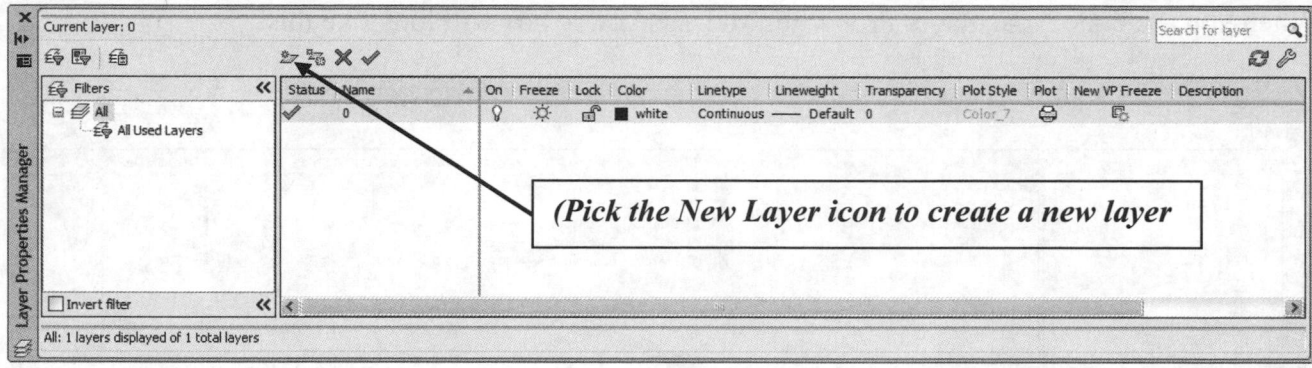

(Pick the New Layer icon to create a new layer

39. Add new layers and name them as shown:

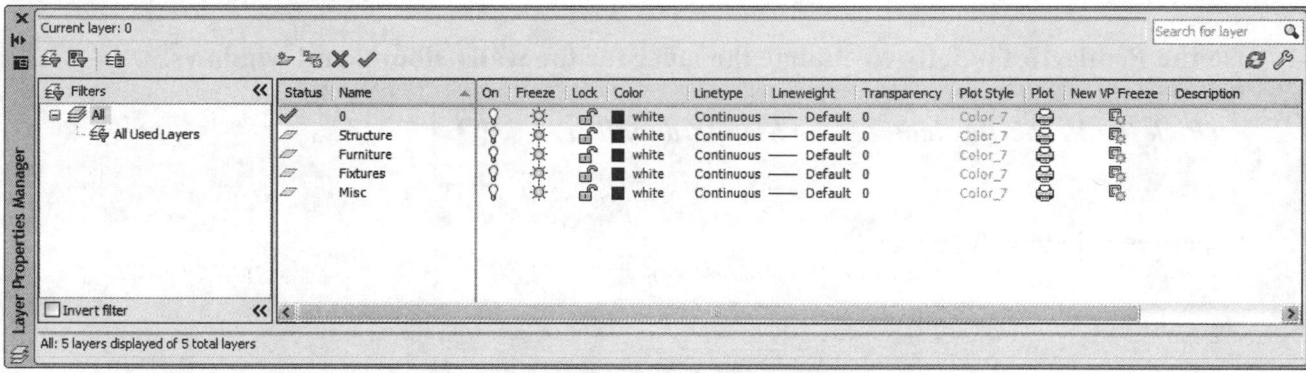

40. Using the Standard colors, change the color of layer "Structure" to green; layer "Furniture" to blue; layer "Fixtures" to magenta, and layer "Misc" to red. In addition, change the Lineweight of layer "Structure" to .012"; layer "Furniture", "Fixtures", and "Misc" to .010".

Standard
Colors

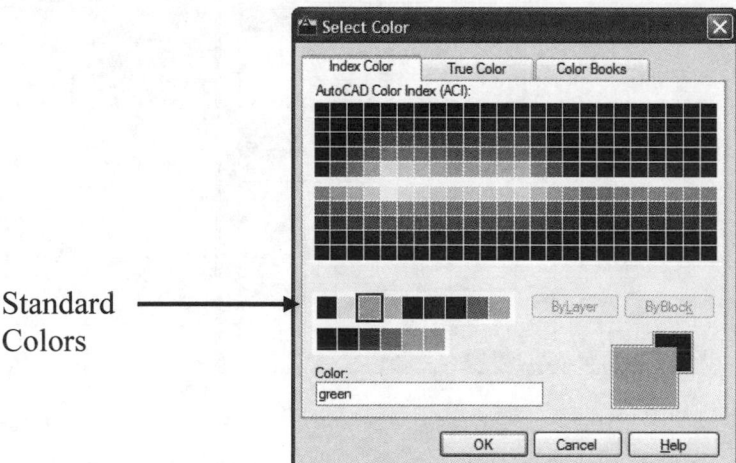

When you are done, your Layer Properties Manager dialog box will look like this:

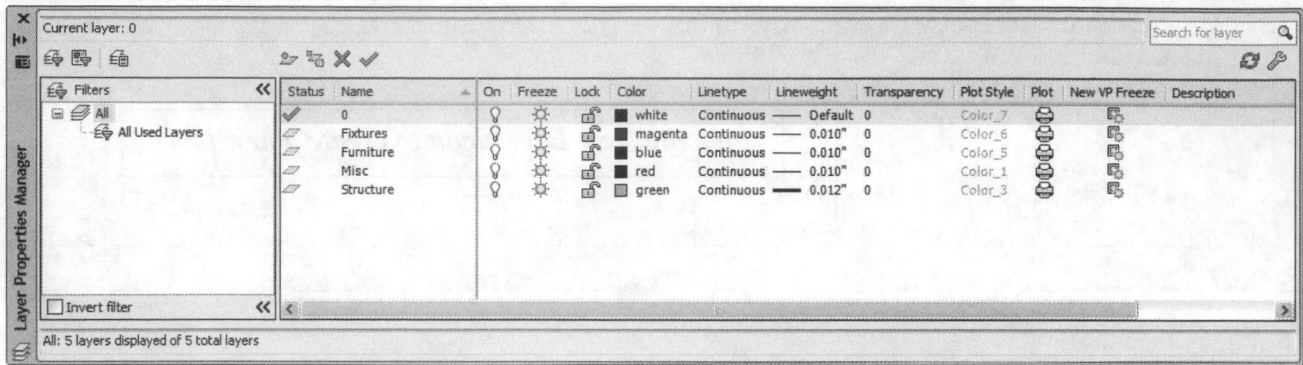

(Pick the "X" in the upper LH corner of the dialog box to close it)

41. Use the Properties palette to change the layer for the walls, doors, and windows.

(Pick the Properties icon on the Standard toolbar)

The Properties palette will appear:

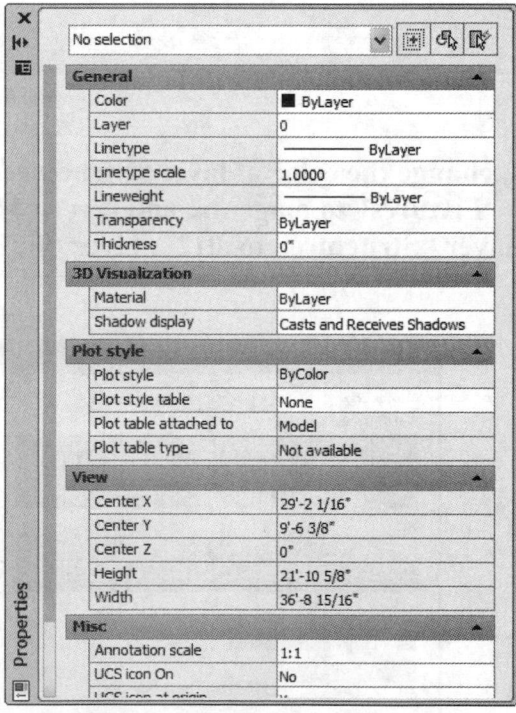

(Pick all the objects that make up the walls, doors, and windows)

It is not necessary to select all the objects at once – you can repeat the process until all objects that belong on this layer have been changed. You can pick anywhere in the drawing space and press the Esc key to eliminate the selection set. This is helpful if you do not pick all the items at once.

After you begin to select the objects do the following:

(Pick Layer and use the pull-down arrow to select layer "Structure")

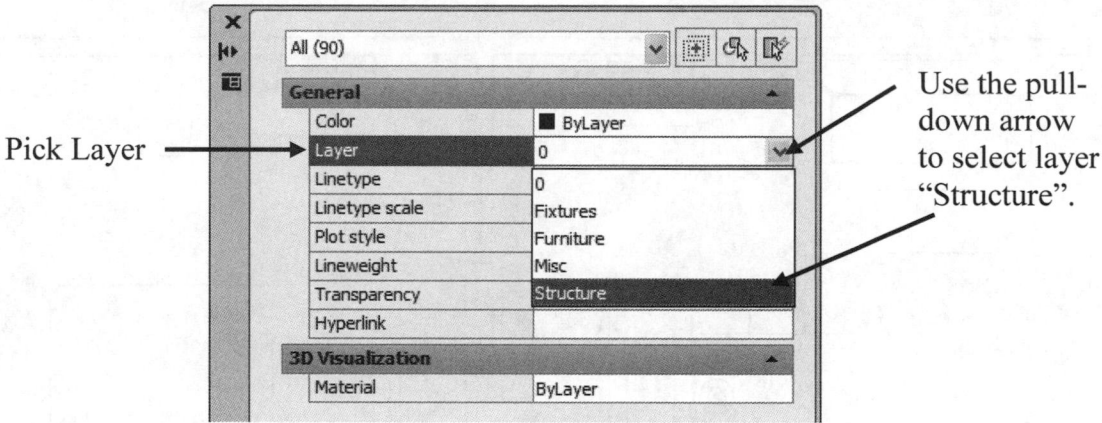

Pick Layer →

Use the pull-down arrow to select layer "Structure".

42. Close the Properties Palette and press the Esc key.

When you are done, your drawing will look like this:

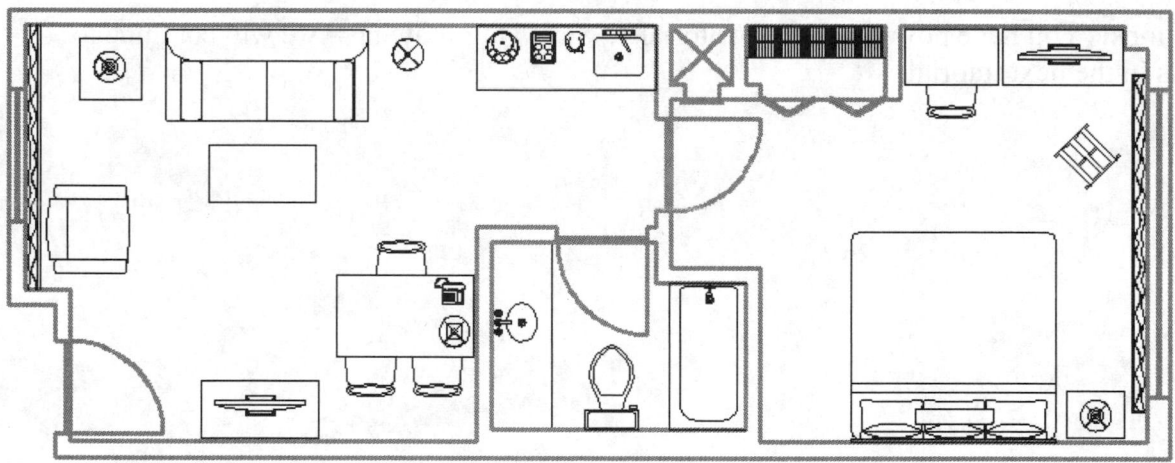

43. Use the pull-down arrow in the Layers toolbar to turn layer "Structure" off.

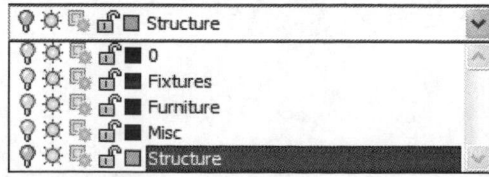

After turning the light bulb off, pick anywhere in the drawing space to close out this pull-down.

With layer "Structure" turned off, it is easier to select the other objects to change their layer.

44. Repeat the process described in Steps 41 and 42 to change the layer for the furniture, fixtures, and miscellaneous items.

You can turn layers on and off as desired to help facilitate selecting the objects.

When you are done, your drawing will look like this:

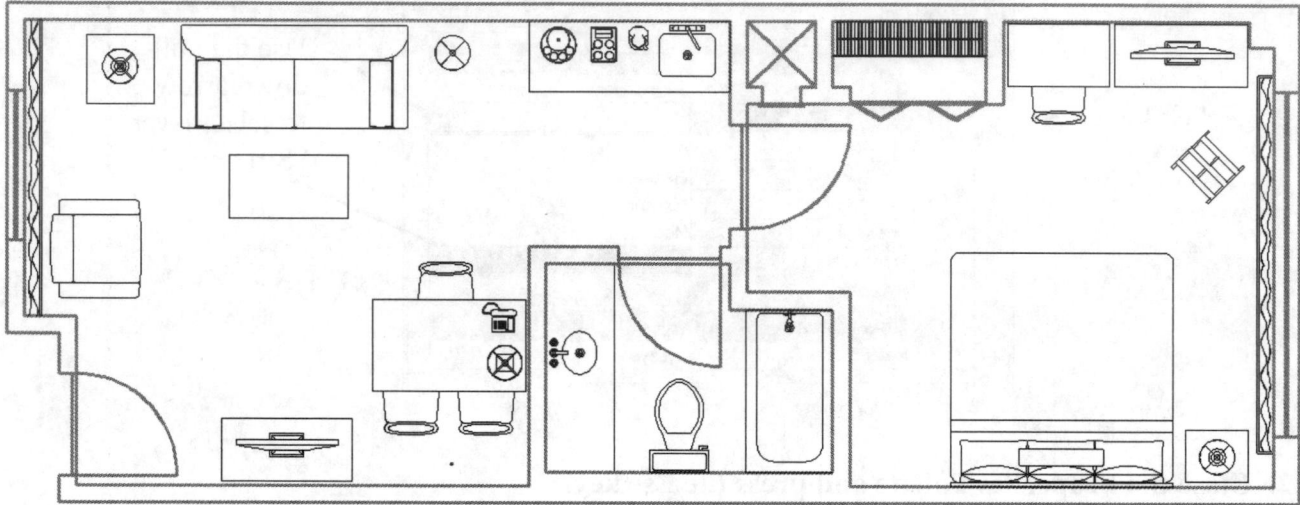

Congratulations! You have now completed Tutorial 4. Save your drawing – we will continue to build on this in the next tutorial.

Chapter 11
Commands – Set 5: Annotating Your Drawing

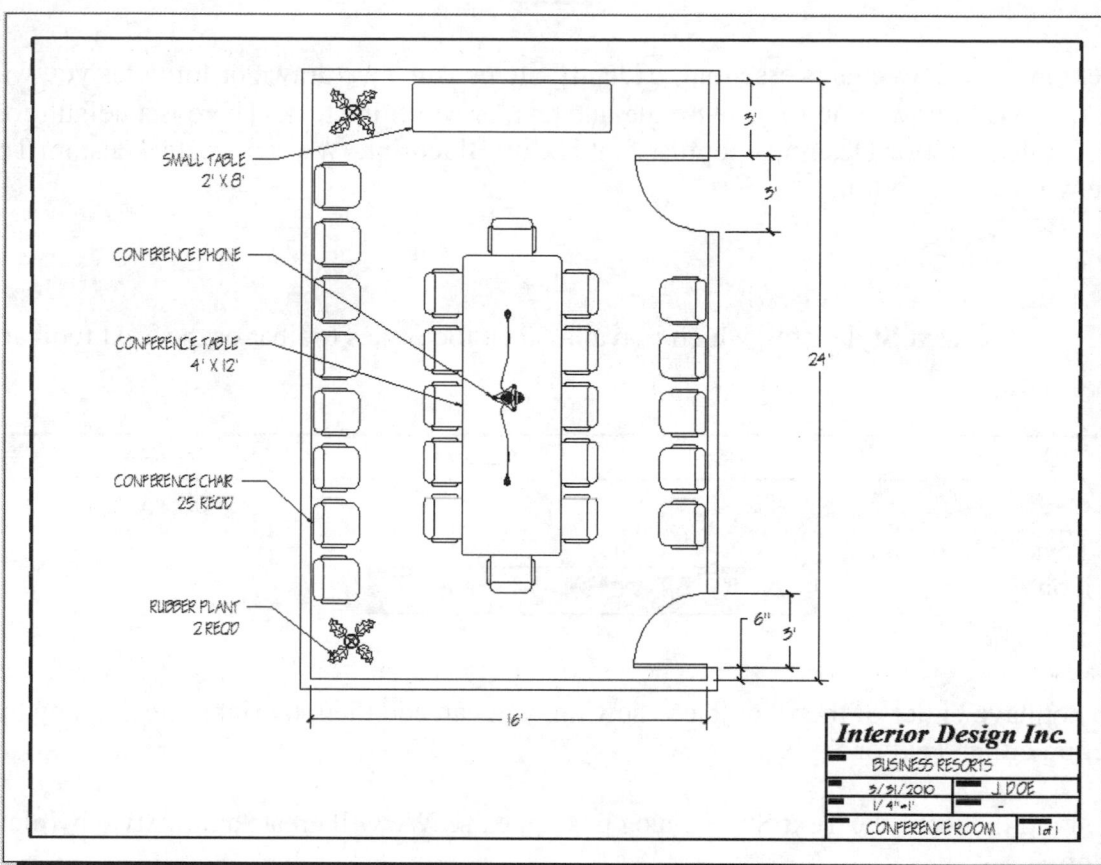

Learning Objectives:

- Creating a style and using Text
- Creating a style and using Dimensions
- Creating labels with the Multileader command

We can now create accurate drawings. Unfortunately, this alone is not enough to convey the information you want to explain your design to a client or to a contractor. All drawings will need text and dimensions to identify what is drawn as well as the size and location of objects.

In this chapter, we will cover Text, Dimensions, and Multileader. The Multileader is the AutoCAD® name for a label.

Text

Putting text in your drawings is essential to identify items you have drawn or for notes you wish to make. AutoCAD® allows you to have Single line text, or Multiline text. There is a default font available, but for Interior Design, a popular font is City Blueprint. We can create a custom Text Style which we will define the font.

Text Style

To begin, pick the Text Style icon, which is available on the Styles toolbar or the Text toolbar as shown:

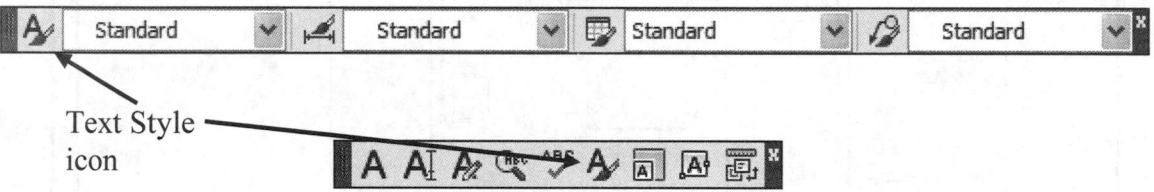

Text Style
icon

If you do not have either of these toolbars showing, you can add them by right-clicking any toolbar and selecting either Text or Styles.

After selecting the icon, the Text Style dialog box appears. We will create a new style by picking the New button.

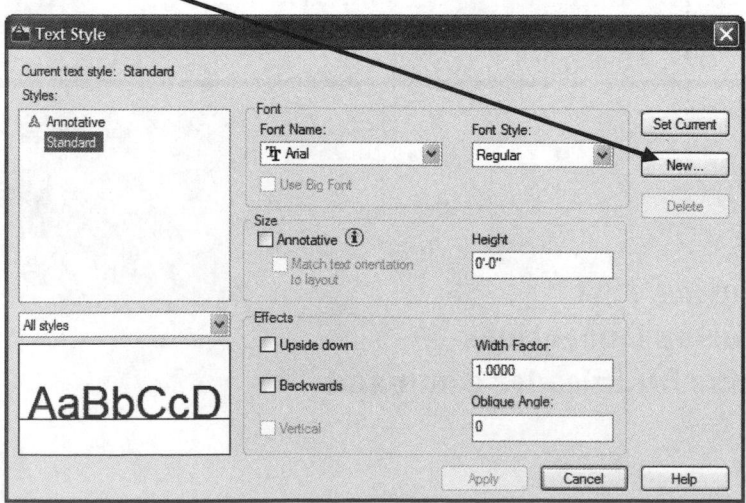

The New Text Style dialog box appears with a default "style1" name, which is ready for editing to a name of your choosing. Let's choose "Notes". Type that in, and then pick OK.

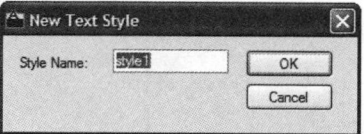 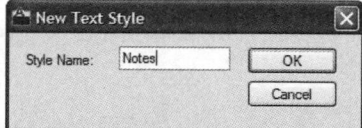

Use the pull-down selection under "Font Name:" to select CityBlueprint as the fonts style. Once you pick the font, the Preview pane shows what the font looks like. Check off "Annotative" under the "Size" portion of the dialog box. Annotative text allows you to scale the text to your drawing so that you do not have to have multiple text styles at different heights. Set the "Paper Text Height" to 1/8″. When done, Pick the Apply button then Pick the Close button.

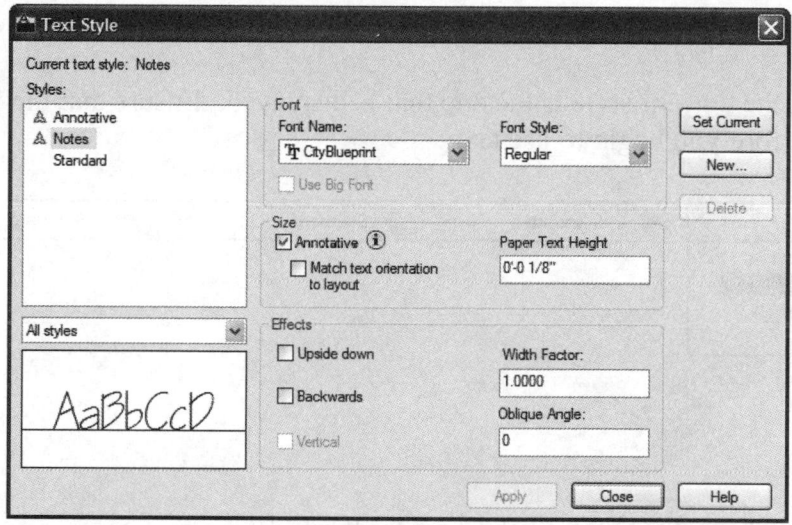

Leaving the height at 0″ will allow AutoCAD to prompt you for text height while placing text in your drawing.

For future use, let's create a second Text Style. Create a style that starts with Notes, but instead of a text height of 1/8″, use 1/4″ instead. Name that new style Titleblock.

Make sure Notes is highlighted before you pick the New button. The new style will be created with all the properties that that the Notes style has. When done, your dialog box will look like the following:

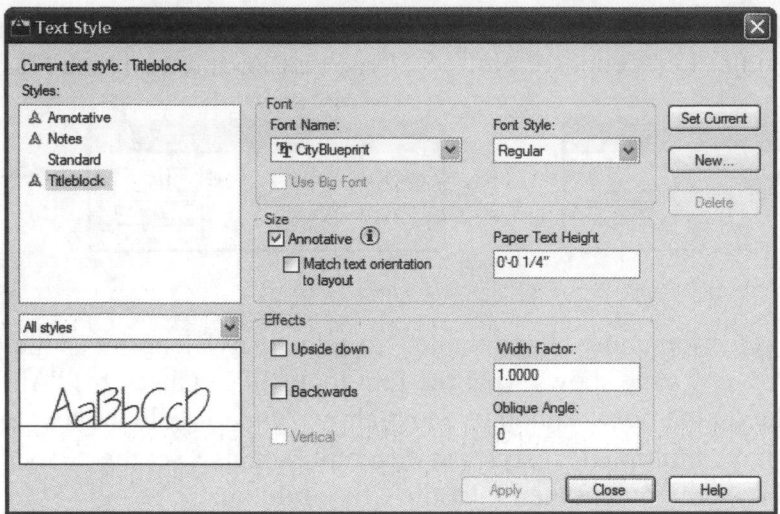

Select the Notes Style and Pick the Set Current button. Pick the Close button to exit the dialog box.

In the Styles toolbar, the current style is the one that is displayed. Ensure that the new style of Notes is the current style before you begin to use text.

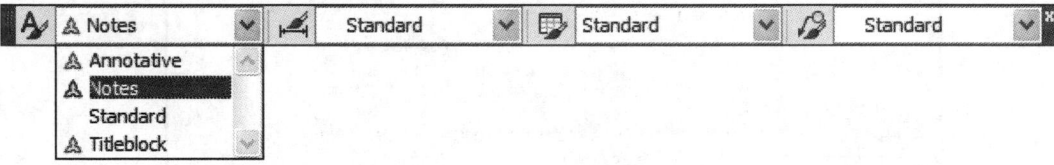

Single Line Text

We will use the Single Line Text icon on the Text toolbar:

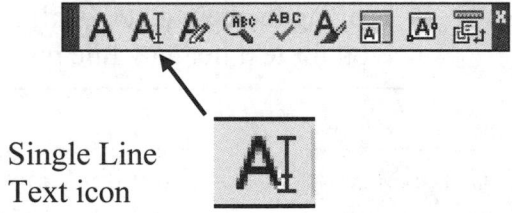

Single Line
Text icon

Procedure:

Pick (left click): **Single Line Text icon** from the Text toolbar.

The command line prompts you with the following:

Command: _text
Current text style: "Notes" Text height: 0'-0 1/8" Annotative: Yes
*Specify start point of text or [Justify/Style]: **(Pick a point on the drawing to place the text)***

Specify rotation angle of text <0>: ↵   **Press the ↵ Enter key to accept the default angle. Key in your text. Your text will appear on the drawing.**

AutoCAD® allows additional lines of text; you press the ↵ Enter key to start the next line of text. When you are done entering text, **Press the ↵ Enter key**.

> If you only want a single line of text, press the ↵ Enter key twice to exit the command.

Note that if you were to place Annotative text onto your drawing while in the Model tab (or in a Layout tab if you haven't set/locked the scale), a dialog box will appear the first time you attempt to do this:

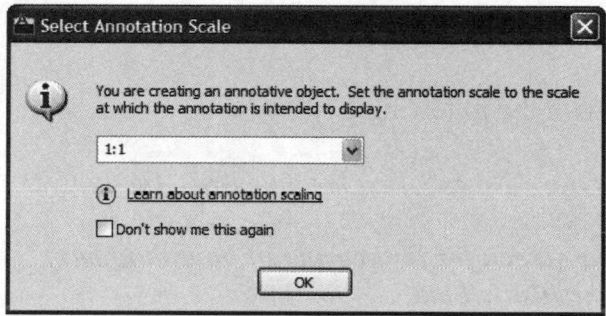

Using Annotative text is best done while you are working in a Layout tab in Model Space. Most times when you wish to apply text to your drawing, you want to apply it when you are laying-out your drawing for printing.

Prior to using Annotative text, set and lock the scale of your Model Space relative to the Paper Space. AutoCAD® will automatically scale the text for you.

> AutoCAD does the scaling for you with Annotative text. If you are using a scale of ¼″=1′, your text height would have to be 48 times bigger to appear on the drawing.
>
> <u>Do the math:</u> ¼″=1′ is the same as ¼″ = 12″ (the units need to be in inches for the math to work). Multiply both sides by 4 (to get rid of the fraction), you get 1″=48″. This means that to get a line of text to appear 3/16″ high on a drawing with a scale factor of ¼″=1′, the text would have to be drawn in the full-scale model 9″ high (3/16 x 48 =9).

As you can see, it is certainly convenient for AutoCAD® to do the math for us when it comes to getting the text to appear at the correct height on our layout.

Multiline Text

Multiline Text
icon

You can create multiple lines of text in a defined area. Before entering or importing text, you specify opposite corners of a text bounding box that defines the width of the paragraphs in the multiline text object. The length of the multiline text object depends on the amount of text, not the length of the bounding box. You can use grips to move or rotate a multiline text object.

Procedure:

Pick (left click): **Multiline Text icon** from the Text toolbar.

The command line prompts you with the following:

Command: _mtext Current text style: "Notes" Text height: 1/8" Annotative:
Yes
Specify first corner: **(Pick on your screen for first corner of bounding box)**
Specify opposite corner or [Height/Justify/Line
spacing/Rotation/Style/Width/Columns]: **(Pick on your screen for the second corner of bounding box)**

After you define the bounding box for the text, a Text Formatting editor appears on your screen:

This is where you type in the text. When you are done, pick the OK button on the Text Formatting editor.

Multiline text is useful for large amounts of text that is cut/pasted from a document. Otherwise, use Single Line Text.

Editing Text

For text that is already on your drawing that you wish to edit, use the Edit Text icon on the Text toolbar. Pick the icon then Pick the text that you desire to edit.

Edit Text
icon

Procedure:

Pick (left click): **Edit Text icon** from the Text toolbar.

The command line prompts you with the following:

(Pick the Edit Text icon)
Command: _ddedit
Select an annotation object or [Undo]: (Pick the text to be edited)

For single line text, the text will highlight for editing. Begin editing the text. The delete key on the keyboard can be used to delete characters as desired. Highlighting text and then typing will overwrite the text that was highlighted. After you finish editing, press the ↵ Enter key.

AutoCAD® will prompt you to select more text to edit. If you have none, press the ↵ Enter key to exit the command.

Select an annotation object or [Undo]: ↵
Command:

For Multiline text, the Text Formatting editor will appear. This is the same Text Formatting editor that appeared when you were creating Multiline text. Editing of Multiline text is done in the same manor as single line text. When done, pick the OK button to exit the Text Formatting editor. You must also press the ↵ Enter key to exit the Edit Text command.

Relocating text

To relocate text on your drawing, it is easily done using grips with the Object Snap feature turned off. Simply pick the text to get the grip, and then pick the grip and move the text to the new location.

Special Characters

There are times when you need to insert a special character or symbol into your line of text. Probably the most commonly used one would be the degree symbol "°".

You can insert a special character while inserting or editing text by keying in the correct code.

The following codes result in special characters:

Code	Resulting Character	Character Name
%%d	°	Degree Symbol
%%p	±	Plus/Minus Symbol
%%c	∅	Diameter Symbol

Example:

Typing: "Door swings through 120%%d", results in "Door swings through 120°".

For Multiline text, you can add symbols and special characters directly from a character map. The character map is found by using the Symbol icon, which is on the Text Formatting editor.

Scaling Text

For non-Annotative style text only, the text height can be changed using Scale Text. Pick the icon then pick the text you want to scale.

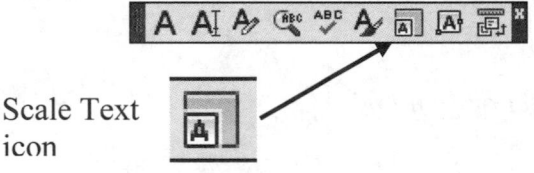

Scale Text icon

Procedure:

Pick (left click): **Scale Text icon** from the Text toolbar.

The command line prompts you with the following:

Command: _scaletext
Select objects: 1 found
Select objects: **(Pick the text)**
Enter a base point option for scaling
[Existing/Left/Center/Middle/Right/TL/TC/TR/ML/MC/MR/BL/BC/BR] <Existing>: ↵
Specify new model height or [Paper height/Match object/Scale factor] <3/16">: **3/8** ↵
1 objects changed
Command:

You cannot change the scale of Annotative text. If you tried, your command line will advise:

1 annotative objects ignored

Dimensions

It is important to use dimensions in your drawing to describe the size and placement of items. AutoCAD® has a variety of dimensions available that can be customized. There are several types of dimensions: linear, aligned, radial, diameter, angular, etc. A standard style is available as the default style. This style is more suitable for engineering than it is for Interior Design. We will create a unique style that is better suited for use in Interior Design.

Dimension Toolbar

Right-click on any toolbar and select the Dimension toolbar to make it available. The icons described below are the ones that we will be using. We will not need all the icons available.

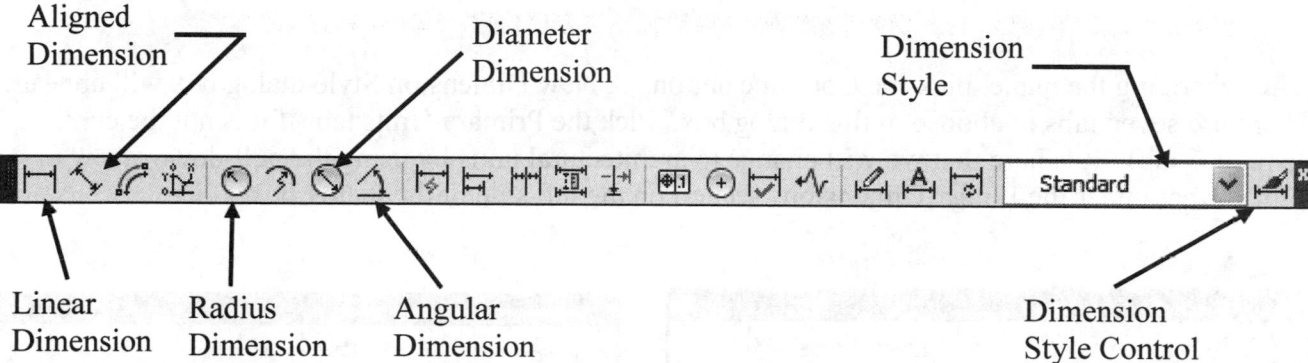

Aligned Dimension

Diameter Dimension

Dimension Style

Linear Dimension

Radius Dimension

Angular Dimension

Dimension Style Control

Creating a Dimension Style

To create a unique dimension style, pick the Dimension Style icon. The Dimension Style Manager dialog box will appear.

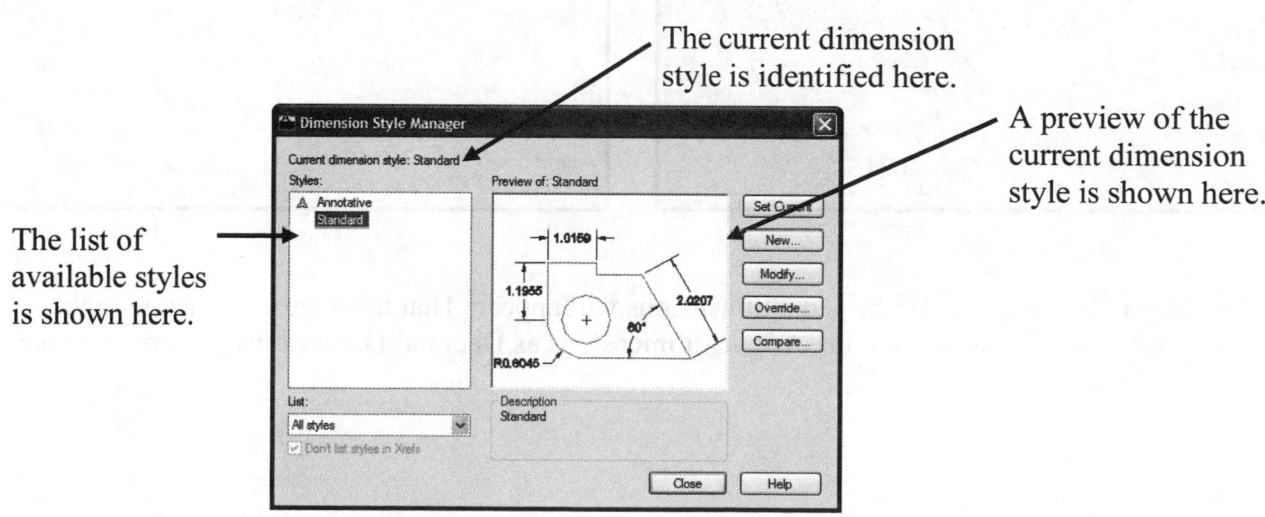

The current dimension style is identified here.

A preview of the current dimension style is shown here.

The list of available styles is shown here.

To create a new dimension style, pick the New… button. A new dialog box will appear. Under New Style Name, the text "Copy of Standard" is highlighted and ready for editing. Let's name the new style Interior Design. Also, check-off Annotative.

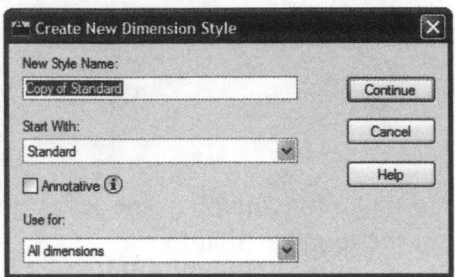 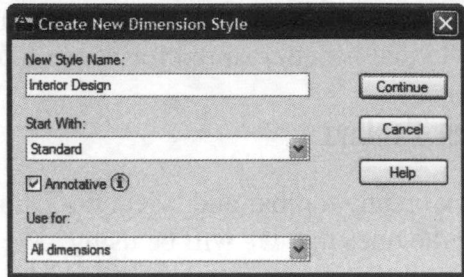

After changing the name, pick the Continue button. A New Dimension Style dialog box will appear. There are seven tabs to choose in this dialog box. Pick the Primary Units tab (if it is not the currently displayed tab). It is here that we will change to architectural units by using the pull-down arrow of Unit format under the Linear Dimensions section on the left side of the dialog box.

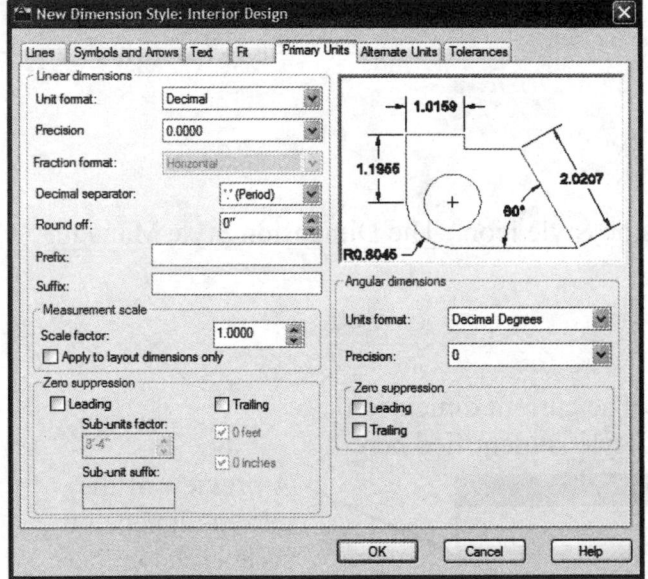 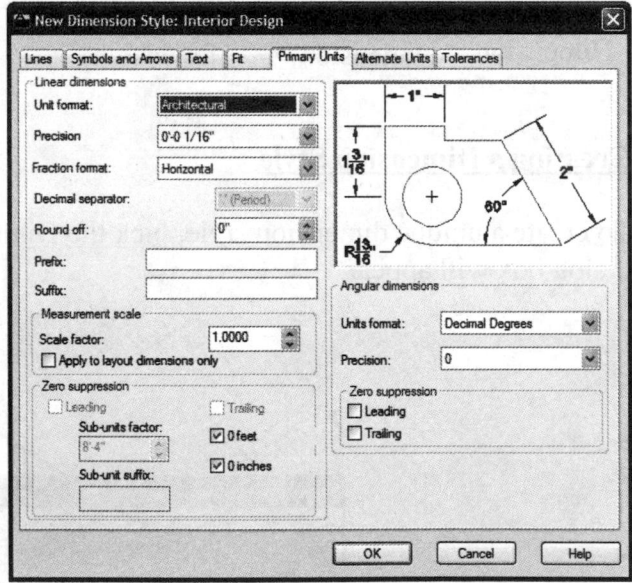

Notice the preview pane shows how the dimensions will appear. That is all we will change in the Primary Units tab. We will leave the Angular dimensions as Decimal Degrees with a zero precision.

Next, pick the Lines tab. It is here we can control the dimension lines and extension lines.

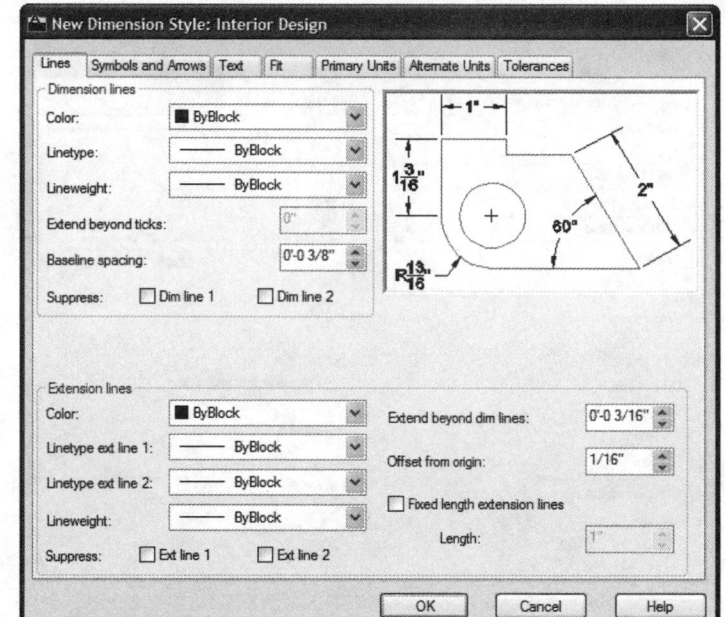

Make the following changes (if these values are not already there):
- Change the value of Baseline spacing to 3/8.
- Change the value of Extend beyond dim lines to 3/32.
- Change the value of Offset from origin to 1/16.
- Change all Color and Lineweights from ByBlock to ByLayer

When done, your dialog box should look like this:

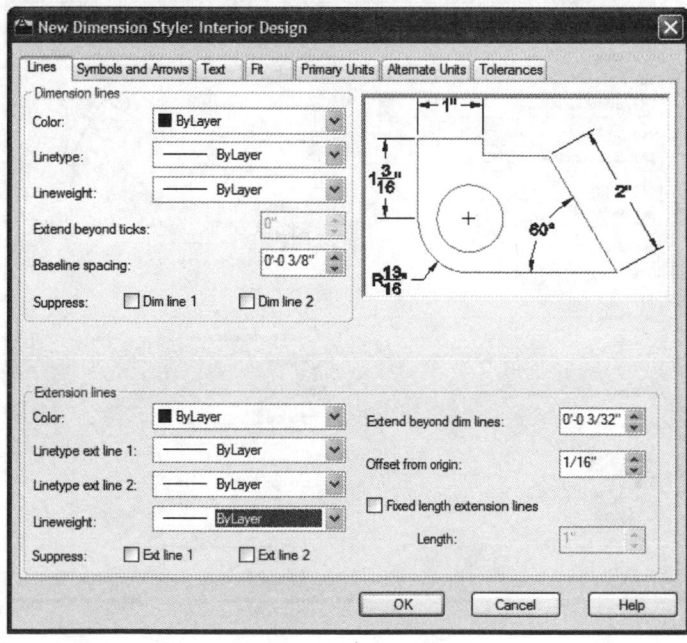

Now, pick the Symbols and Arrows tab. It is here we will control the style and size of the arrowheads.

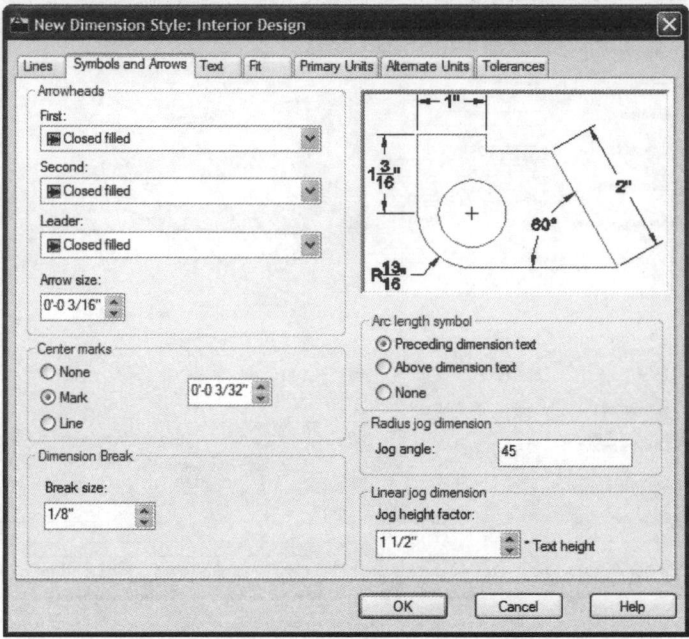

Make the following changes under the Arrowheads portion of the dialog box:
- Change the arrow style to Architectural tick under both First and Second.
- Change the Arrow size to 1/16.

When done, your dialog box should look like this:

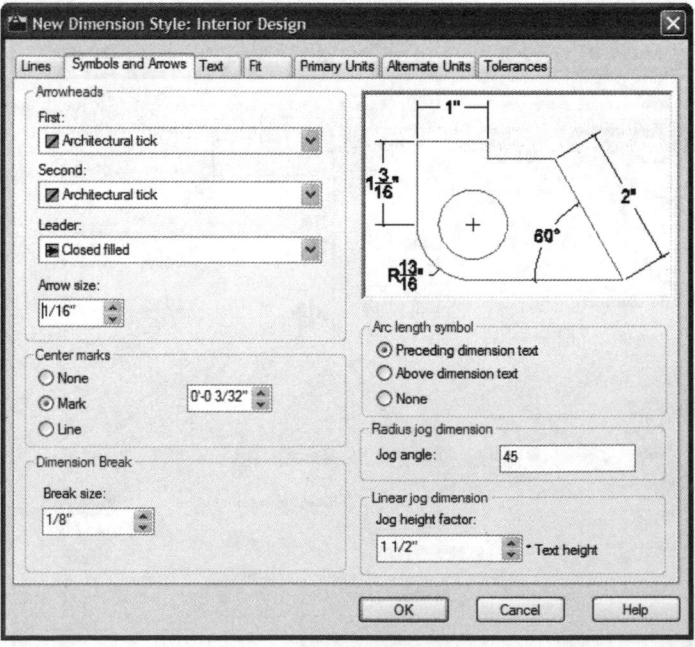

Pick the Text tab. We will change the appearance and placement of the text. For the alignment, we will leave the default value of Horizontal.

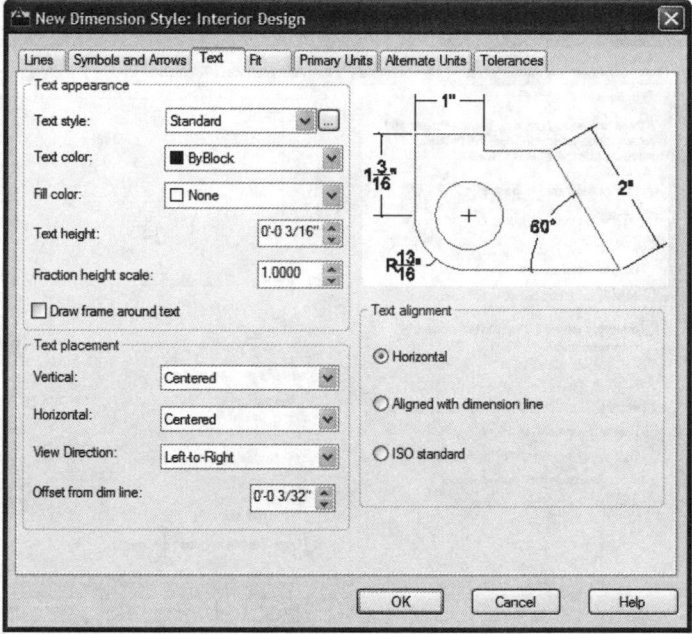

In the Text Appearance portion of the dialog box, make the following changes:
- Change the Text style to Notes (if you have not already created this style, you must create that first before this can be done)
- Change the Text color to ByLayer

In the Text Placement portion of the dialog box, make the following change:
- Change the value of Offset from dim line to 1/16

When done, your dialog box should look like this:

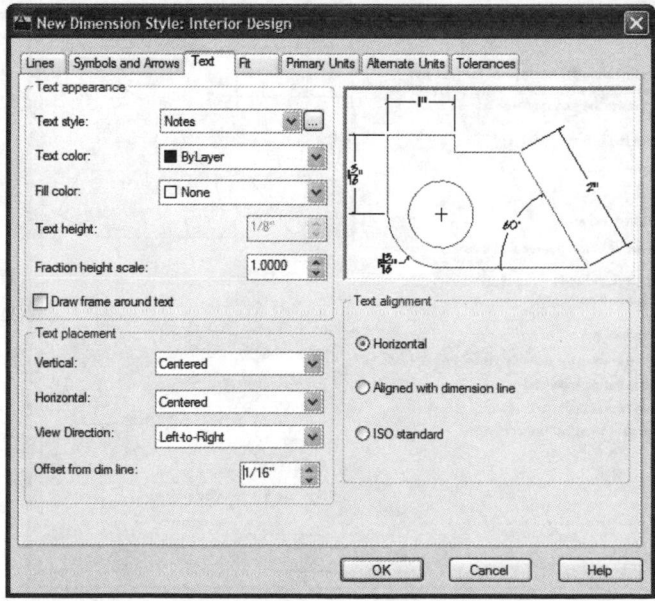

Note that the Text height becomes grayed-out because the Text style of Notes already has a Text height value of 1/8″.

Next, pick the Fit tab. We will change the Scale and Fine Tuning and leave the Options and Placement at the default values.

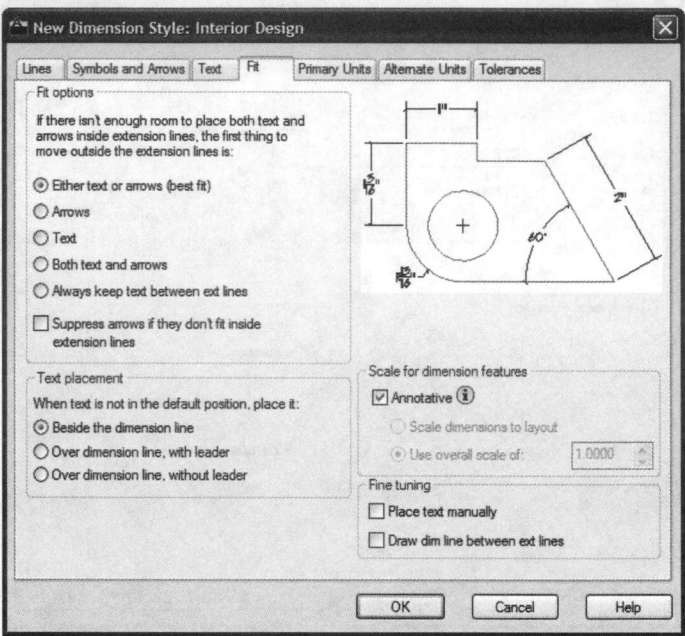

In the Scale for dimension features portion, Annotative should already be checked because the Text Style chosen is an Annotative style.

In the Fine Tuning portion, pick the check boxes for both items available. This will allow us to place the dimension text where we want it (instead of AutoCAD® automatically placing it) and it will draw the dimension lines between extension lines (primarily handy for radius and diameter dimensions).

When you are done making these changes, your dialog box will look like this:

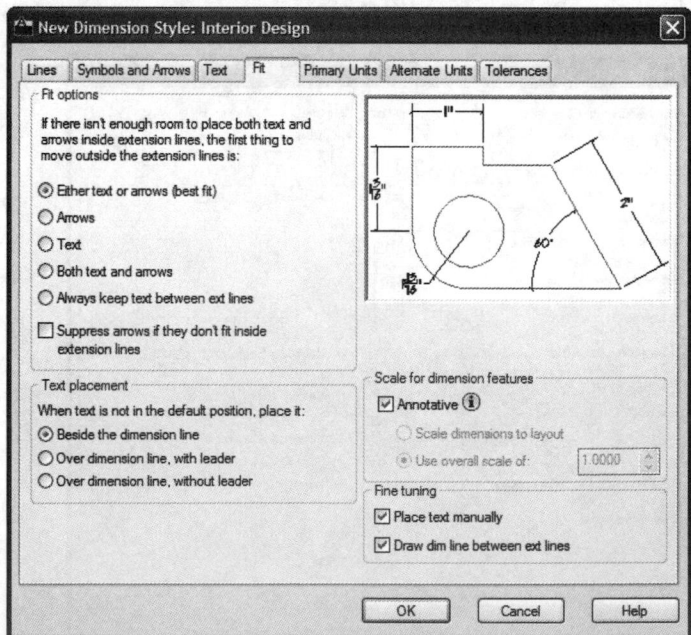

Since these are the only changes we plan to make for our new dimension style, pick the OK button to exit the dialog box. AutoCAD® will return you to the Dimension Style Manager dialog box.

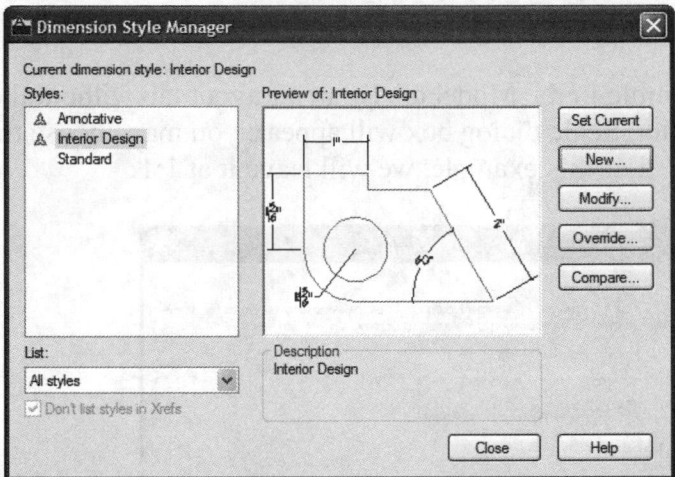

Ensure that Interior Design is the current dimension style. If it is not, pick it to highlight it (on the left side of the dialog box), and then pick the Set Current button. When done, pick the Close button to exit the dialog box.

Using Dimensions

It is important to use dimensions in your drawing to describe the size and placement of items. There are several types of dimensions: linear, aligned, radial, diameter, angular, etc. You have just created a new dimension style. These instructions will show you how to use the various dimension icons.

As an example of using dimensions, we will dimension the faucet:

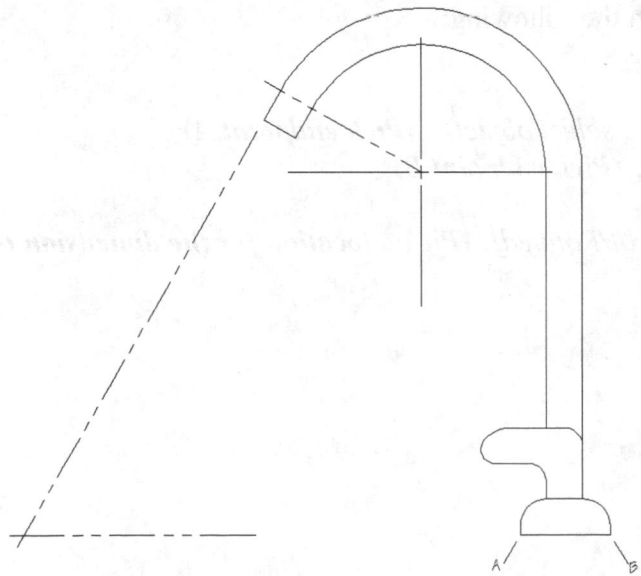

Before beginning to use the dimensions, ensure that OSNAP is turned on and the settings are logical for what you plan to select (example: endpoint, or intersection). Also, select the dimension style, Interior Design, that you just created by using the pull-down arrow in the dimension style control box.

If you are working this example in the Model tab (or in a Layout tab without the Model Scale set and locked), the Select Annotation Scale dialog box will appear; you may choose the annotation scale by using the pull-down arrow. For this example, we will leave it at 1:1.

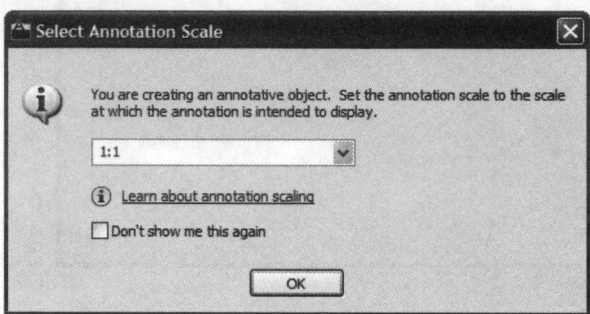

Linear Dimension

Linear dimensions are used to define the horizontal or vertical distances.

Procedure:

Pick (left click): **Linear Dimension icon** from the Dimension toolbar.

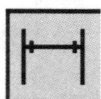

The command line prompts you with the following:

Command: _dimlinear
Specify first extension line origin or <select object>: **(Pick endpoint A)**
Specify second extension line origin: **(Pick endpoint B)**
Specify dimension line location or
[Mtext/Text/Angle/Horizontal/Vertical/Rotated]: **(Pick a location for the dimension text)**
Dimension text = 1 1/4"
Command:

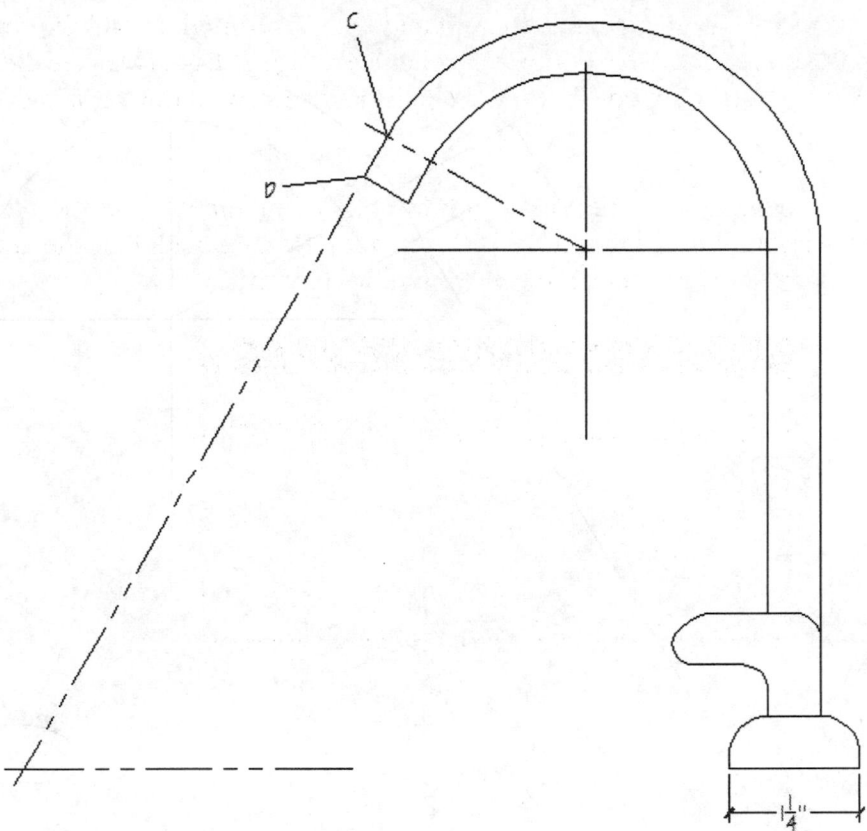

Aligned Dimension

Procedure:

Pick (left click): **Aligned Dimension icon** from the Dimension toolbar.

The command line prompts you with the following:

Command: _dimaligned
Specify first extension line origin or <select object>: **(Pick intersection point C)**
Specify second extension line origin: **(Pick endpoint D)**
Specify dimension line location or
[Mtext/Text/Angle]: **(Pick a location for the dimension text)**
Dimension text = 1/2"
Command:

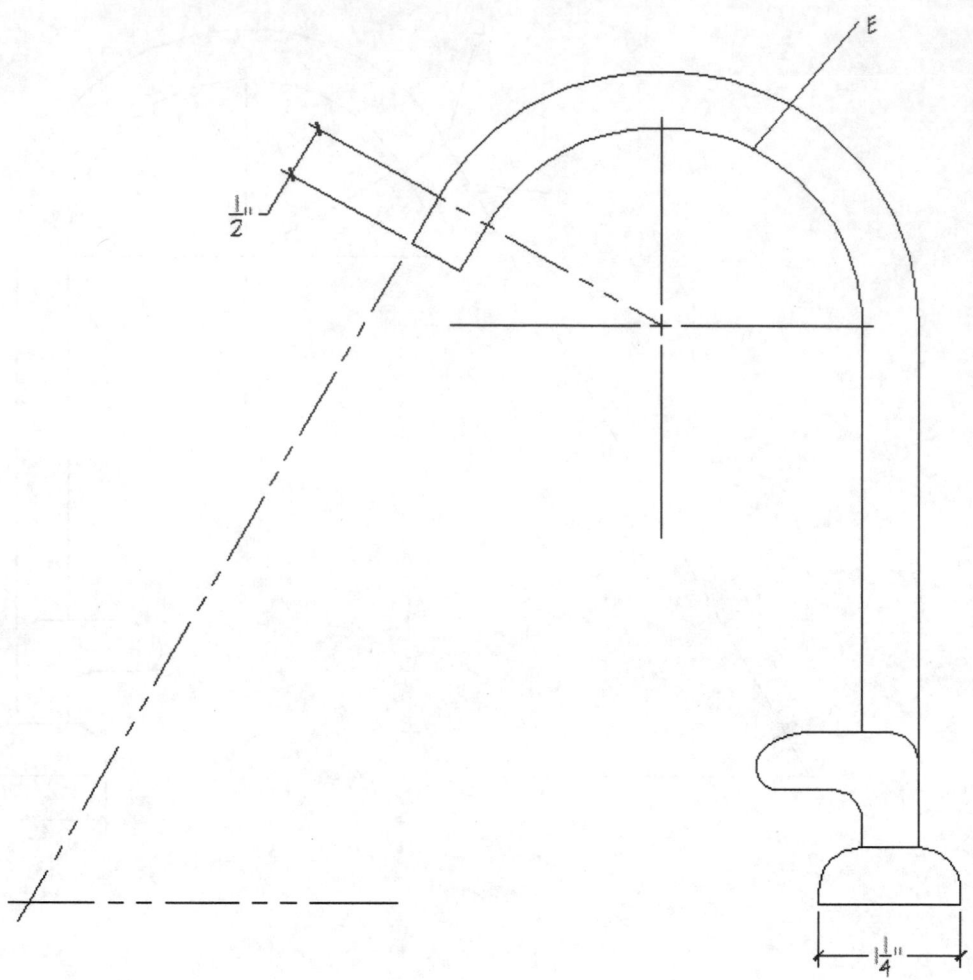

Radial Dimension

Procedure:

Pick (left click): **Radial Dimension icon** from the Dimension toolbar.

The command line prompts you with the following:

Command: _dimradius
*Select arc or circle: **(Pick arc E)***
Dimension text = 1 3/4"
*Specify dimension line location or [Mtext/Text/Angle]: **(Pick a location for the dimension text)***
Command:

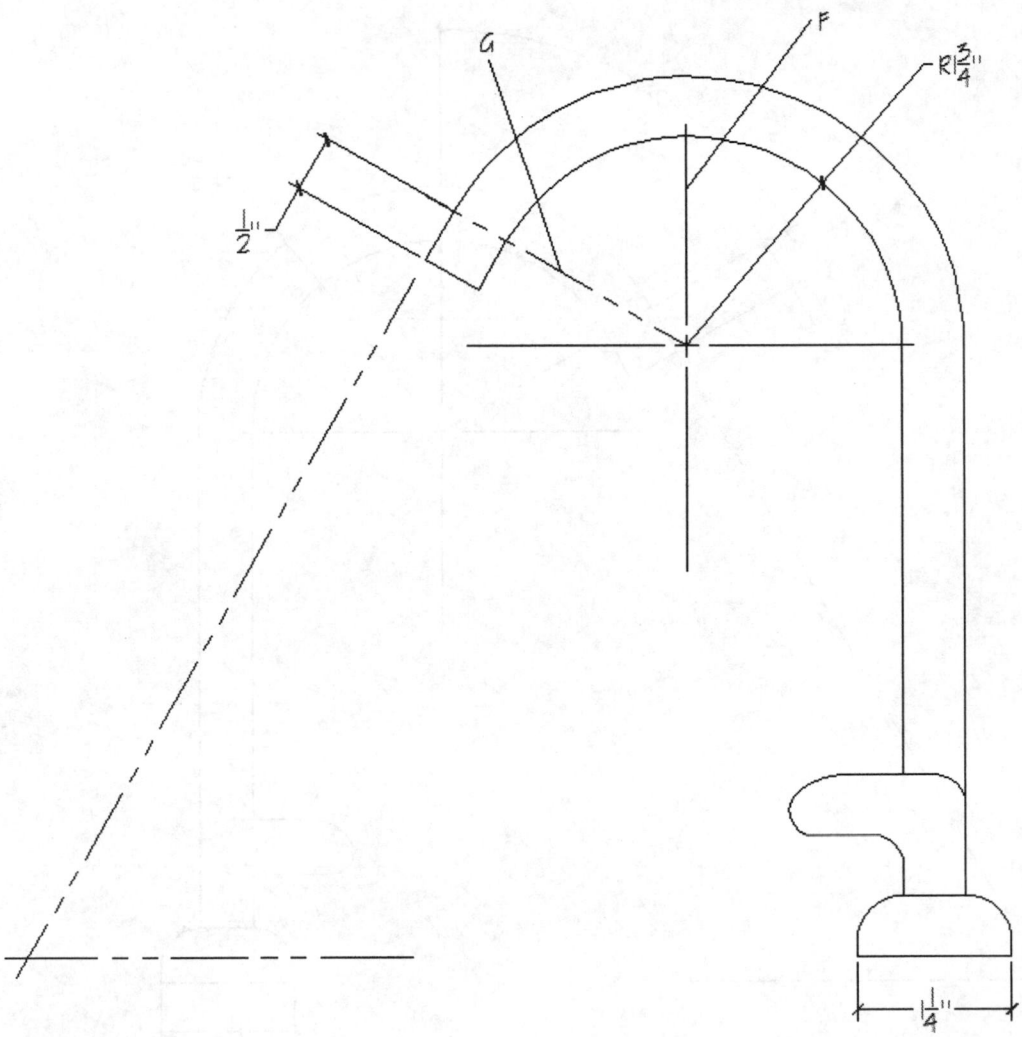

Angular Dimension

Procedure:

Pick (left click): **Angular Dimension icon** from the Dimension toolbar.

The command line prompts you with the following:

Command: _dimangular
Select arc, circle, line, or <specify vertex>: **(Pick line F)**
Select second line: **(Pick line G)**
Specify dimension arc line location or [Mtext/Text/Angle]: **(Pick a location for the dimension text)**
Dimension text = 60
Command:

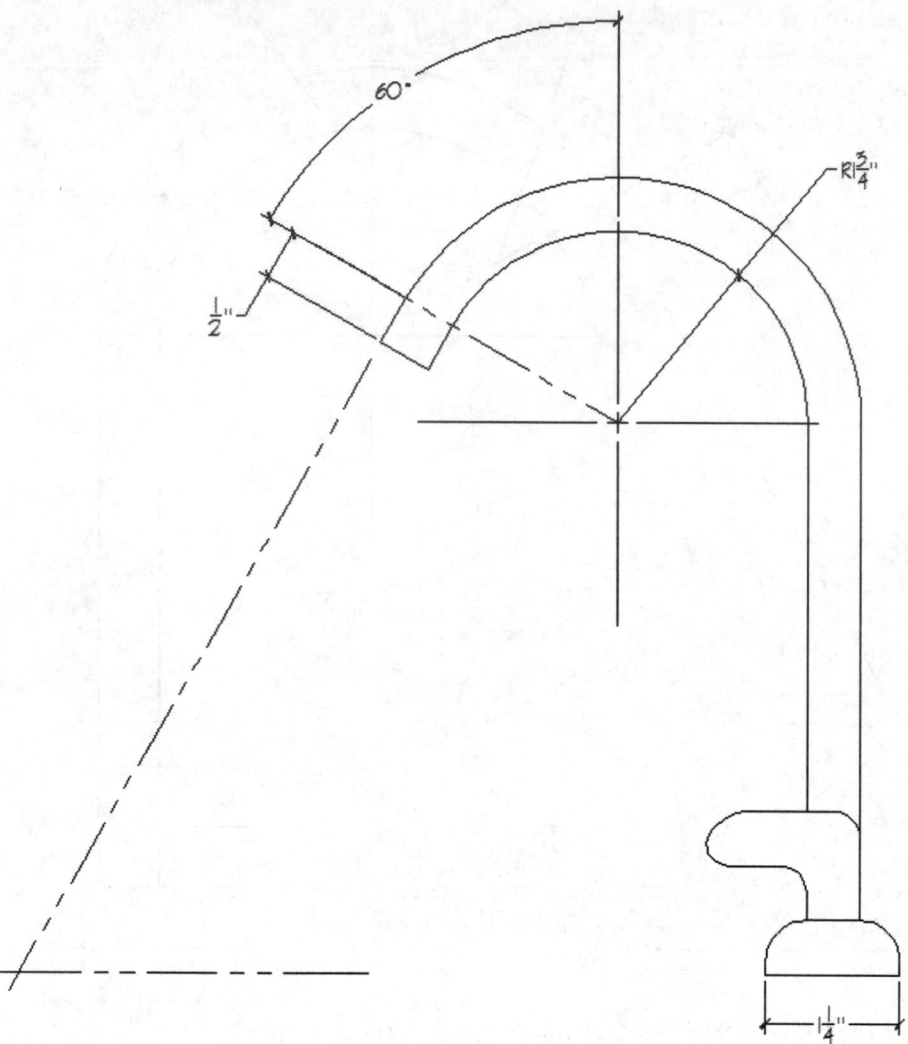

Diameter Dimension

As an example for this dimension type, we will use a simple 4″ diameter circle.

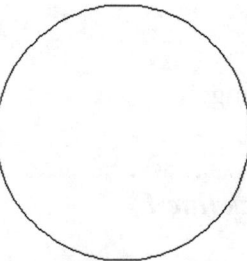

Procedure:

Pick (left click): **Diameter Dimension icon** from the Dimension toolbar.

The command line prompts you with the following:

Command: _dimdiameter
*Select arc or circle: **(Pick the circle)***
Dimension text = 4"
*Specify dimension line location or [Mtext/Text/Angle]: **(Pick a location for the dimension text)***
Command:

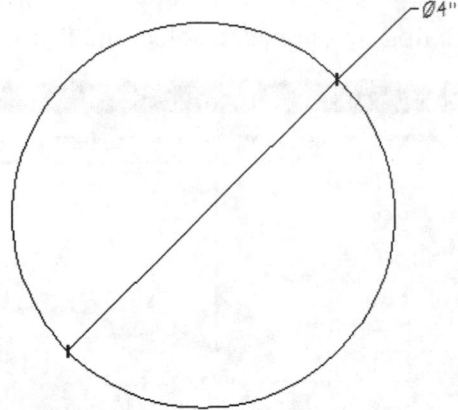

The default setting for AutoCAD® diameter dimension is to use the diameter symbol:

We can change that by modifying the existing style. Pick the Dimension Style icon. When the Dimension Style Manager dialog box appears, select the New button.

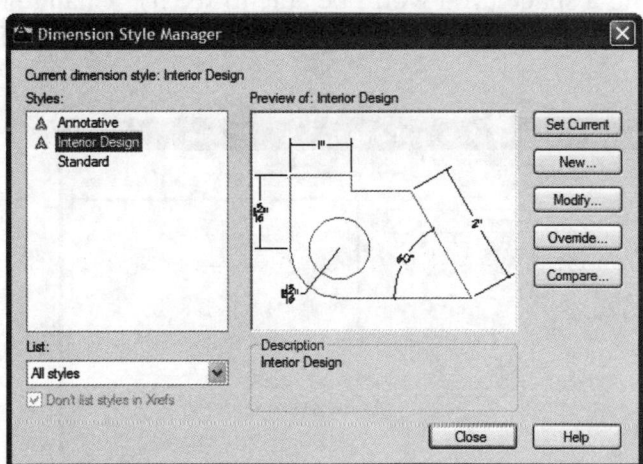

In the Create New Dimension Style dialog box, use the pull-down arrow under Use for: to select the Diameter dimensions, then pick the Continue button.

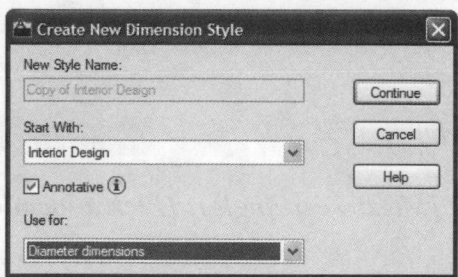

When the New Dimension Style dialog box appears, select the Primary Units tab.

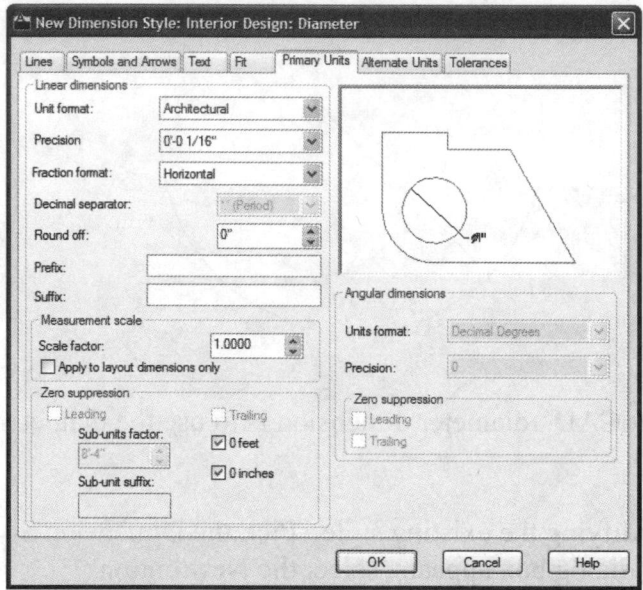

Change the Prefix text by typing a space (you won't be able to see it). Change the Suffix text by typing a space and the word DIA. Notice how it changes in the preview pane. Pick the OK button when you are done.

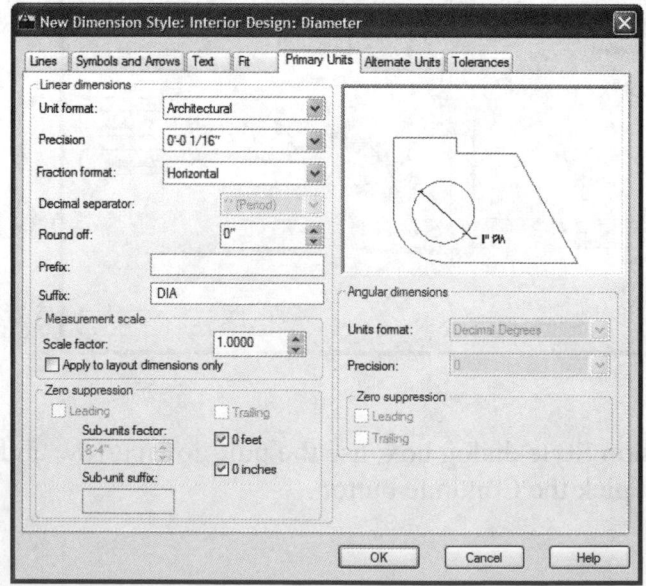

AutoCAD® returns to the Dimension Style Manager dialog box. Notice that the new diameter style that was just created is a subset of the dimension style Interior Design.

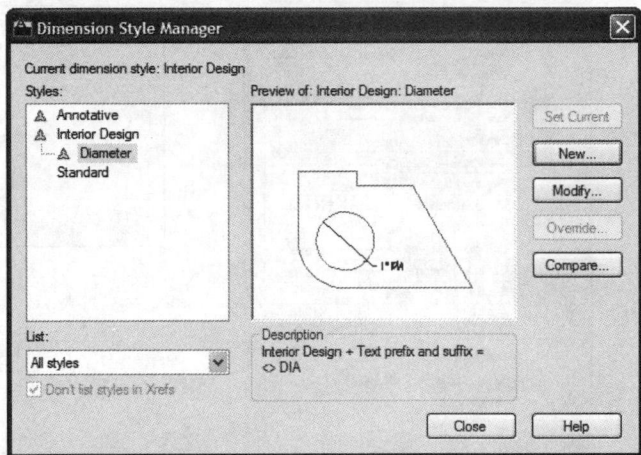

Now when a diameter dimension is created using style Interior Design, the diameter dimension will look like this:

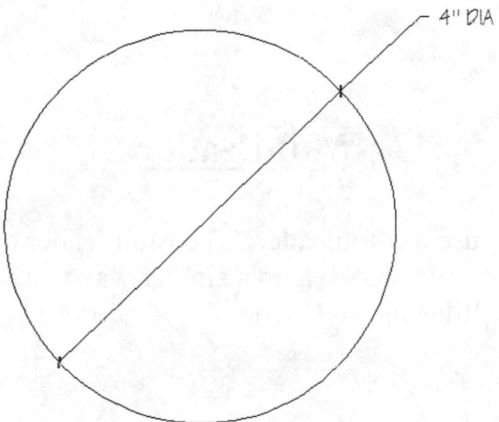

Modifying Existing Dimensions

There are times when dimensions share the same extension lines. Rather than create a unique style with the dimension line suppressed, this can be accomplished by using the Properties icon. In the Properties dialog box, after the dimension is selected, either extension line 1 or 2 or both can be turned off.

This example shows
the Properties Palette
was used to turn Ext
line 2 off.

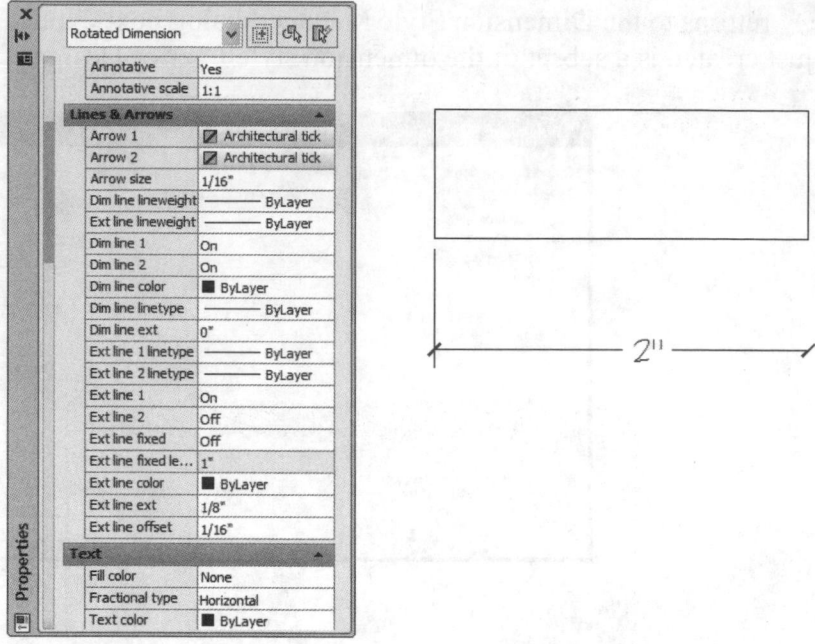

Multileader

To label items on your drawing, use a Multileader. The Multileader can have an arrow with line and text. You can create a unique Multileader style in a similar way that we created a unique dimension style. This is done using the Multileader Style icon.

Multileader Toolbar

Right-click on any toolbar and select the Multileader toolbar to make it available. The icons described below are the ones that we will be using. We will not need all the icons available.

Multileader   Multileader Style

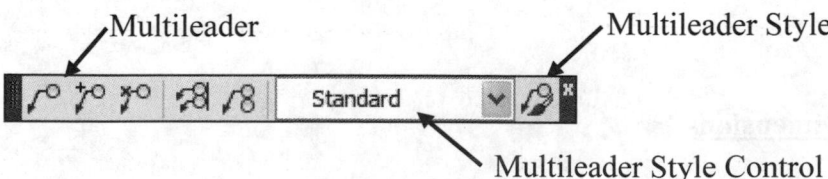

Multileader Style Control

Creating a Multileader Style

To create a unique Multileader style, pick the Multileader Style icon. The Multileader Style Manager dialog box will appear.

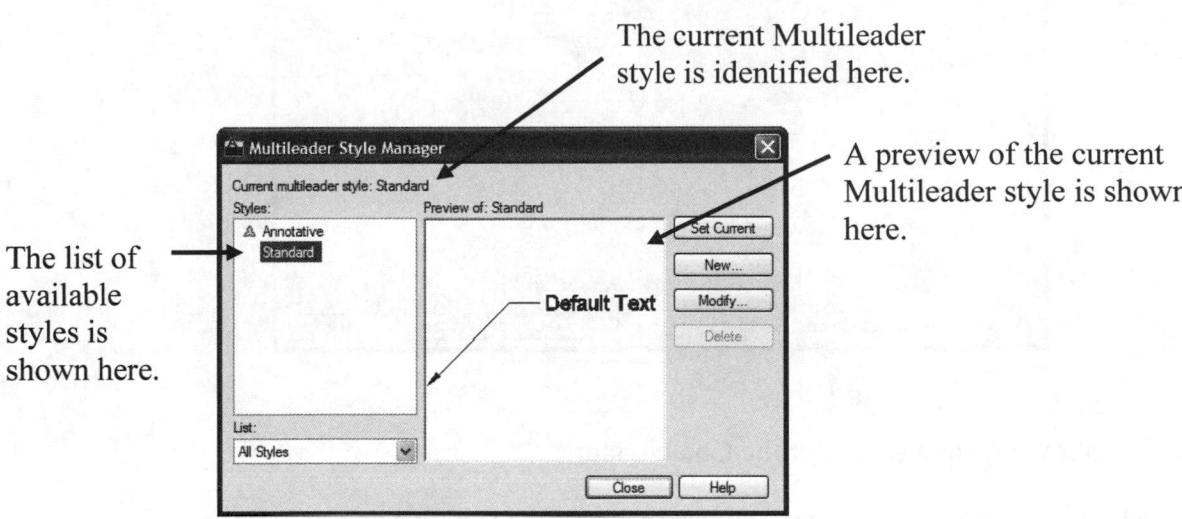

The current Multileader style is identified here.

A preview of the current Multileader style is shown here.

The list of available styles is shown here.

To create a new Multileader style, pick the New... button. A new dialog box will appear. Under New Style Name, the text "Copy of Standard" is highlighted and ready for editing. Let's name the new style Label. Also, check-off Annotative. Pick the Continue button when done.

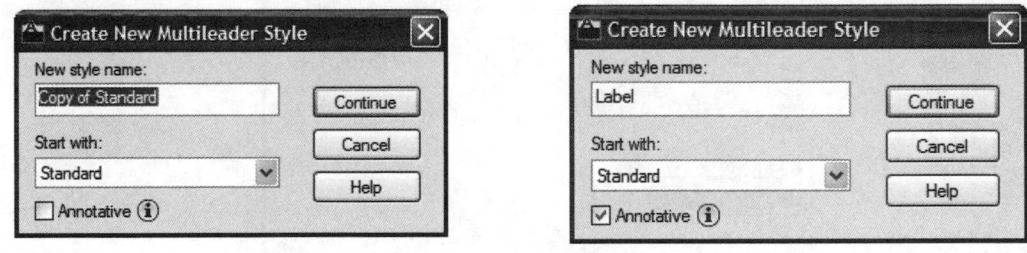

A Modify Multileader Style dialog box will appear. This is where you will make the setting changes. There are three tabs to choose from.

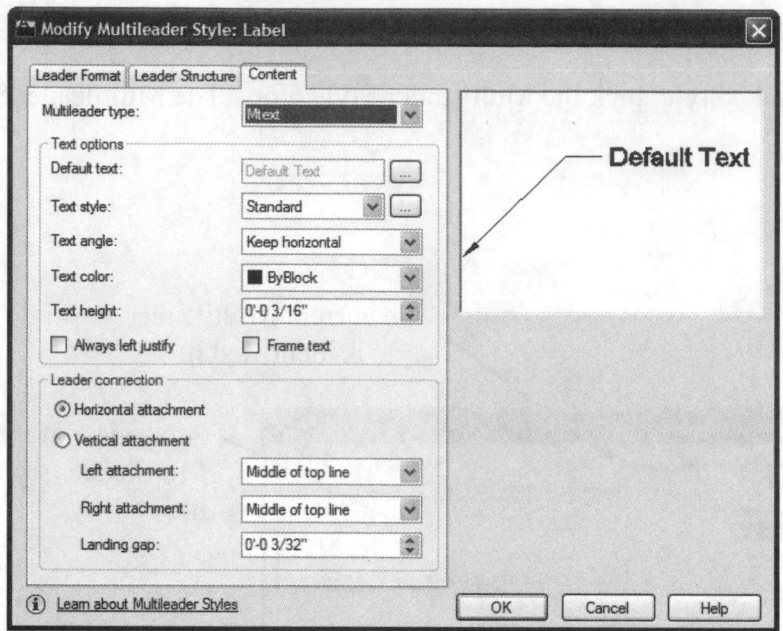

Make the following changes under the Content tab:

- Change the Text style to Notes (as created in previous chapter)
- Change the Text color from ByBlock to ByLayer

When done, your dialog box should look like this:

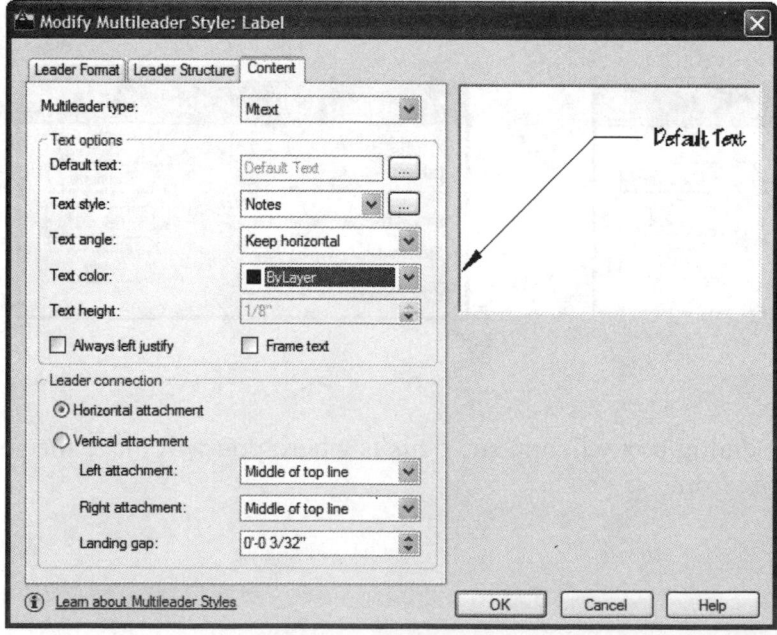

Pick the Leader Format tab. This is where the style of leader (straight or spline), and the choice of multiple arrowheads are made.

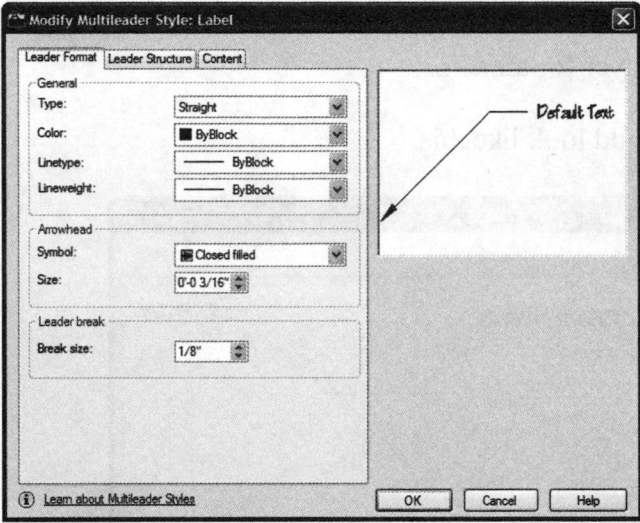

The following shows the difference between a Straight Leader and a Spline Leader:

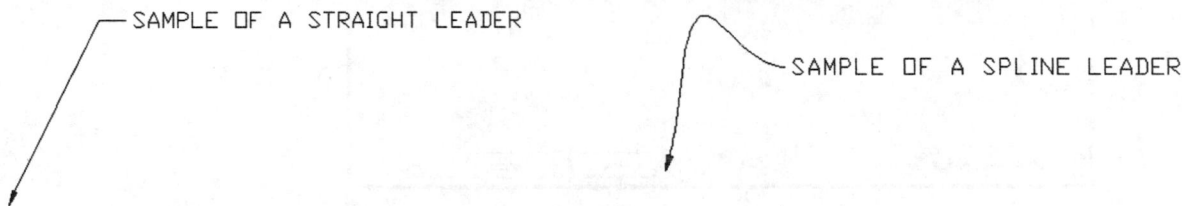

For this style, we will leave the Type as Straight.

The multiple arrowhead choices are found by using the pull-down arrow in the Arrowhead section of the dialog box:

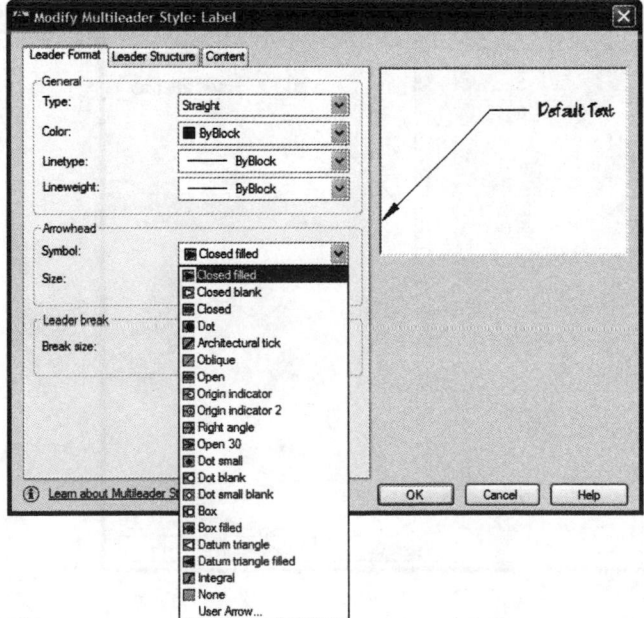

For this style, we will leave the Arrowhead Symbol as Closed filled.
Make the following changes under the Leader Format tab:

- Change the Arrowhead Size to 1/4.
- Change ByBlock to ByLayer for all items.

When done, your dialog box should look like this:

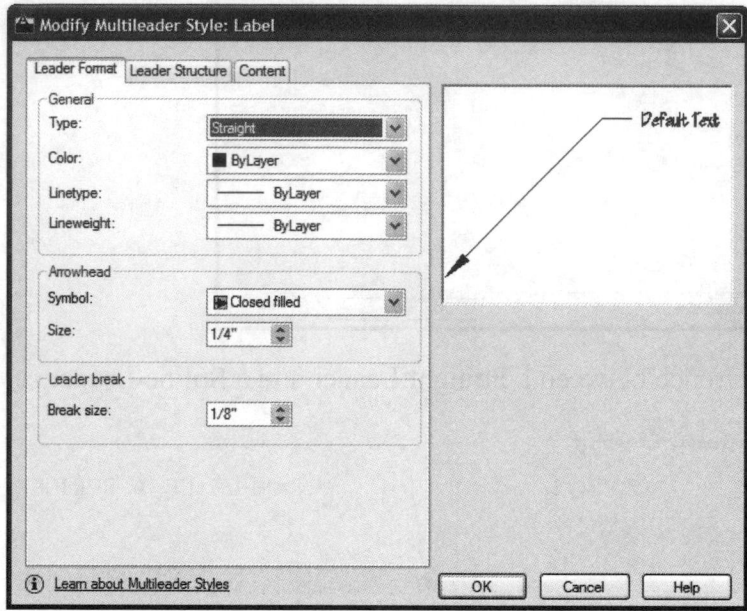

Pick the Leader Structure tab.

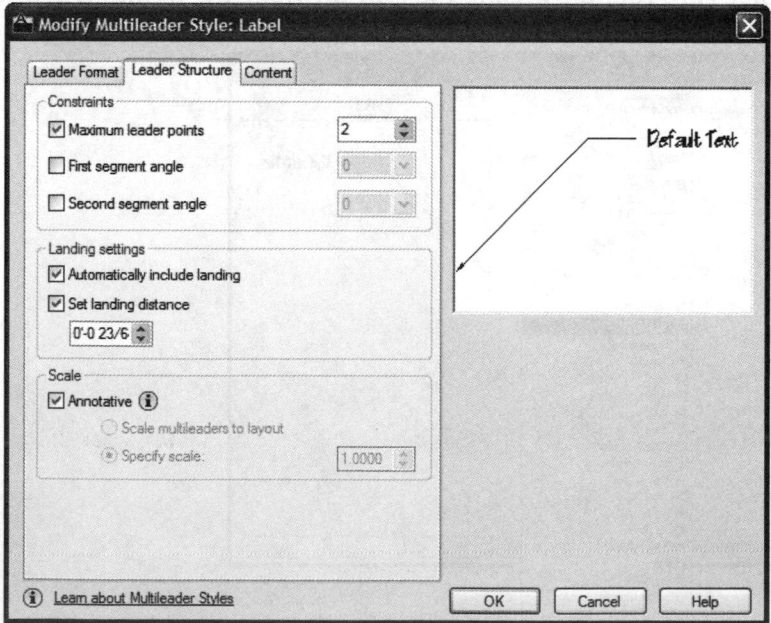

Each line segment can be constrained as you desire.

Make the following changes under the Leader Structure tab:

- Change the landing distance to 1/4.

When done, your dialog box should look like this:

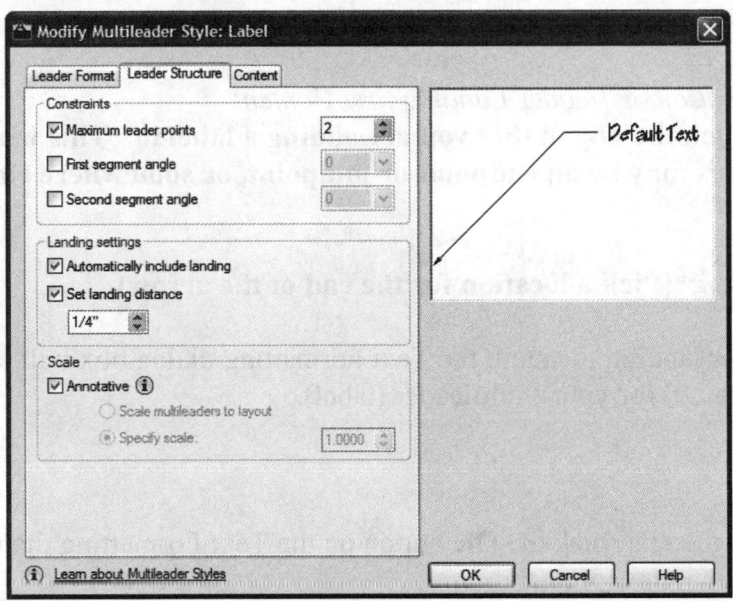

Note that if you desired, you can change the Maximum number of leader points. Below is an example of 3 leader points:

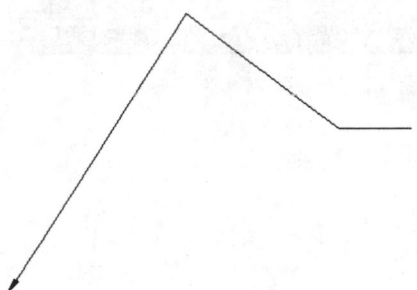

Example of 3 leader points

Pick OK to exit the dialog box. Pick Close to exit the Multileader Style Manager dialog box.

The current style should now be set to Label:

Inserting a Multileader on Your Drawing

Procedure:

Pick (left click): **Multileader icon** from the Multileader toolbar.

The command line prompts you with the following:

Command: _mleader
Specify leader arrowhead location or [leader Landing first/Content
first/Options] <Options>: **(Pick the object that you are adding a label to. This will be the Arrow end of the first segment. This may be an endpoint or midpoint, or somewhere close to the object with OSNAP off)**

Specify leader landing location: **(Pick a location for the end of the arrow)**

As soon as you pick the leader landing location, the Text Formatting dialog box will appear. This is where you type in the information for your Multileader (label).

(Key in the desired text).

When you are done typing in the text, pick the OK button on the Text Formatting dialog box. This will close the dialog box and exit the command.

OK Button

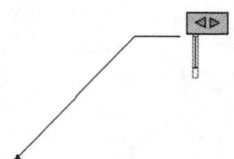

As an example, let's assume we are labeling a coffee table. When done, your Multileader should look like this:

COFFEE TABLE

Summary

In this chapter you have learned to:

- Create different styles of text
- Create a style for dimensions that is suitable for interior design
- Use various types of dimensions, including linear, aligned, radial and angular
- Modify existing dimensions
- Create a label style for Multileader
- Use Multileaders for labeling objects

Review Questions

1. What does "Annotative" style mean?

2. What does "current style" mean?

3. What does a text height of 0″ mean?

4. What are the differences between Single Line Text and Multiline Text?

5. What is an easy way to relocate text on your drawing?

6. After text is already on the drawing, how can you change its size?

7. What is the difference between a dimension line and an extension line?

8. What is an easy method to turn a dimension extension line off?

9. How do you change the default diameter symbol?

10. What is a Spline Leader?

Exercises

1. Draw the bookshelf. Use the 8-1/2″ x 11″ layout to set and lock the scale to 1″ = 1′. Create layers "Object", "Viewport", and "Dimension and Text". Set the Lineweight of layer Object to .012″ . Place the viewport border on layer Viewport and Freeze the layer. The bookshelf is drawn on layer Object. Use the dimension, text, and multileader styles created in this chapter. The dimensions and multileaders must be Model Space objects and placed on the Dimensions and Text layer. The text items are Paper Space objects and belong on Dimensions and Text layer.

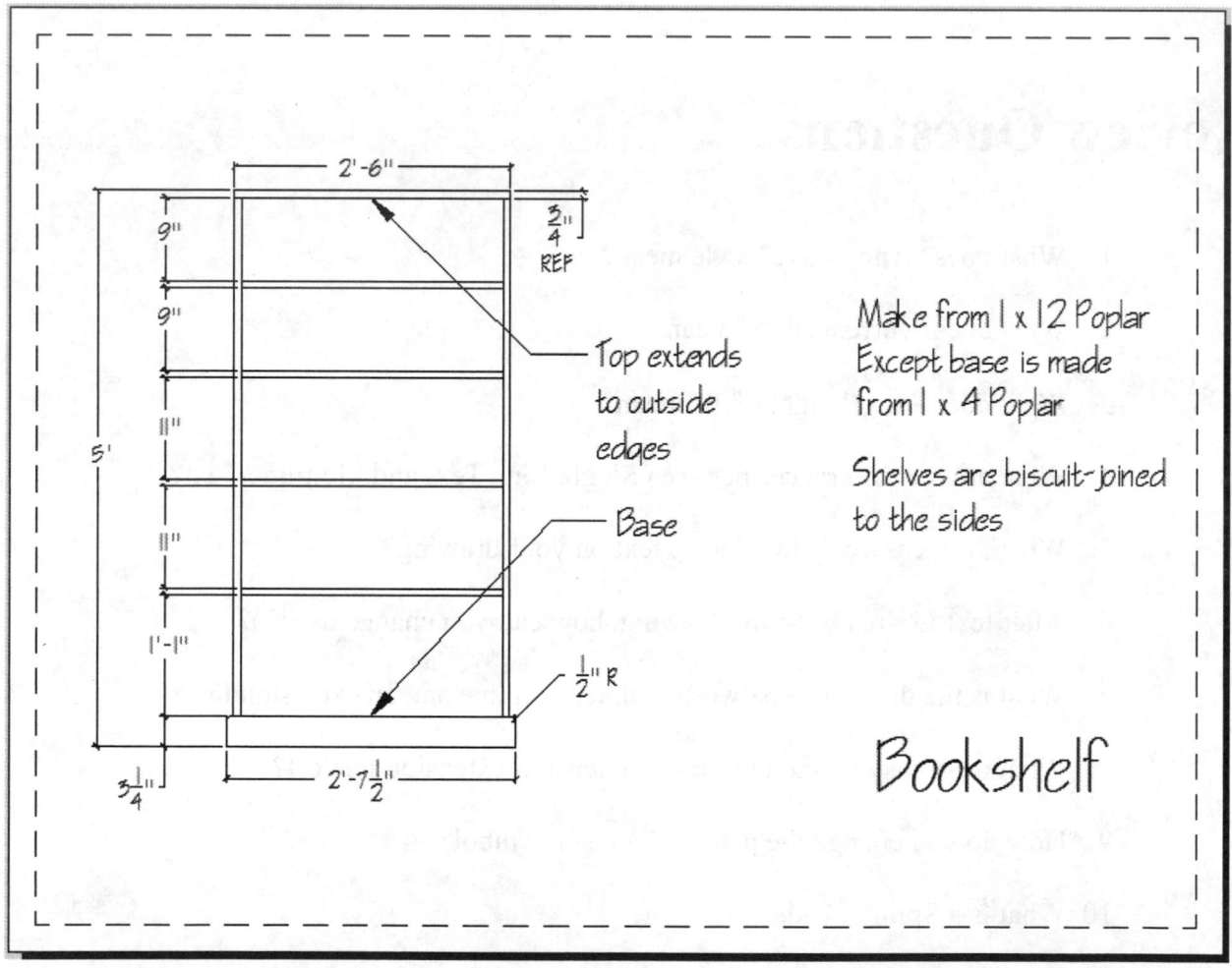

2. Draw the Hinge.

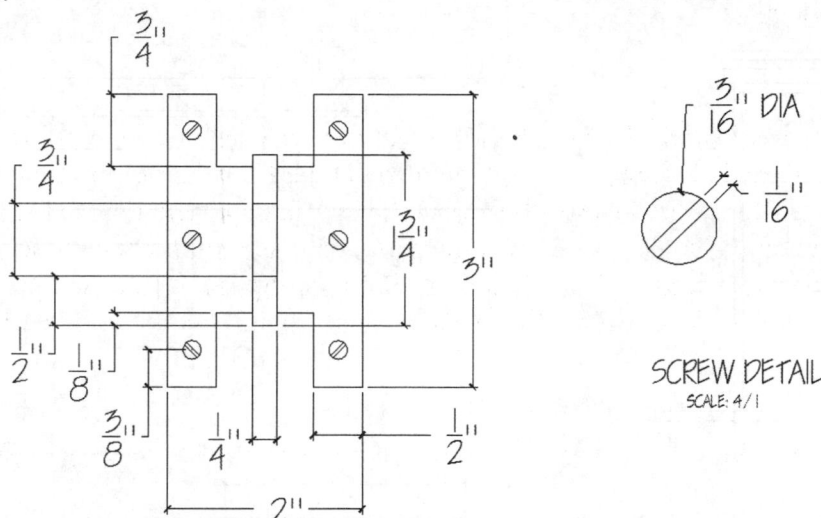

SCREW DETAIL
SCALE: 4/1

3. Draw the country hutch. Use the drawing format sheet, layers, dimensions, text, multileaders, and create viewports and layouts.

The hutch drawing details are on the following three drawing sheets:
(Hint for side view: draw the arcs as circles, draw a line tangent to the circles for the angled line (use Snap-to-Tangent), and trim the circles so they become arcs).

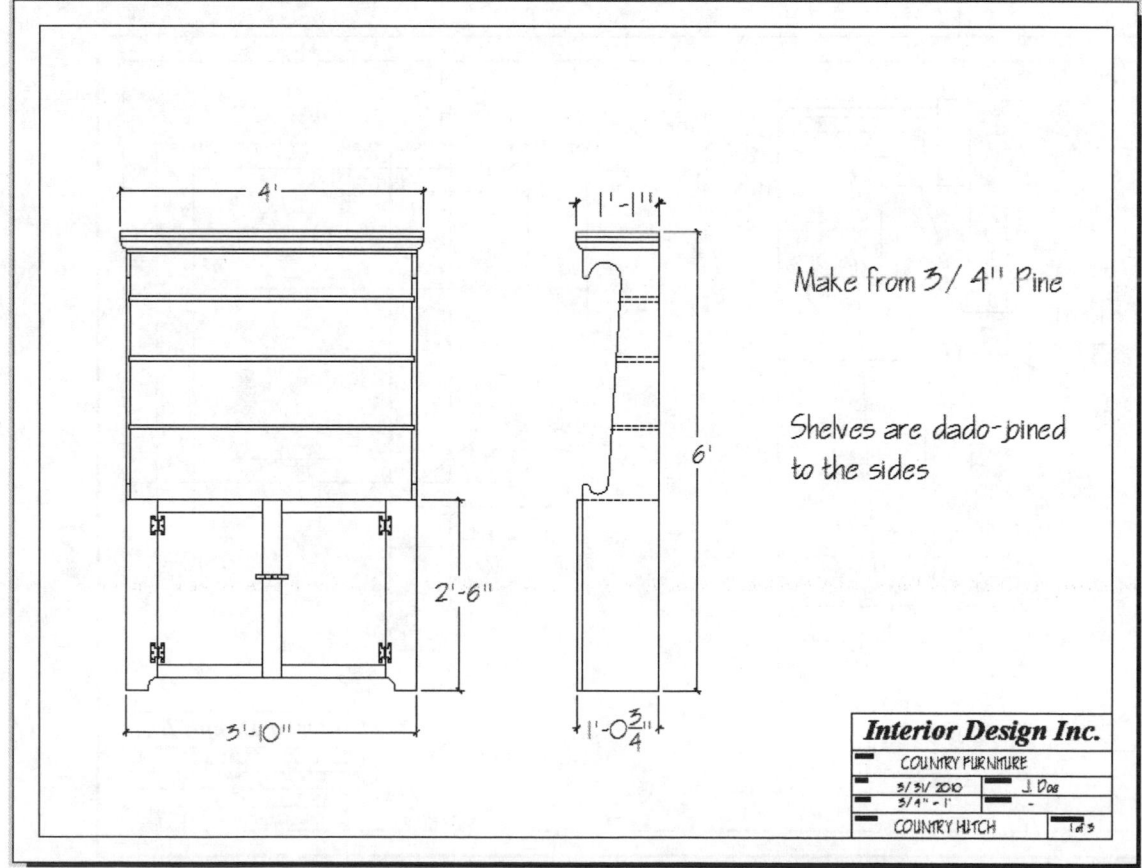

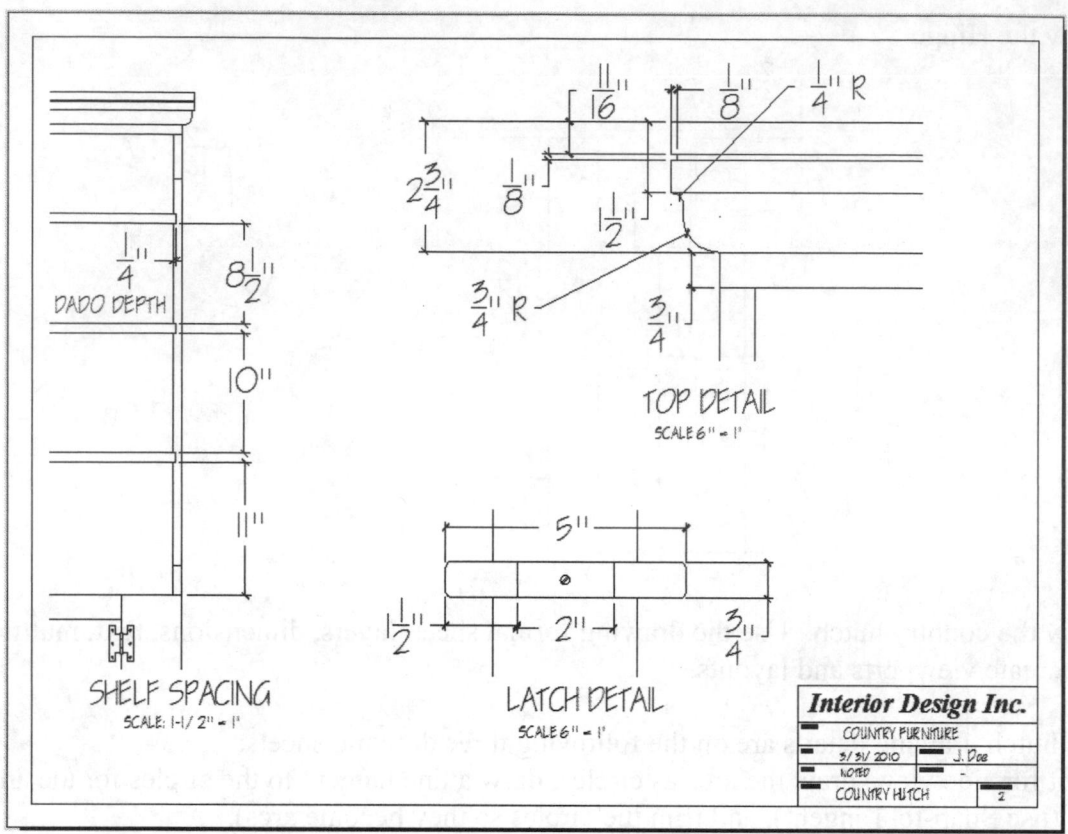

SHELF SPACING
SCALE: 1-1/2" = 1'

TOP DETAIL
SCALE 6" = 1'

LATCH DETAIL
SCALE 6" = 1'

Interior Design Inc.
COUNTRY FURNITURE
3/31/2010 — J. Doe
NOTED —
COUNTRY HUTCH — 2

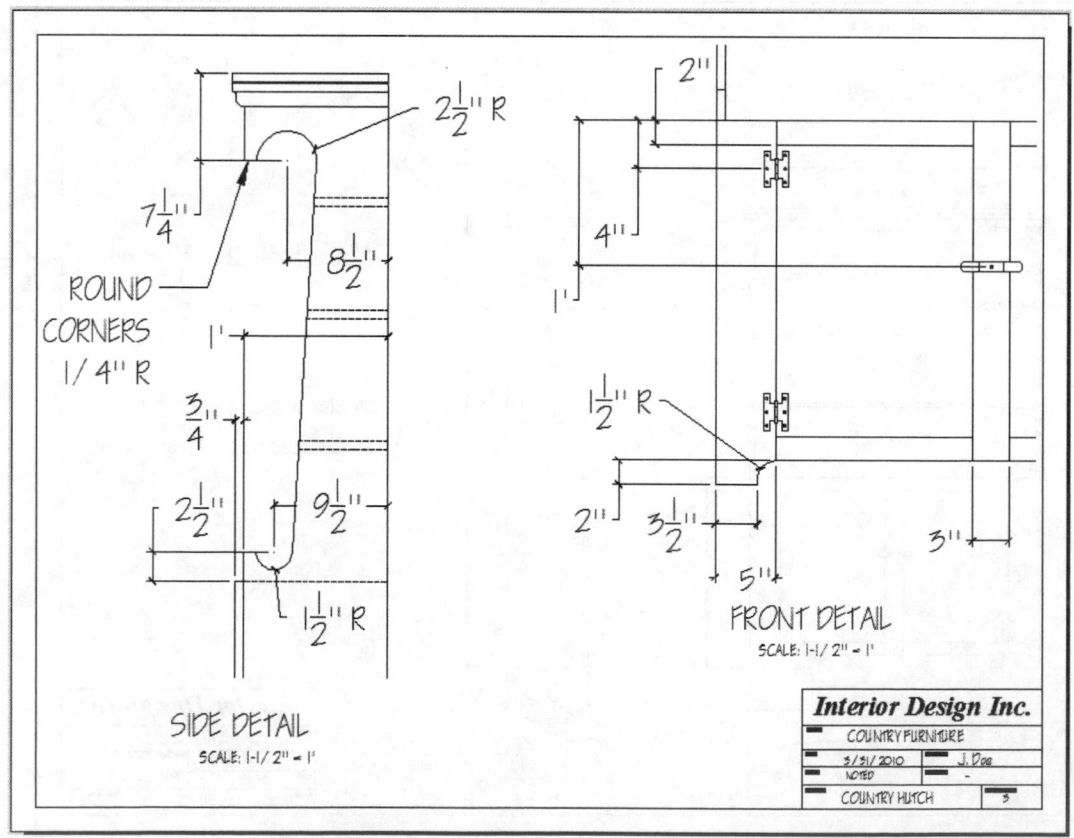

SIDE DETAIL
SCALE: 1-1/2" = 1'

FRONT DETAIL
SCALE: 1-1/2" = 1'

Interior Design Inc.
COUNTRY FURNITURE
3/31/2010 — J. Doe
NOTED —
COUNTRY HUTCH — 3

Chapter 12
Hotel Suite Project – Tutorial 5

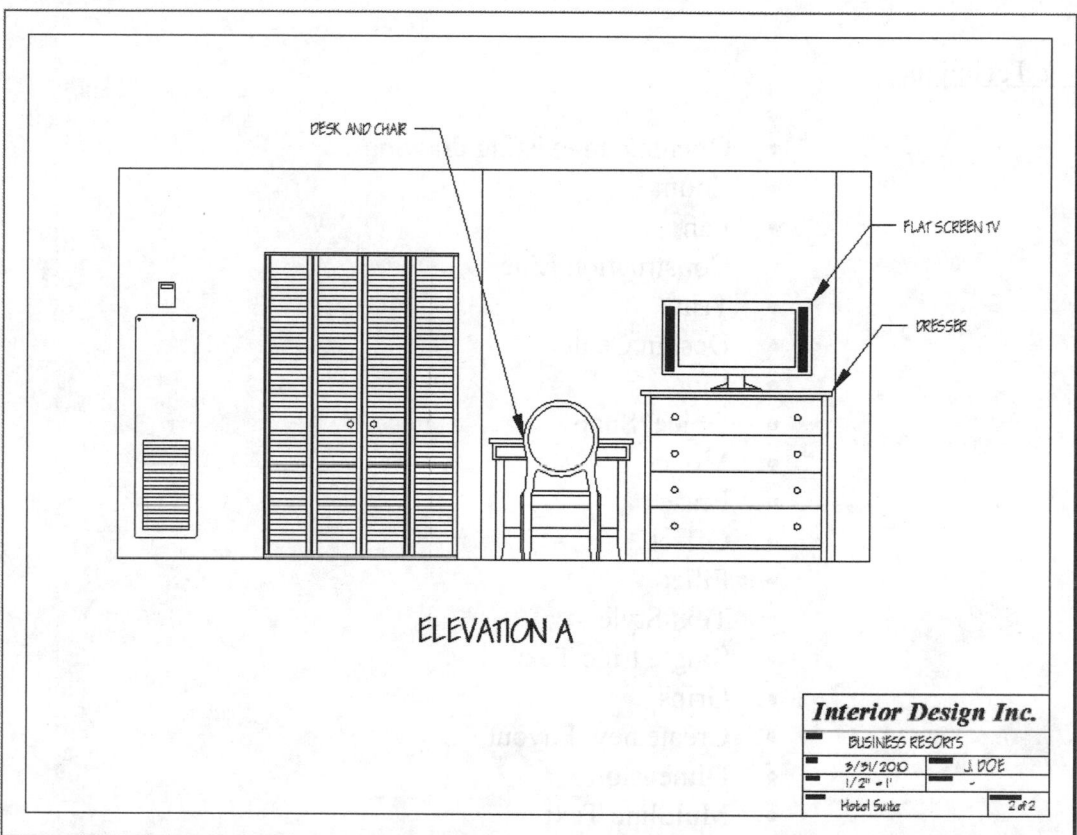

ELEVATION A

Learning Objectives:

- To continue creating a drawing of a real-world application of AutoCAD®
  - Create an elevation view
  - Annotate with Text, Dimensions, and Multileader
  - Create multiple layouts
- To utilize and reinforce the use of the AutoCAD® commands learned in the previous chapters

This tutorial builds on Tutorial 4 found in Chapter 10. In this tutorial, we will create an elevation view of the bedroom. We will also create additional layers and annotate the drawing. When you are finished with this tutorial, the bedroom elevation will be completed and you will have dimensions, labels, and text your printable 8-1/2″x 11″ sheets.

Commands & Techniques:

- Opening an existing drawing
- Zoom
- Pan
- Construction Line
- Trim
- Design Center
- Line
- Object Snap
- Move
- Erase
- Offset
- Fillet
- Text Style
- Single Line Text
- Grips
- Create new Layout
- Dimension
- Multiline Text
- Multileader
- Save

Create an Elevation View

Before beginning, open the Hotel Suite drawing that you updated in Tutorial 4. Note, for this tutorial, the author has changed the colors of the layers back to white and hidden the lineweights to make it easier to see in the textbook. Make sure layer "Structure" is the current layer.

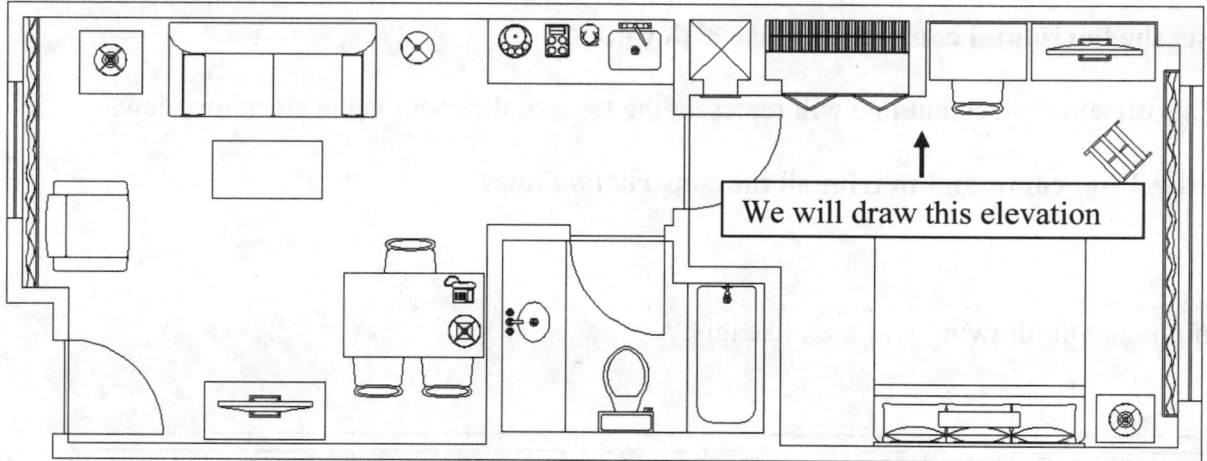

We will draw the elevation view of the bedroom as shown above. As you already know from drawing elevation views by hand, the best way to start the new view is to project from the plan view. In AutoCAD®, the projection lines will be construction lines.

1. **Create vertical construction lines to project below the plan view.**

    You do not need to project all the lines. In fact, for the utility closet, it is best to project the midpoint instead of the endpoints because the access panel will cover the opening. The same is recommended for aligning the furniture – project the midpoints of the desk and dresser instead of the endpoints.

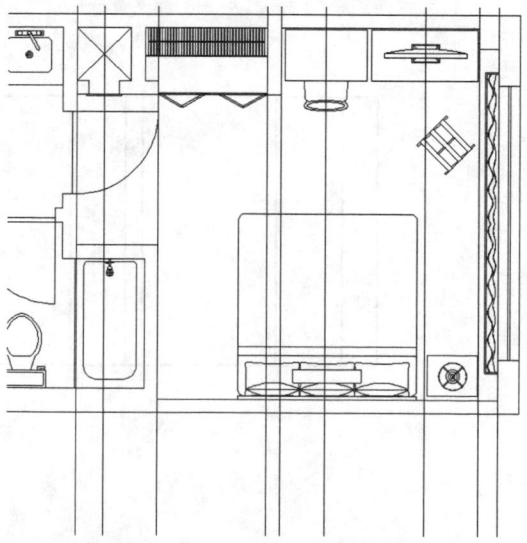

Vertical construction lines are used to project either endpoints or midpoints (as appropriate) from the plan view into the elevation view.

We will build the elevation view directly below the plan view. Leave some space between the plan and elevation views. It is important to note that the ceiling height is 8′.

2.   Create a horizontal construction line a reasonable distance below the plan view.

This horizontal construction line will represent the ceiling of the room in the elevation view.

3.   Offset the horizontal construction line 8′ down.

This offset construction line will represent the floor of the room in the elevation view.

4.   Use the Trim command to trim all the construction lines.

After trimming, your drawing will look like this:

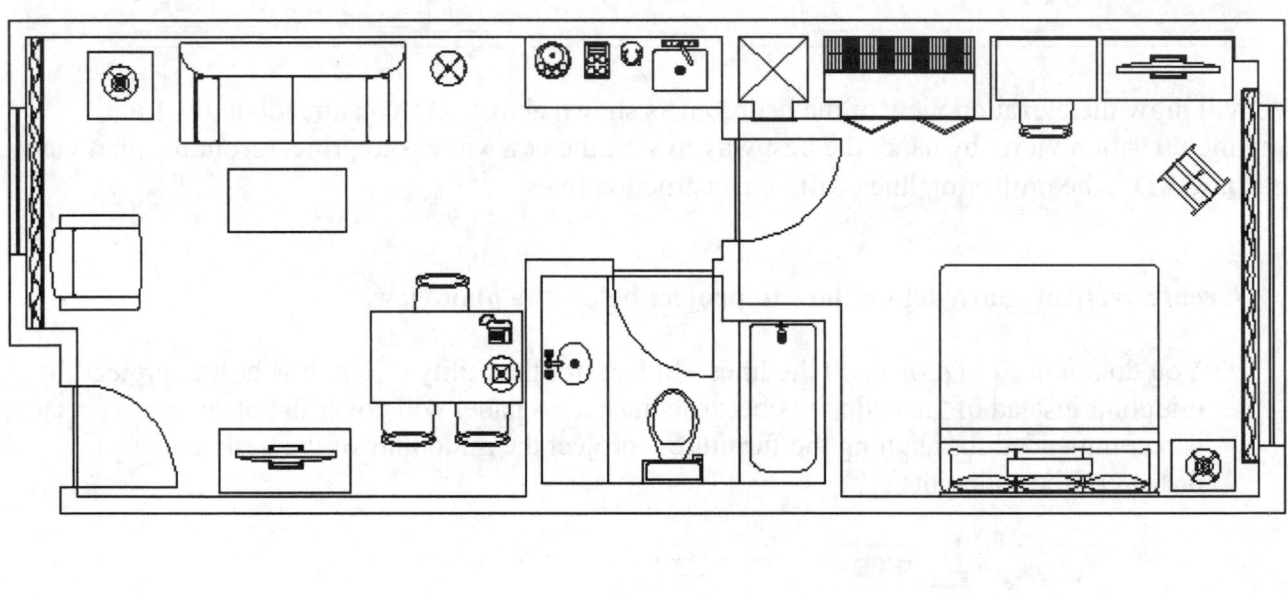

Adding the Blocks to the Drawing

Prior to inserting the block, you must have the Hotel Suite Blocks – Bedroom Elevation drawing that you can download from the publisher's web site.

The Blocks that we are going to use for the bedroom elevation view are shown below:

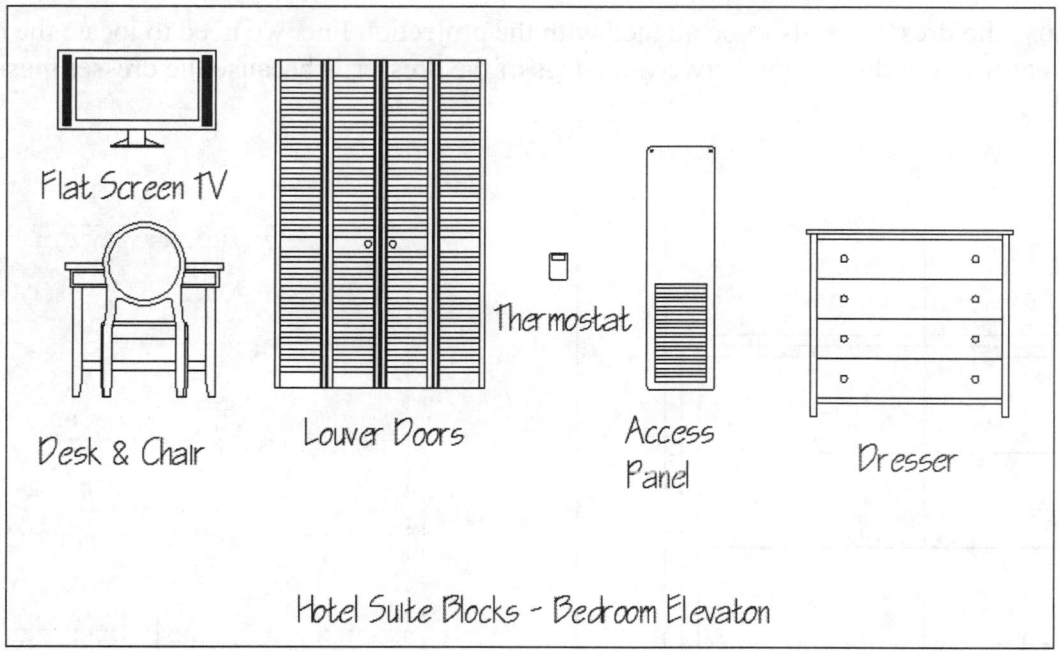

Adding Blocks to the Bedroom Elevation

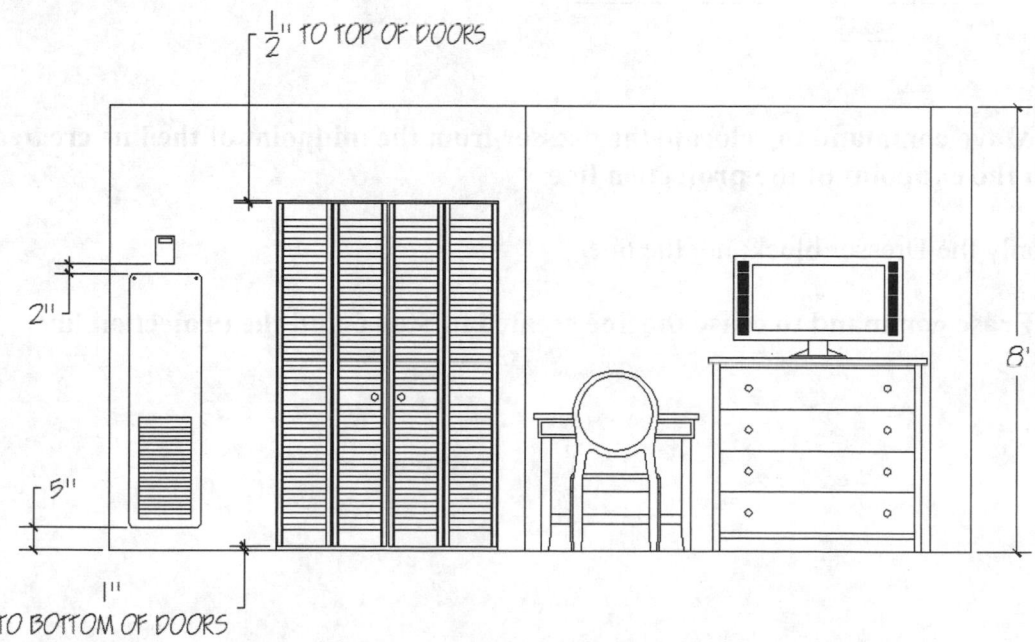

Let's insert the blocks one at a time. Before inserting the furniture blocks, make sure layer "Furniture" is the current layer.

5. **Use Design Center to insert the Dresser block.**

6. **Use the Line command to draw a line between the legs of the dresser.**

   Because the dresser needs to be aligned with the projection line, we need to locate the center. The reason for adding a line between the legs of the dresser is because the dresser must set on the floor.

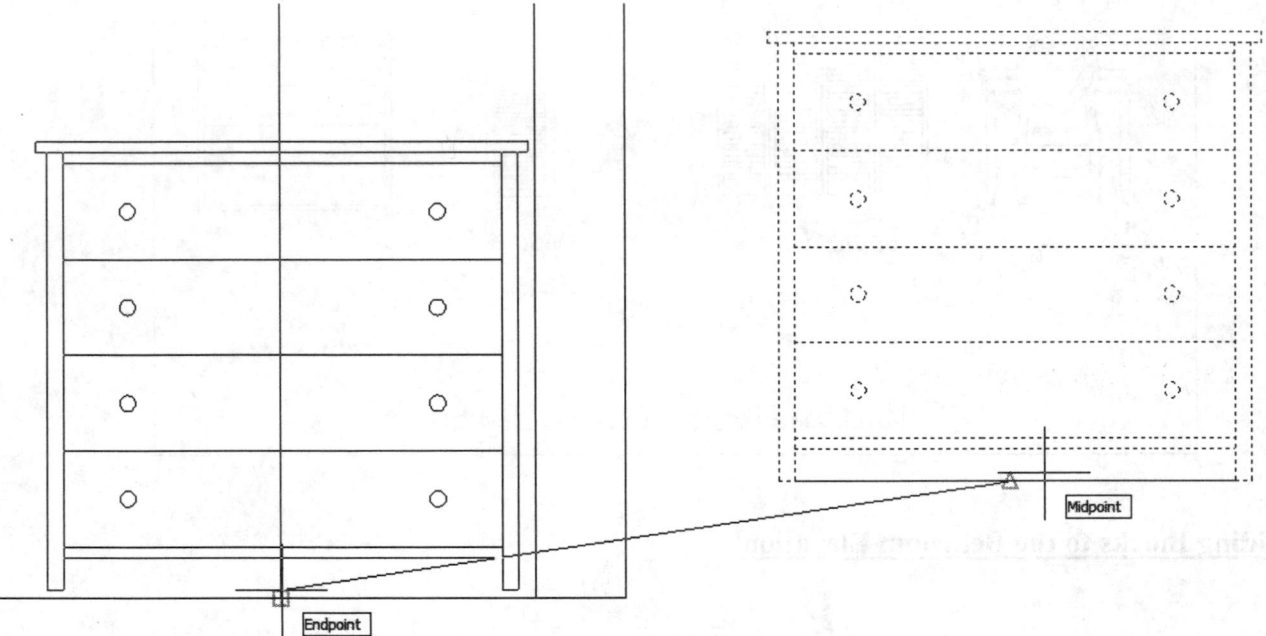

7. **Use the Move command to relocate the dresser from the midpoint of the line created in Step 6 to the endpoint of the projection line.**

   Pick only the Dresser block, not the line.

8. **Use the Erase command to erase the line created in Step 6 and the projection line.**

When you are done, your elevation view will look like this:

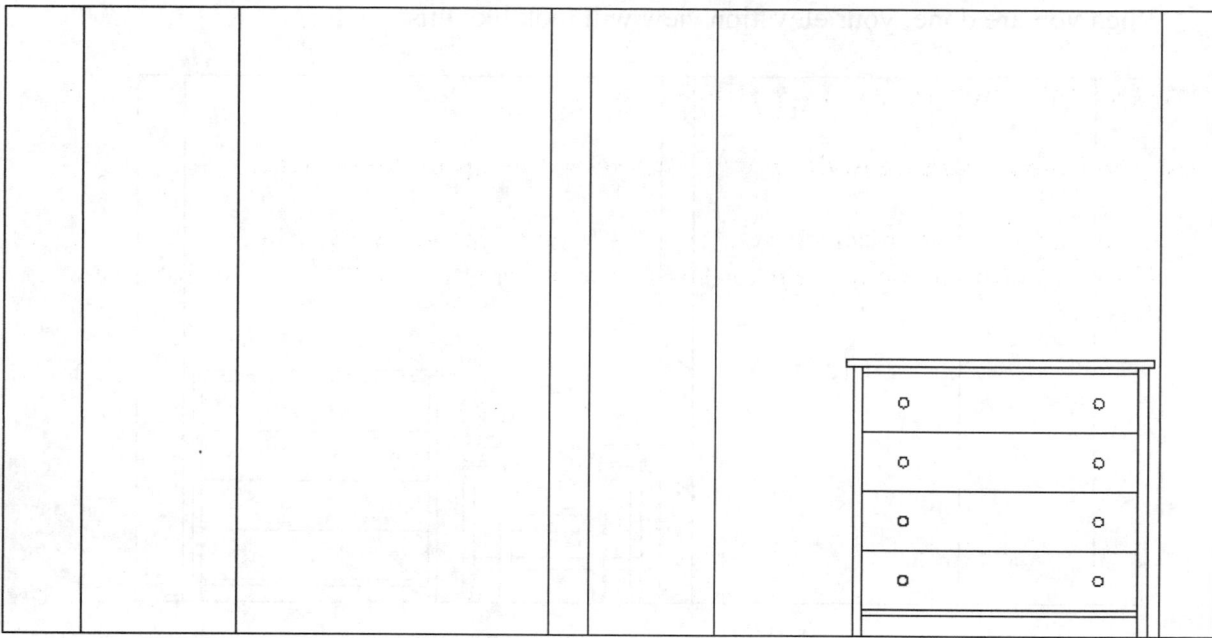

9. **Use Design Center to insert the Desk & Chair block.**

10. **Use the Line command to draw a line between the legs of the desk.**

    Because the desk needs to be aligned with the projection line, we need to locate the center. The reason for adding a line between the legs of the desk is because the desk must set on the floor.

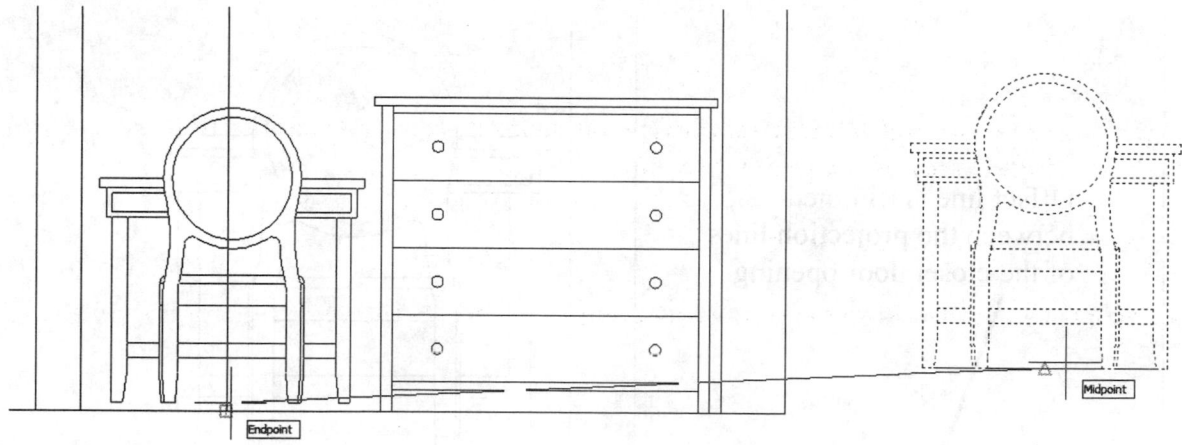

11. **Use the Move command to relocate the desk from the midpoint of the line created in Step 10 to the endpoint of the projection line.**

    Pick only the Desk & Chair block, not the line.

12. Use the Erase command to erase the line created in Step 6 and the projection line.

When you are done, your elevation view will look like this:

The bottom of the louver doors is 1″ above the floor to provide adequate clearance for opening and closing. Before we bring in the block for the doors, we will create the location off the floor. In addition, we will change the current layer to "Structure".

13. Offset the floor 1″ upward.

14. Trim the offset line between the door opening.

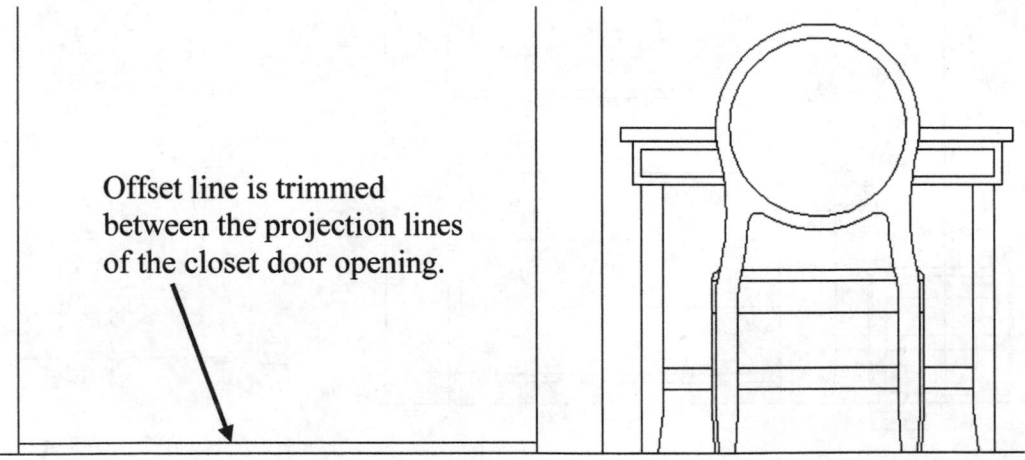

Offset line is trimmed between the projection lines of the closet door opening.

15. Use Design Center to insert the Louver Doors block.

16. Use the Line command to draw a line at the bottom and between the two middle doors.

Because the doors must be centered in the opening and above the floor, we need to locate the center.

Line added between middle doors at the bottom of the Louver Doors block.

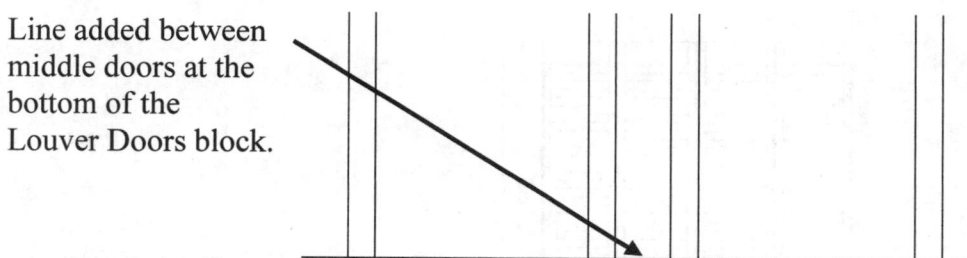

17. Use the Move command to relocate the doors from the midpoint of the line created in Step 16 to the midpoint of the line created in Step 14.

Pick only the Louver Doors block, not the line.

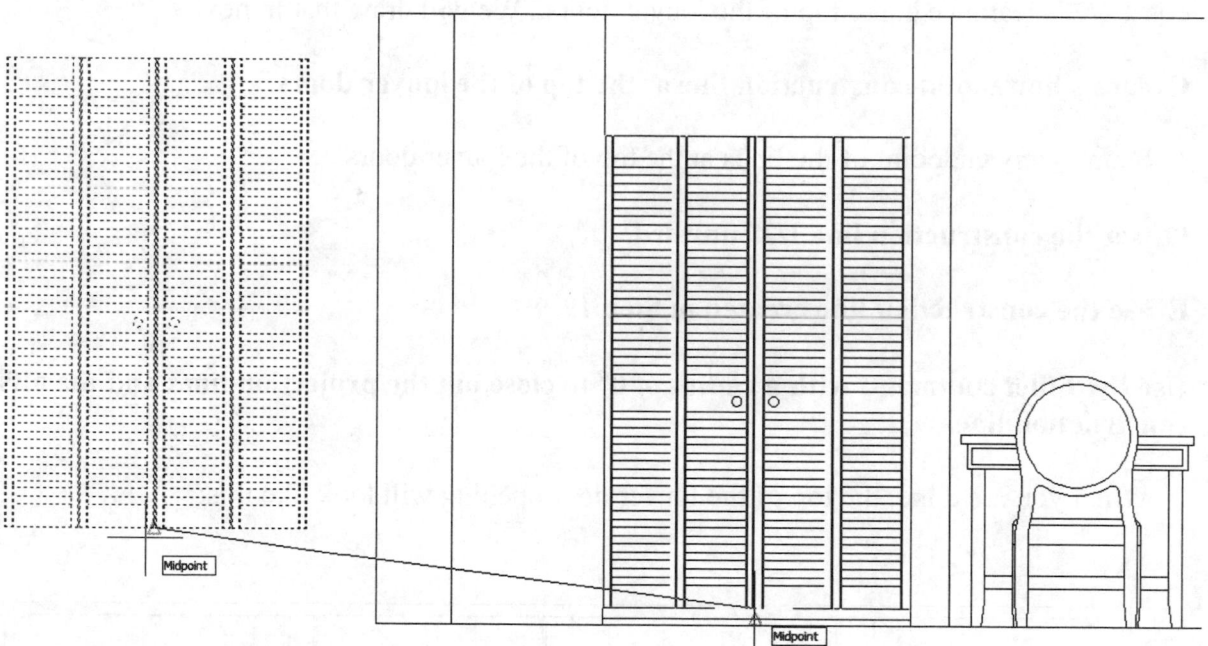

18. Use the Erase command to erase the lines created in Steps 14 and 16.

When you are done, your elevation view will look like this:

There is a 1/2″ clearance at the top of the louver doors. We will draw that in next.

19. Create a horizontal construction line at the top of the louver doors.

Snap to any endpoint of the lines at the top of the louver doors.

20. Offset the construction line 1/2″ upward.

21. Erase the construction line created in Step 19.

22. Use the Fillet command with a radius of 0″ to close out the projection lines and the offset construction line.

When you are done, the top of the louver door opening will look like this:

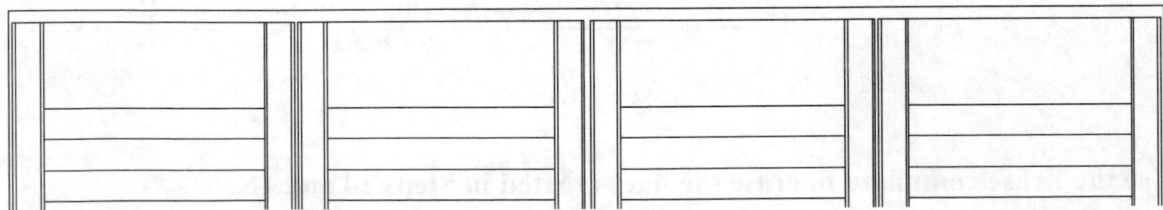

23. Use Design Center to insert the Access Panel block.

Because the bottom of the access panel is 5″ off the floor, we will need to create an offset line from the floor.

24. Use the Offset command to offset the floor 5″ upward.

25. Use the Move command to relocate the Access Panel.

> Snap to the Midpoint of the bottom horizontal line of the access panel and to the intersection of the projection line and the offset line created in Step 24.

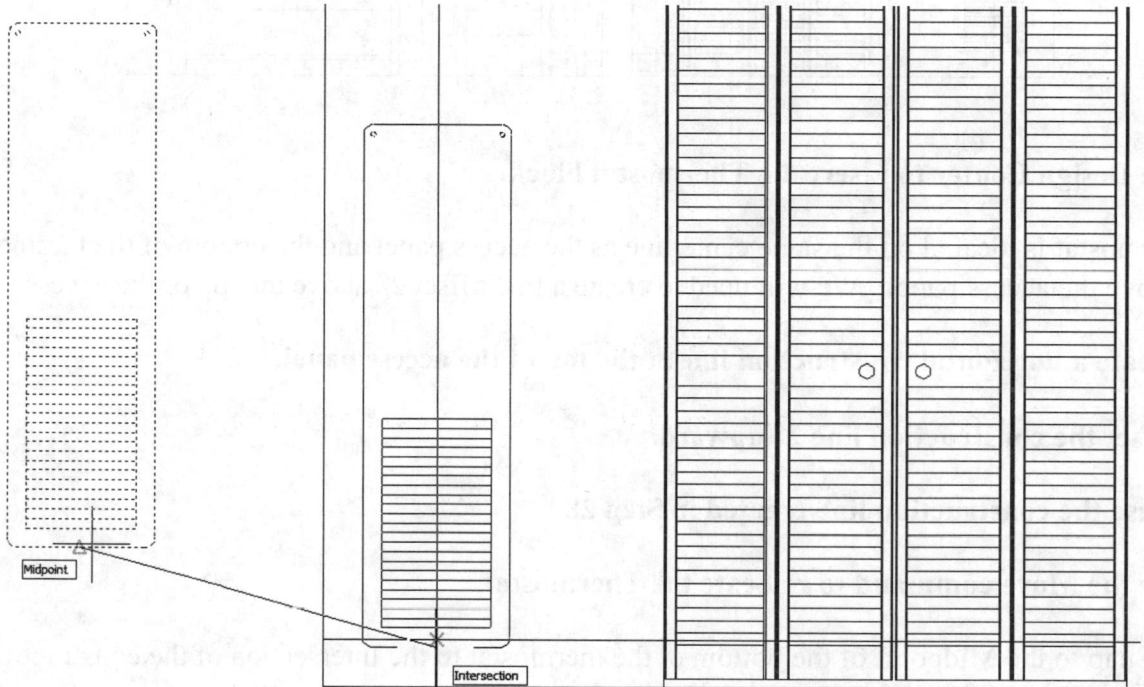

26. Use the Erase command to erase the line created in Step 24.

> For now, we will keep the projection line. We will need it to locate the thermostat.

When you are done, your elevation view will look like this:

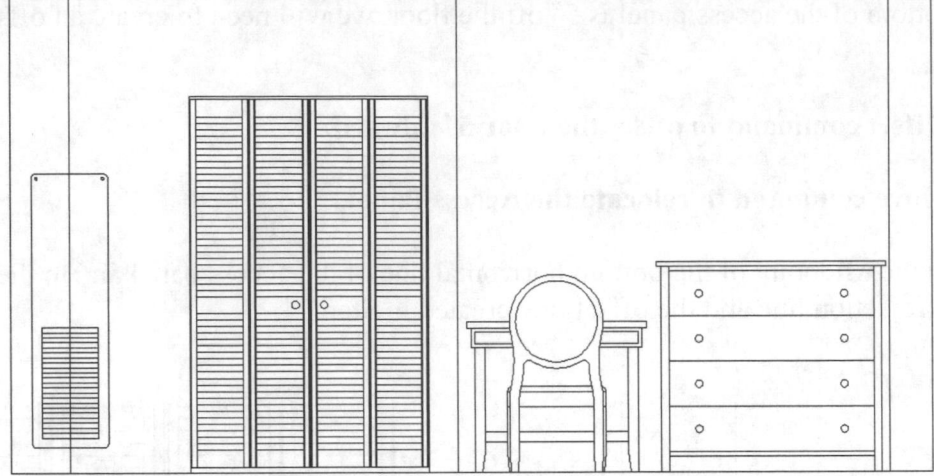

27. Use Design Center to insert the Thermostat block.

The thermostat is located on the same centerline as the access panel and the bottom of the thermostat is 2″ above the access panel. We will need to create a line offset 2″ above the top of the access panel.

28. Create a horizontal construction line at the top of the access panel.

29. Offset the construction line 2″ upward.

30. Erase the construction line created in Step 28.

31. Use the Move command to relocate the Thermostat.

Snap to the Midpoint of the bottom of the thermostat to the Intersection of the construction line of Step 29 and the projection line.

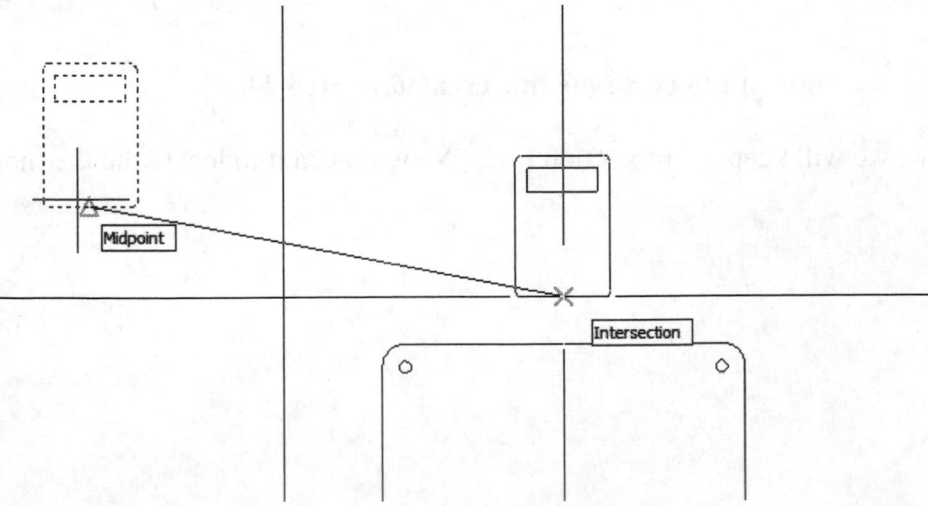

32. Use the Erase command to erase the projection line and the line created in Step 29.

When you are done, your elevation view will look like this:

Before we insert the Flat Screen TV block, change the active layer to "Misc".

33. Use the Design Center to insert the Flat Screen TV block.

34. Use the Move command to relocate the TV to the top of the dresser.

Snap to the Midpoint of the bottom of the TV to the Midpoint of the top of the dresser.

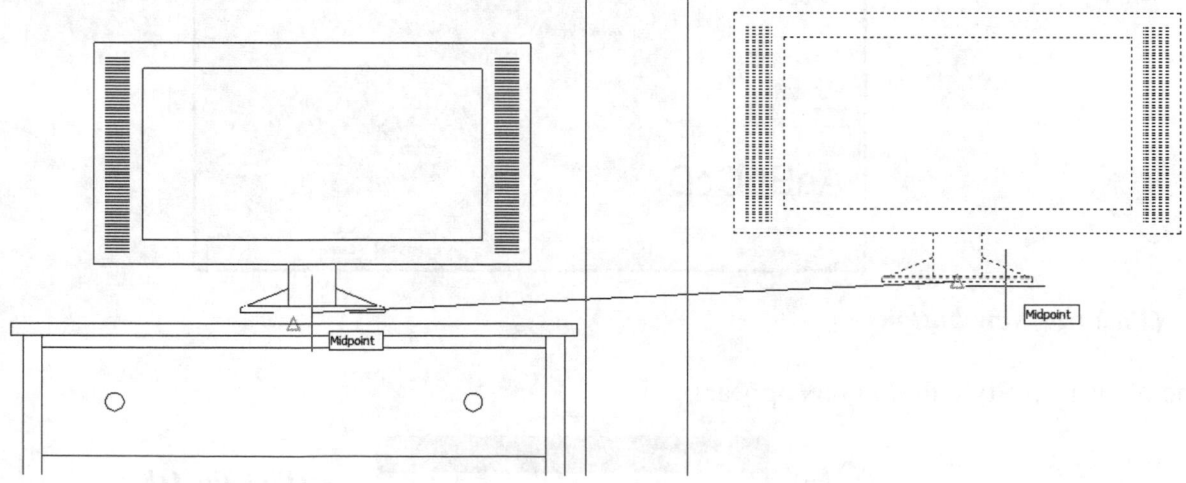

When you are done, your elevation view will look like this:

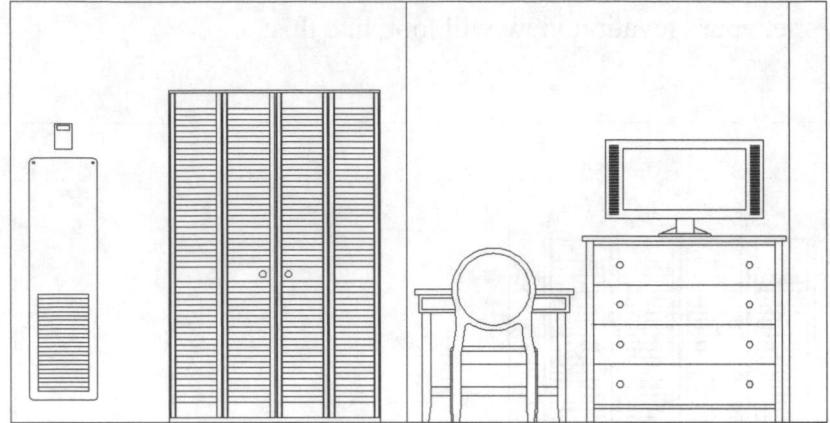

Layout the Drawing

Before we begin a layout of the bedroom elevation should fill out the titleblock that was created for the Plan View layout tab in Tutorial 4.

35. Create text styles so that we can fill in the titleblock.

(Pick the Text Styles icon)

The Text Style dialog box appears:

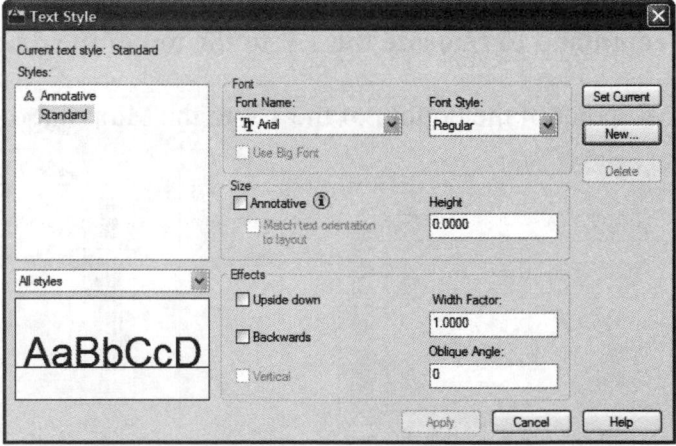

(Pick the New button)

The New Text Style dialog box appears:

**Key in the name
"Titleblock"**

*(Pick the OK
button when done)*

36. Use the pull down arrows to select the font of Times New Roman for the Font Name and Bold Italic for the Font Style.

We will leave the Height at 0″ so that we can key in the value as we place the text on the drawing.

37. While still in the Text Style dialog box, we will create an additional style and name it "Notes". The new style will have the following properties:

Font: CityBlueprint
Annotative: yes – place a check mark in the box
Text Height: 1/8″

38. While in the Plan View layout tab, place Single Line text in the titleblock as shown:

Make sure you are in Paper Space before you attempt to insert text.

3/16″ Titleblock style

1/16″ Titleblock style

Notes style

38a. Use the pull-down arrow on the Text Style portion of the Styles toolbar to make Titleblock the current style.

38b. Use the Single Line Text command on the Text toolbar to insert the company name in the titleblock.

(Pick the Single Line Text icon)

Command: _text
Current text style: "Titleblock" Text height: 0'-0 3/16" Annotative: No
Specify start point of text or [Justify/Style]: (Pick a location in the titleblock)
Specify height <0'-0 3/16">: ↵
Specify rotation angle of text <0>:↵

Key in the text "Interior Design Inc." and press the ↵ Enter key twice to exit the command.

38c. Use Single Line Text to insert the remaining titleblock text.

Press the ↵ Enter key to repeat the single line text command.

Command:
TEXT
Current text style: "Titleblock" Text height: 0'-0 3/16" Annotative: No
Specify start point of text or [Justify/Style]: **(Pick a location in the titleblock)**
Specify height <0'-0 3/16">: **1/16** ↵
Specify rotation angle of text <0>: ↵

Key in the text to fill in the remainder of the titleblock. Press the ↵ Enter key twice to exit the command.

38d. Change the current Text Style to Notes.

38e. Complete the titleblock.

The text you placed in the titleblock may not be placed exactly where you want it. Use grips to relocate the text. Turn off Object Snap before moving the text around.

Now that we have the titleblock in the Plan View layout filled out, we can create another layout for the bedroom elevation view.

39. Create a layout for the bedroom elevation view.

(Right-click the Plan View tab)

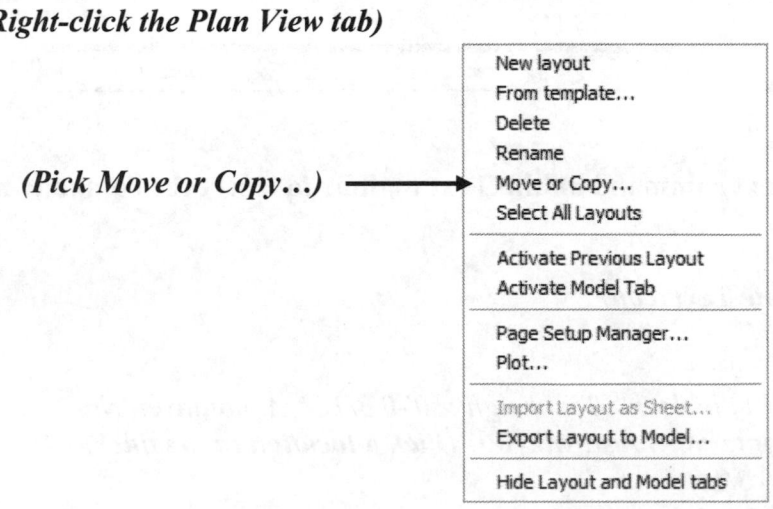

After the Move or Copy dialog box appears:

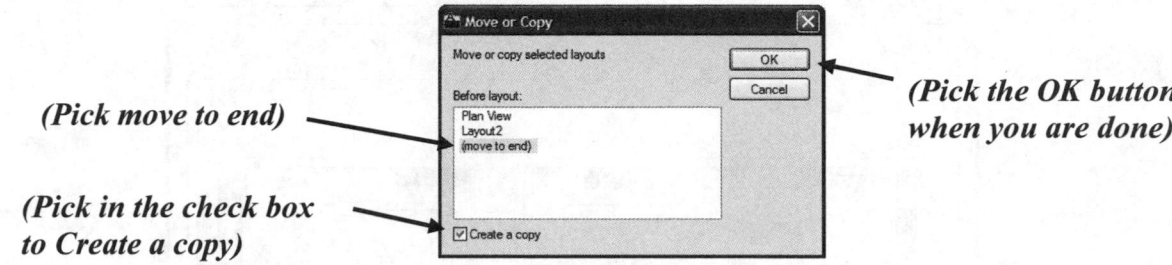

(Pick move to end)

(Pick the OK button when you are done)

(Pick in the check box to Create a copy)

40.   Rename the new layout tab to "Bedroom Elevation".

41.   While in the Bedroom Elevation layout tab, switch to Model Space.

42.   Pan the view of your model so that you center the bedroom elevation. Change the scale to 1/2″ = 1′, and lock the viewport scale.

If the plan view is still showing in the viewport, switch back to Paper Space and re-size the viewport so that only the bedroom elevation view is showing. Leave enough empty space around it to allow for dimensions and text.

43.   Switch back to Paper Space and edit the scale and sheet number in the titleblock.

The text for scale should read: 1/2″ = 1′
The text for the sheet number should read: 2/2

(Pick the Edit Text icon)

Command: _ddedit
Select an annotation object or [Undo]: (Pick the text and edit it) ↵
Select an annotation object or [Undo]:↵
Command:

44.   Delete the Layout 2 tab.

You will now have two layouts – Plan View and Bedroom Elevation.

Your Plan View layout will look like this:

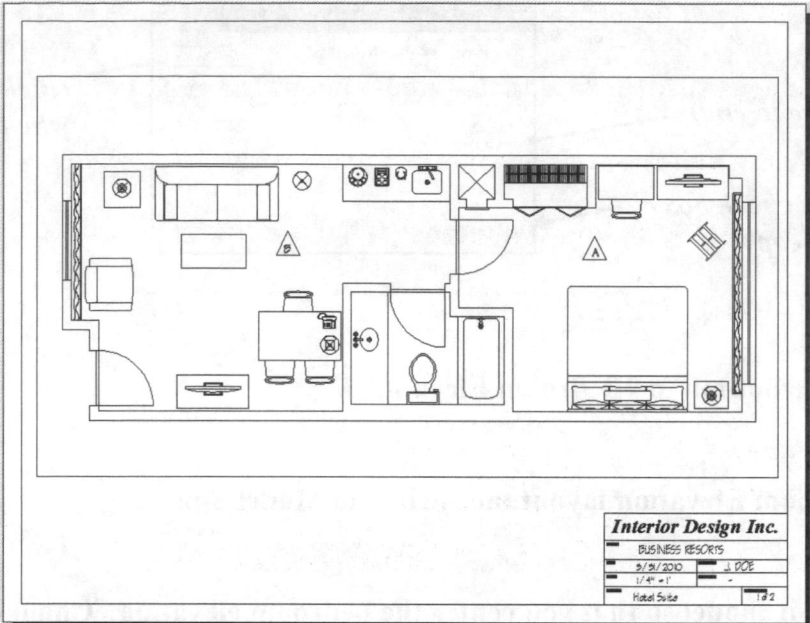

Your Bedroom Elevation layout will look like this:

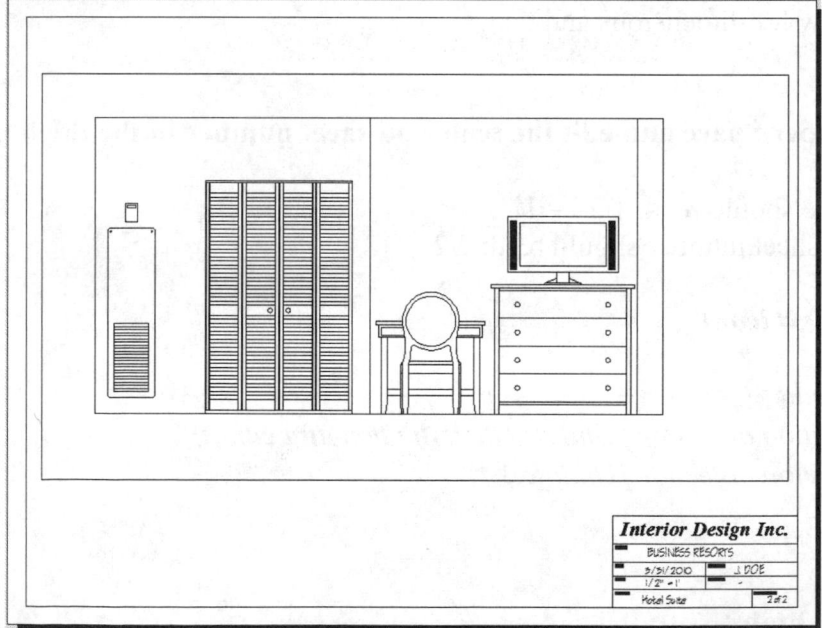

Notice that the viewport border is visible. When you print your drawing, it is not desirable to have the viewport border on the printout. We cannot delete it because it will leave us with a blank drawing. To get around this, we can create a unique layer and we can freeze the layer from visibility.

45. Create a new layer and name it "Viewport".

Remember, to create a new layer you must use the Layer Properties Manager icon.

46. For each layout, change the layer that the viewport is currently on, to layer Viewport.

47. For each layout, use the pull-down arrow on the Layers toolbar to freeze layer Viewport.

You must be in Paper Space before you freeze layer Viewport.

(Pick the Freeze or thaw in current viewport icon for layer Viewport)

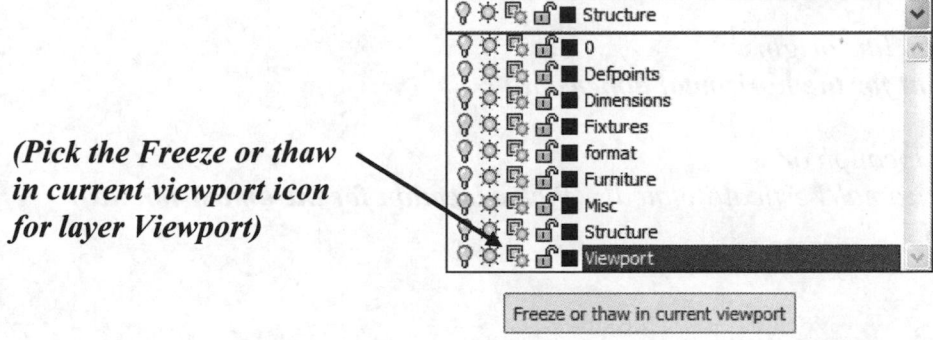

Annotating the Drawing

We are done setting up the drawing layouts. We can now annotate the drawing with dimensions and labels. First, we will need to create styles for both Dimensions and Multileader. We will use the same styles that we created in Chapter 11. The steps to creating those styles will not be repeated here. Please refer to that chapter to create the styles.

Before you begin, create a new layer and name it "Dimensions and Text", and make it current.

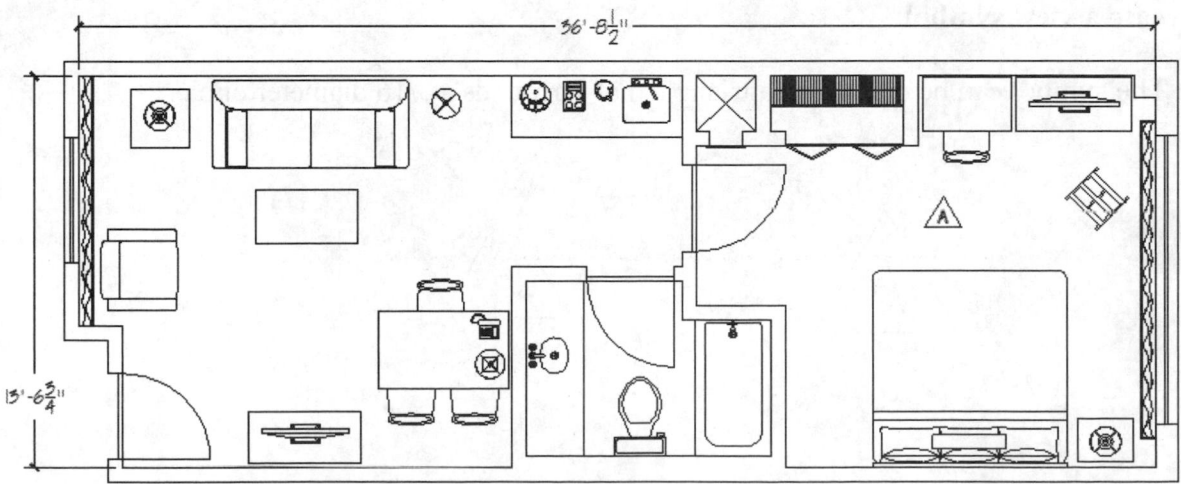

48. Add two linear dimensions to the plan view.

Make sure you are in the Plan View layout tab and working in Model Space with Object Snap set to Endpoint. Also, if you haven't already done so, bring up the Dimension toolbar.

(Pick the Linear icon on the Dimension toolbar)

Command: _dimlinear
Specify first extension line origin or <select object>:
(Pick one of the endpoints for the horizontal dimension at the top of the drawing)

Specify second extension line' origin:
(Pick the other endpoint for the horizontal dimension)

Specify dimension line location or
[Mtext/Text/Angle/Horizontal/Vertical/Rotated]: (Pick a location for the dimension text)
Dimension text = 36'-8 1/2"
Command:

Press the ↵ Enter key to repeat the command.

DIMLINEAR
Specify first extension line origin or <select object>:
(Pick one of the endpoints for the vertical dimension at the side of the drawing)

Specify second extension line origin:
(Pick the other endpoint for the vertical dimension)

Specify dimension line location or
[Mtext/Text/Angle/Horizontal/Vertical/Rotated]: (Pick a location for the dimension text)
Dimension text = 13'-6 3/4"
Command:

49. Create a view symbol:

The symbol can be created as a triangle that surrounds a 3/16 diameter circle.

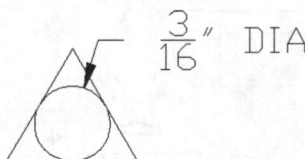

We will create a view symbol as a Paper Space object. As a Paper Space object, the size of the symbol will remain constant, regardless of the scale of the drawing.

49a. Draw a circle that is 3/16″ diameter in the area that you want the symbol to appear.

49b. Draw a horizontal construction line that will Snap to Quadrant on the lower quadrant of the circle.

49c. Use the Array command to rotate and copy around the circle via a Polar Array.

Set "Total number of items" to 3.
(Pick the construction line) under "Select object"
(Pick the center of the circle) as the "Center point"

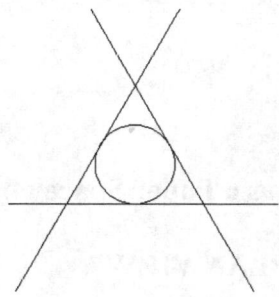

49d. Use the Trim command to trim the construction lines.

49e. Use the Erase command to erase the circle.

49f. Change the Lineweight of the three lines to .012″.

49g. Use Multiline Text to insert the symbol text.

Make sure the text style is set to Notes.

(Pick two points to straddle the triangle to define the text field)

(Pick the Bold button)   *(Pick the OK button when done)*

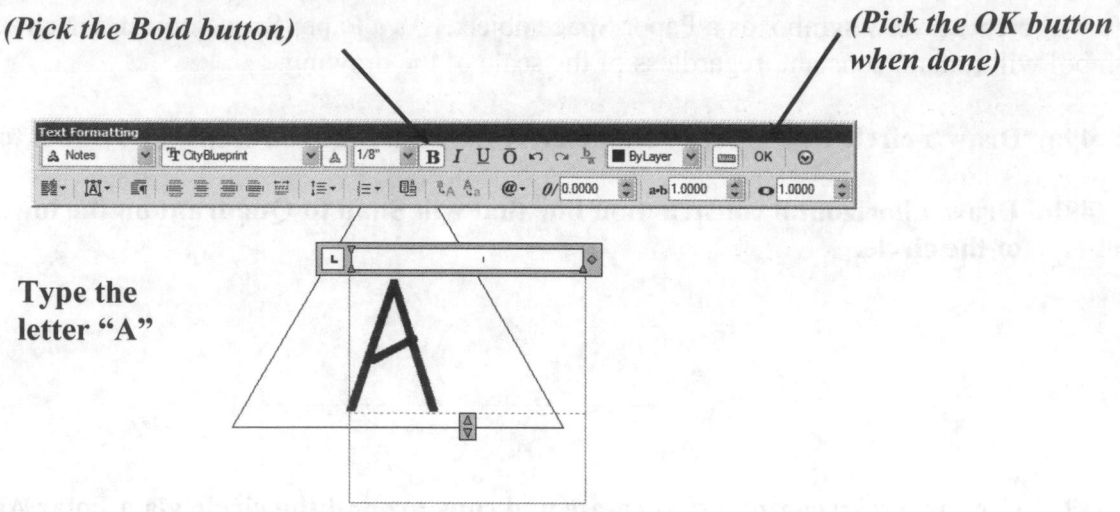

Type the letter "A"

After you insert the Multiline text, you may need to reposition it within the triangle. Use grips to relocate the text – it works best if Object Snap is turned off.

When you are done, your symbol looks like this:

50. Add Multiline Text to the Plan View layout as a Paper Space object.

    Using 1/4″ Bold letters, type the words "PLAN VIEW".

51. Add labels to the elevation view by using Multileader.

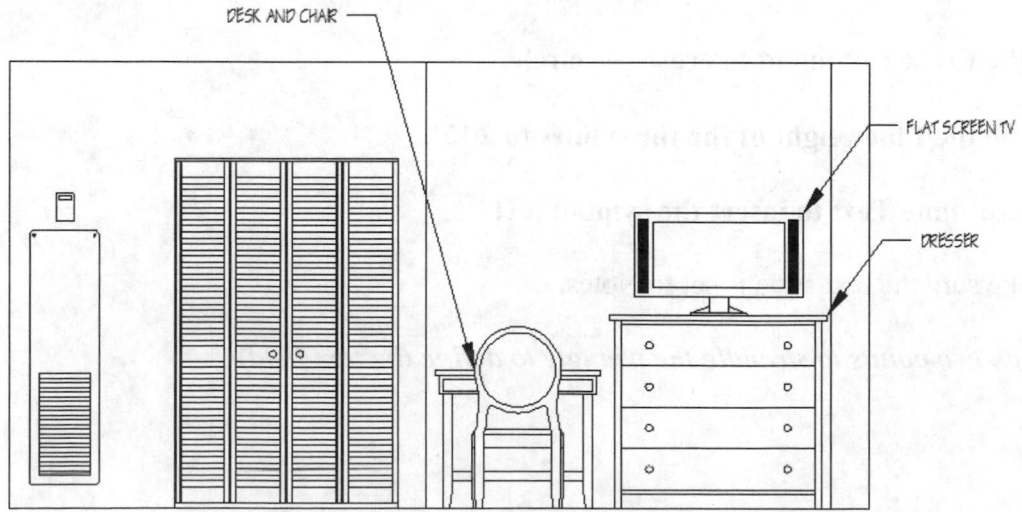

52. Add Multiline Text to the Plan View layout as a Paper Space object.

   Using 1/4″ Bold letters, type the words "ELEVATION A".

Congratulations! You have now completed all the tutorials. Be sure to save your drawing.

Your two drawing sheets will now look like this:

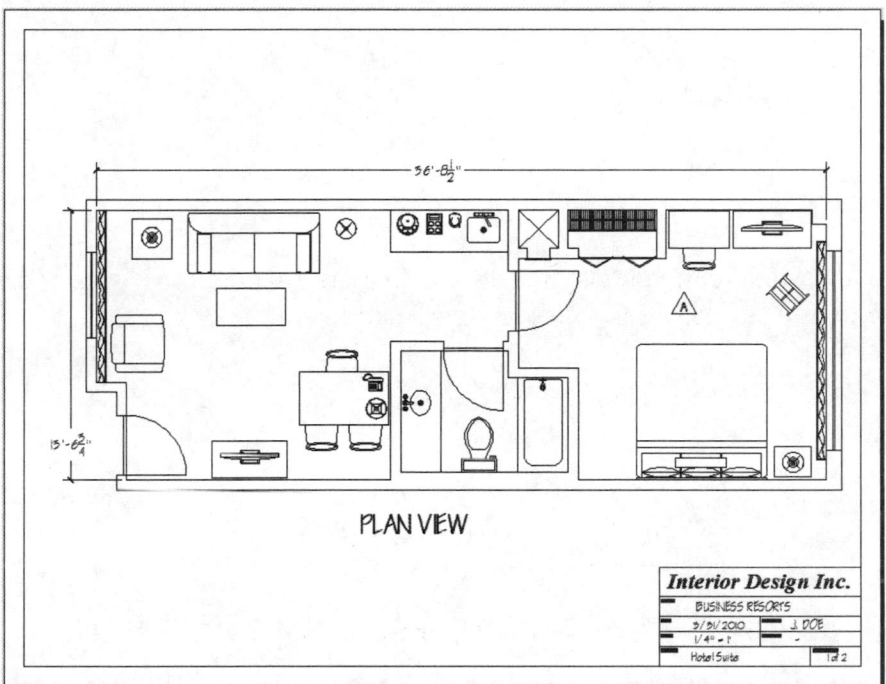

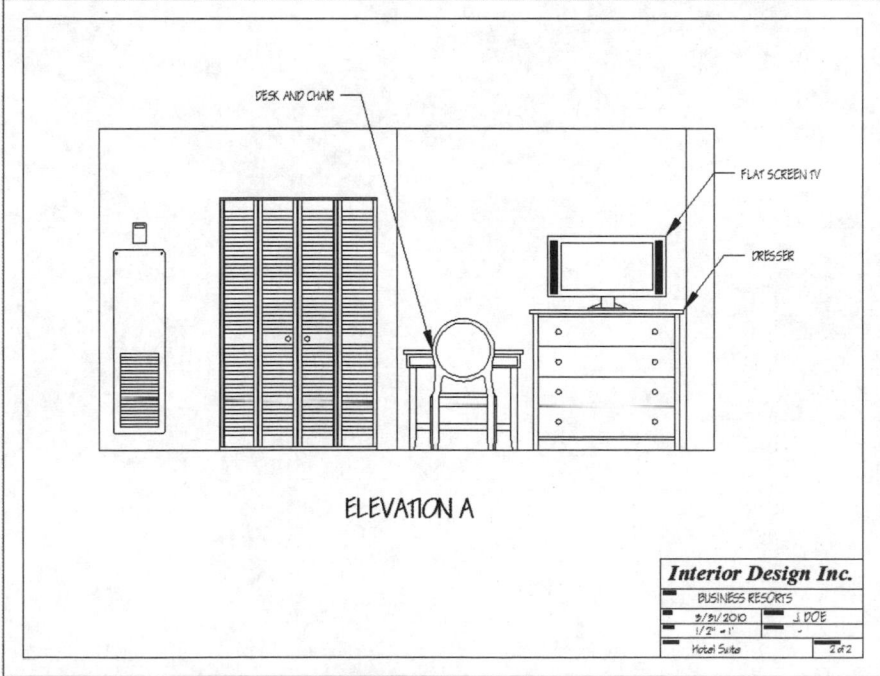

Notes:

Chapter 13
Commands – Set 6: Creating and Editing Schedules

Paint Schedule			
Room	Walls	Ceiling	Trim & Doors
Dining Room	California Paints Tomahawk Red, 7856A Latex, Eggshell Finish	Glidden Paints Ceiling Whitec GC3070 Latex	Benjamin Moore Navajo White, N31973 Acrylic, Eggshell Finish
Living Room	Behr Paints Forest Green Latex, Eggshell Finish	Glidden Paints Ceiling Whitec GC3070 Latex	Benjamin Moore Navajo White, N31973 Acrylic, Eggshell Finish

Learning Objectives:

- Creating a style for your Schedule using Table Style
- Use the Table feature to create a Schedule
- Edit an existing Table

Tables – Creating a Schedule

You can create a schedule by using the AutoCAD® Table command. Tables can have any number of rows and columns that you define. Defining a Table Style allows you to customize how the table will look.

Creating a Table Style

The current Table Style is shown on the Styles toolbar. For a new drawing, the default style is Standard. To create a Table Style, pick the Table Style Manager icon on the Styles toolbar.

Table Style
Manager icon

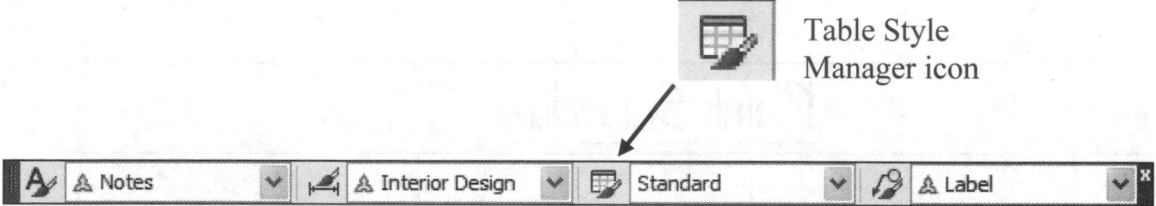

The Table Style dialog box will appear:

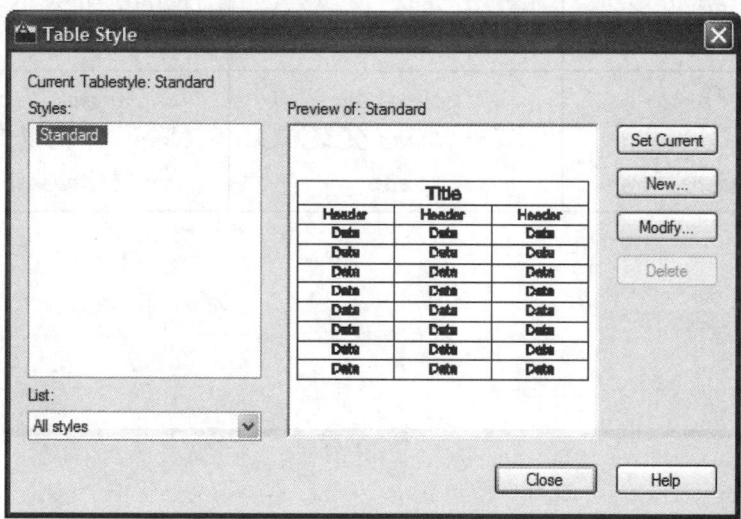

Pick the New button in the dialog box and a Create New Table Style dialog box will appear. Let's create a style named Schedule:

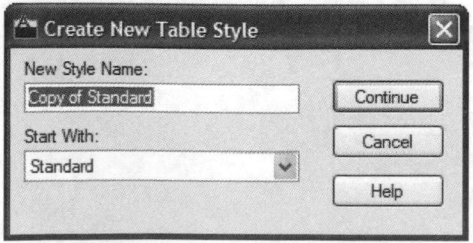
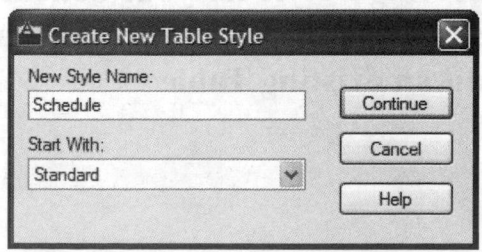

Pick the Continue button. Another dialog box will appear. This dialog box will allow you to define several features for your Table Style.

Properties for each section are controlled using the choices within each of these three tabs.

Each section is selected by using pull-down under Cell styles.

There are three sections to the table: Title, Header, and Data. This is illustrated in the preview pane.

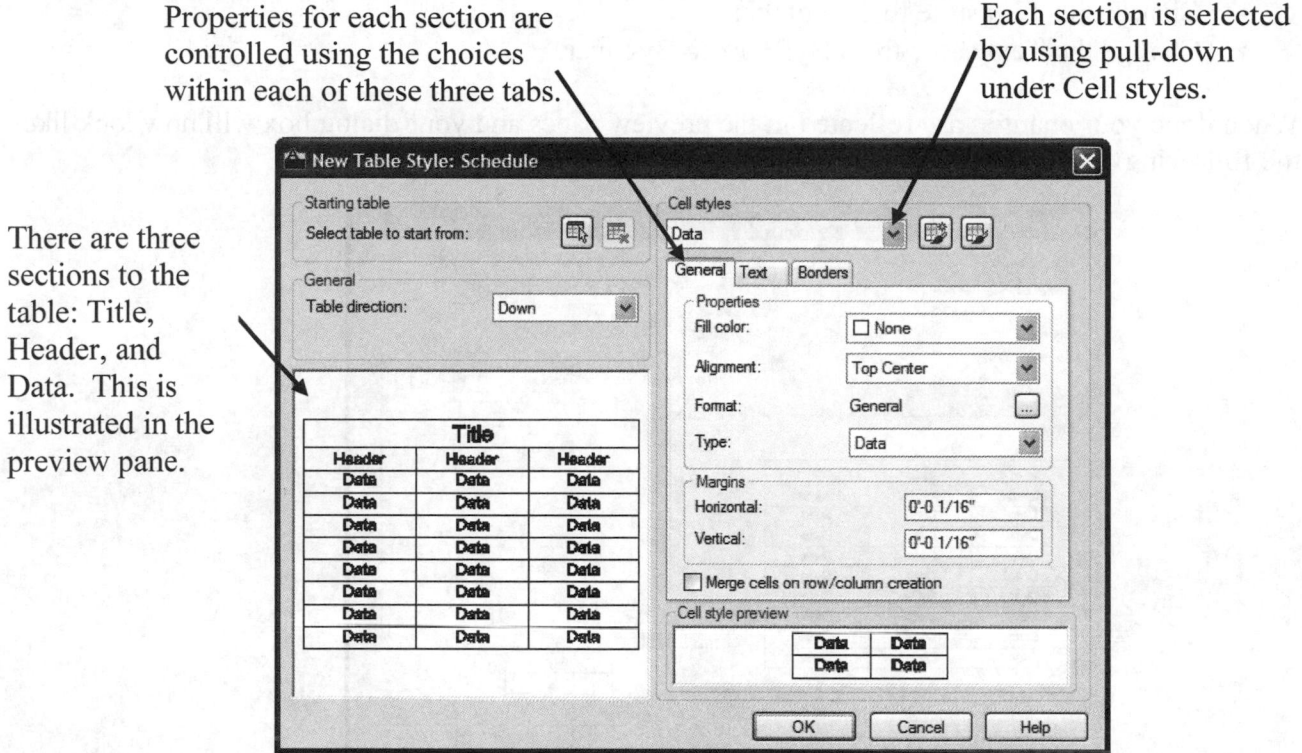

There are three sections that comprise the AutoCAD® table: Title, Header, and Data. These can each have their own properties for Alignment and Color, Text Style, and Border style. Each section is selected by using the pull-down under Cell styles. Once selected, the properties for that section are controlled using the tabs General, Text, and Borders.

Prior to choosing the style of text for each section, we need to have a style already defined. Previously, we created a style and named it Notes. We also set the text height for Notes to 1/8″. Notice that the Title text height is larger than the Header and Data text heights. By setting the text height in Text Style, we are not able to change that height to a larger size for the Title section. That is why we created the second style: Titleblock.

Table Title

Use the pull-down to select Title under Cell styles.

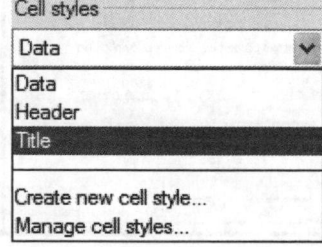

We will not make any changes under the General tab.
Pick the Text tab and make the following changes:

- Change the Text style to Titleblock.
- Change the Text color from ByBlock to ByLayer.

When done your changes are reflected in the preview panes and your dialog box will now look like the following:

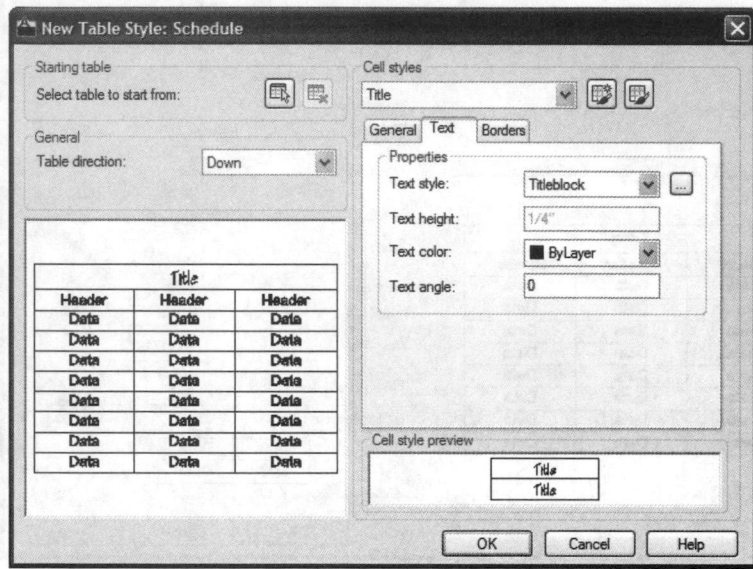

Pick the Borders tab and make the following changes:

- Change ByBlock to ByLayer for all choice selections.
- Pick the left-most button for the grid border.

When done, your dialog box will now look like the following:

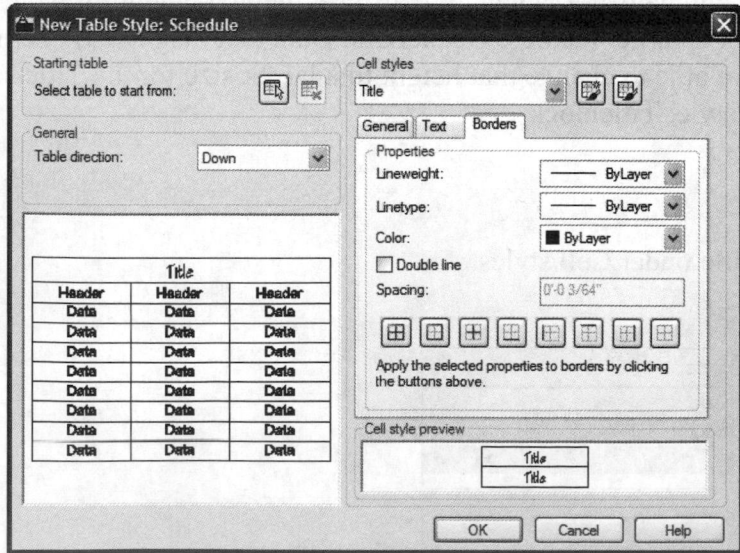

Table Header

Use the pull-down to select Header under Cell styles.

Pick the Text tab and make the following changes:

- Change the Text style to Notes.
- Change the Text color from ByBlock to ByLayer.

When done, the dialog box will now look like the following:

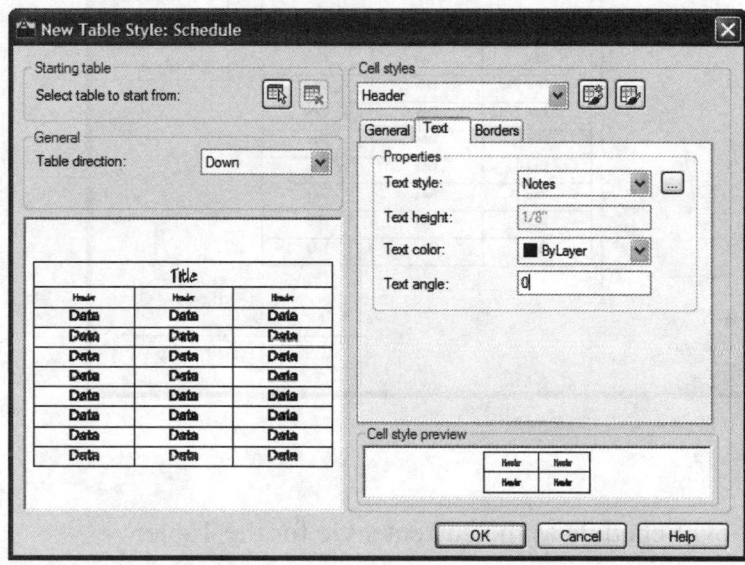

Pick the Borders tab and make the same changes for Header as you did for the Title style:

- Change ByBlock to ByLayer for all choice selections.
- Pick the left-most button for the grid border.

Table Data

Use the pull-down to select Data under Cell styles.

Pick the Text tab and make the same changes for Data that you made for the Header style:
- Change the Text style to Notes.
- Change the Text color from ByBlock to ByLayer.

Pick the Borders tab and make the same changes for Data as you did for both the Header and Title styles:

- Change ByBlock to ByLayer for all choice selections.
- Pick the left-most button for the grid border.

The table style of Schedule is now complete. Pick the OK button to exit the New Table Style dialog box and return to the Table Style dialog box. Pick the Schedule Style on the left side of the dialog box, and then pick the Set Current button to make it the current style. Pick the Close button to exit the dialog box.

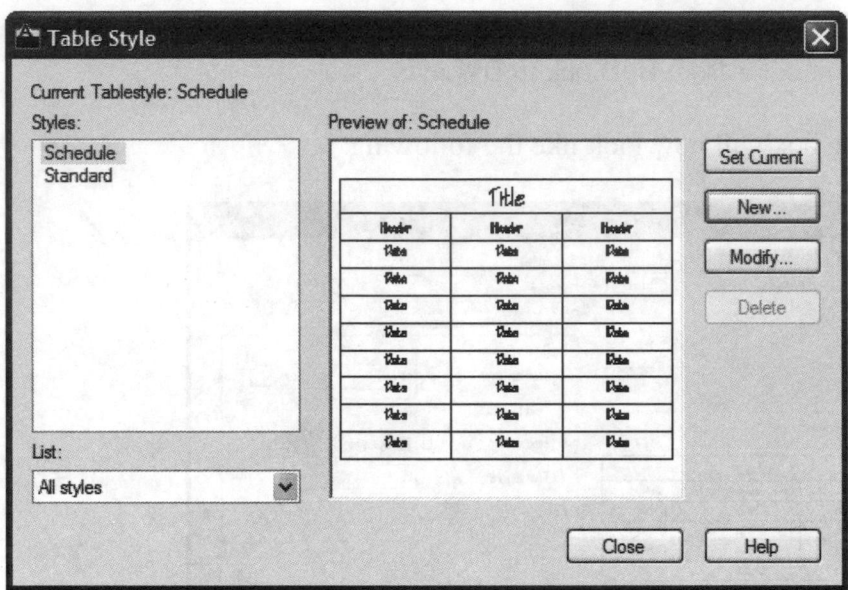

The Styles toolbar will now show Schedule as the current style for the Table:

Inserting Tables on the Drawing

To insert a table on the drawing, it is best done on the Layout tab in Paper Space.

<u>Procedure:</u>

Pick (left click): **Table icon** from the Draw toolbar.

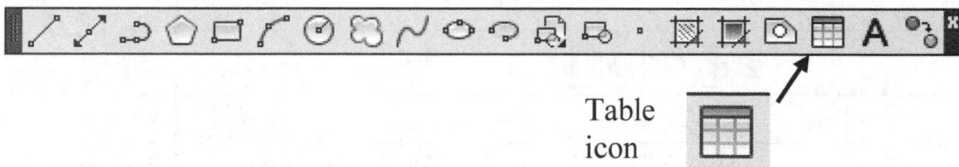

Table
icon

The Insert Table dialog box will appear. In this dialog box, the number of rows and columns can be specified, as well as the height and width of the rows and columns. For this example, change the number of columns to 3. Pick the OK button to insert the table.

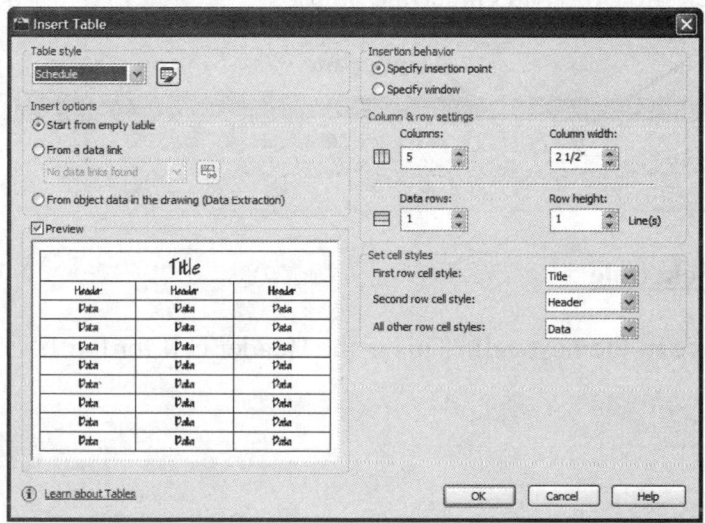

An image of the table will appear on the screen and will follow the cursor. Left-click to place the table in a desired location on the drawing sheet.

A Text Formatting dialog editor will appear.

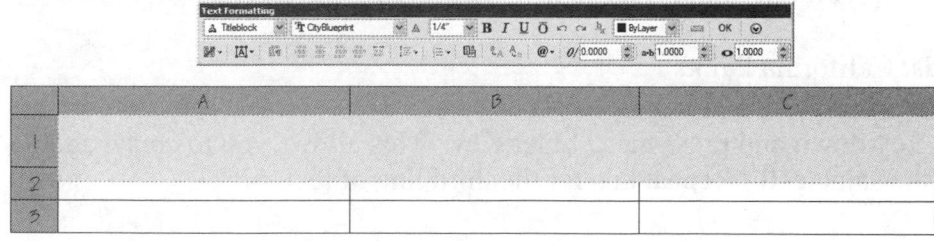

The cell that you will add text to will be highlighted. Enter the text as desired.
- To add lines within a cell, hold down the ALT key and press the Enter ↵ Key.
- To move to the next cell use the Tab key.

Try it:

We will create a schedule on the Layout 1 tab. The schedule will be a Paper Space object. Before we insert the Table, erase the viewport that is on Layout 1 – we will not need to see any part of our Model so we won't need any viewports.

Let's create the following paint schedule:

Paint Schedule		
<u>Walls</u>	<u>Ceiling</u>	<u>Trim & Doors</u>
California Paints Tomahawk Red, 7856A Latex, Eggshell Finish	Glidden Paints Ceiling White, GC 3070 Latex	Benjamin Moore Navajo White, N319 73 Acrylic, Eggshell Finish

1. For the Title section, Pick the Bold and Underline buttons:

Bold   Underline

2. Type the words: **Paint Schedule**

3. Press the Tab key to move to the next cell. This is the Header cell for the 1st column.

4. Pick the Underline button.

5. Type the word: <u>Walls</u>

6. Press the Tab key to move to the next cell. This is the Header cell for the 2nd column.

7. Fill in the remaining Header cells. You will need to pick the Underline button for each Header cell. Use the tab key to change cells. After the last Header cell, the tab key will move you to the 1st column of the Data cell.

8. Type the words: California Paints

9. Hold the ALT key down and press the ↵ Enter Key. This allows you to create another line of text within the same cell. Repeat this for the third line of text.

10. Press the tab key to move to the next Data cell. Continue entering the information for all the cells.

11. Pick the OK button to exit the command and complete the table.

Editing an Existing Table

If you simply want to add text to an existing cell, double-left-click inside the cell. The cell will highlight and the Text Formatting dialog box will appear. All methods used to enter information to the table are the same as when the table was initially created.

To edit an existing table, such as adding rows or columns, pick in a cell (single left click), then right-click. The following menu choices will appear:

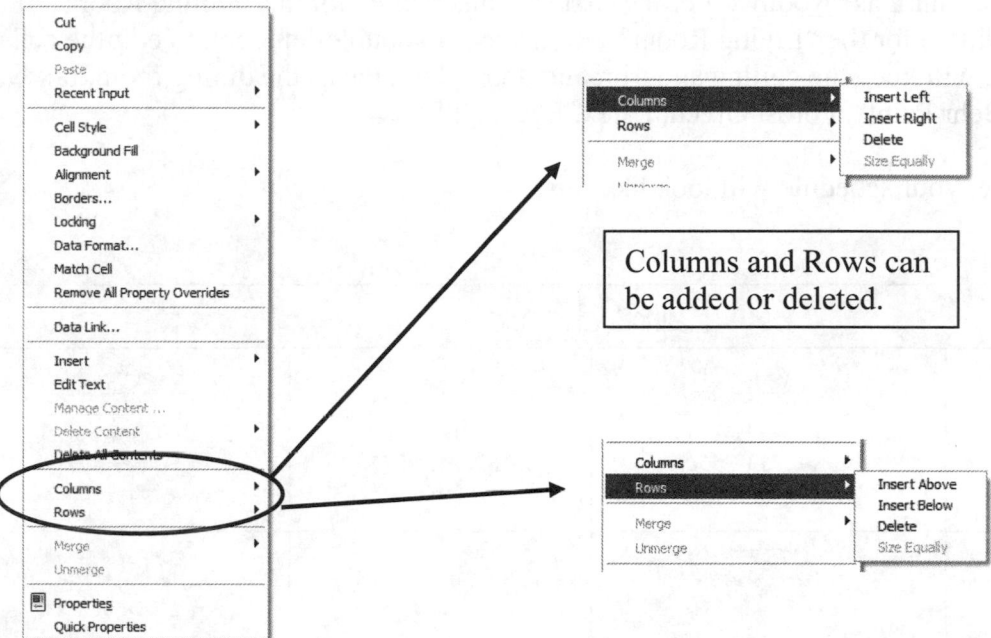

Columns and Rows can be added or deleted.

Try it:

Let's modify the Paint Schedule we just created by adding another column to identify the room that the paint scheme applies to:

1. *(Pick a cell in Column A of the Paint Schedule)*
2. *(Right-click to bring up the menu choices)*
3. *(Pick Columns from the menu choices)*
4. *(Pick Insert Left)*

A new column will appear to the left of the column labeled Walls.

1. *(Pick a cell in Row 3 of the Paint Schedule)*
2. *(Right-click to bring up the menu choices)*
3. *(Pick Rows from the menu choices)*
4. *(Pick Insert Below)*

A new row will appear below the bottom row of the schedule.

Paint Schedule			
	Walls	Ceiling	Trim & Doors
	California Paints Tomahawk Red, 7856A Latex, Eggshell Finish	Glidden Paints Ceiling Whitec GC5070 Latex	Benjamin Moore Navajo White, N51975 Acrylic, Eggshell Finish

Let's title the new column as "<u>Room</u>". For the first row this will be for the "Dining Room". For the second row, this will be for the "Living Room". Remember to double-left click to edit the cells. For the living room we will keep the ceiling and trim and doors the same as the dining room, but we will make the walls a **Behr Paints, Forest Green, Latex, Eggshell Finish.**

When you are done, your schedule will look like this:

Paint Schedule			
Room	Walls	Ceiling	Trim & Doors
Dining Room	California Paints Tomahawk Red, 7856A Latex, Eggshell Finish	Glidden Paints Ceiling Whitec GC5070 Latex	Benjamin Moore Navajo White, N51975 Acrylic, Eggshell Finish
Living Room	Behr Paints Forest Green Latex, Eggshell Finsh	Glidden Paints Ceiling Whitec GC5070 Latex	Benjamin Moore Navajo White, N51975 Acrylic, Eggshell Finish

Notice that the columns are wider than they need to be. We can change the column widths and row heights by using grips. You can get the grips by using a single left-click on any cell.

Let's reduce the size of the first column:

(Pick in the cell that has the word <u>Room</u>)

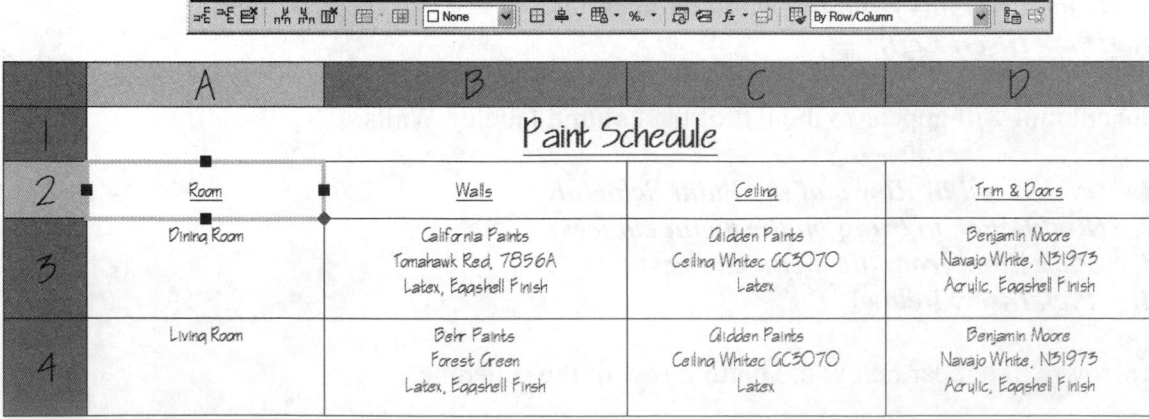

(Pick the right grip and drag it left to reduce the column width. Press the Esc key when done.)

When you are done, your Paint Schedule will look like this:

Paint Schedule			
Room	Walls	Ceiling	Trim & Doors
Dining Room	California Paints Tomahawk Red, 7856A Latex, Eggshell Finish	Glidden Paints Ceiling Whitec GC3070 Latex	Benjamin Moore Navajo White, N31973 Acrylic, Eggshell Finish
Living Room	Behr Paints Forest Green Latex, Eggshell Finish	Glidden Paints Ceiling Whitec GC3070 Latex	Benjamin Moore Navajo White, N31973 Acrylic, Eggshell Finish

You can continue to re-size each column and row until you are satisfied.

Paint Schedule			
Room	Walls	Ceiling	Trim & Doors
Dining Room	California Paints Tomahawk Red, 7856A Latex, Eggshell Finish	Glidden Paints Ceiling Whitec GC3070 Latex	Benjamin Moore Navajo White, N31973 Acrylic, Eggshell Finish
Living Room	Behr Paints Forest Green Latex, Eggshell Finish	Glidden Paints Ceiling Whitec GC3070 Latex	Benjamin Moore Navajo White, N31973 Acrylic, Eggshell Finish

Summary

In this chapter you have learned to:

- Create a Table Style
- Create a schedule using the Table command
- Add and Edit Text for a Table
- Modify an existing Table by adding and re-sizing columns or rows

Review Questions

1. What does AutoCAD® call Schedules?

2. Why is it better to make a schedule in Paper Space than Model Space?

3. Where can you find the Table Style icon?

4. Which toolbar has the Table command icon?

5. To edit text on an existing Table, how do you get the text editor?

6. How do you add a row or a column to an existing Table?

7. How do you change the size of a column or row in a Table?

Exercises

1. Create the following Door and Hardware Schedule in Paper Space:

Door & Hardware Schedule		
Location	Door Style	Hardware
Entrance	Jeld-Wen Prehung Solid Core Molded 6-Panel 2'6"	Stanley Hardware Square Privacy Mortise Bolt
Living Room to Study	Jeld-Wen Pocket Solid Core Molded Smooth 2'6"	Stanley Hardware Rectangular Flush Pull
Closet	Jeld Wen Prehung Solid Core Molded 6-Panel 2'	Stanley Hardware Square Privacy Mortise Bolt

Notes:

Chapter 14
Commands – Set 7: Creating Curves and Rendering

ELEVATION B

SCALE: 1/4" = 1'

$\frac{2}{4}$

Learning Objectives:

- **Creating curved shapes using Arc, Polyline, and Spline**
- **Creating an Ellipse**
- **Using Hatch for sections and to fill shapes**
- **Using Gradient Hatch to render your drawing**

Up to this point, we have focused primarily on straight-line shapes. This covers the majority of items we will draw: walls, doors, windows, etc. There are many times that we will need to draw curved shapes. This is especially true for items such as curtains, bedding, upholstery, etc.

Although AutoCAD® is a drafting program, not a drawing program, it has the ability to draw curved shapes. This will take some practice, but once you get used to it, it is easy to do.

Arc

The Arc command creates an arc. We have created arcs from circles by using the Trim command. There are multiple ways to create an arc. We have used the Circle command with trimming in the previous chapters. Although that may not have been the most efficient method, it was intuitive and straightforward. This section will only cover one method of creating arcs. It is left to the student to explore other methods.

The method covered here is the 3-point arc. This is an arc that is created by picking 3 points. The arc created will have the first and last point picked as the endpoints. The second point picked will define the amount of curvature the arc will have. This type of arc comes in handy when you are working a design where you want to have a curvature bounded by a fixed distance.

Procedure:

Pick (left click): **Arc icon** from the Draw toolbar.

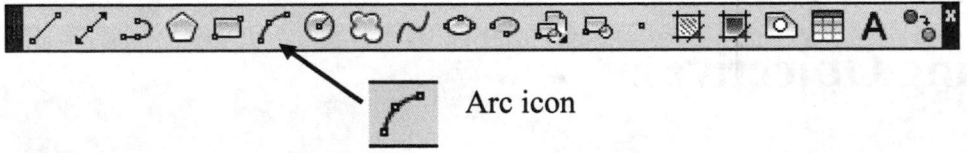

Arc icon

The command line prompts you with the following:

Command: _arc Specify start point of arc or [Center] **(Pick the first endpoint of the arc – Point "A")**
Specify second point of arc or [Center/End]: **(Pick the second point which defines the curvature – Point "B")**
Specify end point of arc: **(Pick the third point which is the endpoint of the arc – Point "C")**
Command:

Once the arc is created, AutoCAD® automatically ends the command.

Try it:

As an example, let's draw an arc that is the shape for the top of a cabinet door. Before beginning, make sure that you have the Object Snap turned on with Endpoint and Midpoint selected.

This is the cabinet door before the arc is created:

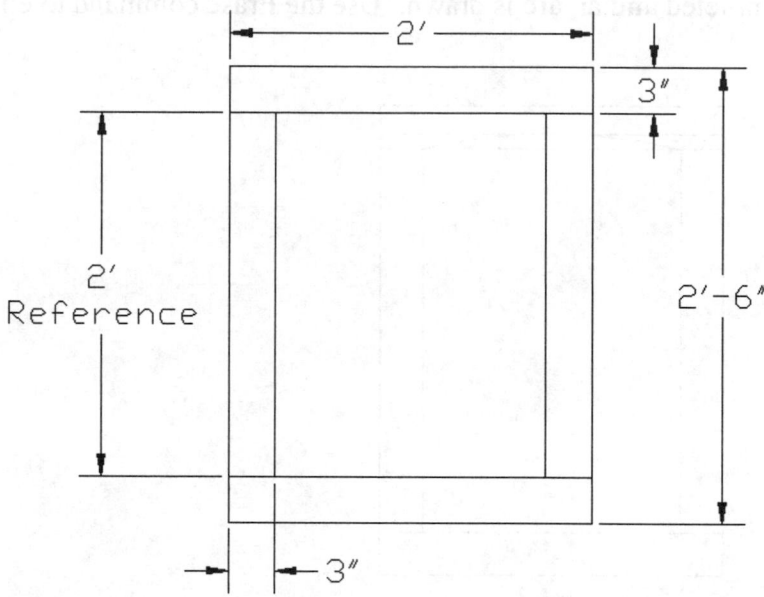

To create an arc that curves within a 1″ distance from the bottom of the top frame, let's first Explode the top rectangle.

Use the Offset command and offset the bottom line of the top frame up 1″.

(Pick the Arc icon)

Command: _arc
Specify start point of arc or [Center]: **(Pick endpoint 1)**
Specify second point of arc or [Center/End]: **(Pick the centerpoint of the offset line)**
Specify end point of arc: **(Pick endpoint 2)**
Command:

The command is completed and an arc is drawn. Use the Erase command to eliminate the offsite line.

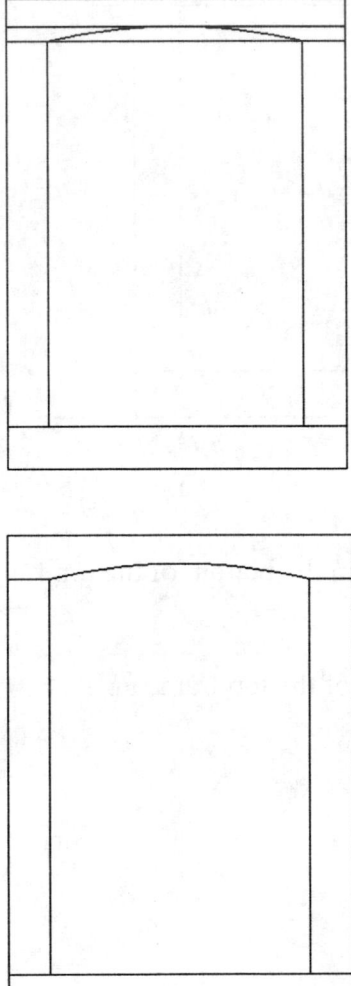

Ellipse

The Ellipse command creates an ellipse. An ellipse looks similar to an oval, but it is a unique shape. An elliptical shape is how an object with a circular shape appears when it is viewed at an angle. Sometimes the elliptical shape is used for a table, a mirror, or as an architectural feature such as windows or archways.

An ellipse can be created in multiple ways. It is defined with a major and a minor axis. The default method of creating an ellipse using the icon is to define the two end points of the first axis plus the distance for the second axis.

Prior to creating the ellipse, it is easier to define the boundary of the ellipse by using a rectangle. Make sure the size of the rectangle is the size that you want the ellipse to be. In addition, make sure you have your object snap setting to Midpoint.

Example:

Let's draw the elliptical shape of the coffee table shown:

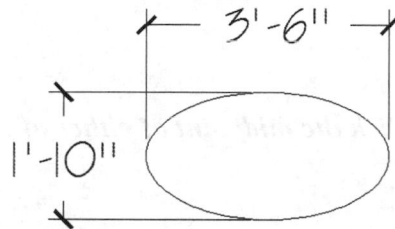

First, start with a rectangle that is the same dimensions as those shown for the ellipse:

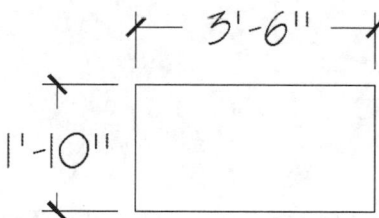

Procedure:

Pick (left click): **Ellipse icon** from the Draw toolbar.

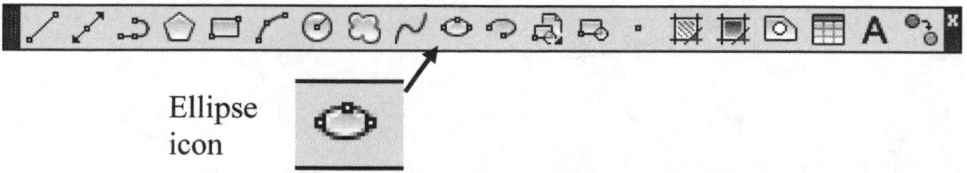

Ellipse
icon

The command line prompts you with the following:

Command: _ellipse
Specify axis endpoint of ellipse or [Arc/Center]: **(Pick the midpoint of the first line)**

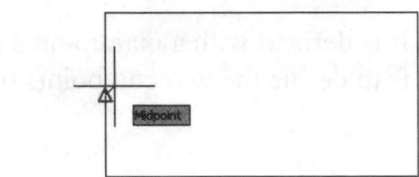

Specify other endpoint of axis: **(Pick the midpoint of the line opposite the first line)**

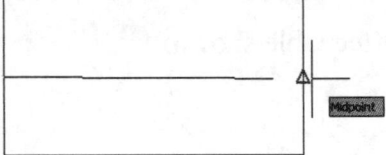

Specify distance to other axis or [Rotation]: **(Pick the midpoint of either of the two remaining lines)**

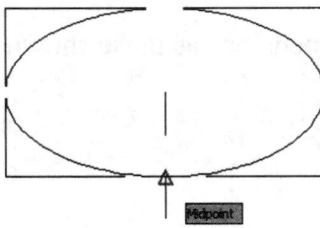

Once the ellipse is drawn, use the Erase command to erase the rectangle. The result will be an ellipse to the exact dimensions as shown:

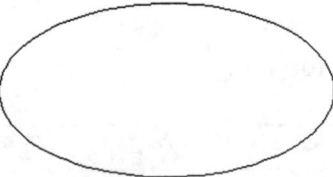

Polyline

Another command that allows you more freedom to draw curved shapes is Polyline. This command allows you to draw straight lines and arcs in a free form (as well as precision).

For fun, let's draw a heart shape. Let's do this in a free form without worry of a specific size, and we can approximate the shape. Note, however, that the heart shape is symmetrical. We can take advantage of that fact by drawing only half the heart shape and then mirroring that about the line of symmetry.

First, draw the vertical line that we will use to mirror about. Use the construction line, with vertical as the option, to draw a vertical line somewhere on the screen. Once that is done, we can draw the shape of the half-heart. We will intentionally draw the half-heart crossing the construction line.

Polyline:

The Polyline command is located on the Draw toolbar.

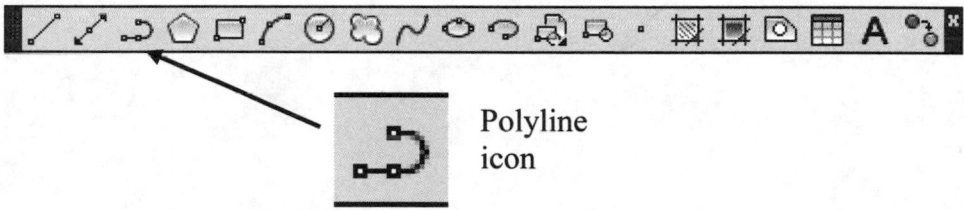

Polyline
icon

Procedure:

Pick (left click): **Polyline icon** from the Draw toolbar.

The command line prompts you with the following:

Command: _pline
Specify start point: **(Pick a location on the left side of the vertical construction line)**

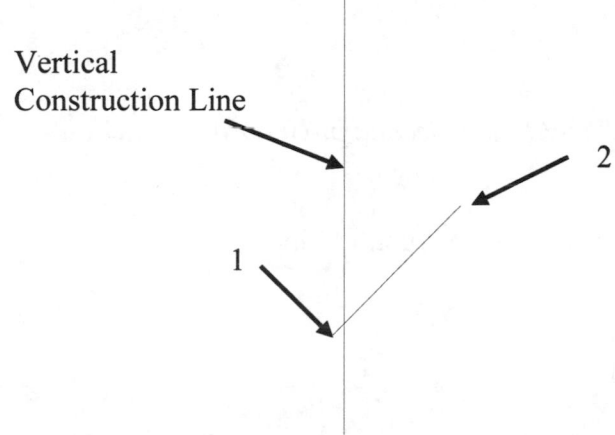

Vertical
Construction Line

1

2

The polyline will rubber-band to follow your cursor. As you pick the second point, the polyline will be a point-to-point line.

Current line-width is 0.0000
Specify next point or [Arc/Halfwidth/Length/Undo/Width]: **(Pick the second point, up and to the right of the first point)**

Specify next point or [Arc/Close/Halfwidth/Length/Undo/Width]: **a** ↵

An arc will begin to be drawn. The radius and endpoint will change as it rubber-bands with your cursor movement.

Specify endpoint of arc or
[Angle/CEnter/CLose/Direction/Halfwidth/Line/Radius/Second pt/Undo/Width]: **(Pick a location on the opposite side of the construction line to form the rounded part of the half-heart)**

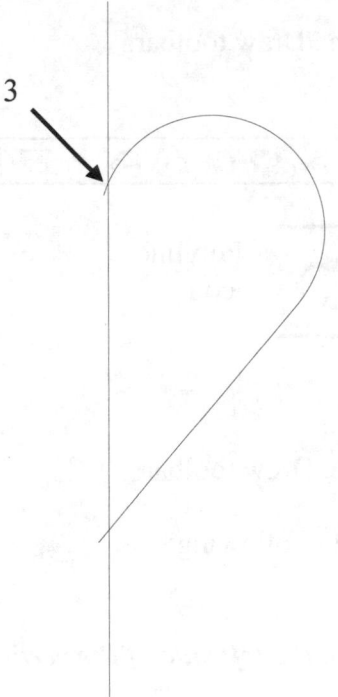

3

Specify endpoint of arc or
[Angle/CEnter/CLose/Direction/Halfwidth/Line/Radius/Second pt/Undo/Width]: ↵
Command:

Use the Trim command to trim the half-heart to the Construction Line.

Use the Mirror command to mirror and copy the half-heart shape to become a complete heart shape.

Try using the Polyline for any other shapes you would like. If you want to change its shape, use the grips. For multiple hearts, try the Array command. Have fun with it!

Spline

Another command that comes in handy for free-form drawing is the Spline command. The spline is drawn by picking multiple points on the drawing. As you pick those points, the shape will rubber-band with your cursor. To end the command, press the ↵ Enter key multiple times (ignore the Start and End Tangent requests).

The Spline command is located on the Draw toolbar.

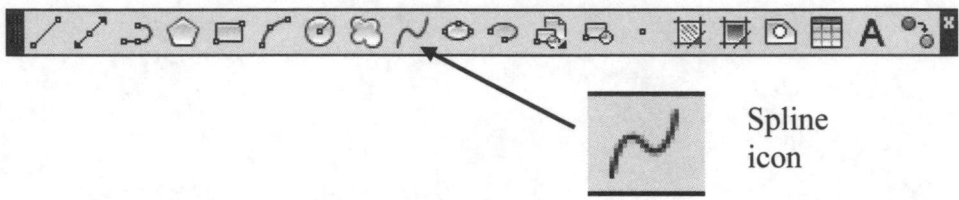

Spline icon

Procedure:

Pick (left click): **Spline icon** from the Draw toolbar.

The command line prompts you with the following:

Command: _spline
Specify first point or [Object]: (Pick a point on the screen)
Specify next point: (Pick a point on the screen)
Specify next point or [Close/Fit tolerance] <start tangent>: (Pick a point on the screen)
Specify next point or [Close/Fit tolerance] <start tangent>: (Pick a point on the screen)
Specify next point or [Close/Fit tolerance] <start tangent>: (Pick a point on the screen)
Specify next point or [Close/Fit tolerance] <start tangent>: ↵
Specify start tangent: ↵
Specify end tangent: ↵
Command:

Resulting Spline shape

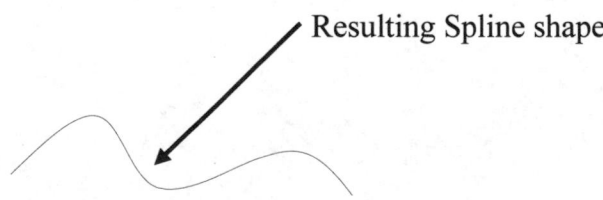

Hatch

Hatch is used to fill an enclosed area with either a pattern or a solid color. It can be most useful for section views or for the solid fill color of walls for a plan view.

Procedure:

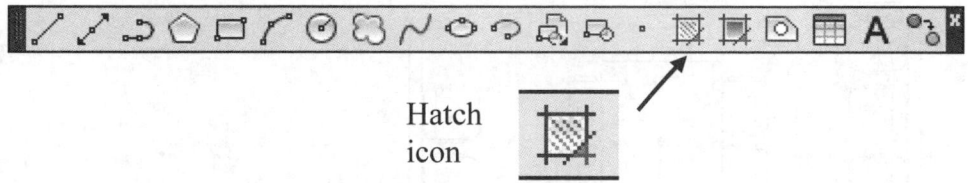

Hatch icon

Pick (left click): **Hatch icon** from the Draw toolbar.

The Hatch dialog box will appear. The various sections of that dialog box are described below:

Hatch Pattern display button

Choose a pre-defined pattern using the pull-down or display button.

A preview of the pattern is shown here.

Using the Annotative option is similar to using Annotative Text and Dimensions – The scale of the Hatch pattern will coordinate with the scale of the Paper.

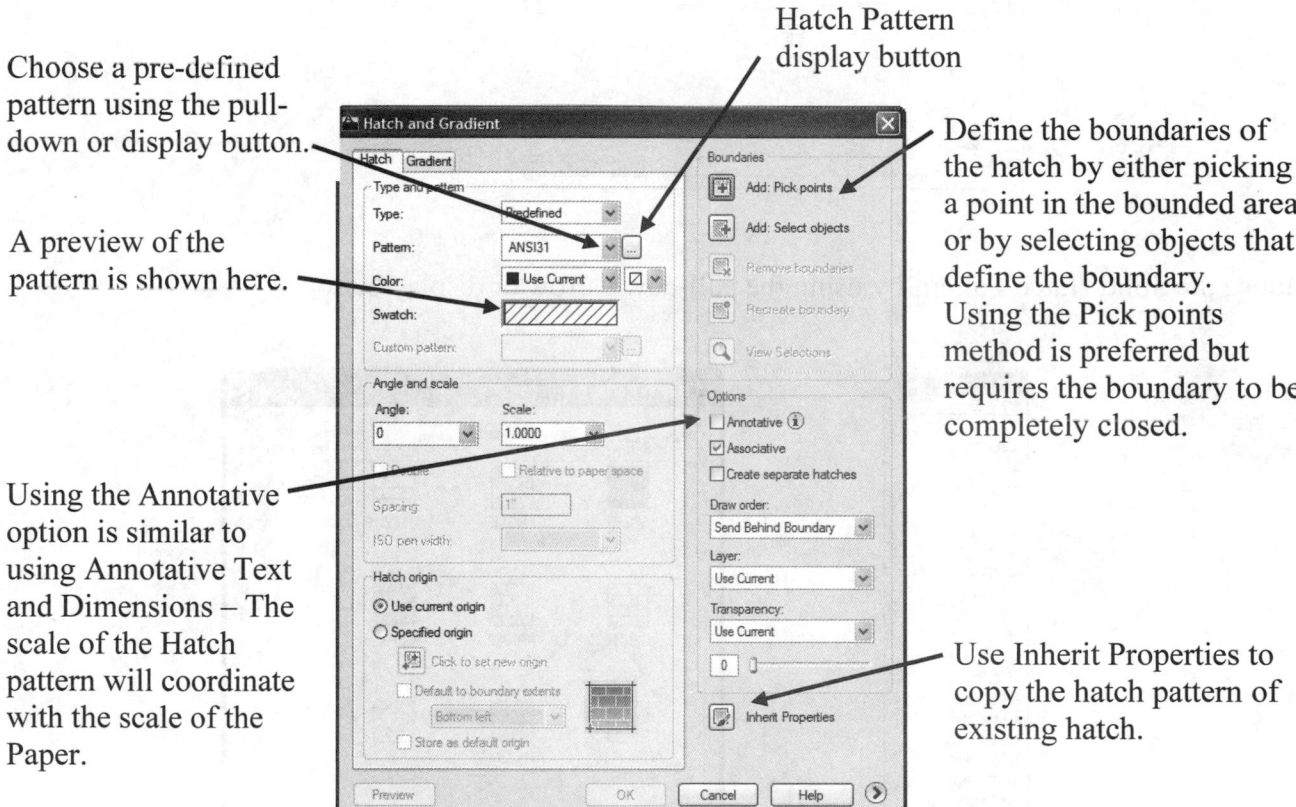

Define the boundaries of the hatch by either picking a point in the bounded area or by selecting objects that define the boundary. Using the Pick points method is preferred but requires the boundary to be completely closed.

Use Inherit Properties to copy the hatch pattern of existing hatch.

<u>Example:</u>

Let's use a solid color Hatch to fill in the walls of the conference room:

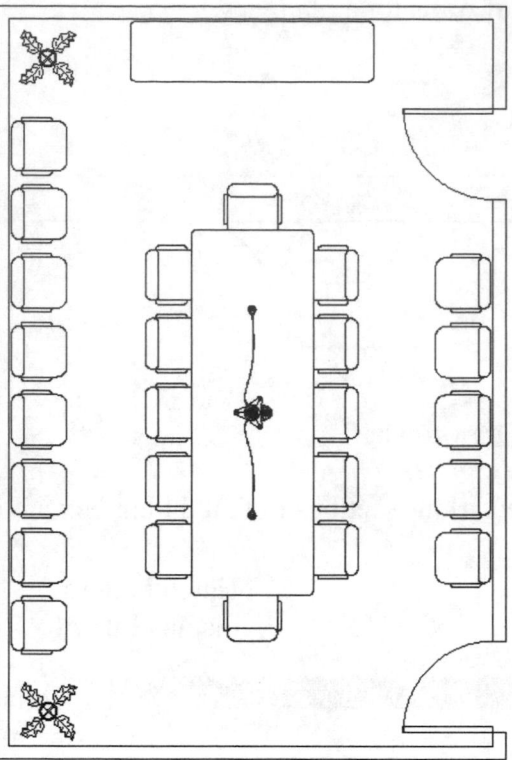

Choose the Solid Hatch Pattern by using the pull-down arrow or display button:

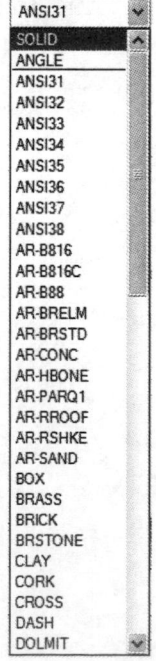

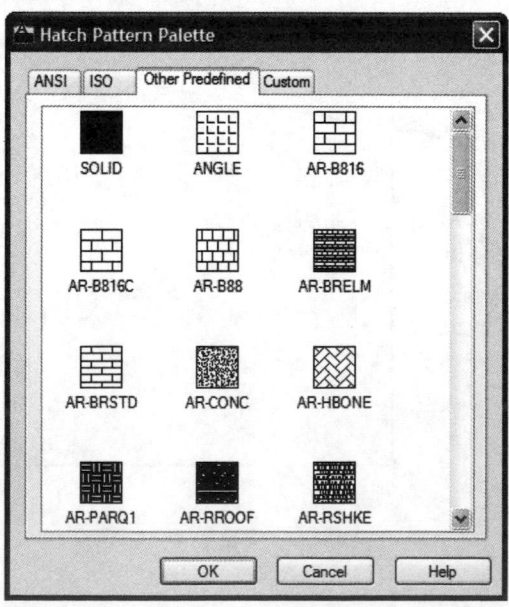

Choosing a pattern by using the display button allows you to see the pattern while you are choosing it. The patterns are categorized and tabulated. Select each tab to see which patterns are available. The Solid pattern is found under the Other Predefined tab. Simply pick on the icon of the Solid pattern, and then pick the OK button to exit the Hatch Pattern Palette and return to the Hatch dialog box.

The Swatch display now has a pull-down selection for the solid color. We will select ByLayer for this example. By choosing ByLayer, the color of the Hatch will be the same color as the Layer that it is created in.

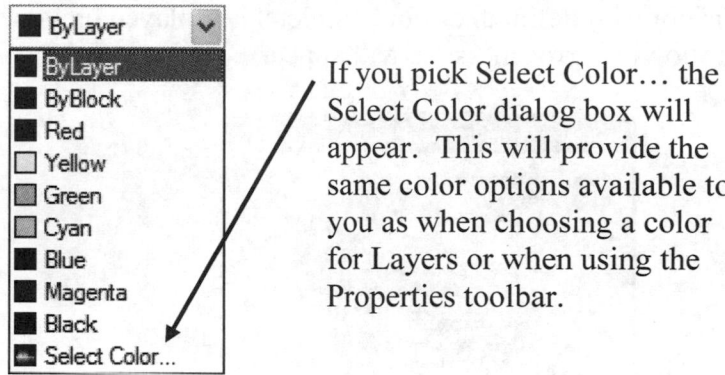

If you pick Select Color… the Select Color dialog box will appear. This will provide the same color options available to you as when choosing a color for Layers or when using the Properties toolbar.

Since we are using a Solid Hatch, the Angle and Scale options of the Hatch dialog box are grayed-out.

Choose the Pick points button to select the area that will define the Hatch boundary. The dialog box will disappear and you will have cursor control again to be able to pick inside the walls:

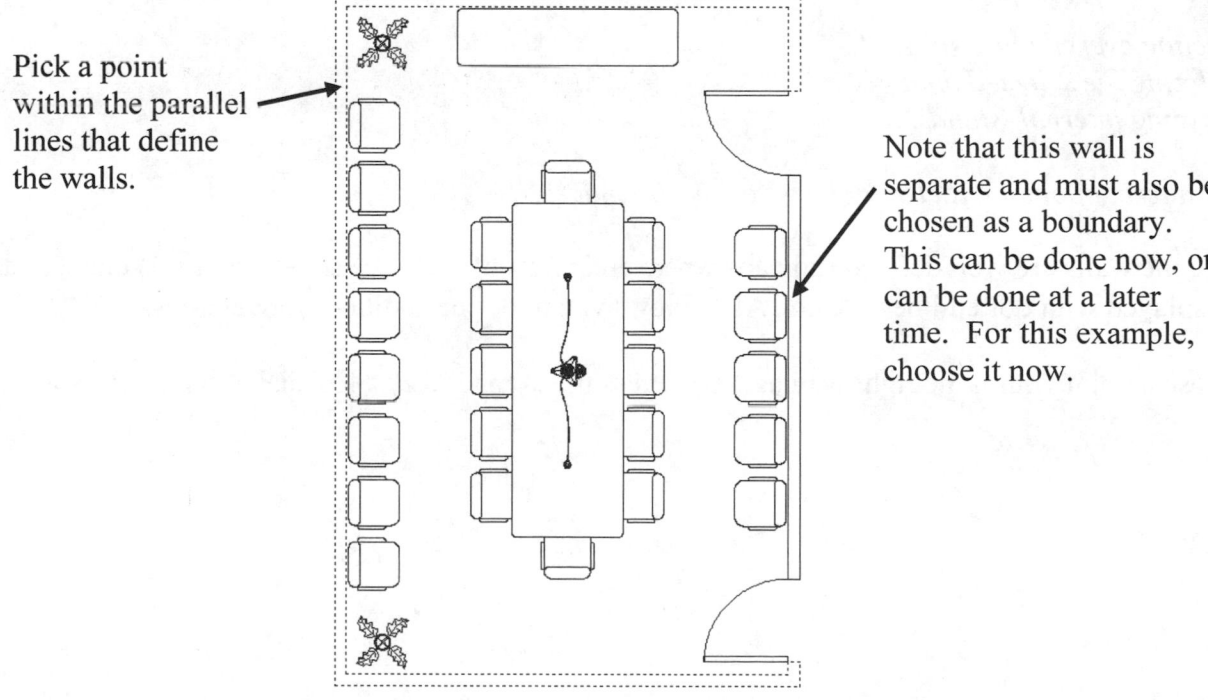

Pick a point within the parallel lines that define the walls.

Note that this wall is separate and must also be chosen as a boundary. This can be done now, or can be done at a later time. For this example, choose it now.

Your command line will display the following:

Command: _bhatch
Pick internal point or [Select objects/remove Boundaries]:

(Pick a point within the walls to define the boundary)

> Note: Be patient while AutoCAD searches for the boundary. At first, it
> may not appear that anything happened after you picked a point.

If the boundary is not well defined, or not completely displayed on your screen while you are
selecting it, the following error message will appear:

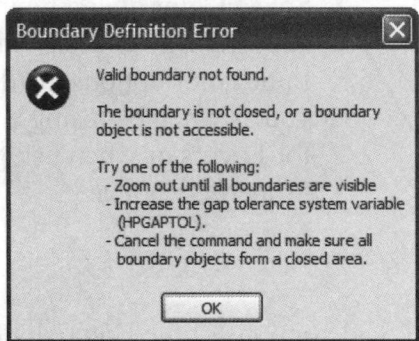

If you get this error message, try to fix the problem via one of the suggested methods given in the
error message.

If there are no issues with the boundary, the command line will display the following:

Selecting everything visible...
Analyzing the selected data...
Analyzing internal islands...

Pick internal point or [Select objects/remove Boundaries]:

Since the walls are well defined (no gaps where endpoints of each line should connect) the boundary
is displayed with dotted lines. AutoCAD® allows you to define additional boundaries.

Choose a point within the right wall as well. Press the ↵ Enter Key. The dialog box will re-appear.

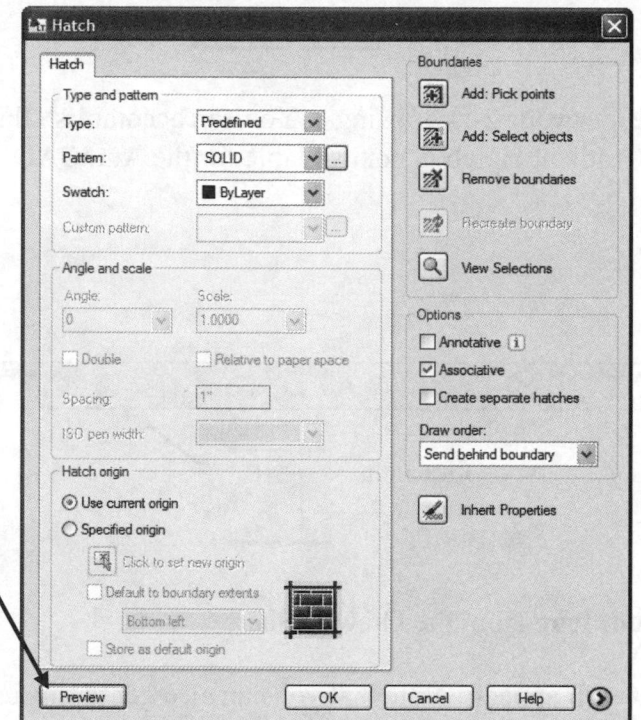

You may pick the Preview button to view how the Hatch will appear. Press the Esc key to return to the dialog box or press the ↵ Enter Key to complete the Hatch command.

Pick the Preview button and the boundaries that you have chosen will now be filled with the selected Hatch pattern:

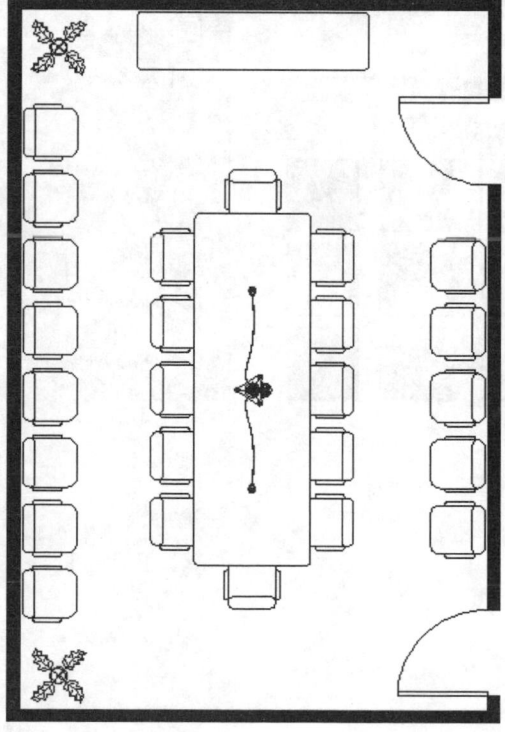

Press the ↵ Enter Key to accept the Hatch pattern. This will end the command.

Rendering

You can use Hatch to render your 2-D drawings. You can accomplish this by using the Gradient Hatch. Unfortunately, Gradient Hatch is not available for the AutoCAD® LT version.

Gradient Hatch

Procedure:

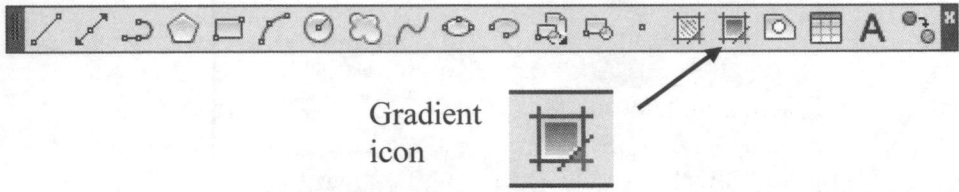

Gradient
icon

Pick (left click): **Gradient icon** from the Draw toolbar.

The Gradient dialog box will appear. Note that you can also get to this using the Hatch icon and then selecting the Gradient tab.

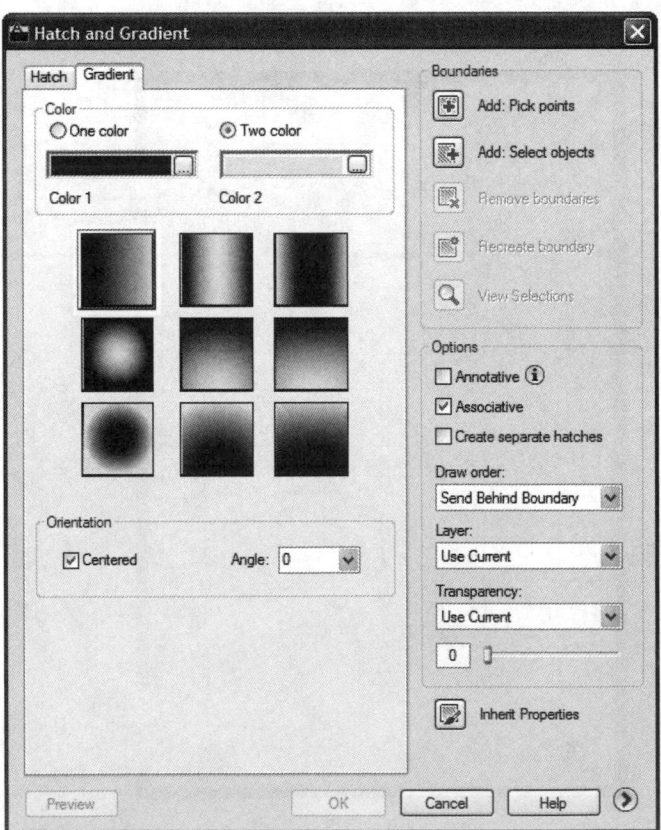

The various styles available are named below:

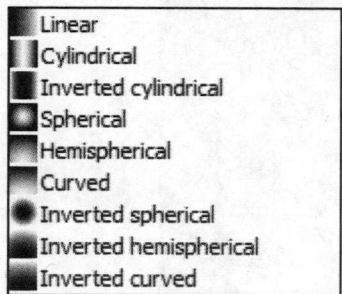

Gradient works the same as a solid Hatch except that it has two color choices. This allows for simulating lighting conditions. To create a good visual rendering of your drawing will take practice and patience. It is likely that you may not be satisfied with the color or style the first time you place the Gradient Hatch on the drawing. This does not mean you need to erase it and try again. Instead, it is better to use the Properties palette to make the changes once the Gradient Hatch is on the drawing.

Another technique that can be employed is to cover small areas at a time. This is especially true when you want to have different effects for different parts of a piece of furniture or areas of a room.

<u>Example:</u>

Let's render the dresser that we created as homework in Chapter 3.

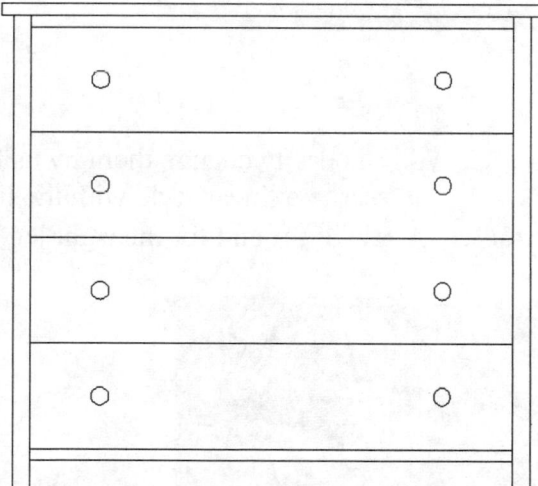

Notice that there are multiple segments that make up the dresser: knobs, drawer fronts, and vertical/horizontal structure. We can add Gradient Hatch to each portion separately. The following is an example of adding 90° Cylindrical style Gradient Hatch to all the sections (except the knobs) at once:

If we choose each section individually, using the same style we will obtain the following effects:

If you are not happy with the color or style, you can easily change them by using the Properties Palette. Let's change the vertical legs of the dresser to a linear style with the lighter portion toward the inside. For the left leg, this is a Gradient Angle of 0°, and for the right leg, it is 180°.

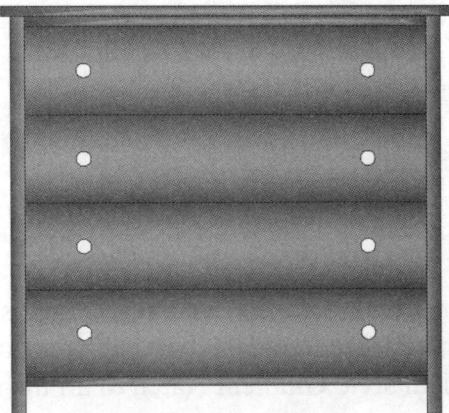

After selecting a Gradient Hatch, the Properties Palette will allow you to change various features. The features that are most commonly changed for Gradient Hatch are Color 1, Color 2, Gradient Angle, and Centered.

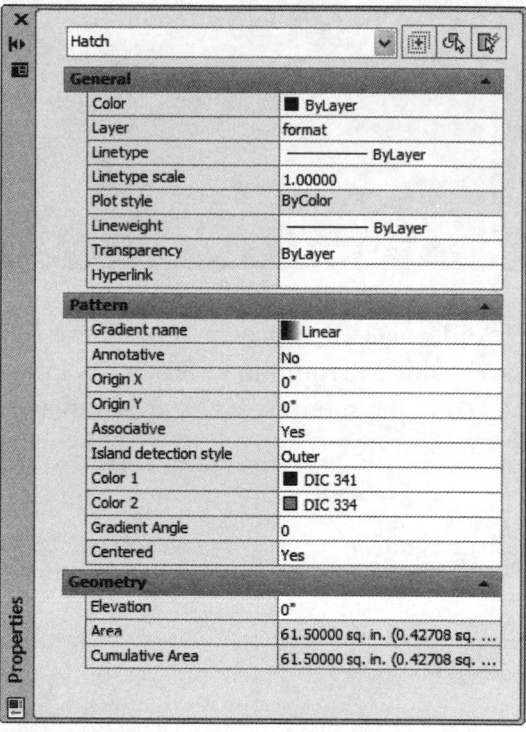

Another technique that can be applied is to divide up the area that you wish to add the Gradient Hatch. As an example, let's say that you have a lamp next to a wall. The color will be lighter nearest the lamp as a result of the intensity of the light in close proximity to the lamp. Let's explore this with two floor lamps. Each lamp will have an affect on the appearance of the wall color.

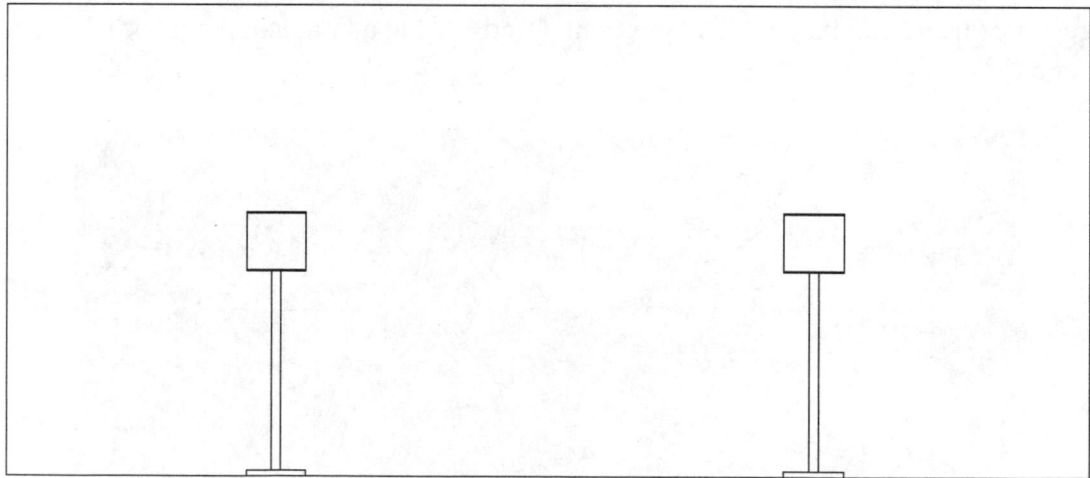

Using Cylindrical style for the wall will not provide the effect we are looking for:

Notice that the Cylindrical style would make it appear as though the light was centered on the wall. One way around this problem is to divide the room in sections. We can draw a vertical line from each floor lamp and another centered in the room to divide it into reasonable sections.

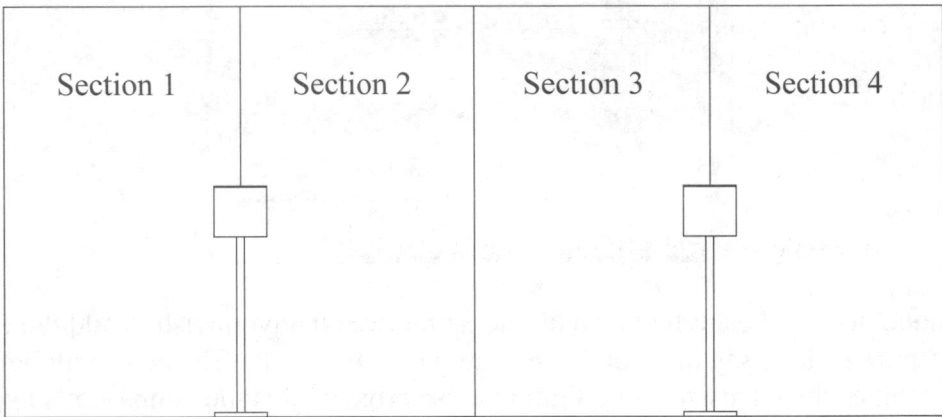

With the room divided into sections, we can add Gradient Hatch to each section. The following shows the result of using Linear style with sections 1 and 3 set at a Gradient Angle of 0° and sections 2 and 4 set at a Gradient Angle of 180°.

It may not produce perfect results, but it certainly provides for a much more realistic appearance.

Summary

In this chapter you have learned to:

- Draw a 3-point Arc
- Create an Ellipse using a rectangle to define the boundaries
- Use a Polyline to draw continuous lines and arcs
- Draw a free-form curve using Spline
- Use Hatch to fill an area with a solid color or other pre-defined patterns
- Render your drawing using Gradient Hatch – Filling an area with two-color solid hatch
- Use various techniques to improve the appearance of your rendered drawing

Review Questions

1. Why would you use an Arc instead of a Circle?

2. How is an Ellipse defined?

3. What situation would you use a Polyline?

4. Why would you use a Spline instead of a Polyline?

5. If your Hatch does not appear the right size, what can you do about it?

6. What can you do if you get an error message while trying to insert Hatch?

7. How is Gradient different than Hatch?

8. How many different styles of Gradient Hatch are there available?

9. If you are not satisfied with the Gradient Hatch you put in, how can you change it without re-creating it?

10. For Gradient Hatch for a locally lit area, what technique can you use to get an improved appearance?

Exercises

1. Add to the drawing that you created through Tutorial 5 by using solid Hatch for the walls in the Plan View. Choose whichever color you desire. In addition, add a view triangle for Elevation B, and change the coffee table from a rectangular shape to an elliptical shape.

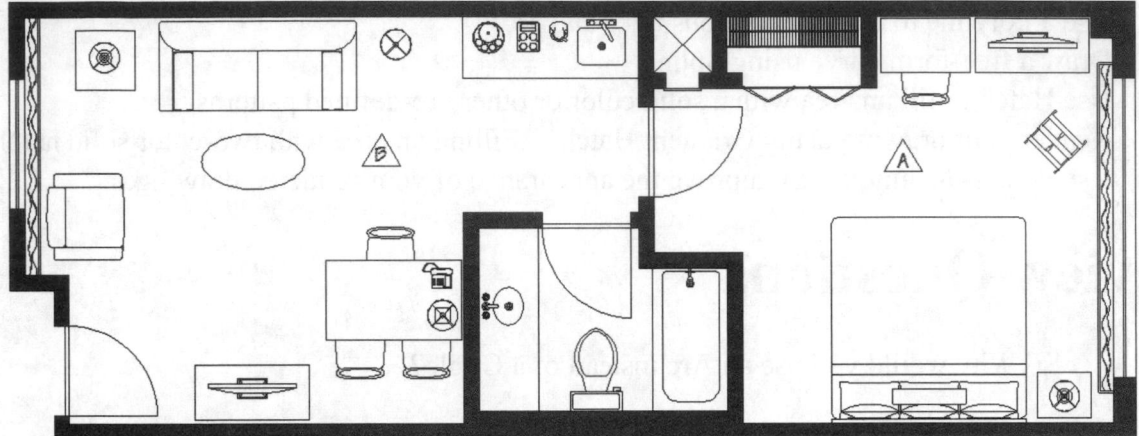

2. Download the Hotel Suite Living Room Elevation Blocks from the publisher's web site. Create Elevation B from the Plan View. Create a Layout tab for Elevation B. Set and lock the scale to a standard scale value. Complete the titleblock and annotate your drawing as desired.

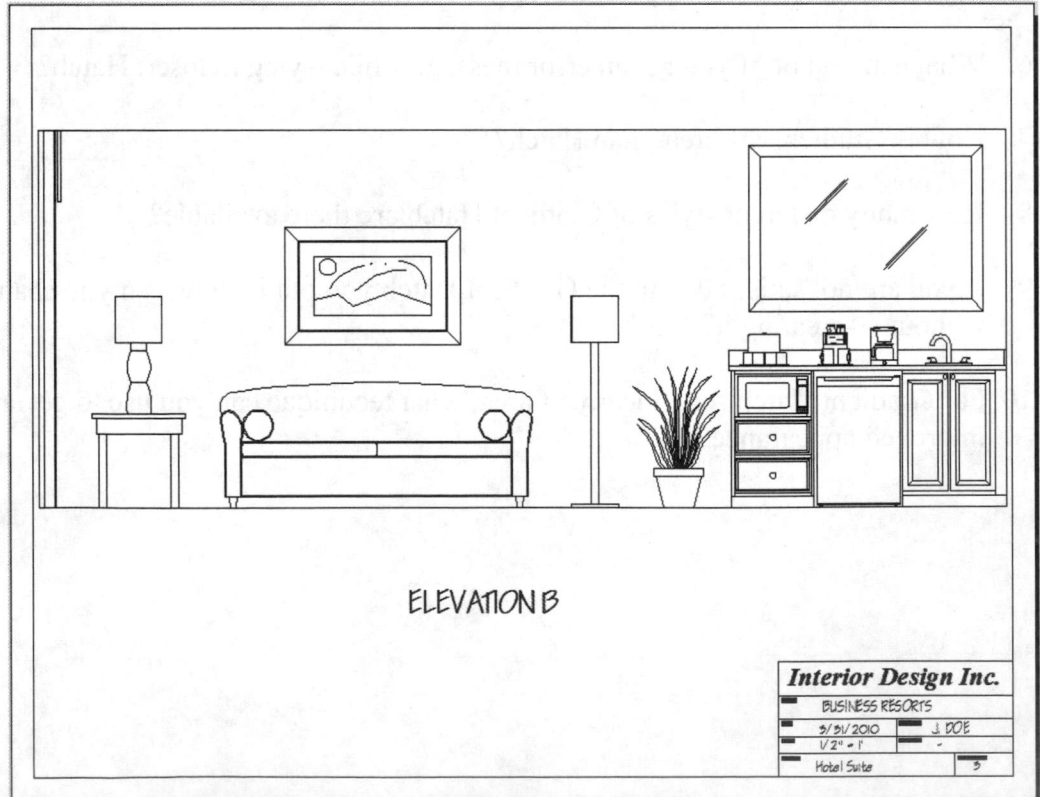

ELEVATION B

3. Create the Radiator Cover. Use NET3 style Hatch with a scale of 6 for the screen. Use a 3-point arc to create the curved top of each side.

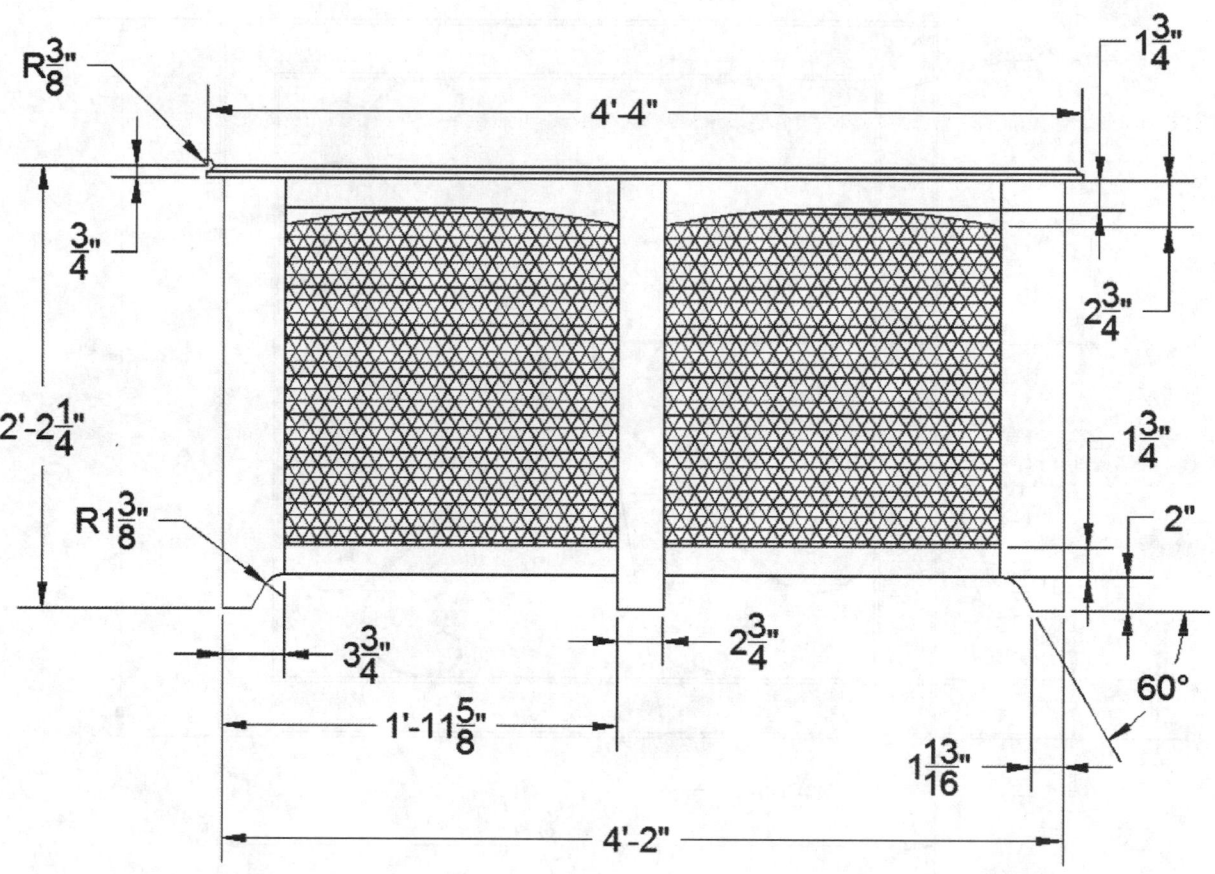

4. Create the cross-section of the radiator cover. Use Hatch and annotate your drawing as shown.

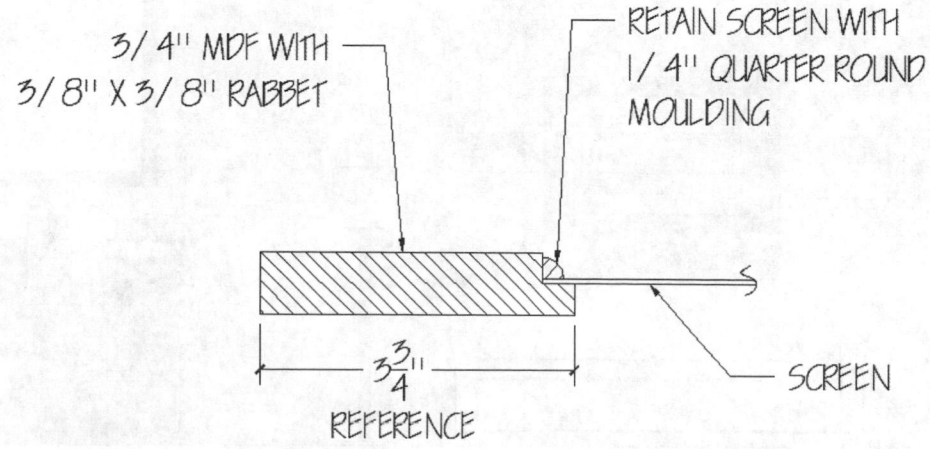

5. Create the wrought iron wall hanging. Use either Polyline or Spline to create one of the shaped end. Use the Mirror command as well as the Array command to complete the design.

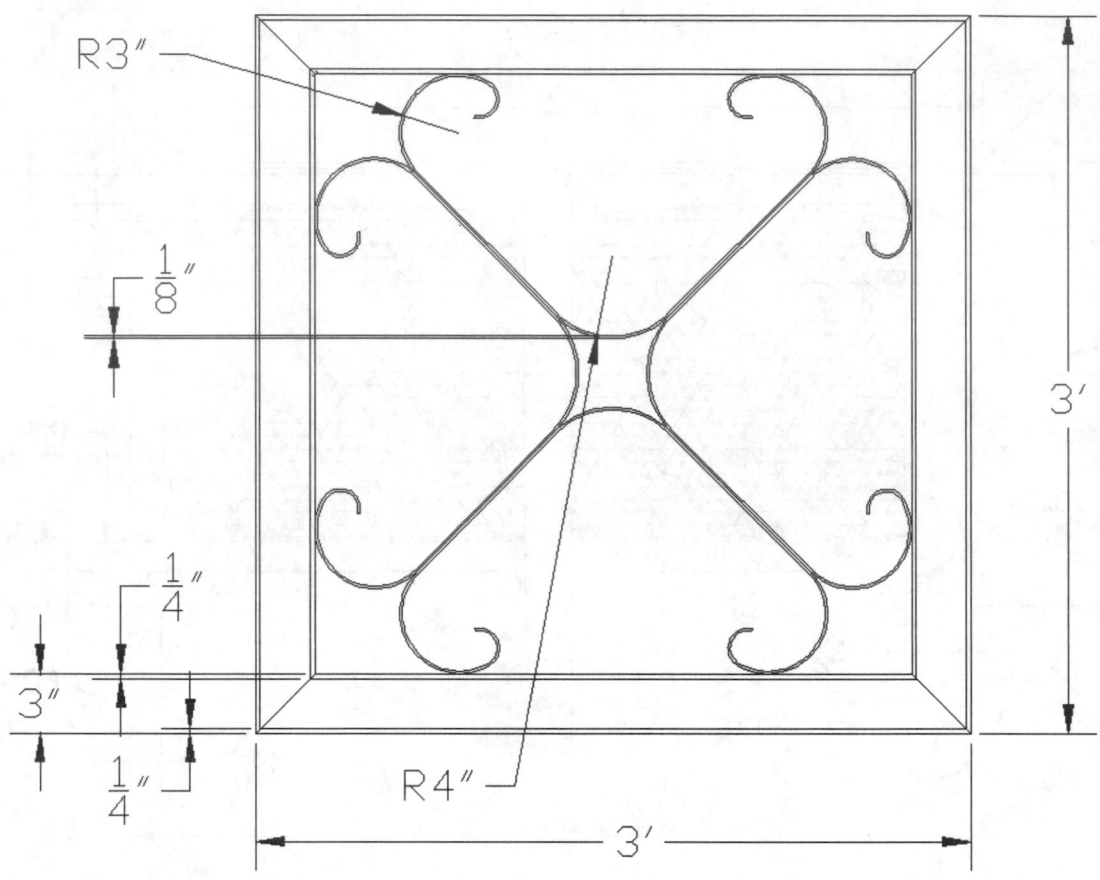

6. Render Elevation B by using both Hatch and Gradient Hatch.

Chapter 15
Miscellaneous – Techniques, Commands, and Options

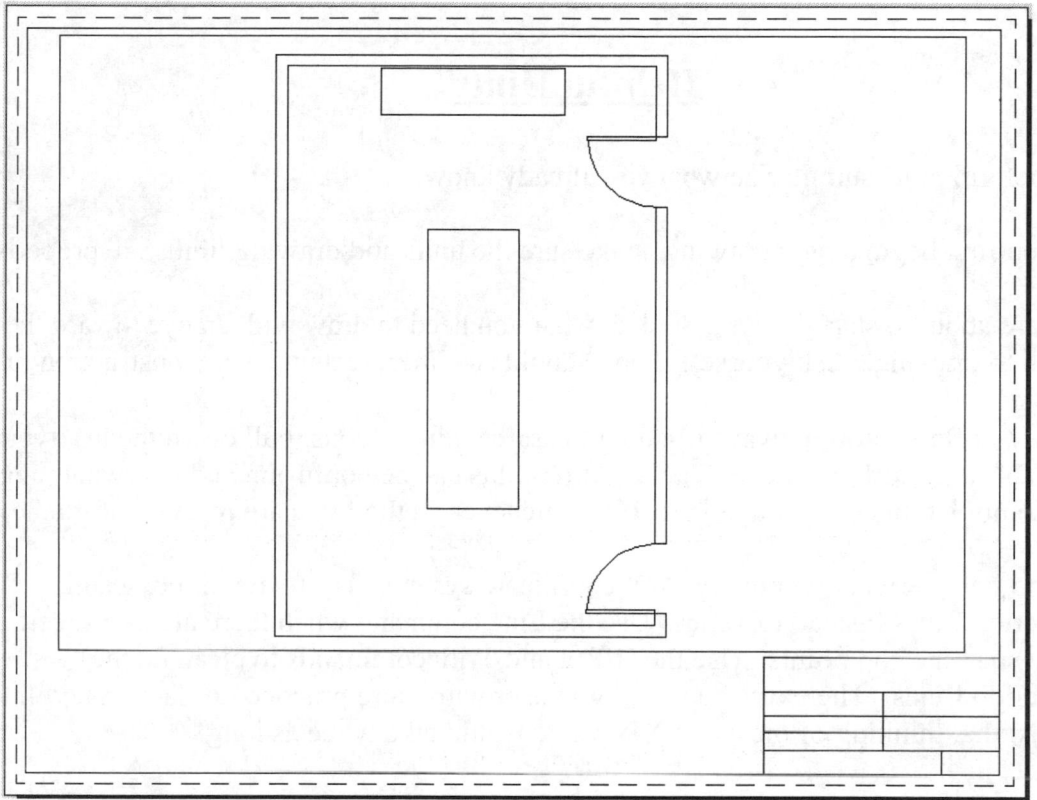

Learning Objectives:

- **Improve drawing techniques**
- **Use several new commands**
- **Explore additional command options**

Up to this point, we have learned enough of the AutoCAD® program to be able to be productive and create our interior designs. This chapter provides some review of what we already know and consolidates them into helpful hints. In addition, there are some occasionally used commands that are explored, as well as some additional options for commands we have already learned. For the most part, you could get by without knowing the commands and options covered in this chapter and you would still be very productive. However, it is certainly worth exploring these since they can come in handy.

Helpful Hints

The following helpful hints summarize what you already know.

1. When you first begin a new drawing, make sure the units and drawing limits are properly set.

2. As you are about to start drawing, look at what you need to draw with an eye toward the best approach to drawing. Ask yourself if you should use lines, rectangles or construction lines.

3. AutoCAD® offers multiple ways of doing the same thing. Icons, pull down menus, typing commands, and shortcuts are available. At first this can be confusing and overwhelming. Please do not let this discourage you. Use whichever method you are most comfortable with.

4. Try not to get overwhelmed by the X-Y coordinate system. Try to avoid it by using Construction Lines instead of Lines. Use the Line command when there are two specific points to snap the end points. Use the Offset and Trim commands to clean up the Construction Lines. The extra steps will go faster with more practice. In fact, you will likely get so fast that thinking of the exact X-Y value would take twice as long.

5. Any time you need to start a line or other geometry a specific distance away from another line, use the Offset command (or Construction Line/Offset) to find an intersection point. Use the Object Snap/Intersection setting to find your start point. After you are done, simply erase the construction line. This can also be done by using Circles for construction purposes and erasing them when you are done.

6. I find the Grid/Snap to be a hindrance; I do not use them, and did not cover it in this text. Instead, I make extensive use of Object Snaps.

7. Use the Fillet command with a radius of zero to trim/extend lines simultaneously, such as a corner for an outside line for a wall.

8. When using a fly-out style icon, such as Measure Geometry (Distance), remember that the icon displayed was the last one used. So if the last measurement made was Angle, and now you want to measure a Distance, move the cursor over the Angle fly-out icon, press and <u>hold</u>

the left mouse button. The remaining icons "fly-out". While still holding the left mouse button, move your cursor down to the Distance icon and then release the left mouse button.

9. An alternate method of moving around the drawing instead of the Zoom and Pan commands is to use the wheel on the mouse. Rolling the wheel forward and backward will Zoom in and out of the drawing. Pressing the wheel down and dragging will allow you to Pan around your drawing. For zooming the entire drawing, double-click the mouse wheel.

Finding the Center of a Rectangle

There are times when you need to locate the center of a rectangle. As an example, if you are creating a reflected ceiling plan, you may want to locate a fixture in the middle of the room. If you have a rectangular room, it is easy to find the center.

If you were drawing this by hand, you would likely draw two diagonal lines from corner to opposite corner to form an "X". The intersection of the lines would be the exact center of the rectangle.

With AutoCAD®, you do not need to draw two lines. You can take advantage of the Snap to Midpoint feature and just draw one line between opposite corners. Of course, when you are done, simply erase the diagonal line.

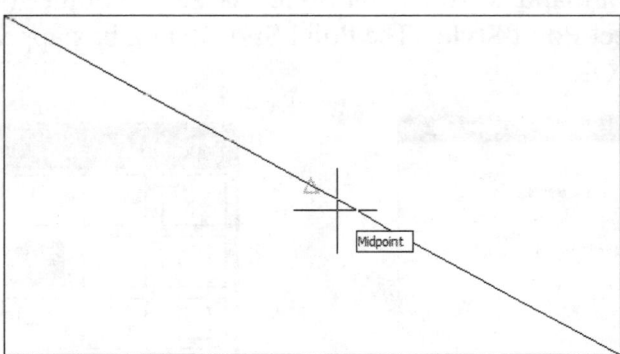

Divide

There are times when it is desired to divide an object into equal segments. Typically, this would be a line or a circle. However, AutoCAD® will allow you to divide other objects as well. AutoCAD® will divide the object in equal perimeter true distance.

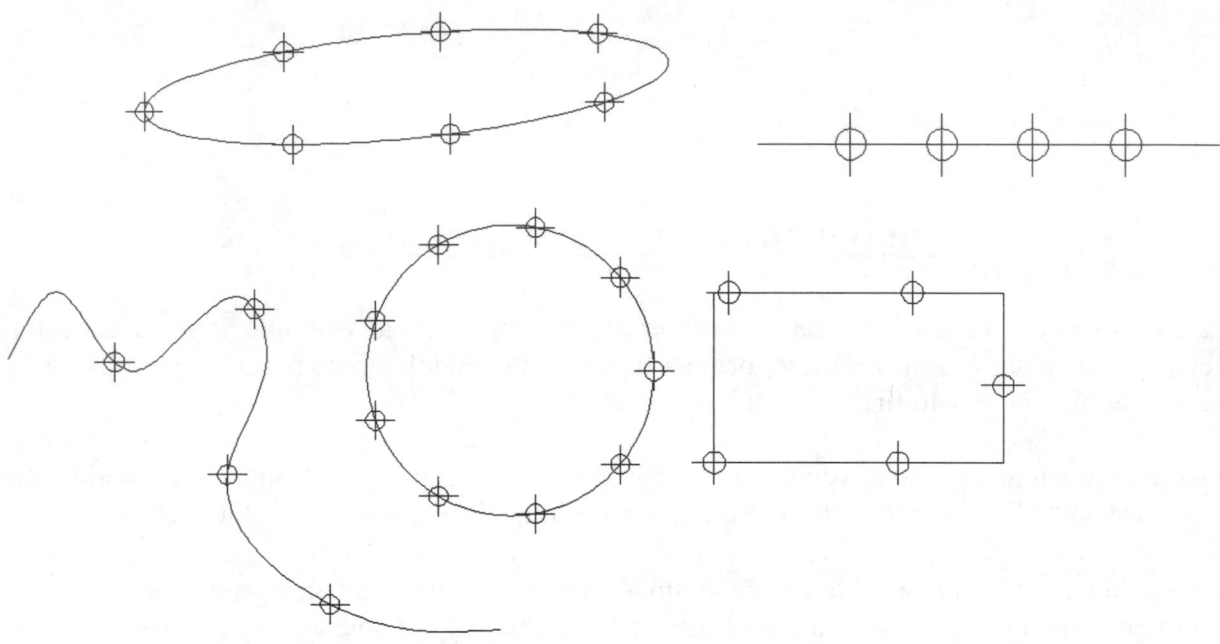

Before using the Divide command, set the Point Style. To set the Point Style, use the pull-down menu item Format and select Point Style. The Point Style dialog box appears. Choose a style, set the desired size, and then pick OK.

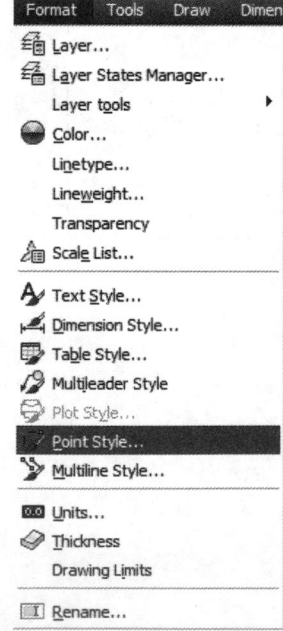

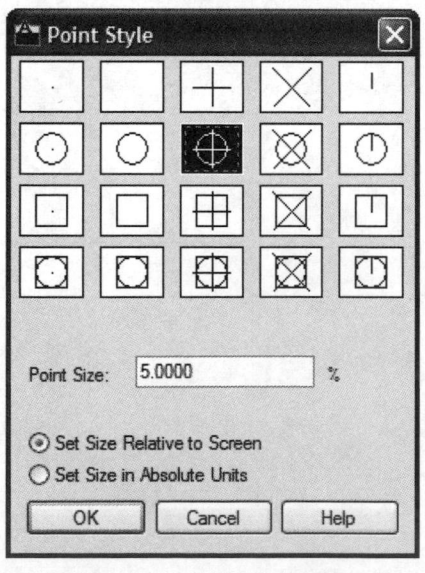

Procedure:

Type: **div⏎** in the command line

The command line prompts you with the following:

Command: div
DIVIDE
Select object to divide: **(Pick the object that you want to divide)**
Enter the number of segments or [Block]: **Type a number and then press the ⏎ Enter key**
Command:

AutoCAD® ends the command.

In order to snap to a point, set Snap to Node on. AutoCAD® refers to points as nodes.

Try it:

After you set the Point Style using the Format pull-down menu, draw a line that is arbitrarily long at any angle on your screen:

Use the Divide command to divide the line into 5 equal segments. When you are done, your drawing will look like this:

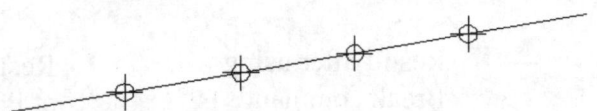

Let's draw vertical construction lines through the points that were just created. Make sure Snap to Node is selected in the Object Snap setting. Now use the Construction Line icon and choose the Vertical option. Pick each point for the vertical construction line to snap to. When you are done, your drawing will look like this:

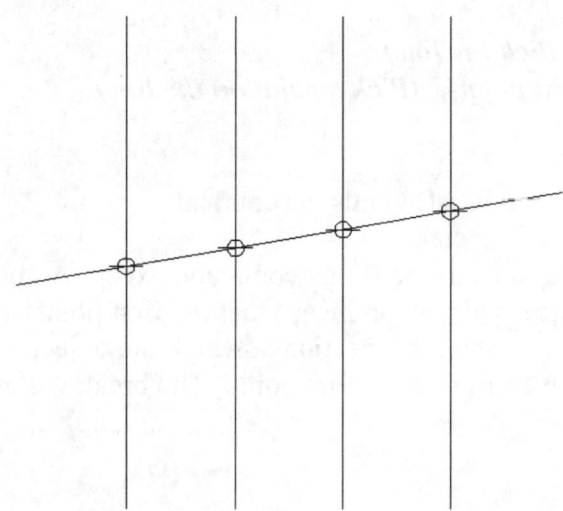

Break & Break at Point

There are times when it is desired to split a line, arc, etc. into two segments. This can be accomplished by using either the Break command or the Break at Point command. These are both located on the Modify toolbar.

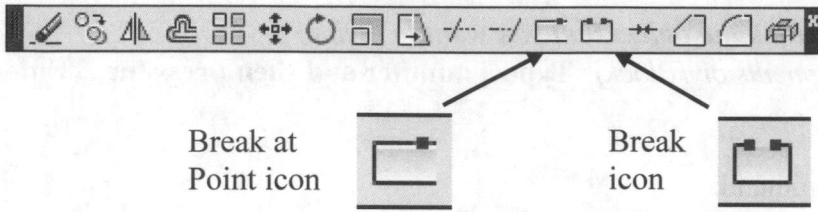

Break at
Point icon

Break
icon

The Break command will break the object into two segments and trim away a portion of the object that you selected. The amount that is trimmed away is dependent on where the object was selected and the location picked for the break point.

Let's use a line as an example of the Break command.

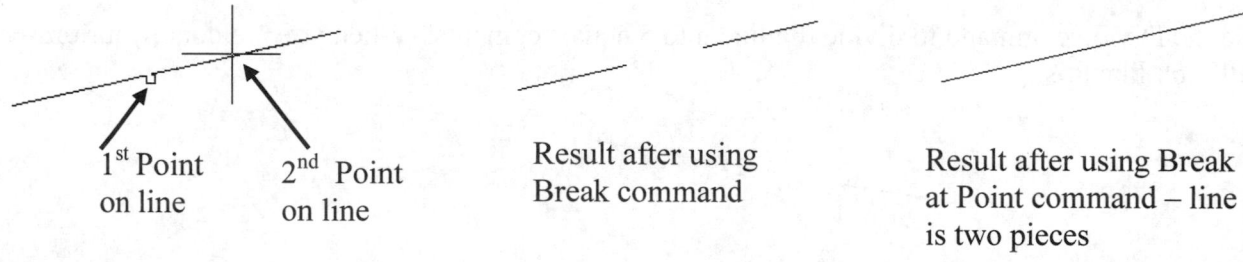

1st Point
on line

2nd Point
on line

Result after using
Break command

Result after using Break
at Point command – line
is two pieces

Procedure:

Pick (left click): **Break icon** [or **Break at Point icon**] from the Modify toolbar.

Command: _break Select object: **(Pick the line)**
Specify second break point or [First point]: **(Pick a point on the line)**
Command:

AutoCAD® ends the command.

The Break at Point command is the same as the Break command except AutoCAD automatically selects the First point option for you. This option means that the first point selected for the break will be defined by picking a location rather than the location at which the object was selected. The second point selected will automatically be chosen as the first point. The break will not be obvious because no gap will be shown.

Stretch

You can change the shape of an object by using the Stretch command. You can make several objects longer or shorter in one direction. An example would be if you wanted to modify the size of a room. This could be handled using the Move command and then trimming/extending the remaining objects to match. You need to exercise caution when using stretch because the objects could easily become distorted. It is important to have set up the base and target points to stretch from and to.

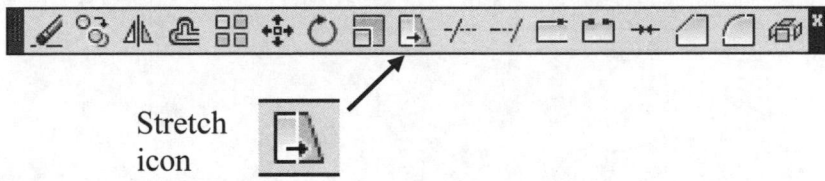

Stretch icon

Example:

Below is an 8′ x 10′ room. The client desires to change the 8′ direction to 12′.

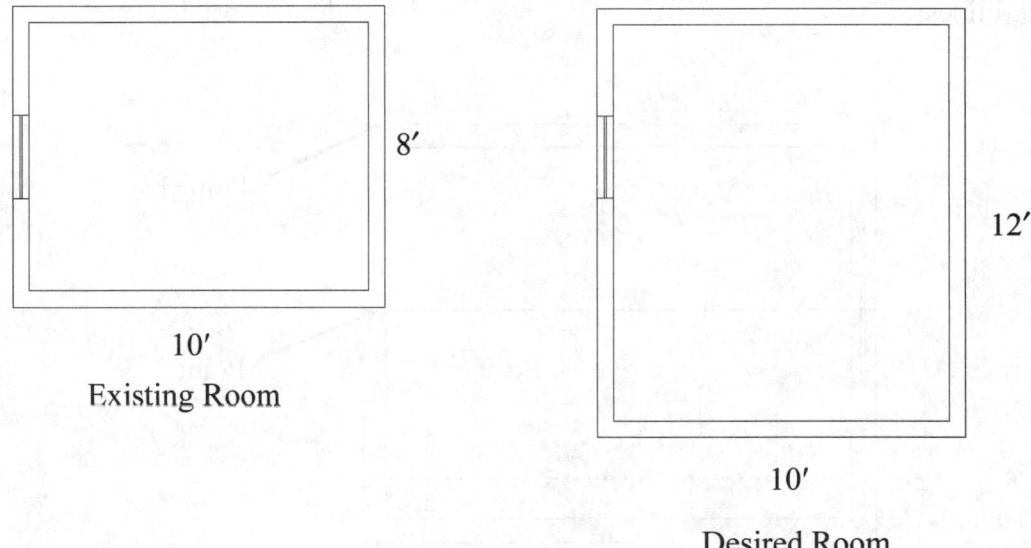

8′

10′

Existing Room

12′

10′

Desired Room

In order to use the Stretch command, offset the top horizontal line 4′ down. This will allow us to use Snap to Endpoint for the base and target points.

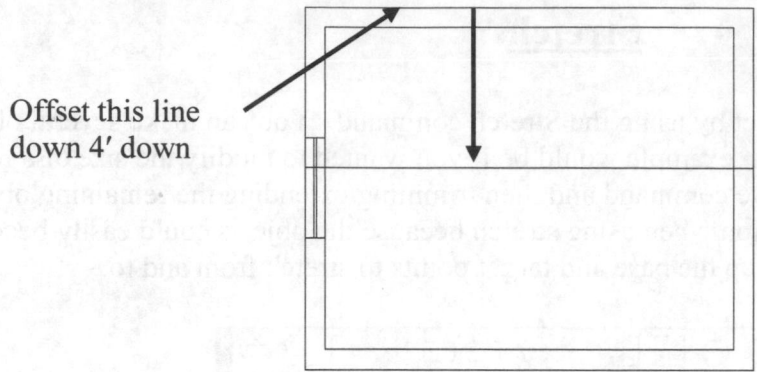

Offset this line
down 4' down

Procedure:

Pick (left click): **Stretch icon** from the Modify toolbar.

When prompted to select the objects, use a crossing window to select the 4 vertical lines and the bottom horizontal lines:

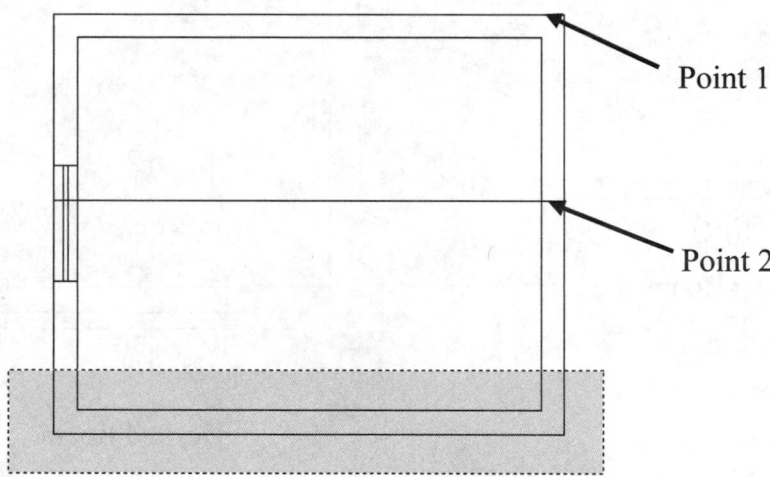

Point 1

Point 2

Since no more objects are to be selected, press the ↵ Enter key. This will bring us to the second part of the command.

*Specify base point or [Displacement] <Displacement>: **(Pick Point 1)***
*Specify second point or <use first point as displacement>: **(Pick Point 2)***
Command:

The result of the Stretch command looks like this:

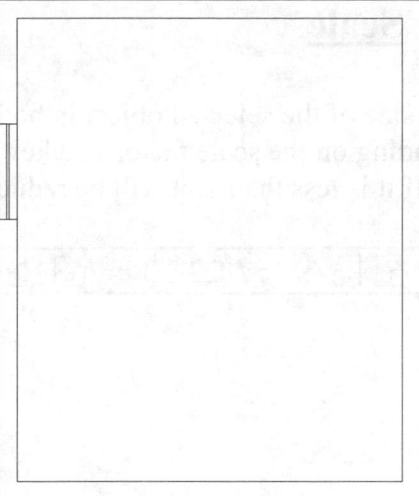

Without good base and target points, the room could end up distorted:

It is because of this that you need to exercise caution and set things up first to avoid this.

Scale

The Scale command allows you to change the size of the selected object in both directions. The object can either be enlarged or reduced depending on the scale factor you key in. If the scale factor is greater than 1, the object will be enlarged. If it is less than 1, it will be reduced.

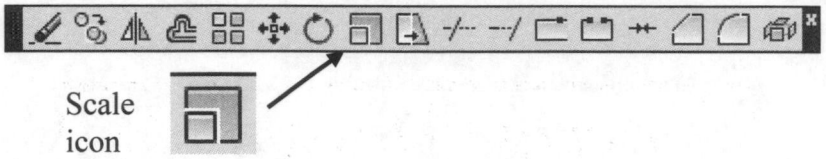

Scale
icon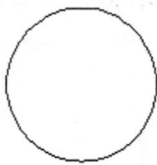

Example:

Let's enlarge a 1′ radius circle. We want the circle to be twice as big as it is, so the scale factor will be 2.

Procedure:

Pick (left click): **Scale icon** from the Modify toolbar.

Command: _scale
*Select objects: (**Pick the circle**) 1 found*
Select objects: ↵
*Specify base point: (**Pick the center of the circle**)*
*Specify scale factor or [Copy/Reference]: **2**↵*
Command:

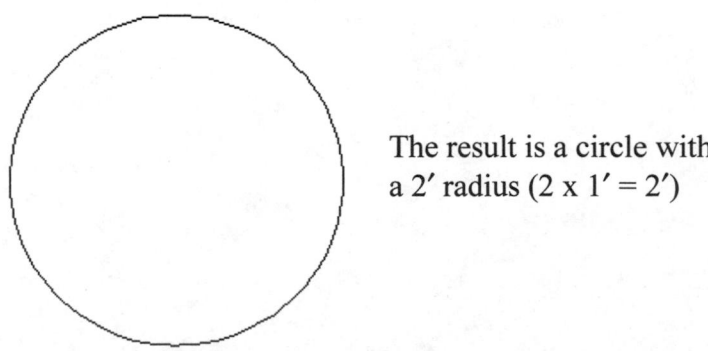

The result is a circle with
a 2′ radius (2 x 1′ = 2′)

Cut (or Copy)/Paste – Using the Clipboard

Changing Objects from Model Space to Paper Space

You can easily move an object that you created in Model Space to Paper Space by using a cutting and pasting technique. For example, let's say you have created the Titleblock, in Model Space, shown below:

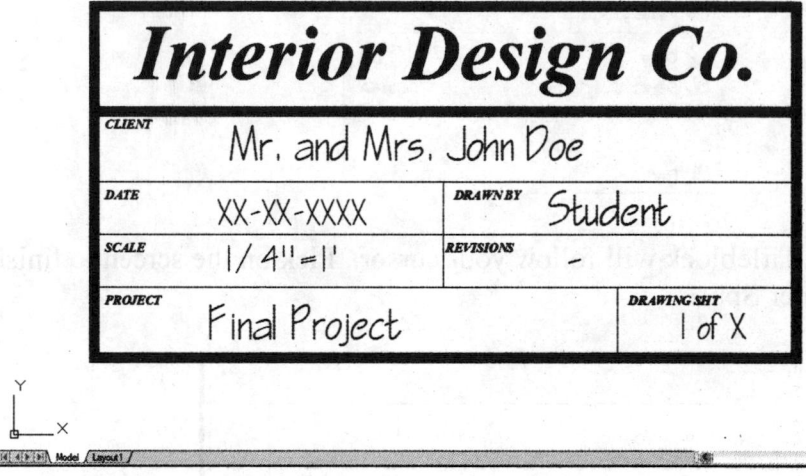

In order to get it out of model space and into paper space, use the following instructions:

1. Use the pull-down menu Edit command and select Cut from your selection choices. Use a Selection Window (or a Crossing Window) to select all the objects. Press the ↵ Enter key.

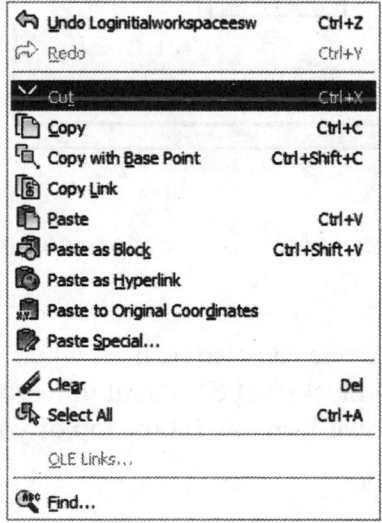

2. Pick one of the Layout tabs.

3. Use the pull-down menu Edit command and select paste from your selection choices.

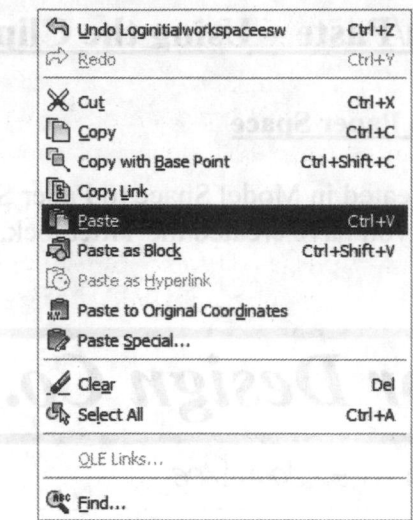

4. An image of the Titleblock will follow your cursor. Pick on the screen to finish pasting the Titleblock in Paper Space.

Now that the Titleblock is a Paper Space object, use the move command to re-locate it on your layout.

This same cut/paste or copy/paste technique can also be used when you want objects from another drawing that are not already defined as blocks to be brought in to your drawing. You must have both drawings open and use the pull-down Window (at the top of your screen) to switch between drawings.

Use the pull-down Window to toggle between open AutoCAD drawings

Circle Options

In Chapter 2, we learned the basic concept of the Circle command. We were able to define the circle by specifying the center point and either the radius or diameter. This is not the only way to create a circle.

AutoCAD® offers many options of specifying a circle. These options are shown in the square brackets of the circle command prompt: *[3P/2P/Ttr (tan tan radius)]*. The following describes each of those options.

Define the Circle with 3 points

This option allows you to define a circle using 3 points that lie on the circumference of the circle.

To use this option after selecting the Circle icon, type **3p↵**
Command: _circle Specify center point for circle or [3P/2P/Ttr (tan tan radius)]: **3p↵**

The command line prompts you to specify the points on the circle:
Specify first point on circle: **(Pick a point on the screen)**
Specify second point on circle: **(Pick a point on the screen)**
Specify third point on circle: **(Pick a point on the screen)**
Command:

This can come in very handy for a situation where you want a circle (or an arc after trimming the circle) to be between 3 lines and you don't know (or care) what the diameter of the circle will be. Use Snap to Tangent as you pick each of the three lines.

Example:

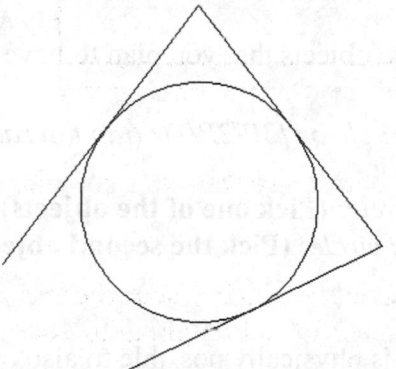

Using the 3 point option for creating a circle comes in handy when you want a circle to be nested between three lines. You must use Snap to Tangent when selecting the lines.

Define the Circle with 2 points

This option allows you to define a circle by using 2 points that define the endpoints of the diameter of the circle.

To use this option after selecting the Circle icon, type **2p↵**

Command: _circle Specify center point for circle or [3P/2P/Ttr (tan tan radius)]: **2p↵**

The command line prompts you to specify the points on the circle:
Specify first end point of circle's diameter: **(Pick a point on the screen)**
Specify second end point of circle's diameter: **(Pick a point on the screen)**
Command:

This could be useful in a situation such as drawing piping on an upholstered chair or a full bullnose for the edge of a countertop. After drawing the circle, it can be trimmed and you would now have a semi-circle.

Example:

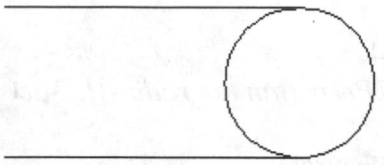

2 point circle drawn using the
endpoints of two parallel lines

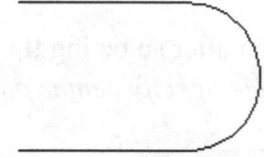

The same 2 point circle can be
trimmed resulting in a semi-circle

Tan Tan Radius

This option allows you to define a circle that is tangent to two objects of a specific radius. The two objects can be circles, arcs, lines, or combinations of two of these object types. The radius specified must be large enough to be tangent to the two objects.

To use this option you must already have two objects that you plan to have the circle be tangent to. After selecting the Circle icon, type **t↵**
Command: _circle Specify center point for circle or [3P/2P/Ttr (tan tan radius)]: **t↵**

Specify point on object for first tangent of circle: **(Pick one of the objects)**
Specify point on object for second tangent of circle: **(Pick the second object)**
Specify radius of circle: **1↵**

If the radius that you specify is smaller than is physically possible to also be tangent to the two objects, AutoCAD® will provide you with the following message in the command line and end the circle command:
Circle does not exist.
Command:

This can come in handy when you want to draw circles between two arcs/circles, or lines/circles, etc.

Example:

Varying diameter round
objects, such as oranges,
in a glass container:
These make contact
with each other or the
container at two points.

Rectangle Options

In Chapter 3, we learned the basic concept of the Rectangle command. We were able to define the rectangle by specifying one corner point, specifying the distance in both the horizontal and vertical directions, and the location of the opposite corner. This method provided a rectangle with square corners.

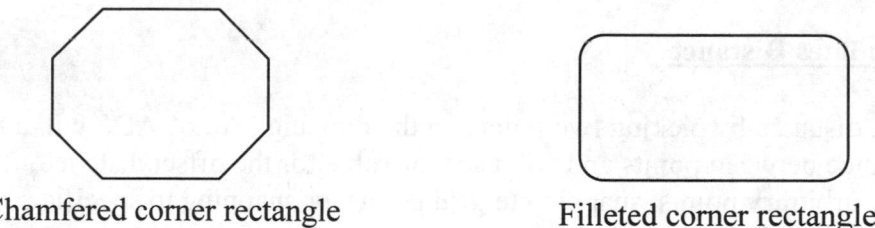

Chamfered corner rectangle   Filleted corner rectangle

Chamfered Corner Rectangle

For rectangles with chamfered corners:
Specify first corner point or [Chamfer/Elevation/Fillet/Thickness/Width]:

Type "**c**" and then press the ↵ Enter key.

Specify first chamfer distance for rectangles <X'-X">:

Type in the chamfer value then press the ↵ Enter key.

Specify second chamfer distance for rectangles <X'-X">:

Type in the chamfer value then press the ↵ Enter key. Note that both first and second values should be the same for a 45° chamfer.

After the chamfer values have been keyed in, AutoCAD® prompts for the location of the corner points of the rectangle as described before.

Filleted Corner Rectangle

For rectangles with filleted corners:
Specify fillet radius for rectangles <X'-X">:
Type in the fillet radius value then press the enter key.

After the fillet value has been keyed in, AutoCAD® prompts for the location of the corner points of the rectangle as described before.

Offset Options

In Chapter 3, we learned the basic concept of the Offset command. We were able to offset lines, circles, or rectangles by specifying a distance first, and then selecting the object and direction to offset. This method is most commonly used because you usually know the distance you desire to offset. In some instances, you may wish to offset to a specific location without knowing the distance.

AutoCAD® Calculates Distance

You can specify a distance by picking two points on the drawing. AutoCAD® will automatically calculate the distance between points and will use that value for the offset distance. The points chosen can be any arbitrary points, snapping to grid points, or snapping to specific parts of objects (such as endpoints of a line).

After picking the first point, the command line prompts you with the following:

Specify offset distance or [Through] <X'-XX>: Specify second point:

After you pick the second point the remainder of the prompts are the same as what you learned in Chapter 3.

Pick Object First, then Specify Distance

Use this option if you don't know the distance you plan to offset. First, the object is selected, and then the distance is defined by picking in the drawing. Typically, you would choose an end point or intersection, or some specific location for the offset value.

Select object to offset or <exit>:
Specify through point:

AutoCAD® will continue to prompt for more objects to offset:
Select object to offset or <exit>:

To exit the command, press the ↵ Enter key or press the Esc key.

Trim/Extend Options

Edge

Use this choice when the cutting edge (or boundary edge for Extend) does not cross the object to trim/extend, but it would if it was extended. Type **e** in the command line and press the ↵ Enter key for this choice.

> *Select object to trim or shift-select to extend or [Project/Edge/Undo]:* **e**↵

AutoCAD® prompts you with the following:

Enter an implied edge extension mode [Extend/No extend] <No extend>:

For extend mode, type **e** in the command line and press the ↵ Enter key.

> *Enter an implied edge extension mode [Extend/No extend] <No extend>:* **e**↵

Drafting Settings

We have only taken advantage of a few Drafting Setting features: Object Snap and Show/Hide Lineweights. There are other settings that you may have a preference to use. A very brief description of some of these will be given here. Since you already know about Object Snap, that will not be described here. If you are interested in exploring others, or these any further, the best way is to try them and to also check the Help menu.

Access to Drafting Settings is obtained by using the toggle icons on the left side of the Status Bar.

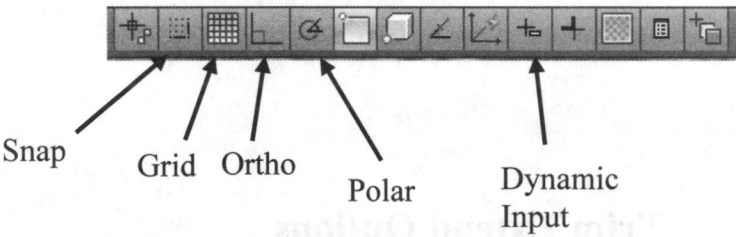

Snap   Grid   Ortho   Polar   Dynamic Input

Changing any settings for any of the drafting features is accomplished by bringing up the Drafting Settings dialog box. This is accomplished by right-clicking on any of the toggle icons and selecting drafting settings:

After right-clicking a toggle icon, select Settings...

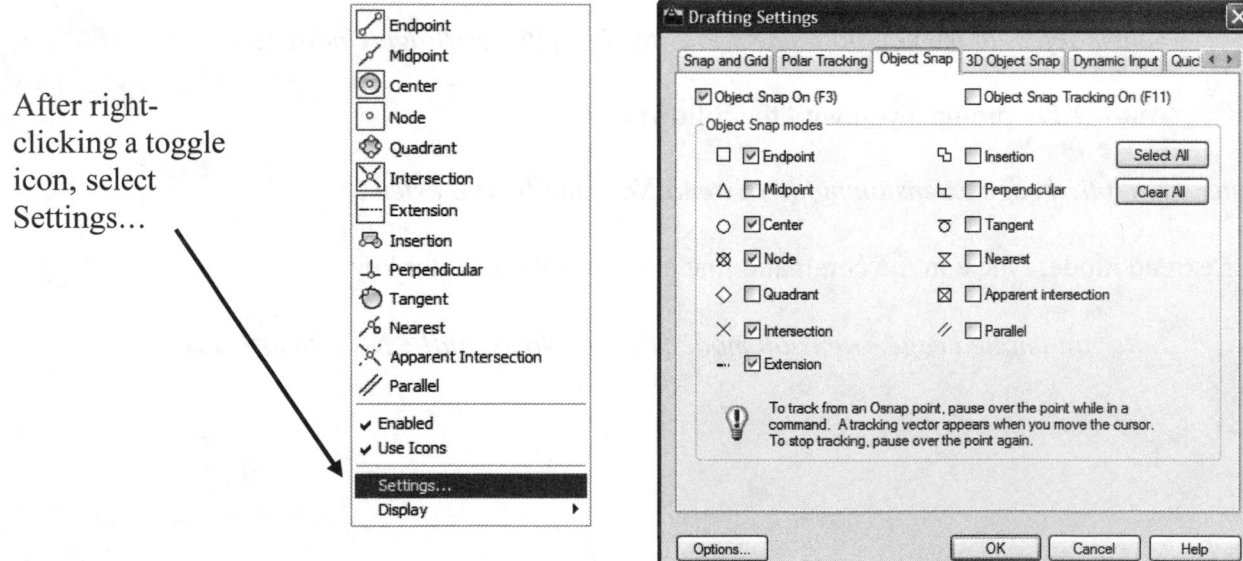

There are several tabs across the top of the dialog box. Use these to change settings.

Snap and Grid

You can use a grid and allow your cursor to snap to the grid when you make your drawing. Some people work with this, but I find it more tedious than it is worth. The grid and snap settings are to the nearest increment that you choose. One reason for not using it is because real-world dimensions never fall exactly on a grid. The best way to get familiar with the grid and snap feature is to try it. For further info, it is recommended that you check the Help menu.

Ortho and Polar

Ortho restricts you to horizontal (0°) and vertical (90°) directions only. This could be used on occasion when you prefer to insert a line instead of a construction line for either a horizontal or vertical direction. Otherwise, this has limited use.

Polar is similar to Ortho except it allows you to have more than 0° and 90° increments.

Dynamic Input

The Dynamic Input feature allows you to key in values and provides prompts at the location of the cursor. This is a personal preference whether to have this turned on or not.

Drawing Template

You do not need to set up your drawing every time you start a new one. Instead, you can create your own drawing template that has all the features and settings that you use. To create a template drawing, start with a new drawing and make all the features and settings that you would like:

- Units
- Drawing Limits
- Text Styles
- Dimension Styles
- Multileader Styles
- Table Styles
- Layouts and drawing format
- Layers
- Etc.

Remember, if you already created these styles on another drawing, these can be imported by using the Design Center.

After you set up the blank drawing, save it as a .dwt (instead of a .dwg) file. AutoCAD® automatically looks in the template folder when you start a new drawing. Saving a drawing as a .dwt will automatically save it to the template folder.

Congratulations! You are now ready to become a valuable and productive AutoCAD® designer.

Notes:

Index